American Art Appreciation Activities Kit

Ready-to-Use Lessons, Slides, and Projects for Grades 7-12

HELEN D. HUME

PRENTICE HALL
Paramus, New Jersey 07652

Library of Congress Cataloging-in-Publication Data

Hume, Helen D., 1933–.
    American art appreciation activities kit : ready-to-use lessons,
slides, and projects for grades 7–12 / Helen D. Hume.
      p. cm.
    ISBN 0-13-299521-2
    1. Art appreciation—Study and teaching (Secondary)—United
States. 2. Art, American—Study and teaching (Secondary)—United
States. 3. Project method in teaching. 4. Activity programs
in education—United States. I. Title.
N363.H84 1996   95-54178
707'.1'273—dc20   CIP

FRONT COVER: Grant Wood, American, 1891–1942. *American Gothic*, oil on
beaver board, 1930, 74.3 x 62.4 cm, Friends of American Art Collection, © 1996
The Art Institute of Chicago and VAGA, New York, NY, 1930. 934

Printed in the United States of America

10 9 8 7 6 5 4 3 2

ISBN 0-13-299521-2 NB2I

ATTENTION: CORPORATIONS AND SCHOOLS

Prentice Hall books are available at quantity discounts with bulk purchase for
educational, business, or sales promotional use. For information, please write to:
Prentice Hall Special Sales, 240 Frisch Court, Paramus, New Jersey 07652.
Please supply: title of book, ISBN number, quantity, how the book will be used,
date needed.

PRENTICE HALL
Paramus, NJ 07652

A Simon & Schuster Company

On the World Wide Web at http://www.phdirect.com

Prentice-Hall International (UK) Limited, *London*
Prentice-Hall of Australia Pty. Limited, *Sydney*
Prentice-Hall Canada Inc., *Toronto*
Prentice-Hall Hispanoamericana, S.A., *Mexico*
Prentice-Hall of India Private Limited, *New Delhi*
Prentice-Hall of Japan, Inc., *Tokyo*
Simon & Schuster Asia Pte. Ltd., *Singapore*
Editora Prentice-Hall do Brasil, Ltda., *Rio de Janeiro*

*To my husband, Jack, and
my children, Connie, Susan, David*

ACKNOWLEDGMENTS

A book of this scope does not come together without support from many students, colleagues, professional art educators, and other researchers and writers who recorded the lives of American artists. I include one of my former professors, Leon Hicks, whose research on African-American artists has been invaluable.

A special debt is owed to editors Connie Kallback and Win Huppuch, whose review, input, and encouragement got the book off to a good beginning, and whose continued support has been invaluable. My gratitude to the professional staff at Prentice Hall, especially Diane Turso and Mariann Hutlak, who saw this book through to completion. I am especially grateful to all my students from Parkway West High School and Florissant Valley Community College who encouraged me and were willing to allow me to use their artwork in this book, and to colleagues John Dunivent, Timothy Smith, Sue Trent, Mary Ann Kroeck, Sue Hinkle, Linda Bowers, Katie Wendel, Pamela Hellwege (formerly on the St. Louis Art Museum staff), Bonnie Enos, Lois and Steve Rufer, and Cyndi Shepard, who generously agreed to allow me to use projects they had developed. Other artists who allowed me to adapt projects they had shown at National Art Education Association conferences were John Rozzelle of the School of Chicago Art Institute, Helen Fleming Stone, and Bill Camptin.

The staff of The Saint Louis Art Museum has been unfailingly encouraging, in particular: Dr. Elizabeth Vallance, Louise Cameron, Sue Hooker, Cheryl Benjamin, Kate Guerra, Barbara Decker-Franklin, and Carlene Fullerton. Pat Woods deserves a special accolade for her help and encouragement in selecting the many artworks used in this book.

Parkway West librarians Barb Kellams and Paula Lucas have been particularly supportive, and I am also indebted to The Saint Louis Art Museum librarians under the direction of Stephanie Sigala who have helped me with research. The museum professionals who have worked with me in obtaining reproductions from their collections have had infinite patience. I would like to thank the following: Stacey Sherman of The Nelson-Atkins Museum of Art, Claudia Goldstein of Art Resource, Julie Zestel and Pamela Stuedemann of The Art Institute of Chicago, Ann Stetser of The Hirshhorn Museum and Sculpture Garden, Laura Jolley of Missouri State Archives, Barbara Guthrie of Kemper Museum of Contemporary Art and Design, Bernice Epstein of The Metropolitan Museum of Art, Tina Douglas of The Minneapolis Museum of Art, Mikki Carpenter of The Museum of Modern Art, Sarah Sibbald and Barbara Bernard of The National Gallery of Art, Felicia Pickering and David Burgeven of The National Museum of Natural History, Virginia Dooley of Navajo Gallery in Taos, New Mexico, Caroline Demaree of Philadelphia Museum of Art, and Joseph Ketner of Washington University Gallery of Art.

We thank the following for permitting us to use their artwork:

Art Resource
Arrangement in Gray and Black No. 1, The Artist's Mother, James Abbott McNeill Whistler, The Louvre, Paris; *The Library,* Jacob Lawrence, National Museum of American Art, Washington, D.C.; *George Washington, 1732–1799, First President of the United States,* Rembrandt Peale, National Portrait Gallery, Washington, D.C./Art Resource

The Boatmen's National Bank of St. Louis
The Verdict of the People, George Caleb Bingham

Louise Bourgeois (permission from Robert Miller Gallery)
The Winged Figure, 1948; *Untitled,* 1950

The Art Institute of Chicago
Gulfstream, Winslow Homer; *American Gothic,* Grant Wood; *AARRRRRRHH,* Red Grooms; *Flying Dragon,* Alexander Calder; *Whirligig,* Frank Memkus; *The Herring Net,* Winslow Homer; *The Advance Guard or The Military Sacrifice,* Frederick Remington; *Nocturne in Grey and Gold,* 1872, James Abbott McNeill Whistler; *No. 6,* Jackson Pollock; *City of Chicago,* 1967, Red Grooms

Mr. and Mrs. Barney Ebsworth Foundation
Classic Landscape, 1931, Charles Sheeler

Hirshhorn Museum and Sculpture Garden
Rapt at Rappaports, Stuart Davis; *Hollywood,* Red Grooms; *Beach at Gloucester,* Maurice Prendergast; *Holy Mountain III,* Horace Pippin; *The Beware-Danger American Dream No. 4,* Robert Indiana; *Maquette for Way Down East,* Red Grooms

Kemper Museum of Contemporary Art and Design, Kansas City, Missouri
Still Life With Open Book, Janet Fish

Mercantile Library
Tri-colored Heron, John James Audubon

Metropolitan Museum of Art
Washington Crossing the Delaware, Emanuel Gottlieb Leutz; *Still Life—Violin and Music,* William Michael Harnett

Minneapolis Museum of Art
Reminiscences of 1865, John Frederick Peto

Museum of Modern Art, New York
Washington Crossing the Delaware, Larry Rivers; *Map of USA,* Jasper Johns; *The American Dream 1,* Robert Indiana; *Robert,* Chuck Close; *Dove,* Romare Bearden; *Visa,* Stuart Davis; *Target with Four Faces,* Jasper Johns

National Gallery of Art
Voyage of Life, Youth, Thomas Cole; *Snow in New York,* Robert Henri; *Jack in the Pulpit No. IV,* Georgia O'Keeffe; *Number 1 (Lavender Mist),* Jackson Pollock; *The Loge,* 1882, Mary Cassatt; *Cutout of Animals,* artist unknown; *The Return of Rip Van Winkle,* John Quidor; *Peaceable Kingdom,* Edward Hicks; *The White Cloud, Head Chief of the Iowas,* George Catlin

National Museum of American Art
Washington Crossing the Delaware, Alex Katz; *The Library,* 1960, Jacob Lawrence; *Young Omahaw, War Eagle, Little Missouri, and Pawnees,* Charles Bird King

National Museum of Natural History
Bear Tipi, Bear Bringing It

Navajo Gallery, Taos, New Mexico
Flower of Las Lunas, R. C. Gorman; *Morning Star,* R. C. Gorman; *Seated Woman,* R. C. Gorman

Nelson-Atkins Museum of Art, Kansas City, Missouri
Horse, Deborah K. Butterfield; *At the Theater (Woman in Loge),* Mary Cassatt; *Winter Count,* Hunkpapa
Lakota; *Himmel,* Marsden Hartley; *Teaching a Mustang Pony to Pack Dead Game,* Frederic Remington; *Apple
Blossoms,* Georgia O'Keeffe; *Berdie with the American Flag,* Larry Rivers; *Vase of Flowers,* artist unknown;
Serape Blanket, artist unknown; *No. 6, 1952,* Jackson Pollock

People of Missouri
Young Boatman, George Caleb Bingham

Philadelphia Museum of Art
The Peaceable Kingdom, Edward Hicks

Professional Artists
Jo Baker's Birthday and *The Dinner Party,* Faith Ringgold; *Still-Life With Blue Pitcher,* LuWayne Stark; *My
Inspiration,* Dycie Madsen; *Mural with Blue Brush Stroke,* Roy Lichtenstein

St. Louis Museum of Art
Sea Captains Carousing in Suriname, John Greenwood; *The Jolly Flatboatmen in Port,* George Caleb Bingham;
Flowering Cherry Tree and Peony, John LaFarge; *Steerage,* Alfred Stieglitz; *Bathers Verso,* Maurice
Prendergast; *Classic Landscape,* Charles Sheeler; *Jo Baker's Birthday,* Faith Ringgold; *Storage Jar,* Pueblo
Anasazi; *Headpiece,* Bella Coola People; *Travelling Tents of the Sioux Indians called a Tepe* (sic), Seth Eastman;
Album Quilt, Mary Ann Hudgins, Eliza Garrett, and Mary Jane Smith; *George Washington,* Gilbert Stuart;
Benjamin Franklin, Jean-Antoine Houdon; *The Boston Massacre,* Paul Revere; *In Memory of General
Washington and His Lady,* artist unknown; *The Bronco Buster,* Frederick Remington; *The Wrecked Schooner,*
Winslow Homer; *With the Staats Zeitung,* William M. Harnett; *Still-Life Feasible #2,* Stuart Davis; *Weehawken,
New Jersey,* John Marin; *Goldfish Bowl II,* Roy Lichtenstein; *Head,* Roy Lichtenstein; *Cubi XIV,* David Smith;
Keith IV - State 1, Chuck Close; *Untitled,* Keith Haring; *Painted Deerhide,* collection of William Webster;
Raftsmen Playing Cards, George Caleb Bingham; *Supermarket - Produce,* Jacob Lawrence

State of Missouri
Social History of the State of Missouri, Detail: Politics, Farming, and Law in Missouri, 1935–1936, Thomas
Hart Benton

Utah Travel Council
Newspaper Rock

Washington University Gallery of Art, Steinberg Hall, St. Louis, Missouri
The Iron Cross, Marsden Hartley

ABOUT THE AUTHOR

Helen Hume has been an art educator for almost thirty years. An art specialist, she has taught general art to students from kindergarten through university level, and specific courses such as art history, painting, photography, ceramics, printmaking, sculpture, and crafts. While living in Europe and studying painting at Het Vrij Atelier in Antwerp, Belgium, she established the art program at the Antwerp International School. She also taught art at the International School of Sao José dos Campos in Brazil for several years. She currently creates and writes about art and is part of the Education Department at Florissant Valley Community College in St. Louis, where she teaches an Art Methods course.

Mrs. Hume has written articles for professional magazines such as *School Arts* and *Arts and Activities,* and been involved in art curriculum development for the Parkway School District. She was recently involved in writing a model curriculum as part of the "Curriculum for the 21st Century" Project for the State of Missouri. She is also the author of *A Survival Kit for the Secondary School Art Teacher,* and *Art History and Appreciation Activities Kit: Ready-to-Use Lessons, Slides, and Projects for Secondary Students.* Her fourth book, *An Art Teacher's Book of Lists,* is already in progress.

Mrs. Hume has represented the Parkway School District on the Educational Advisory Board of the St. Louis Art Museum. She is a member of the National Art Education Association, and has presented art methods at many national conferences. Her degrees are from Webster University in St. Louis, Missouri. She is a photographer, painter, and printmaker as well, and is on the Board of Governers of the St. Louis Artists' Guild.

ABOUT THIS RESOURCE

American Art Appreciation Activities Kit was written to bring alive the history of American art by involving students in projects based on their heritage. Most of these activities are suitable for interdisciplinary studies in art, humanities, social studies, foreign languages, and language arts classes. Although the techniques are based on historical examples, students are encouraged to make personal interpretations drawn from their own lives and contemporary culture. Studio activities give students a greater understanding and appreciation for the skills developed by earlier artists. Suggestions are given for a number of group activities. Many of the projects can be worked on for short periods of time or for one or two days.

The book includes some writing activities, architectural handouts, and time-lines. It is arranged chronologically, with over 75 projects and 225 additional suggestions, to complement secondary American history textbooks. Because many secondary schools stress post-1865 history, greater emphasis is given to the artwork from 1865 to modern times. An overview of the entire visual art history of the United States is covered, relating to the work of major artists and themes. Artwork based on that of various social groups is included as it occurred, chronologically. Works by female artists, Native-Americans, African-Americans, and Americans of Hispanic, Asian, and European descent are represented. (It was with regret that I was not able to adapt the artwork of many of our influential artists for use in this book, but their names will be found in the Appendix.) Several projects are based on American symbols such as the flag, George Washington, the eagle, and state capitol buildings.

The activities in this book explore that heritage while allowing students to bring their own personal identities to traditional arts and crafts. The book encourages students not only to learn about the work done by their forebears, but to carry on the tradition of American art.

This teacher resource book may be used in any manner you wish, but it contains a number of special features that you may want to take advantage of. The Introduction contains suggestions for teaching about the Elements and Principles of Art, with a reproducible handout, and suggestions for activities in architecture and aesthetics. In addition, there is a slide script to accompany the slides which will give you a quick overview. Individual chapters contain more information on the artists whose work is featured in the slides. Each chapter contains a brief overview of American art trends, "schools" of art, and artists, with specific information on painting, sculpture, and architecture throughout American history. Each chapter features reproducibles: a time-line, an architectural handout, student activity handouts, as well as information for you, the teacher.

Helen D. Hume

CONTENTS

Section 6—Early Twentieth Century (1900 to 1920) • 169

Section 7—Art Between the Wars (1920 to 1940) • 199

FOR THE TEACHER

INTRODUCTION

American art is like America itself: rich in cultural traditions from all over the world, diverse in its many forms, flourishing, and constantly changing. Sometimes it is crude and untutored, sometimes quite sophisticated, but its art is always reflective of the time period and culture in which it was made.

Students can learn about the art and history of their country by studying its artists, techniques, and innovations. Because American students take history courses, they will already be aware of the forces that formed a given era, but they may not be familiar with the art that was produced during that time. Learning "old" techniques, and sometimes applying them to their own lives, brings art alive to students.

This book explores not only painting, but also folk art, sculpture, and architecture. Many of the artists are known by name, but many were anonymous, perhaps because what they did was not even considered "art" at the time they made it. Many American artists were "naive" (not formally trained) folk artists, whose art might be painted on the side of a barn or embroidered into a "sampler." Works such as weathervanes constructed by artisans, quilts made by the women of a family, and beaded work placed on practical Native American items reflect the practical application of decorative art.

In the years of the founding of the country, American painters who could afford it usually went to Europe to complete their education. Many early American portraits were painted, however, by anonymous "limners" (slang for illuminators) who went from town to town painting portraits. It was speculated that some painted the bodies during the winter, then painted in "portrait" heads during the summer when they traveled. Wealthy Americans wished to have their portraits painted for posterity, but had little interest in other forms of art such as landscape, religious paintings (as evidenced by the plain churches of the pilgrims), or mythology.

There was little need for sculpture in a country that was formed on the premise of religious freedom. Carved images in churches were rare. The earliest form of decorative carving was on gravestones. Images made to identify shops such as "Cigarstore Indians," or shop "signs" were necessary for a society that was only partially literate. Carved figureheads (of which few examples survived shipwrecks and fires) for sailing ships were among the finest in the world.

The daily occurrences of life have always been reflected in paintings or sculpture. In the art of the twentieth century, industrial symbols were often incorporated into paintings. The automobile culture is reflected in today's paintings, and often automobile parts are found as parts of sculpture or the entire automobile itself is decorated as an "art car."

As the twentieth century ends, the ease of travel and communication leads to an "international style," yet American artists continue to retain a national identity. The cultural heritage of well over 500 years continues to make its impact on the arts in America. Each culture that immigrates to America brings with it certain innovations or traditional art forms that are assimilated into American art, just as the people themselves are assimilated into the country's social fiber. National symbols such as the American flag, the Statue of Liberty, the president, and the White House continue to be incorporated into artwork. Individual cultures that add their threads to the American tapestry reflect a personal artistic heritage, whether it is Asian, African, Native American, Hispanic, or European. These individual differences keep American art alive and vital.

LOOKING AT ART AND WRITING ABOUT IT

The following writing and discussion projects are "filler" projects—many of them take from five to ten minutes, but I find students enjoy the change-of-pace at times.

- Students may keep an art journal. From time to time put something in the front of the room such as a slide, poster, or art object and have students make a journal entry. Collect the journals occasionally and read them. It will be helpful to students and you.

- Teach students to look analytically at a painting, sculpture, or example of architecture through looking at slides, books, and posters. A handout on the elements and principles of art is included here, which will aid them in learning the vocabulary of art. Have them:

  Look for triangles in a composition.

  Look for a composition that is largely composed of lines, or where a line leads your eye to the point of emphasis.

  Look for a picture where color is the main element.

  Look for a diagonal line.

- Have students write a short descriptive essay about an artwork concentrating on using adverbs and adjectives.

- Hang posters around the room and have students select one about which to write a poem. When you ask them to read the poem, have students look at the posters and see if they can identify which artwork was described.

The Diamante (literally a diamond-shaped poem) is perfect for the project:

Line 1: a one-word equivalent for the picture

Line 2: an action phrase

Line 3: a simile or metaphor

Line 4: a summation, again a single word

A *Haiku* poem is a three-line poem that consists of 17 syllables:

Line 1: 5 syllables

Line 2: 7 syllables

Line 3: 5 syllables

A *sonnet,* a fixed verse originating in Italy, has 14 lines (typically rhyming). I've had better luck having students *not* make their poems rhyme, but when they ask how long it *has* to be, I find that "at least 14 lines" is a good answer and gets good results. They especially enjoy writing poetry about photography.

- The following is a brief overview of some of the information contained in the book that will give students food for thought and discussion. As with anything, pick and choose what you might want to discuss at any one time.

  Teach students to recognize the different *media used in painting* such as water-color, gouache (watercolor with white added), tempera, oil and acrylic paints, and ink.

  Drawing media such as oil pastels, pastels, conté crayon, and charcoal might be experimented with so students will recognize them when they see them. If you are short of time, have each student experiment with or research a different medium and share results with the class.

  Printmaking techniques such as woodcuts, linocuts, silkscreen, and intaglio printing can be explained by getting a library book and showing differences.

  Have students research different *sculpture techniques* such as assemblage with found materials, carving, and modeling. They can find examples of each.

  New media in art—such as computer graphics, photography, environmental art, the use of sound, light, and space—all could be discussed with students to further their appreciation for non-traditional art methods.

  Crafts such as basketry, weaving, ceramics, jewelry-making, glass-blowing, and paper making are ages-old, but continue their popularity, and ever-new ways of using these old techniques keep them popular.

  Subject matter in art changes as taste changes, but the traditional painting and sculpture subjects are: animals, religious art, mythological, literary and historical subjects, portraiture, narrative art, landscape / seascape, interiors, fantasy art, and still-life.

  Style has to do with whether an artist works realistically or emotionally. Stylistic methods are called romantic, realistic, abstract, non-objective, and classical.

ELEMENTS AND PRINCIPLES OF ART

ELEMENTS OF ART

- **Line:** The path of a moving point. It can be vertical, horizontal, diagonal, curved, angular, zigzag, bent, straight, interrupted, thick, thin.
- **Color:** What the eye sees when light is reflected from it. *Hue* is the color in its most intense form. *Value* refers to the differences in hue ranging from lightest to darkest. Primary colors (red, blue, yellow) cannot be produced by mixing other colors together. Secondary colors (orange, violet, green) are created by mixing primary colors.
- **Shape:** The area enclosed by an outline; the flat area created by lines, colors, and tones; geometric; amorphous (without clarity); and bio-morphic (living or dead). Shapes can be indicated by line or color.
- **Form:** Shape with three dimensions—height, width, and depth. Form can be realistic, abstract, idealized, naturalistic, or non-representational.
- **Value:** The gradual change of lightness or darkness, white to black, used to suggest roundness or depth.
- **Texture:** Surface treatment ranging from very smooth to quite rough. It can be real or implied.
- **Space:** Actual (open air around sculpture or architecture) or implied (can be shown by control of size, color, overlapping).

PRINCIPLES OF DESIGN

- **Proportion:** The pleasing relationship of all parts to each other and to the whole of the design.
- **Variety:** Differences in scale, surface, line, value, and shape that give interest to a composition.
- **Contrast:** Differences between the elements of art: texture, color, value, line.
- **Emphasis:** The center-of-interest; one feature is most important and everything else works with it.
- **Pattern and repetition:** Use of line, color, or a motif in more than one place in a composition.
- **Rhythm:** Repeated use of similar elements such as color, line, or shape. The smooth transition from one part to another.
- **Balance:** The equilibrium of various elements in the work of art. It can be symmetrical or asymmetrical.
- **Harmony:** The unity of all the visual elements in a composition.

AESTHETIC EXPERIENCES

Aesthetics was a term first used by the German philosopher Alexander Baumgarten in 1744 to mean "The Science of the beautiful." Educating students in art today means that we will teach its history, the process of doing it, criticism of the student's own artwork and that of other artists, and aesthetics. Dealing with aesthetics seems to yield more questions than answers, but it encourages students to develop and express opinions.

In conducting an aesthetic lesson with students, here are a few suggestions:

- Assemble a group of items such as a T-shirt, really disreputable jeans (most kids own them), a natural object such as a shell, a manufactured item such as a decorated coffee mug, a mask or artwork from a foreign culture, a photograph, a print, an ad from a magazine, etc. Display these, with a number on each one. Before explaining this exercise, have each student write a definition of art. By the definition they just wrote, students must decide whether these objects in front of them are art or not. To get a discussion going, ask them first to give you their definitions. Then ask questions such as: Does something have to be one of a kind to be art? Is art always beautiful? Does it have to be made by hand to be an artwork? If it is part of nature, is it a work of art? If you only see something beautiful to you (such as a sunset), is that a work of art?

- Hang posters around the room. Make some small tokens of construction paper (such as green strips to represent dollar bills, a "blue ribbon," a red heart). Have some tape, and have students tape their tokens on the one they love best (the blue ribbon), the one they think cost the most money (green "dollars"), the one they think a museum curator might buy (a yellow "frame"), and the one they think their mother would love (the heart).

Here are some suggestions that may be useful in beginning discussions:

Have a few questions with obvious answers to get the conversation rolling and involve shy students.

Help students develop the ability to deal with disagreement and uncertainty and to value ways of looking at something from a different perspective.

Avoid yes / no questions because they tend to cut off discussion.

Avoid rote definitions from a dictionary. These give the impression there is only one answer.

Avoid questions that have their own answers.

Have students play "devil's advocate" by presenting counter-arguments.

Avoid long questions. Be clear and concise, because the question sometimes determines the answer.

Wait for a time, then sum up or clarify.

Play off one student's answers against another's. "Do you agree with David? Why?"

Keep all students involved, not just the ones nearest you.

Don't ask a question if you don't have time to listen to an answer.

Try the pair-share method of inquiry. Have students get into groups and come up with one answer.

Set down rules before you begin an aesthetic discussion such as: Try to be open to a point of view that is different from yours, and when possible, try to give a clear reason to support your statement.

Questions like the following often get students thinking and talking about their own opinions, and offer lively discussions:

What do we mean by the word "beautiful"?

What is art?

Without an artist, is there art?

Does the intention to be an artist make you one?

What purposes does art serve?

How can we tell if one artwork is better than another?

Do artists have a responsibility to society in what they choose to depict?

In what ways are aesthetic values related to other values?

What function does this serve for a society?

Does a particular object mean more to one society than to another?

What are some examples of something that means more to one society than to another? (depictions of the human form, for example)

Why is this object art and that object not art?

Can art be made of something that is not beautiful? or something that is actually ugly?

ARCHITECTURAL ACTIVITIES

- Take students on an architectural tour of their own city or region of the country. Allow time to stop and, if at all possible, make arrangements to go inside several buildings or houses. Old and brand new houses constantly evolve, and students enjoy comparing and contrasting architecture. Before going, find information about various building techniques so students know what to look for.

- Suggest a group of students make slides, prints, or videos of the buildings in their city or old buildings around the countryside. This project works well in either the country or city, as students make an architectural record of their region. This could be presented to the class as a brochure (photocopies could be made), travel video, or slide show.

- Tell students that they are creating a brochure for the local Chamber of Commerce. The purpose is to attract business to the city. This is a very good interdisciplinary project as students can find out the impact of bringing in a factory or business from outside the city. They could find out the impact on the local environment as it affects water supply, sewage facilities, school, fire, and police systems. They can collect information about the city that a business would want to know, such as the population, school system (how many schools, state rankings, etc.).

- Have students discuss what the ugliest building in town is, which is the best looking, and why they think it is. Ask them if an ugly building should be torn down. Who should make the decision? Let them know that they may have to be involved if they want to preserve something just because it is old.

- Have students find out when their own families first immigrated to the United States. If they are not sure, have them "adopt" a nationality to research. Questions they should find answers to are:

  What was housing like in their "mother" country when their families came here?

  What is it like today?

  Did the homes of their ancestors influence architecture of the United States? (for example, adobe buildings/Spanish architecture)

  How much do available materials influence a building style?

- Divide groups of students to find out about architecture of different regions of the country or different periods of time. This research can be presented to the class through showing books or videos.

- Students may make a clay facade of a building, perhaps their own home, or one of the better-known landmarks of the city. This could also be made of tagboard, building up layer after layer to make details.

- Students can make an architectural time line showing how public buildings have changed. They can identify famous buildings.

• Have students design a model city such as Washington, D.C. Discuss what the hub of a city is—for many it is the courthouse square. They could redesign their own city (much as some government agencies have done). Ask how they could make areas of their own city more accessible for disabled people. Considerations should be parking, public restrooms, parks, water supplies, waste treatment, green space around the city, transportation such as circumferential highways, buses, underground transportation, etc.

SUGGESTIONS FOR USING THE SLIDES

Showing slides and getting students to talk about them is fun for the students and the teacher. This is a good opportunity for them to use the vocabulary of art, noticing how the artist uses the elements of art: color, line, form, texture, shape, and space. The principles of art: repetition, proportion, contrast, variety, rhythm, harmony, emphasis, and movement are used to organize the elements of art. Naturally the content of an artwork is important, but when you encourage each student to analyze and say something about a sculpture or painting, they find that this is one part of learning about art that they truly love. Here are some teaching suggestions that work when showing slides:

- Use the slides (which are organized chronologically) to give an overview of American art, or select individual slides to illustrate a particular concept or project.

- In each chapter, specific slides are listed that would give further information about a certain artist or time period. The slides fit into a number of categories. Contrasting and comparing them is sometimes a useful teaching tool. The slides included in this book also can be grouped. Students tend to remember best those artworks about which *they* have talked.

- Tell the students that each of them will have to say something about the painting. (Suggest they have two or three things ready in case someone else "uses" theirs.)

- Sometimes have one student be "the teacher" by standing next to and analyzing an entire projected painting, using a pointer or yardstick to show specific items about which he or she is talking.

- Have students write a five-minute essay about a slide, telling them that they can first put down exactly what they see, then analyze it, using the elements and principles of art, then perhaps writing about what they think the artist was trying to show.

- A ten- or twenty-minute essay comparing and contrasting two slides shown side by side really causes students to stretch, but allows them more time to plan their essay in advance.

Examples of categories for comparing and contrasting are:

George Washington

Portrait of George Washington, Gilbert Stuart

Washington Crossing the Delaware, Emanuel Leutz

Washington Crossing the Delaware, Larry Rivers

George Washington Crossing the Delaware, Alex Katz

Watercolor

Tricolored Heron, John James Audubon

The Gulfstream, Winslow Homer

Bathers, Verso, Maurice Prendergast

Weehawken, New Jersey, John Marin

The Library, Jacob Lawrence

Oil Paint

Portrait of George Washington, Gilbert Stuart

Sea Captains Carousing in Suriname, John Greenwood

The Peaceable Kingdom, Edward Hicks

Still Life with Open Book, Janet Fish

The Jolly Flatboatmen in Port, George Caleb Bingham

Voyage of Life—Youth, Thomas Cole

Young Omahaw, War Eagle, Little Missouri, and Pawnees, Charles Bird King

Arrangement in Gray and Black No. 1: The Artist's Mother, James Abbott McNeill Whistler

Reminiscences of 1865, John Frederick Peto

Snow in Winter, Robert Henri

Himmel, Marsden Hartley

Rapt at Rappaport's, Stuart Davis

Jack-in-the-Pulpit No. IV, Georgia O'Keeffe

Classic Landscape, Charles Sheeler

Social History of the State of Missouri, Thomas Hart Benton

American Gothic, Grant Wood

Number 1, (Lavender Mist), Jackson Pollock

Pastel

At the Theater (Woman in a Loge), Mary Cassatt

Print (Lithographs)

Flower of Las Lunas, R. C. Gorman

AARRRRRRHH, Red Grooms

Sculpture

George Washington Crossing the Delaware, Alex Katz

City of Chicago, Red Grooms and Mimi Gross

Horse, Deborah K. Butterfield

Other

Album Quilt, Mary Ann Hudgins, Eliza Garrett, and Mary Jane Smith (crafts)

Jo Baker's Birthday, Faith Ringgold (quilt)

Tipi Model (crafts)

Hollyhocks and *Flowering Cherry Tree and Peony,* John LaFarge (stained glass)

The Steerage, Alfred Stieglitz (photography)

Landscape / Seascape

Peaceable Kingdom, Edward Hicks

Washington Crossing the Delaware, Emanuel Leutz

The Jolly Flatboatmen in Port, George Caleb Bingham

Flower of Las Lunas, R. C. Gorman

Voyage of Life—Youth, Thomas Cole

The Gulfstream, Winslow Homer

Snow in New York, Robert Henri

Weehawken, New Jersey, John Marin

Classic Landscape, Charles Sheeler

Map, Jasper Johns

Portrait

Portrait of George Washington, Gilbert Stuart

Young Omahaw, War Eagle, Little Missouri, and Pawnees, Charles Bird King

Arrangement in Gray and Black No. 1: The Artist's Mother, James Abbott McNeill Whistler

At the Theater (Woman in a Loge), Mary Cassatt

The Dove, Romare Bearden

American Gothic, Grant Wood

Flower of Las Lunas, R. C. Gorman

Hollywood, Red Grooms

Robert, Chuck Close

Jo Baker's Birthday, Faith Ringgold

SLIDE IDENTIFICATION SCRIPT

SLIDE #1: *Winter Count* (?), c. 1912, Painting—American Indian (Great Plains), Ink (?) and colors on muslin, 38-³/₄ × 53-⁵/₈ inches, Hunkpapa Lakota, Lent to The Nelson-Atkins Museum of Art, Kansas City, Missouri, by Conception Abbey, Conception, Missouri.

A Winter Count was a picture record of Plains tribal history from one winter until the next. When written alphabets were introduced in the mid-1800s, the Winter Count became less important, although some are still kept today. Some of the symbols are easily recognizable, such as the white man wearing the tall black hat. A single star was the year a bright comet fell from the sky. The record was generally painted on a buffalo robe or traders' muslin by the keeper of the count, and featured a symbol (agreed upon by the tribal elders) for the year's most important event. The *Winter Count* shown here has years numbered, beginning at the upper left corner and going clockwise around the outside toward the inside. Although the artist is not known, it is *very* similar to one created in 1912 by Swift Dog of the Hunkpapa Lakota. The drawing is stylized (much as Egyptians had stylized rules for painting), and similar to that of many personal and tribal exploit robes.

SLIDE #2: *Bear Tipi of Bear Bringing It,* c. 1904, Kiowa (Gaigwa), hide/wood/pigment, approximately 30 × 33 inches, National Museum of Natural History, Smithsonian Institution.

When Native Americans were forced to move to reservations, traveling tipis were rarely used. An archaeologist commissioned groups of Cheyenne and Kiowa men who had made and lived in tipis to create model tipis such as this. These were to show in the Exposition of 1893 and the World's Fair of 1904. Tipi designs "belonged" to certain families and were passed from generation to generation. The bear and bear pawprints had special meaning to Bear Bringing It, the creator of this tipi. Bears shared many characteristics with humans, and were considered to have spiritual healing and protective powers. Often leaders were shown wearing bearpaw necklaces. An original tipi would have been made with the tanned hides of 14 buffalo, with 22 poles, and the opening facing east.

SLIDE #3: *Flower of Las Lunas,* 1987, Courtesy of R. C. Gorman, lithograph, 33 × 28 inches, edition of 200. Courtesy of the Artist, Navajo Gallery, Taos, New Mexico.

"There's magic in the canyon. There's the eerie feeling they're looking down at you. It makes you feel you should have brought a gift." R. C. Gorman's own words about the area where he lived are shown in his artwork—the wide open spaces, the magical colors, all convey a feeling of mysticism. This lithograph (print) shows a Native American woman looking at chards of ancient pots from the Anasazi (translated Ancient Ones). The flowering cactus is one that opens during the night, and you can almost smell its fragrance. Gorman's most frequently used subjects are female Native Americans, usually showing only head, hands, and feet, often depicted in front of ruins such as Taos, New Mexico. He said he was always in awe of the ruins, which were built by the Anasazi, and he felt like they were still inhabited.

SLIDE #4:   *Album Quilt,* 1848, Mary Ann Hudgins, Eliza Garrett, and Mary Jane Smith, cotton and sepia ink, 100-¼ × 100-¼ inches, Gift of Mrs. Stratford Lee Morton, The Saint Louis Art Museum.

This "show" quilt was appliqued before being finely quilted, and was made by three women working together to honor Elizabeth Morrison. Quilts such as this *Album Quilt* (sometimes called a Baltimore Quilt because so many of this style were made in Baltimore) were made with a collection of squares in a horizontal and vertical grid, and finished with a unifying border. They often were made as a very special presentation quilt for a young man on his 21st birthday or to honor someone in the community. The use of the flag, eagle, and shield in the center is typical of the pride in the United States that is often seen in artwork. The eagle is tinted with sepia ink, and occasionally squares are written on with sepia to identify the artist. Notice the different interpretations of baskets of flowers, wreaths, cornucopias, and stems and leaves with flowers. This quilt is in stark contrast to the crudely patched pioneer quilts made from homespun begun in the early days of the colonies.

SLIDE #5:   *Portrait of George Washington (1732–1799), First President of the U.S.,* 1796, Gilbert Stuart, oil on canvas, 48 × 37 inches, National Portrait Gallery, Smithsonian Institution (owned jointly with the Museum of Fine Arts, Boston); Art Resource, New York.

This unfinished portrait of George Washington was commissioned by Martha Washington and was the third and last portrait of George Washington that Stuart painted from life. The *Athenaeum Head* (named for its purchase from the Boston Athenaeum) served as the model for 70 copies and many of Stuart's 104 subsequent portraits of Washington. Stuart demonstrates his classical English training under Joshua Reynolds and George Romney. He shows Washington as "aloof and commanding, strong, yet sensitive." The head was placed high to show Washington's imposing presence and, although it is unfinished, it is considered the most famous of his portraits. Stuart said of this painting that Washington had just had false teeth inserted, and this accounts for the "constrained expression and set look of the lower part of his face." It is the model for Washington's portrait on the dollar bill, and was copied throughout the colonies by artists such as Raphael Peale in his famous porthole paintings, and folk artists through the ages. A number of Pop artists used paintings of George Washington satirically.

SLIDE #6:   *Sea Captains Carousing in Suriname,* c. 1758, John Greenwood, oil on bed ticking, 37-³⁄₈ × 75-¼ inches, Museum Purchase, The Saint Louis Art Museum.

American sea captains frequently stopped in the Dutch port of Suriname which was on the route between the West Indies and America, and obviously enjoyed themselves while at port. This picture was believed to be the first genre picture (showing everyday life) painted in the Americas. It shows the artist, John Greenwood, vomiting in the doorway, and a number of other well-known colonists such as the seated figure of Captain Nicholas Cooke (with the hat and long pipe) who later became the Governor of Rhode Island. Cooke is shown talking with Captain Esek Hopkins who later commanded the Continental Navy. The Governor of Rhode Island (and a signer of the Declaration of Independence), Stephen Hopkins is pouring rum on the head of Jonas

Wanton. A man is shown cheating at cards (with a card stuck in his hat), and another hasn't noticed that his coat is catching fire from a candle. This scene is reminiscent of tavern scenes by Dutch artist Jan Steen. It is the first of many narrative (story-telling) paintings done in the United States.

SLIDE #7: *The Peaceable Kingdom,* **1826, Edward Hicks, oil on canvas, 32-½ × 41-½ inches, Bequest of Charles C. Willis, Philadelphia Museum of Art.**

This painting is one of approximately eighty similar paintings of this same general subject by Edward Hicks. Not all of them have writing around the border as this one does, but most of them feature a small child, a number of animals, and William Penn (wearing a blue sash) signing a treaty with the Indians in the background. The writing around the outside is based on a Biblical verse of Isaiah's prophecy, "The Lion shall lie down with the lamb" (Isaiah 11: 6-9). William Penn was a Quaker, as was Edward Hicks, and the painting represented the peace hoped for by both men. There are many inconsistencies in the painting, but Hicks was trained as a sign painter, not an academic artist, and his unfamiliarity with exotic animals has made his almost human-faced animals charming. The writing around the edges says: "When the great Penn his famous treaty made, With indian chiefs beneath the Elm-tree's shade. The lion with the fatling on did move. A little child was leading them in love. The leopard with the harmless kid laid down, and not one savage beast was seen to frown. The wolf did with the lambkind dwell in peace. His grim carnivorous nature there did cease."

SLIDE #8: *Washington Crossing the Delaware,* **1851, Emanuel Gottlieb Leutz, oil on canvas, 149 × 255 inches, The Metropolitan Museum of Art, Gift of John Stewart Kennedy, 1897.**

This painting represents Christmas night, 1776, when Washington and 2400 of his troops crossed the Delaware at Trenton during a sleet storm, surprising the Hessians at dawn, winning the battle and turning the tide of the war. It is one of the great icons of American painting, although it was painted in Dusseldorf by German-born-American Emanuel Leutz while he was living there. This particular painting is a copy of his 1848 original which was severely damaged by fire in 1850. It shows Washington at the helm of a boat which is surrounded by ice floes. In the background one sees horses and men. This huge painting, with its romanticized painting of a heroic moment, symbolizes the American Revolution, and has been reproduced more than any other American painting.

Have students point out pictorial devices used by Leutz to make Washington the visual center of the composition. Compare this with two other versions of the same subject by Alex Katz and Larry Rivers. Have students talk about similarities and differences. Why could this have become so famous?

SLIDE #9: *The Jolly Flatboatmen in Port,* **1857, George Caleb Bingham, oil on canvas, 47-¹⁄₁₆ × 69-⅝ inches, Museum Purchase, The Saint Louis Art Museum.**

George Caleb Bingham enjoyed painting small-town political life and life on the Mississippi and Missouri rivers. His paintings and drawings often had triangular or pyramidal compositions of people, many of which he combined into one large composition. His scenes were usually painted at dawn or dusk, allowing him to use light masterfully. *The Jolly Flatboatmen in Port,* while somewhat idealized, demonstrates the need to while away time on the long journeys up and down the river. This scene is in the port of St. Louis, after the cargo has been unloaded, and includes visitors as well as rivermen. While the eye is drawn to the central figure of the young man through the use of light, there are a number of other figures involved in activities of their own (such as the man writing, who might be a reporter or a boat owner checking on a bill of lading). The "pan thumper" to the left of the central figure was used in a number of compositions. This is one of three known versions of the painting, and was painted in Dusseldorf, Germany, while Bingham was there on a visit. He wished to create a painting that would show an important event in the life of the American West.

SLIDE #10: *The Voyage of Life—Youth,* 1842, Thomas Cole, oil on canvas, 52-⅞ × 76-¾ inches, Ailsa Mellon Bruce Fund, National Gallery of Art, Washington, D.C.

Cole was the acknowledged leader of the Hudson River School, a group of American painters who had great reverence for the American landscape and sought to render it in all its grandeur. The group "considered nature as a manifestation of the goodness of God." This romantic painting is one of a series of allegories, following a hero through a series of four stages (childhood, youth, middle age, and old age) along the "river of life." (One analysis suggests that the youth might represent America itself, at an early, idealistic stage.) Cole's early work consisted of detailed, romantic landscapes, but his later work, such as this, suggests surrealism. Cole said of this work, "(This) picture represents youth on the verge of manhood. In that season of life all is hope and expectation. The World spreads out before us a wide paradise. Visions of happiness and glory rise in warm imagination."

SLIDE #11: *Tricolored Heron* (Louisiana Heron), 1821, John James Audubon, hand-colored engraving, 19-½ × 39-½ inches, Mercantile Library, St. Louis.

Audubon, who was born in the West Indies, was always fascinated with birds. He came up with a grandiose scheme of painting all the birds of North America, and spent much time away from home to achieve this goal. To achieve the life-like poses of the birds he painted, Audubon took freshly killed birds and pinned or wired them into lifelike positions. Until that time, drawings of such wildlife had been done from stuffed birds. This tricolored heron was painted on an excursion in 1820 to Louisiana. A student of Audubon's, Joseph Mason (who was only thirteen when Audubon invited him on this trip), painted many of the plants and backgrounds of paintings including this one. The painting was part of Audubon's portfolio of *Birds of America* which contained 435 paintings of birds. He mixed mediums at times, combining pencil, ink, pastel, watercolor, and even oil. Audubon's name today is synonymous with conservation and protection of birds and wildlife.

SLIDE #12: *Young Omahaw, War Eagle, Little Missouri, and Pawnees,* 1821, Charles Bird King, oil on canvas, 91.8 × 71.1 cm., Gift of Helen Barlow, National Museum of American Art, Smithsonian Institution/Art Resource, New York.

Charles Bird King was a well-known painter in Washington, D.C., mostly concentrating on portraits of government officials and delegations of American Indians. The Native Americans came in groups to Washington to safeguard their rights in the forced sale of their lands. He contributed many paintings to the Indian Gallery begun in 1821, which was the first government-sponsored collection of art. Although the title of this picture names four separate individuals, in actuality these portraits are based on portraits of two or three Native Americans (*Petalesharro, Peskelechaco,* and *Sharitarish*) that he had previously done in his studio. The Native Americans' earlobes have been slit to allow them to suspend wampum (shell) ornaments. They are also wearing necklaces, including a peace medal containing the profile of President Monroe on War Eagle (second from left). Their shaved heads have been decorated with dyed deer hair. The use of highlights on several of the faces against the dark background gives drama to the painting, and the use of red throughout (as in the war club next to the peace medal) and the paint on the faces makes this a dynamic painting.

SLIDE #13: *Arrangement in Gray and Black No. 1: the Artist's Mother,* **1871, James Abbott McNeill Whistler, oil on canvas, 57-¼ × 64-¾ inches, Musee d'Orsay, Paris, France, Giraudon/ Art Resource, New York.**

Whistler called his work "arrangements," "nocturnes," "harmonies," or "symphonies," rather than the name of the subject. "Whistler's Mother" is the popular name of this "arrangement," and it has been one of the most satirized works of American art. This painting is as much about overall arrangement of color, contrast, and form as it is a portrait. The straight lines of the picture frames, wallboards, chair, and draperies contrast with the curved lines of the lace bonnet and sleeves. Whistler once said of this painting, "Yes, one does like to make one's mummy just as nice as possible."

SLIDE #14: *Reminiscences of 1865,* **after 1890, John Frederick Peto, oil on canvas, 30 × 20 inches, The Julia B. Bigelow Fund, The Minneapolis Institute of Arts.**

This type of trompe l'oeil (fool the eye) "back of door" painting was popular in the latter half of the nineteenth century. The artist shows his admiration for "Abe" by the "carving" of his birth and death dates, and the photograph of Lincoln. (Peto did almost a dozen pictures featuring an image of Abraham Lincoln.) Peto's work was very similar to that of William Harnett, and many of Peto's unsigned paintings bear Harnett signatures that were later forged. (Because Harnett was better-known, his signature carried greater value.) The coin and bill may be references to corruption of the 1890s when this was painted, and the torn and aged cards show the passage of time.

SLIDE #15: *At the Theater (Woman in a Loge),* **c. 1879, Mary Cassatt, pastel on paper, 21-¹³/₁₆ × 18-⅛ inches, Purchase: Acquired through the generosity of an anonymous donor, The Nelson-Atkins Museum of Art, Kansas City, Missouri.**

Mary Cassatt was the only American who exhibited with the French Impressionists, and gets a great deal of credit for their popularity in the United States. She was from a wealthy Philadelphia family, and when she visited the United States, she introduced the work of her French colleagues to her family and friends. Her mentor was Edgar Degas, and the lightness of her palette, fresh brushwork, and her facility with pastels shows his influence and that of other Impressionists such as Renoir. Her frequent subjects were women and children. This *Woman in a Loge* is one of a series of paintings, prints and pastels showing women in a theater. It demonstrates how beautifully pastel lends itself to the display of light and reflections, as shown in the mirror behind the figure. Notice in particular the way contrasting color is used in underpainting to give a glow to the skin tones, and how loosely she rendered parts of the background.

SLIDE #16: (Left) *Hollyhocks,* 1882, 87-¼ × 37-¼ inches, (Right), *Flowering Cherry Tree and Peony,* 1882, 87-¼ × 37-¼ inches, John LaFarge, windows, Funds given by the Decorative Arts Society in honor of the Twentieth Anniversary of the Friends of The Saint Louis Art Museum, The Saint Louis Art Museum.

John LaFarge and Louis Comfort Tiffany were the two best-known stained-glass artists of the late nineteenth century. LaFarge designed these two windows for the Frederick Lothrop Ames house in Boston's Back Bay. Two more windows created for the same house are in the National Museum of American Art in Washington, D.C. They reflect LaFarge's interest in Japanese design and the interest in nature that inspired Victorian artists to use sinuous Art Nouveau forms. LaFarge incorporated a variety of glass such as the opalescent border, and molded or rough cut glass. The fusing of several layers of glass created a rich, shimmering luminescence with great depth.

SLIDE #17: *The Gulfstream,* 1889, Winslow Homer, watercolor, 11-⅜ × 20-¹/₁₆ inches, Mr. and Mrs. Martin A. Ryerson Collection, The Art Institute of Chicago.

Winslow Homer was an illustrator before he turned to full-time painting, and it was his ability as a storyteller in paint that makes his artwork so memorable. Homer is one of the eminent American watercolorists, but was equally as proficient as an oil painter. Most of his watercolors were done while he was on hunting trips or vacationing in the Carribean. He said, "You will see, in the future I will live by my watercolors." He lived near the sea, and often painted violently realistic paintings such as this. The curve of the wrecked and listing sailboat is echoed in the curve of the shark. A more detailed version of this painting was painted ten years later in oils, and is at The Metropolitan Museum of Art in New York. As with all great paintings, it was somewhat controversial (because of its violence), and Homer replied to his critics, "You may inform these people that the Negro did not starve to death. He was not eaten by the sharks. The waterspout did not hit him. And he was rescued by a passing ship."

SLIDE #18: *Snow in New York,* 1902, Robert Henri, oil on canvas, 32 × 25-¾ inches, Gift of Chester Dale, National Gallery of Art, Washington, D.C.

Considered the leader of the Ashcan School, Robert Henri was one of the most influential teachers in the history of American art. The Ashcan School was noted for its dark, realistic interpretations of city life, as in this example. Henri had studied in Europe, and after working in an Impressionistic manner for some time, began to work with the darker colors based on Frans Hals, Rembrandt, Manet, Courbet, and Whistler. He and his followers tried to record their feelings and the vitality of the scenes they painted with quick, slashing brush strokes. His intent was to fill all his students "with a concern for life and adventure in art." Even in a scene such as this somber and dreary winter day in New York, the vigorous brushstrokes and vitality of the city are captured.

SLIDE #19: *Bathers, Verso,* c. 1916–1919, Maurice Prendergast, watercolor, 35.2 × 50.3 cm., Gift of Mr. and Mrs. G. Gordon Hertslet, The Saint Louis Art Museum.

Prendergast was a member of The Eight, sometimes called the Ashcan School because of their interest in realistically portraying the world around them. He worked in both oils and watercolors. This watercolor painting has the spontaneity of a sketch made on the spot. Prendergast loved to paint crowds of people, and usually organized them in horizontal planes, with people grouped in the foreground, middleground, and background. Even the horizontal waves in the ocean were in planes. A Saint Louis Art Museum catalogue states, "Prendergast blended Impressionist subjects, Fauve color, and Pointillist applications of paint to create a distinctive style." His colors were usually bright, and his crowds of people, even though they were faceless, still gave the impression that all was right in the world.

SLIDE #20: *Weehawken, New Jersey,* 1910, John Marin, watercolor, 47.6 × 39.1 cm. Bequest of Marie Setz Hertslet, The Saint Louis Art Museum.

There is no mistaking what the subject is in a John Marin painting, although he was considered a modernist painter. This seascape of a busy New Jersey port is simple, with the subject concentrated near the bottom of the painting, yet the picture plane is filled. Observe how one horizontal stroke of a flat brush can indicate a boat or a building. The clouds were painted in the wet-in-wet technique which makes them appear so fluid. In later paintings, Marin sometimes concentrated his subject near the center of the painting and made flat lines around the edges. Marin was a member of Gallery 291 and, with Winslow Homer, was one of the eminent American watercolorists.

SLIDE #21: *The Steerage,* 1907, Alfred Stieglitz photogravure, 13-3/16 × 10-1/2 inches, Funds given by Mr. and Mrs. Warren McKinney Shapleigh, The Saint Louis Art Museum.

Stieglitz is credited with being the father of modern photography through his founding of The Little Galleries of the Photo Secession. He sponsored exhibits by such artists as Georgia O'Keeffe (whom he later married), Edward Steichen, John Marin, Arthur Dove, Cezanne, Matisse, and Picasso. His own words about *The Steerage* provide a perfect analysis of the photo:

". . . Coming to the end of the deck I stood alone, looking down. There were men, women, and children on the lower level of the steerage. A narrow stairway led up to a small deck at the extreme bow of the steamer. A young man in a straw hat, the shape of which was round, gazed over the rail, watching a group beneath him. To the left was an inclining funnel. A gangway bridge, glistening with fresh white paint, led to the upper deck. The scene fascinated me: A round straw hat; the funnel leaning left, the stairway leaning right; the white drawbridge, its railings made of chain; white suspenders crossed on the back of a man below; circular iron machinery; a mast that cut into the sky, completed a triangle. I stood spellbound. I saw shapes related to one another—a picture of shapes, and underlying it, a new vision that held me: simple people; the feeling of ship, ocean, sky; a sense of release that I was away from the mob called rich. Rembrandt came into my mind and I wondered would he have felt as I did."

SLIDE #22: *Himmel,* 1915, Marsden Hartley, oil on canvas with original-painting wood border, 120.4 × 120.4 cm., Gift of the Friends of Art, The Nelson-Atkins Museum of Art, Kansas City, Missouri.

Marsden Hartley exhibited his series of paintings about pre-World War I Germany at Gallery 291 in 1916, but they were not well received because of anti-German sentiment in the United States at that time. While in Europe from 1912 through 1916, he exhibited in Munich and Berlin with the Blaue Reiter (Blue Rider) group that included artists Wassily Kandinsky and Franz Marc. He became very good friends with a German officer who was killed in 1914, and this painting is a reaction to his friend's death. Himmel (Heaven) and Holle (Hell), the soldier on horseback, and the strong colors and abstract symbols of this series included epaulettes and medals of the German Army uniform. Although he later painted other subjects, these abstractions painted in Germany were considered his strongest work. He was also a poet and the author of four books and numerous articles.

SLIDE #23:   *Rapt at Rappaport's*, October 1952, Stuart Davis, 52 × 40 inches, oil on canvas, Hirshhorn Museum and Sculpture Garden, Smithsonian Institution, Gift of Joseph H. Hirshhorn Foundation, 1966. Photograph by Lee Stalsworth.

Stuart Davis was one of the early modernists, exhibiting five realistic paintings at the 1913 Armory Show while he was still a student. His version of European Cubism combined with American Abstract Expressionism paved the way for many American painters to follow. Davis abstracted objects such as a gas pump or bridge that one might find in a city until they no longer resembled real objects, but were simply shapes. His use of the word "any" on a painting means that to him any subject matter is equal to any other in art. His word "eydeas" refers to ideas in art. His fascination with using words—combined with his characteristic geometric shapes, letters, symbols, and numbers—often resulted in the title becoming part of the composition as in this painting, *Rapt at Rappaport's*. (Rappaport's was a toy bazaar on Third Avenue in New York that was founded in 1892.) He said of this work (and two others, *Owh! in San Paó* and *Amazene*) that they were as simple to understand as a tabloid headline.

SLIDE #24:   *Jack-in-the-Pulpit No. IV,* 1930, Georgia O'Keeffe, oil on canvas, 40 × 30 inches, Alfred Stieglitz Collection, Bequest of Georgia O'Keeffe, National Gallery of Art, Washington, D.C.

This *Jack-in-the-Pulpit* was the fourth of a series of six paintings. The first painting was quite realistic, and each succeeding flower became progressively more abstract until the last one showed only the Jack (pistil) from the flower. The rich dark colors, made more dramatic with the use of white, were wonderful examples of her work in the 1930s. O'Keeffe said she remembered a high school art teacher who "pointed out the strange shapes and variations in color—from the deep, almost black earthy violet through all the greens, from the pale whitish green in the flower through the heavy green of the leaves. She held up the purplish hood and showed us the Jack inside. I had seen many Jacks before, but this was the first time I remember examining a flower . . . Maybe she started me looking at things—looking very carefully at details."

SLIDE #25:   *Classic Landscape,* 1931, Charles Sheeler, oil on canvas, 25 × 32-¼ inches, Collection of Mr. and Mrs. Barney A. Ebsworth Foundation, The Saint Louis Art Museum.

Sheeler was considered a "precisionist" because of his carefully painted and deceptively simple interpretations of barns, factories, machinery, trains, and manufactured products. He was one of many artists who tried to show the mechanization of America through paintings and photographs of these subjects. Sheeler was as fine a photographer as he was a painter. Many of his paintings, with their relatively quiet color schemes and dramatic use of light, might well have been based on his black-and-white photographs of the same subjects. Details have been eliminated in his paintings to the point that they have become abstract. This painting is of the Ford factory at River Rouge, Detroit that was built to manufacture the Ford Model A that replaced the Model T. The factory had 23 main buildings, 93 miles of railroad tracks, and thousands of employees, yet there is a total absence of human activity, assembly lines, or machinery. A French critic stated of Sheeler's work, "There is an almost puritanical rigidity of his studies, but these should not blind us to the inner force and beauty of his work."

SLIDE #26: *The Library,* **1960, Jacob Lawrence, tempera on fiberboard, 24 × 29-⅞ inches, Gift of S. C. Johnson & Son, Inc., National Museum of American Art, Smithsonian Institution / Art Resource, New York.**

Lawrence is one of the foremost painters of the African American. Although he was too young to be part of the Harlem Renaissance, he learned from many of those artists who were. He had his first one-man show in Harlem in 1939, and was one of the participants in the Federal Arts Projects that created jobs for artists so they could support themselves. He had a number of series of paintings that were meant to be seen as the entire set to tell a complete story. These were *Toussaint L'Ouverture; Frederick Douglass; Migration; John Brown; War; Struggle;* and *Harriet Tubman.* His work was usually painted in gouache or casein (opaque colors similar to tempera). He applied areas of flat color, shapes that looked almost as if he had used paper cut-outs. Lawrence seldom created large works as did many artists of his time, but his work was dynamic, nonetheless, because of the strong diagonals and the way the eye was led through the painting through repetition of color and bright accents, as in this example.

SLIDE #27: *The Dove,* **1964, Romare Bearden, collage on masonite, 13-⅜ × 18-¾ inches, Blanchette Rockefeller Fund, The Museum of Modern Art, New York.**

Romare Bearden, whose work was considered a combination of Cubism / Surrealism, was considered America's foremost collagist (working with cut, torn, and pasted images). He was one of the pioneers in using technical reproduction methods and having them accepted as fine art. An African-American, he was an active participant in the 1963 Civil Rights Movement, and was a founding member of "Spiral," a group of artists who originally "planned to limit their palettes to black and white as a symbol of racial conflict." Bearden resumed using limited color in his artwork after a time, organizing his work within a shallow space.

This collage was created for a show called "Projections" that contained 27 works of art about his life in Charlotte, Pittsburgh, and Harlem. The collage *The Dove* represents a gathering for a funeral farewell, as did two other collages, *Evening, 9:10* and *417 Lenox Avenue.* He created photomontages using black-and-white photographs and magazine cutouts of faces, feet, hands, etc. These were then photographically enlarged, and the photostats (sometimes further cut up or torn) were adhered to masonite boards. He said, "Naturally I had strong feelings about the Civil Rights Movement, and about what was happening in the sixties. I have not created protest images."

SLIDE #28: **Detail,** *Social History of the State of Missouri: Politics, Farming, and Law in Missouri,* **1935–1936, Thomas Hart Benton, 55 × 14 feet, 2 inches, Courtesy of the Capitol Museum, Jefferson City, Missouri.**

This slide represents only one section of a wall of the Thomas Hart Benton mural in the Missouri State Capitol. It contains several scenes of people farming or at other work, or listening to a politician. The politician is Benton's father, shown delivering a speech in front of a poster of Champ Clark, a Missourian who was a competitor of Woodrow Wilson's in the 1919 presidential convention. One of the most controversial vignettes was of the woman wiping a baby's bottom. At a luncheon where diners were complaining because there wasn't enough military history, and also about the diaper scene, Benton answered his critics by saying, "First, there couldn't have been any military history if there weren't any babies to put diapers on. Second, if I'd had more space I would have done it—that is, put in more military history." The upper right-hand corner shows one of the James brothers with a gun drawn (they were robbing both a bank and a train in the mural). The mural was controversial because many felt that it was too bright, or that the Missourians were portrayed as hicks, and many critics were in favor of covering it with whitewash. Near the end of his career, Benton looked back and felt that the Missouri mural was his finest work.

SLIDE #29: *American Gothic*, 1930, Grant Wood, oil on beaverboard, 74.3 × 62.4 cm., Friends of American Art Collection, The Art Institute of Chicago.

American Gothic may be one of the most popular and frequently reproduced paintings in America. Grant Wood, an American Scene Painter, was known for tongue-in-cheek satire in many of his paintings such as *Parson Weems' Fable* and *Daughters of Revolution*. His paintings were frequently controversial. Apparently Wood's neighbors in Iowa found this one an insulting caricature of simple farmers (in actuality, the models for the painting were Wood's dentist friend and his sister, Nan). He was inspired by the Gothic window of a house in Iowa, and imagined long faces to go with the window. He painted everything in fine detail in the manner of Flemish painters whose work he had recently studied.

SLIDE #30: *Number 1, (Lavender Mist)*, 1950, Jackson Pollock, oil/enamel/aluminum paint on canvas, 87 × 118 inches, Ailsa Mellon Bruce Fund, National Gallery of Art, Washington, D.C.

Pollock studied at the Art Students' League with Thomas Hart Benton, but his best-known works—the drip paintings—are far removed from Benton's work. Pollock's paintings of this time period were a combination of paint splatters, drips, spills, and lines, applied (at times with a turkey baster) to a canvas that was on the floor. (One critic nicknamed him "Jack the Dripper.") His work had in common with many others that there was no center of interest, a beginning or an end; rather there was a feeling of continuous movement and energy. He had intended his work to be flat in appearance, but the web that he created with overlapping lines does allow a movement in and out, creating a rhythm. The application of paint to a work of this size led to the phrase "action painting." Pollock's work was unique, departing from the traditional Renaissance painting style. While no one else actually worked in the same method, he led the way for other Abstract Expressionist painters.

SLIDE #31: *The American Dream I*, 1960–1961, Robert Indiana, oil on canvas, 72 × 60-⅛ inches, Larry Aldrich Foundation Fund, The Museum of Modern Art, New York.

The American Dream 1 was one of a series of paintings by Robert Indiana based on commonplace images and symbols. The title comes from Edward Albee's play *The American Dream*. It is an ironic title that expresses the disenchantment Indiana was feeling with certain aspects of the American experience at that time. The basic symbols come from the pinball machines and juke boxes that existed in thousands of roadside cafes and bars across the country. The pinball machines, with their glittering lights, bells, and whistles, promised a get-rich-quick existence to all (much like gambling and lotteries do today). In the upper left circle, the white-and-black stripes resemble road signs and the numbers 40, 29, 66, and 37 are highway route numbers that he associates with his father. The use of stars, "Tilt," and "Take All" appear to have a movement all their own. Indiana said that as the series of paintings evolved, they became much brighter and "negative aspects have pretty well disappeared. They are all celebrations."

SLIDE #32: *Washington Crossing the Delaware,* **1953, Larry Rivers, oil/graphite/charcoal on linen, 212.4 × 283.5 cm., Given anonymously, The Museum of Modern Art, New York. Photograph © 1995 The Museum of Modern Art.**

After reading Tolstoy's *War and Peace,* Larry Rivers was inspired to paint a large composition on the subject of War. His painting entitled *Washington Crossing the Delaware* is based on a variety of sources in addition to Emanuel Leutz's *Washington Crossing the Delaware,* such as Revolutionary War illustrations from children's books and a Rubens drawing. Although Rivers selected what he considered a "corny" painting to "quote," his painting gives an entirely different aspect of the event. Where Leutz's painting shows nighttime and the storm, River's interpretation shows dawn on the horizon (which is when the battle of Trenton took place). He said, "I kept wanting to make a picture out of a national myth, to accept the 'impossible' and the 'corny' as a challenge." The size of the painting and the many open areas simply emphasize the larger-than-life central figure of George Washington and the separate groups of his soldiers with their horses. The painting was received with hostility by the general public because it seemingly was an "inappropriate subject." It was a precursor of Pop Art and, within a few years, many Pop artists were using the image of George Washington in their art.

SLIDE #33: *George Washington Crossing the Delaware* **(Stage Set for Kenneth Koch's Drama), 1961, Alex Katz, acrylic on wood/oil on wood/china, Gift of Mr. and Mrs. David K. Anderson, Martha Jackson Memorial Collection, National Museum of American Art, Smithsonian Institution/Art Resource, New York.**

Larry Rivers's *George Washington Crossing the Delaware* was the inspiration for a one-act play with the same title written by Kenneth Koch in 1955. Pop artist Alex Katz was the set designer, and his *Dream of George Washington* was the result. He used flat, cut-out, almost toy-like figures of Washington and his soldiers and the Redcoat soldiers. Katz's later paintings had large areas of flat color, figures dramatically cropped, and harsh contrasts. Katz was one of many Pop artists who made use of the face or figure of George Washington in their compositions.

SLIDE #34: *Map,* **1961, Jasper Johns, oil on canvas, 198.2 × 314.7 cm., Gift of Mr. and Mrs. Robert C. Scull, The Museum of Modern Art, New York. Photograph © 1995 The Museum of Modern Art, New York.**

Jasper Johns was a leader in the movement away from Abstract Expressionism with its complete lack of subject. Instead, he took icons such as the flag of the United States, targets, letters and numbers, and—through painting them realistically—made them objects of art rather than the commonplace objects they were. A critic once said he "immortalized the commonplace." Occasionally his work was done in the ancient technique of encaustic (wax mixed with pigment). His bronze sculptures of beer cans, a lightbulb, and a coffee can filled with brushes were painted to look like the real thing, taking away from the reverence that is often accorded a work of bronze simply because it *is* bronze. Johns had a passage in his notebook that says:

Take an object

Do something to it

Do something else to it

  "   "   "   "

The map shown here was one of a series. Johns's method of working was to carefully transfer the map outline to a large canvas, then to paint all over the canvas at once, using a number of different brushes and colors, occasionally stenciling a state name or abbreviation, but at times obliterating state lines and even differences between land and sea. Squint through your eyelashes and observe how abstract and balanced the painting is, with its brilliant splashes of red and yellow. The blues and whites almost seem to retreat. Imagine the energy that went into creating such a large painting.

SLIDE #35:   *AARRRRRRHH* (from "No Gas" portfolio), 1971, Red Grooms, lithograph, 70.5 × 55.6 cm., Gift of William E. Hartman, The Art Institute of Chicago.

The title of this lithograph obviously is pronounced the way a firetruck sounds. Red Grooms was a master of many media, including painting, collage, printmaking, drawing, and sculpture. Throughout his career he used these skills almost interchangeably, doing sketches, paintings, or prints for ideas that would be interpreted in collages (which he and his crew then painted). He had a dread of and fascination with fire, and one of his happenings was called *The Burning Building*. One of his friends, Allan Kaprow, said of Red that he was "a Charlie Chaplin forever dreaming about fire." The dalmatian on the firetruck and other sights of the city are vividly portrayed in this scene of a firetruck on its way to a fire. Grooms studied for a short time with the great Abstract Expressionist painter, Hans Hofmann, but found that in his own artwork he wanted to have a recognizable subject. And what subjects! Grooms loved to interpret people, cities, and events. He managed to convey the excitement, humor, and skewed perspective with which he sees the world. This print is full of visual humor, clichés, and movement.

SLIDE #36:   *Hollywood*, 1965, Red Grooms, construction of acrylic on wood/metal foil/ nails/plaster, 31-⅛ × 36 × 12-⅜ inches, Gift of Joseph H. Hirshhorn, 1972, Hirshhorn Museum and Sculpture Garden, Smithsonian Institution.

Grooms said that he started making "stick-outs" to make his paintings have a clearer image and because there was an almost inexhaustible amount of wood and cardboard to be found in New York City (and one presumes Los Angeles) wastebaskets. This construction was one of a number of similar Hollywood cutouts that featured artists such as *Carole Lombard,* and typical 1930s and 1940s movie scenes such as *Tango Dancers,* and *Western Pals.* Paintings and prints of the Hollywood scene were done before his huge (as he called them) "sculpto-picto-ramas" *City of Chicago* (1967) and *Ruckus, Manhattan* (1975). Found materials were frequently used in the assemblages. Grooms said of his work when doing some of his collages that they (he and his collaborators) put 75 percent of their effort into the idea, 10 percent into aesthetic problems, and 15 percent into visiting the hardware store.

SLIDE #37: *Robert,* **1973–1974, Chuck Close, 9 × 7 feet, synthetic polymer paint and ink with graphite gessoed canvas, Gift of J. Frederic Byers III, promised gift of anonymous donor, The Museum of Modern Art, New York.**

Chuck Close is an artist who loves to experiment with many different media. He has used airbrush, charcoal, hand-cast paper, acrylic, oil, charcoal, ink, and even thumbprints to interpret his one subject, the human face. He has worked for years from photographs of close friends and family. Although it looks as if the work were simply projected onto a screen and drawn on, Close actually makes a grid on the photograph and works from the grid. The sheer size of many of these faces is the fascinating thing about them—many of them are painted on canvases 6 by 9 feet!

SLIDE #38: *Still Life with Open Book,* **1990, Janet Fish, oil on canvas, 48 × 60 inches, Gift of the William T. Kemper Foundation, Kemper Museum of Contemporary Art and Design, Kansas City, Missouri.**

Janet Fish's early "reflections" paintings were of fruits and vegetables packaged in plastic from the grocery store, or commonplace objects like water-filled tumblers and goblets. Her paintings are composed of carefully arranged shells, mirrors, china and glassware, water in glass, and other reflective surfaces. They sometimes include animals and flowers. Her interest in collecting depression and Murano glass from flea markets, and her prowess as a gardener are demonstrated in the diversity represented in her compositions. The large scale of her watercolor and oil paintings, the (mostly) light palette, the shallow space, and the carefully composed paintings have made her one of the foremost painters of the late twentieth century.

SLIDE #39: *Jo Baker's Birthday,* **1993, Faith Ringgold, acrylic on canvas with pieced fabric border, 73 × 78 inches. Purchase: Museum Minority Artists' Purchase Fund: The Honorable Carol E. Jackson, Mr. and Mrs. Steven M. Cousins, Mr. and Mrs. Lester R. Crancer, Jr., Mr. and Mrs. Solon Gershman, Mr. Sidney Goldstein in memory of Chip Goldstein, The Links, Inc., Gateway Chapter, The Honorable and Mrs. Charles A. Shaw, Donald M. Suggs, Casually Off-Grain Quilters of Chesterfield, Thimble & Thread Quilt Guild, and funds given in honor of Questa Benberry, The Saint Louis Art Museum.**

Josephine Baker was a beautiful star of the Parisian Folies Bergere who was born in St. Louis, Missouri. In this quilt/painting, she is shown reclining and resting for her birthday party while a maid prepares the food and table in the background. Actually, the maid is based on the Matisse painting *Harmony in Red* and the bright wallpaper background with its bouquets also resembles Matisse wallpaper. Around the edges of the quilt Ringgold has written a "letter" to her "Aunt Melissa." In it she says, "Josephine is colored, a negro, as Josephine calls herself . . . and that would never let her seek fame and fortune in the states. And her talent would be no talent at all. Her voice would be no voice at all. Her dance would be no dance at all . . . Her life would be no life . . . no beauty."

Ringgold combined her love for storytelling, quilting, and painting in this one art form. Her quilts are in many museum and private collections, and are used to illustrate the books she writes for children.

SLIDE #40: *Horse*, 1979, Deborah K. Butterfield, chicken wire/sticks/mud/paper/dextrine/ grass on steel armature, 75-¼ × 26 × 96 inches, Purchase, The Nelson-Atkins Museum of Art, Kansas City, Missouri.

Deborah Butterfield said she would have liked to be a political activist during the Vietnam War, but decided she had to do the only thing she knew how to do well, which was to make art. She said that her horses seemed to make a political statement after all, because all horse sculptures she had ever seen were stallions, carrying generals to war. She decided instead to make a pregnant mare. She said, ". . . in my own quiet way, I was making art that was against war. And it was about the issues of procreation and nurturing rather than destruction and demolition."

Butterfield lives in the West and says that because horses are important in her life, the horses she creates are also important. Her life-sized horses give the same feeling of power that real horses have. Butterfield feels that the materials she uses, such as straw, mud, sticks, and scrap metal, are important because they portray the horse as being inseparable from the environment.

NATIVE AMERICAN
ART
(Prehistory to Present)

NATIVE AMERICAN
TIME LINE

	100 A.D.	500	1000	1200	1400	1600	1800	Present
Painting Sculpture Architecture Folk Art	Snake 200–500 450–700 Basketmaker Burial Mounds 100–400 Effigy Pipe, c. 200–400	Deer Mask 800–1400 Anasazi, 700–1750	Mimbres Pot 1000–1200 Rock Engraving, Utah, c. 1150 Mesa Verde Cliff Palace 1150	Shell Mask 1200–1700 Head pot 1200–1600 Basket—California 1499	Kachina Doll Hopi Powhatan's Mantle, c. 1607 Mask, 19th Cent. Kwakiutl	Painted Muslin Pictographs, c. 1880 Ghost Dance Shirt, c. 1870 Chief's Blanket, c. 1850	Pouch, c. 1870 Storytelling Dolls, c. 1960 Warbonnets	
Politics					Nachez people met DeSoto, 1547 League of the Iroquois 1570	Reservation Period, c. 1850 to present		
Literature						Cherokee Written Alphabet, 1821		
Science	Cultivation of potato, tobacco, corn, chocolate, and tomatoes				c. 1560—Native Americans breed horses			
Music								
Current Events			Vikings reach North America, c. 1000		1513—Ponce de Leon 1519—Cortez brings horses to America Columbus sails to West Indies, 1492 John Cabot to Nova Scotia, 1497	Jamestown settled, 1607	Trail of Tears, 1839 1876—Battle of Big Horn	

NATIVE AMERICAN DWELLINGS

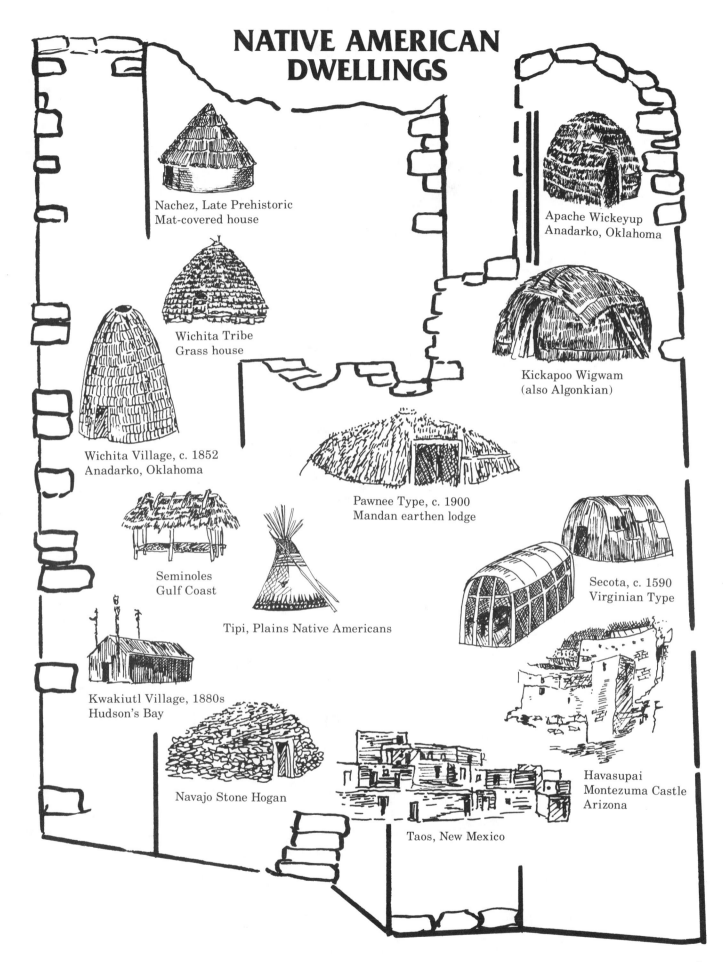

Nachez, Late Prehistoric
Mat-covered house

Apache Wickeyup
Anadarko, Oklahoma

Wichita Tribe
Grass house

Kickapoo Wigwam
(also Algonkian)

Wichita Village, c. 1852
Anadarko, Oklahoma

Pawnee Type, c. 1900
Mandan earthen lodge

Seminoles
Gulf Coast

Secota, c. 1590
Virginian Type

Tipi, Plains Native Americans

Kwakiutl Village, 1880s
Hudson's Bay

Havasupai
Montezuma Castle
Arizona

Navajo Stone Hogan

Taos, New Mexico

3

EASTERN WOODLANDS

SOUTHEAST WOODLANDS

MIDWEST

NORTHERN PLATEAU

PLAINS

HIGH PLAINS

GREAT BASIN

SOUTHWEST

NORTHWEST COAST

CALIFORNIA

Southwest

ACOMA
APACHE
COCHITI
COMANCHE
HAVASUPAI
HOPI
ISLETA
JEMEZ
MARICOPA
MOJAVE
NAMBÉ
NAVAJO
PAIUTE
PAPAGO
PIMA
SAN ILDEFONSO
SANTA ANA
SANTA CLARA
SANTO DOMINGO
SAN JUAN
SIA
TAOS
YAQUI
ZIA
ZUNI

Northwest Coast

BELLA BELLA
BELLA COOLA
CHILKAT
CHINOOK
COWICHAN
HAIDA
KLAMATH
KWAIKUTL
MAKAH
NOOTKA
QUINAULT
SALISH
SKOKOMISH
SQUAMISH
TLINGIT
TSIMSHIAN
WASCO
WISHRAM
YAKIMA

Eastern Woodlands and Midwest

ALGONQUIN
CAYUGA
CHEROKEE
CREE
DELAWARE
FOX
HURON
IROQUOIS
KASKASKIA
KICKAPOO
MENOMINEE
MICMAC
MOHAWK
MOHICAN
OJIBWA
ONONDAGA
ONEIDA
OTTAWA
PASSAMAQUODDY
PENOBSCOT
POTAWATOMI
SAUK
SENECA
SHAWNEE
WAMPANOAG
WINNEBAGO

Plains

APACHE
ARAPAHO
ARIKARA
ASSINIBOINE
BLACKFEET
CADDO
CHEROKEE
CHEYENNE
CHOCTAW
COMANCHE
CROW
DAKOTA
DELAWARE
FOX
ILLINOIS
IOWA
HIDATSA
HUNKPAPA SIOUX
IOWA
KANSA
KIOWA
MISSOURI
OMAHA
OSAGE
OTO
PAWNEE

PLAINS CREE
PONCA
MANDAN
PAWNEE
POTAWATOMI
SAKSI
SIOUX
WICHITA
WYANDOTTE
UTE

Northern Plateau

BLACKFEET
FLATHEAD
GROS VENTRE
KLIKITAT
OSAGE
NEZ PERCE
SHOSHONI
UTE

Southeast Woodlands

BILOXI
CALUSA
CHEROKEE
CHICKASAW
CHITIMACHA
CHOCTAW
CREEK
ETOWA
HOUMA
MISSISSIPPIAN
SEMINOLE
TIMUCUA

California

ACHOMAWI
ATSUGEWI
CAHUILLA
CHUMASH
HUPA
KAROK
KITANEMUK
MAIDU
MIWOK
MODOC
MONO
POMO
TULARE
WAILAKI
YOKUT
YUROK

NATIVE AMERICAN PICTOGRAPHS

Birds		(Hopi) Thunderbird	(Zuni)	(Zuni) Magpie	Thunderbird		
Animals	Horse	(Hopi) Goat	(Zuni) Sheep	Sheep	Deer	Mastodon	Buffalo
Nature	(Zuni) Bird	(Hopi) Plant	(Zuni) Seed		(Ojibway) Seed Pod	Rabbit	(Plains) Owl
Sun		(Hopi) Sun				Sun (Penobscot)	(Navajo) Sun
Animal Forms	(Haida) Frog	Dragonfly	(Zuni) Frog	(Arapaho) Frog	(Arapaho) Bear Foot	(Zuni) Insect	(Plains)
Person Forms		(Hopi)	(Zuni)	(Arapaho)	Squaw	(Hopi)	(Navajo)
Insect Forms	Butterfly	(Hopi) Butterfly	(Zuni)	(Arapaho) Butterfly	Dragonfly	Spider	(Navajo)
Feather		(Hopi)	(Zuni)	Wing (Hopi)		(Penobscot)	
Tents				(Arapaho)	(Ojibway)	(Penobscot)	

NATIVE AMERICAN PICTOGRAPHS

Nature Symbols	Star	(Hopi) Star	(Zuni) Star	(Arapaho) Star	Moon	(Penobscot) Star	(Navajo) Star
Clouds		(Hopi) Clouds		(Arapaho) Clouds			(Navajo) Clouds
Rain		(Hopi) Rain	(Zuni) Rain	(Arapaho) River	Rainbow	(Penobscot) Rain	(Navajo) Rain
Mountains		(Plains) Earth	(Acoma) (Zuni)	(Arapaho)		(Acoma)	(Navajo)
Lightning		(Hopi)	(Zuni)	(Arapaho)		(Plains)	(Zuni)
Plant Forms: Leaf	(Hopi)	(Hopi)	(Zuni)	(Arapaho)	(Ojibway)	(Penobscot)	Reeds (Plains)
Cactus and Corn		Cactus	Corn		(Ojibway)	(Penobscot)	(Navajo) Roots
Flower	(Acoma)	(Hopi)	(Acoma)	Eye (Arapaho)	(Ojibway)	(Hopi)	(Hopi)
Squash Blossom		(Hopi)	(Zuni)			(Acoma)	(Navajo)

OVERVIEW OF THE VISUAL ARTS

Because of the vast differences in America—the climate, availability of water, and natural resources—-the cultures of the various Native American societies are widely dissimilar. Some groups developed a specialty, such as silversmithing, rock art, wood or stone carving, architecture, or birchbark boxes, that was influenced by natural materials found in their surroundings. Most Native American people created variations of masks, carved figures or dolls, baskets, painted hides, pouches, pottery, and weaving. Most of what was produced was not considered "art" at the time it was created but was made for a practical purpose: pots and baskets for cooking and storage, or objects and clothing for ceremonial occasions or burials. However, the beauty of these useful objects is so extraordinary that it is obvious great pride was taken in fine craftsmanship and original design (or a carefully interpreted traditional design).

Ceremonial occasions are frequent, often to please spirits that cause natural phenomena. Native American people feel close to the earth, and their spiritual practices reflect their reverence. The many objects that may be seen on reservations or in museums reflect the skill passed on from generation to generation.

The North American continent is divided roughly into regions where geographic differences (and perhaps other ancient traditions) influenced the way of life and consequently its artwork. The regions are the Northeast Woodlands, the Southwest, California, the Arctic Coast, the Southeast, the Plains, and the Great Basin (between the Rocky Mountains to the east and the Cascades and Northern Sierra Mountains to the west). It has been theorized that the Far Northwest reflects an Asian influence; the Northeast Woodlands, a European or Mediterranean influence (after settlers arrived); the Southwest and California, an Aztec influence; and the Northwest Coast, a relation to New Zealand's Maori or Asian art. As groups traveled or encountered outsiders, they traded and developed new ways of making practical objects (e.g., beading with glass beads rather than quills). Artists usually did more than create art; they were also involved in day-to-day hunting or gathering and preparation of food, making clothing, and creating objects for special use. Women usually did beading, weaving, painting, basketry, and pottery making, while men did sand painting, decorated tipis and "exploit robes," made weapons and tools, and carved masks or bone and horn implements. Hopi men would spin and weave the textiles and were silversmiths.

The accompanying map and list gives the traditional location of major societal groups. Some modern Native American artists continue creating art in the old tradition, while yet another group interprets their background in contemporary artwork, realizing that their heritage is unique. The Native American heritage is appreciated and cherished by contemporary society.

PAINTING

Decoration of useful objects such as tipis, masks, kachina dolls, totem poles, and pottery often followed traditional colors and designs, depending on where the people lived. Painted rock art (pictographs), drums, shields, painted tipi linings, murals inside adobe dwellings, interior and exterior of long houses, and even painting of faces seemed to follow custom, with symbols and colors being understood by the people. The color *white* represented the Great Spirit or creator; *red,* the thunder spirit; *blue,* North in the circle of life; *yellow,* the rising sun and wisdom; and *green,* Mother Earth, the sustainer. Sand paintings (dry paintings) were traditional in the Southwest and used for healing purposes. By the 1770s, commercial paint was available to decorate exploit robes, ledger drawings, and backdrops for altars.

Examples of Paintings

Painted Deer Hide, 1891–1895, White Bird, The Saint Louis Art Museum (Lent by William H. Webster)

Prairie Fire, c. 1953, Blackbear Bosin, Philbrook Museum of Art, Tulsa, Oklahoma

Tipi liner with hunting scenes, c. 1920, American Museum of Natural History, Washington D.C.

Akicita Wasté (Good Soldier), 1991, Martin Red Bear, Minneapolis Museum of the Arts

Events Leading to the Battle of the Little Big Horn, c. 1899, Standing Bear, Foundation for the Preservation of American Indian Art and Culture, Inc., Chicago

Ghost Dance, c.1852, Yellow Nose, National Museum of Natural History

Painting of a Basket Dance, 1920–1930, Tonita Peña, The St. Louis Art Museum

SCULPTURE

The Northwest Coastal and Eastern Native Americans had a plentiful supply of wood, which they used for totems, masks, rattles, fish hooks, bowls, combs, chests, and utensils. They also carved beautiful decorative pipes and other objects of argilite (black stone) or horn. Plains Indians carved pipes and figures of wood and elk horn. Decorated shell amulets have been found in the Mississippi Valley area, and carved animal replicas in the Southeast. Sculptural pots were often made in the Southwest, and decorated stone vessels and other useful objects are still found throughout the continental United States.

Examples of Sculpture

Horse Effigy, c. 1880, Teton Lakota, South Dakota State Historical Society

Buffalo, late 19th century, Montana Crow, American Museum of Natural History, Washington, D.C.

War Club, c. 1880, Sioux, Joslyn Art Museum, Omaha, Nebraska

Raven Rattle, 19th century, Nelson Atkins Museum of Art, Kansas City, Missouri

Mask, Iroquois, Peabody Museum, Salem, Massachusetts

Mask, Alaskan, 19th century, Nelson Atkins Museum of Art, Kansas City, Missouri

Potlatch Hat, late 19th century, Tlingit, The Saint Louis Art Museum

ARCHITECTURE

Architecture varied from the multi-story pueblos found in the Southwest to ancient Mandan earth-covered lodges in the Midwest. Hogans were built in the Southwest. Homes were built of cedar on the Northwest Coast. The Northeastern Senecas built longhouses using poles covered with slabs of bark. The Seminoles of Florida built open platforms covered with thatch. Creek tribal homes were built with log walls and a roof of shake shingles, copied from early settlers' construction methods. Wigwams were rounded houses covered with birch. Some homes of the Havasupai in the Southwest were built with flat roofs and thatched walls. Places of worship and meeting places often used the same construction methods, with the structures built larger to accommodate more people. Most were made of materials that were destroyed with time, so reconstructions of many of these types of architecture may be found in museums.

Examples of Architecture

Three Turkey Ruin, c. 1290, near Canyon de Chelly, Arizona

Navajo Hogans, Canyon de Chelly, Arizona

Taos Pueblo, Taos, New Mexico

Old Kasaan village, Southeastern Alaska

Cliff Dwelling, Manitou Springs, Colorado

Cliff Dwellings, Mesa Verde National Park, Colorado

PROJECT 1-1: NEWSPAPER ROCK

FOR THE TEACHER

"Rock art" refers to the pictographs (painted rocks) and petroglyphs (pecked and incised rocks) left behind by ancient Native Americans. While there are regional differences, most rock art was done by several generations and was a mixture of several traditions. The major concentrations of rock art are found in California, the Columbia Plateau, the Great Basin region (Utah), and the Southwest, with fewer than 200 examples found east of the Mississippi River. Early explorers and travelers made notes and drawings of ancient rock art, much of which has disappeared.

The drawings tend to be naturalistic, although settled tribes' paintings showed an evolution from naturalistic to stylized, then abstract drawings. The rock art might have been related to hunting, as animals often were depicted. Interestingly, if animals were plentiful—such as salmon in the Northwest or buffalo in the Plains, these were seldom seen in rock art of those regions; only difficult ones to hunt (such as the rocky mountain goat) were drawn. Drawings were done at special spiritual places. Some rock art was done to ensure fertility or created during and after puberty rites. Some drawings recorded events such as a supernova seen in A.D. 1054 or the arrival of the Spaniards on horses in A.D. 1519.

Examples of Rock Art

Newspaper Rock, Newspaper Rock State Park, Utah

Nine Mile Canyon, Utah

Canyonlands National Park, Utah

Arroyo San Nicolas, Baja California

Salt River, near New London, Missouri

San Cristobal, New Mexico

Petrified Forest National Park, Arizona

PREPARATION

This project is based on rock art as a means of communication. A large group of petroglyphs in Canyonland National Forest in Utah is called the "Newspaper Rock" because of the many messages on it. Challenge your students to tell a story using only pictures to help them understand the difficulty of communicating without a written language. The pictograph examples that accompany this project are only "starters." Students can think of modern symbols such as logos on cars, hand signals, or traffic signs. If your region has pictographs or petroglyphs, this is an opportunity for students to learn about and appreciate this ancient art form. The class could be broken into groups to find out about differences in rock art depending on the region where they were made.

The format for the project can be like an actual newspaper, with each student contributing one page of pictographs, or designs can be actually made on "rocks."

ADDITIONAL SUGGESTIONS

- Have students "peck" a petroglyph on soft rock with a harder rock (or metal hammer and metal chisel or large steel nail). Create lines as Native Americans did by making individual holes, then "connecting the dots."
- Pick up large flat rocks by the side of the road (or buy them cheaply from a landscaper) and paint a pictographic story on them with acrylic paint, using shades of dark red, black, white, brown, blue, green, or yellow. Flat pieces of cardboard could also be cut into "rock" shapes for painting.

- Make clay "rock-boxes" by mixing terra cotta and white clay for a marbleized effect, forming an orange-sized ball of clay in the palm, smoothing it, then slightly flattening its sides on a table. Have students use a wire or string to cut it in half, hollowing out the inside to a thickness of ½ inch and refitting the two sides together. The smoothed surfaces should have petroglyphs incised on the outside. Fire the two pieces separately, and apply a clear glaze or leave unglazed.

- Flatten small round balls of clay to a thickness of ¼ inch, and incise or paint petroglyphs on them with contrasting slip for use as refrigerator magnets. After firing, these can have magnets glued on the back. This would also work with self-hardening clay.

- Play a newspaper game. Divide the class into groups and have each student in a group draw pictographs on individual 8-½ × 11-inch papers to make a statement that might be found in a modern newspaper, such as "Woman donates money to children's charity," or "Rain and thunderstorms expected in the early afternoon." To make interpretation easier, each student should use a different color (red, white, brown, black, blue, or green). Each student can redraw the same message as pieces of paper are passed around the group. When there is no more room on the paper, each person in the group has to try to figure out and read aloud one message (not his or her own).

Note: A very fine field guide entitled *Rock Art Symbols of the Greater Southwest* by Alex Patterson (Boulder, CO: Johnson Books, 1992) lists locations of hundreds of rock art sites.

Photo 1-1. *Newspaper Rock.* **Courtesy of Utah Travel Council, Salt Lake City.**

PROJECT 1-1: **NEWSPAPER ROCK**

MATERIALS

- Colored fine-line marker, crayon (or red, white, brown, or black crayon or conté)
- Pencil
- Brown paper bags, kraft paper, or lined paper
- Pictograph handouts

Rock art is found throughout America, perhaps not far from where you live. Pictographs (painted images) and petroglyphs (incised images) were created by Native Americans. They might have been made for religious purposes, or to bring luck for a hunt, or to record an event. In Utah, a rock with many symbols on it is called the *Newspaper Rock*. Until 1852, when a standard "alphabet" was introduced for the Dakota language, most written communication among Native Americans was done with pictographs.

A pictographic handout included with this project has symbols shown in different tribal "languages." You can probably interpret some of them. The same is true of contemporary symbols—-they are often universally understood.

You are going to tell a story in pictographic form. It could be about a trip you took recently, your fixing dinner, a story you read in the newspaper, a dispute with a brother or sister, or information about your life that you would like to see published!

1. Tear brown paper bags into shape(s) approximately 8 × 11 inches (the size of notebook paper). Try to make the edges jagged. Dampen and crumple the paper, and spread it out to dry for use the next day. Iron it before using.

2. Meanwhile, use scrap paper to quickly draw familiar symbols such as the "golden arches" and dollar signs. Draw various types of people, simplifying their shapes. Make up a pictograph that represents you or your personality. These are "doodles" just to get you thinking. Now devise a simple message or story.

3. *Lightly* draw the images on the crumpled paper in pencil, making them large enough to fill the page. Use crayon, conté, or marker to draw over the pencil. Most rock art drawings used only one or two colors at a time. Reddish brown was quite common, as were black and white. Some "polychrome" paintings had more than one color.

4. When the class has completed its newspaper stories, display them on a wall or bind them together to make a modern-day "newspaper rock."

Barrier Canyon
2000 B.C.

Freemont
A.D. 600

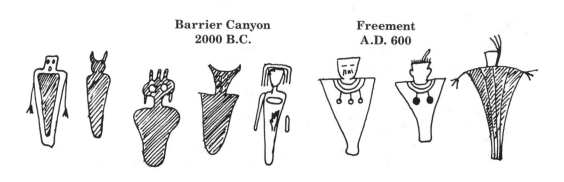

PROJECT 1-2: **WINTER COUNT**

FOR THE TEACHER

SLIDE #1: American Indian (Great Plains), *Winter Count (?)*, Hunkpapa Lakota, c. 1912, Ink(?) and colors on muslin, 38-3/4 3 53-5/8 inches, Lent to The Nelson-Atkins Museum of Art, Kansas City, Missouri, by Conception Abbey, Conception, Missouri

Native Americans of the Plains recorded the most significant event of the year on their "Winter Count," which was an ongoing picture document. It represented the year from the first snowfall to the following year's first snowfall, hence the name "winter count." The elders of a group might help decide what should be recorded by the "keeper of the count" and what one symbol should be used to explain that event. Since written language was introduced, some keepers of the winter count have kept written records instead. Some pictorial winter counts continue to be added to yearly, even in this century. Individuals also created exploit robes or personal winter counts that gave a personal history. Some of the symbols were the white man (wearing a top hat), smallpox (spotted Indian), and dollars (small circles).

Examples of Winter Counts

Winter Count, c. 1931, Blue Thunder, Upper Yanktonai Dakota, State Historical Society of North Dakota

Winter Count, c. 1912, attr. to Swift Dog, Hunkpapa Lakota, State Historical Society of North Dakota

PREPARATION

The drawings on a winter count look natural, including simplified animals and people. Events recorded on one count included the arrival of whiskey (1822), a meteor shower (1834), and a solar eclipse (1870). Students may choose to use some pictographic symbols such as stars or "sacred circles." Show the *Winter Count* slide and discuss some of the symbols on it. Also discuss symbols of your students' lives, having them suggest pictures they could draw to represent milestones such as birthdays, holidays, trips, and families. The symbols can be drawn in rows, beginning at the center and working in a spiral outward, or beginning at the outside and working in. Because your students have not lived that many winters, they might record three or four events a year.

ADDITIONAL SUGGESTIONS

- Create a "ledger drawing" on lined notebook paper with colored pencil. Most exploit robes were originally painted on buffalo or deer hide, but many were also created on ledger paper furnished by traders.

- One personal exploit robe was created on heavy chamois-colored material with black crayon. The cloth was later ironed to make it permanent. Paint personal exploit robes with acrylic on natural or fake chamois from an auto-parts department (which for today's students could, for example, involve their exploits with their car—-emphasize discretion here).

- Create a communal class winter count with each student recording one significant event that happened to him or her in a specific agreed-on year. Remind them that it does not *have* to be personal; occasionally events such as a comet or war were also recorded on winter counts. Hand out 4-½ × 6-inch pieces of drawing paper for students to draw on, having them tear the edges of their drawings to make the winter count more visually interesting when they are mounted together.

After mounting the completed drawings together on large posterboard, use a black marker to divide each event.

• Paint traditional Hopi designs on 3 × 3 tiles, which could be fired, then wiped with shoe polish, and buffed.

Photo 1-2. *Painted Deer Hide,* **1891–1895, White Bird, Northern Cheyenne, Montana, watercolor on buckskin, 65 × 96 cm., Lent by William H. Webster, The Saint Louis Art Museum.**

PROJECT 1-2: **WINTER COUNT**

MATERIALS

- 12 × 18-inch white drawing paper
- Pencils
- Watercolor paint or colored pencils
- Black marker

The Plains Native Americans kept pictorial diaries of significant exploits and events in the life of the tribe. These were painted, sometimes on deer hide or buffalo skin, sometimes on muslin, and usually were rows (registers) of drawings. In an unusual winter count picture, the symbols were drawn clockwise around all four outside edges, continuing in toward the center. Each drawing was considered the most important event of the year. You can make a winter count of your own life, in the style used by the Plains tribes.

1. Begin by listing the important events in your life—-where you were born and went to school, your pets, how many houses you've lived in, details about your family, the birth of a brother or sister, first toys, summer vacations, a visit to an amusement park, or especially memorable birthdays or holidays. Write about your favorite foods, colors, sports, or collections (such as baseball cards). The writing is important, or you will run out of things to draw.

2. Think as far back in your life as you can remember—-either of things you have seen in photographs or what family members have told you. Think about what symbol you will use to represent that event (often it will involve a person—-you). Number these events to organize them chronologically.

3. In reality, winter counts had outlines around the symbols that varied in size. You may prefer to divide the paper before you begin. Several traditional methods of dividing are shown below. Ideally you should have 30 to 40 spaces for drawings.

4. Begin at the upper left corner, filling in each square as you think of something. Remember, you will have quite a few "mileposts" in your life, so plan ahead so you don't run out of something to "say" as you get toward the end. A number of the rectangles may contain something that happened to the world around you, such as memories of presidential elections, memorable TV cartoons, or sights you saw on trips.

5. Outline your pencil drawings with black marker. Fill these in with colors (either opaque or watercolor). It is not necessary to put color on every blank. When you have finished, look at the entire composition critically to decide whether more color needs to be added someplace, or if you should give emphasis to some drawings with marker.

  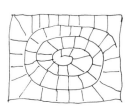  

PROJECT 1-3: **RAVEN MASK**

FOR THE TEACHER

Raven created the world! He put people on the earth; gave them the sun, moon, and stars; caused the tide waters to go in and out; and put fish into the sea, salmon into the rivers, and food onto the lands. He gave the people fire and water; placed the rivers, lakes, and cedar trees over the land. He was a fun-loving trickster whose foolish tricks often backfired.

Artists love interpreting Raven in all media such as stone, horn, wood, and even buttons on blankets. He often has a circle in his mouth as a reminder that he stole the sun from a box and tossed it into the sky to bring light to the world. It is also said:

> "When the sun was released from the box, it roared into the sky, frightening people in all directions. Those wearing nothing at all remained human, and those wearing feathers or animal skins became the birds or animals" (from a St. Louis Art Museum booklet)

Northwest Coast people (from northern Oregon to southern Alaska) used many animals that were clan emblems, or totems. These animals brought luck, and clan members might even paint their own faces with the symbols of their clan before a hunt.

Examples of Northwest Coast Masks

Mask, c. Tsimshian, 1900 A.D., British Columbia, Portland Museum of Art

Mask, Kwakiutl, early 20th century, Denver Art Museum

Mask, Tlingit, c. 1875, Museum of Primitive Art, New York

PREPARATION

Although this project will take quite a bit of clay, it is completely recyclable for other projects afterward, so create larger-than-life masks. It is also possible for two students to work together, making two (or more) masks off the same mold, then painting them differently. The designs could be based on an animal, or made to appear human. Try to have books of Native American art or photocopies of a variety of masks from Northwestern people. Discuss with students the stylization found in artwork from the Northwest Coast.

This is a good opportunity to discuss the potlatch, a ceremony at which a chief or clan tried to prove generosity by giving away worldly goods. Copper was a valued metal, and owning a "copper" in the shape shown on the mask illustrated was of special good luck. If you have copper-colored foil, a mask could be trimmed with a "copper."

ADDITIONAL SUGGESTIONS

- A very popular art form created by modern Northwest people is the silk-screen print based on traditional motifs. Many silk screens are in circular form, and most are restricted to red, black, blue, and green on a white background. These designs would be easy to paint in tempera or acrylic paints. Today they are reproduced on wall hangings, pieces of wood, T-shirts, wooden utensils, boxes, and coasters.

- Create a different form of papier-mâché by applying wallpaper paste with a large brush between five sheets of newsprint (leaving the top and bottom sheets "clean"). While the newsprint is damp, hold it against your face, pushing slightly where the eyes and nose are to allow you to place eye holes and the bottom of the nose. Take it off and make a horizontal slit below the nose. Fold the nose slightly. Cut eyeholes by pinching vertically between the thumb and forefinger where they would be, then cutting an "eye" shape. Cut around the outside of the mask and shape it by making (four) 1-½-inch long slits from the outside toward the center (at the upper "brow" and "chin"). Fold the paper on either side of the slits to make tucks and hold them together with spring clothespins or large paper clips until the mask dries. You can also wad newspaper and put it inside the mask-form (use plastic wrap between it and the mask form, or they will stick together) to help it hold its shape until it dries. When dry, paint traditional decorations and add trim to the outside. This project can also be done with layers of wallpaper samples. You might even find some wood-grained or tan wallpaper with an appropriate texture for the top layer.

Photo 1-3A. *Headpiece,* **19th century, Bella Coola People, wood/paint/abalone shell/copper/mirrored glass, 8-¼ × 8-⅞ inches, Gift of Morton D. May, The Saint Louis Art Museum.**

Photo 1-3B. *Raven Portrait Mask,* **copper shield, c. 1993, 10 × 20 inches, Joe Bolton, Kenno, British Columbia, collection of the author.**

PROJECT 1-3: **RAVEN MASK**

MATERIALS

- 5 pounds of clay per student
- Cafeteria tray, heavy cardboard, or masonite
- Plastic wrap
- Wallpaper paste or Pritt® paste
- Tan kraft paper
- Newspaper
- Masking tape
- Gesso
- Tempera or acrylic paint
- Spray varnish (*Caution:* Use in a well-ventilated room)
- Feathers, jute, beads, or other trim

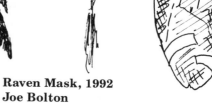

Raven Mask, 1992
Joe Bolton

Carving wooden masks is a continuing tradition among the Native Americans of the Northwest Coast and Alaska. These masks play an important role in the rituals and the life of the people who make them. Other carved objects were wooden rattles, totem poles, house posts, and bas-relief (shallow) animal carvings on storage boxes and bowls. Their designs have a unique, abstract style, but are related to some real animal, which they considered their clan's totem (or good luck symbol). Animals that hold special meaning are the bear, beaver, frog, eagle, whale, wolf, loon, and, of course, the raven.

1. Make a newspaper oval by wadding one piece of newspaper, enclosing it with another, then another, and then taping it with masking tape so it will hold its shape. Place it on masonite, heavy cardboard, or a cookie sheet and flatten it slightly. Cover it with plastic wrap, allowing the edges of the plastic wrap to hang loose.

2. Form a large piece of clay into an egg-like oval. Flatten it so it is approximately 1-½ inches thick. Place it on the plastic-covered paper oval. About halfway down, make indentations for eyes, then form a nose (or beak). Then a third of the way between the nose and the chin, add a mouth. Don't be afraid to exaggerate the features or to make them angry or distorted.

3. When you are satisfied with the contours of the face, cover it *loosely* with plastic wrap and, starting at the center, carefully adhere the plastic to the mask's contours, allowing excess to hang to the table's surface.

4. Mix the paste with water to the approximate thickness of white glue. Tear the kraft paper and newspaper into pieces approximately 1 × 1-inch (small pieces allow greater control in making detail). Fold a long piece of 3-inch wide brown paper in half, and put the folded edge all the way around the outside of the clay to make a strong, even mask edge.

5. Dip a piece of newspaper into the paste and loosely pull it between your first and second fingers to get rid of excess moisture. Smooth it over the clay mold with your fingers, overlapping one piece on another. Alternate layers of newspaper with layers of kraft paper (four layers altogether). Alternating layers allows you to make sure you have covered the mask evenly. You can add decorative motifs by adding heavy string dipped in the paste. Put it in place, then drape and smooth brown paper over it.

6. When the mask has dried, remove it from the clay form and finish the edges by adding paper dipped in paste around them. Allow it to dry completely before painting. The tan background could be left plain. Some masks are painted all over with white; then red, black, or blue-green designs are added. After painting, a layer of varnish protects the paint and makes it shiny. Jute braids, mother of pearl eyes or teeth, copper ornaments, and feathers can be added. The clay should still be moist, and can be recycled.

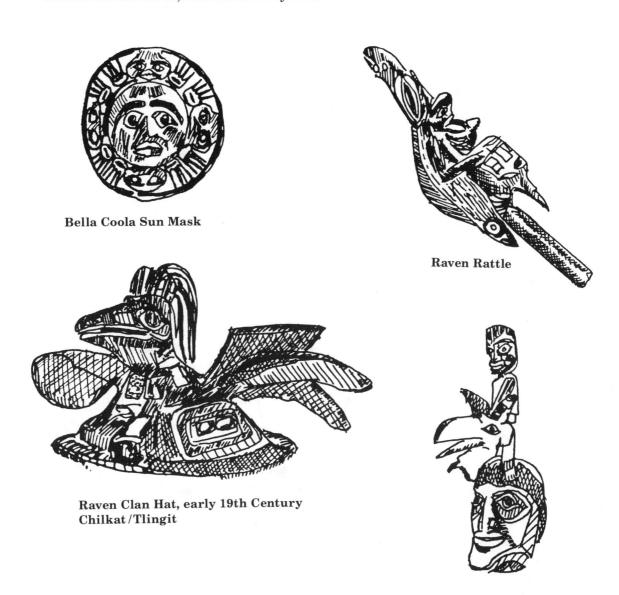

Bella Coola Sun Mask

Raven Rattle

**Raven Clan Hat, early 19th Century
Chilkat/Tlingit**

PROJECT 1-4: MODEL TIPIS

FOR THE TEACHER

SLIDE #2: *Bear Tipi of Bear Bringing It,* c. 1904, Kiowa (Gaigwa), National Museum of Natural History, Smithsonian Institution

James Mooney, an anthropologist, commissioned Kiowa men who had lived in tipis (tepees) to create and design model tipis for the 1893 Columbian Exposition in Chicago. He also commissioned a set of Cheyenne tipis for the 1904 World's Fair in St. Louis. These models are true to scale, with authentic designs. Real tipis might not have had hunting scenes painted on them, as some of the models had, but the Native Americans had found something that appealed to collectors. Small-scale tipis were used by young girls of the Plains tribes as toys, but the majority of them were made as collectors' items.

Tipi designs "belonged" to specific families. Among the Blackfeet people, a painted tipi signified that a sacred prayer bundle was inside and that the owner possessed the rites and rituals of the bundle. Motifs used on a tipi might include bison, horses, turtles, deer, eagles, fish, plants, snakes, stars, and geometric shapes.

Tipi Models

Model Tipi, c. 1900, Cheyenne, American Museum of Natural History, New York

Tipi Model, 1904, Cheyenne, Field Museum of Natural History, Chicago

PREPARATION

Have students research real tipi designs in an effort to be as authentic as possible. Native American symbolism was complicated, and students would find this interesting. For example, stars on a tipi represented the heavens, or triangles might signify mountains, with white circles within the triangles representing the stones of which the mountains were made. Model tipis would make an ideal group project.

ADDITIONAL SUGGESTIONS

- Use 12- to 14-inch pizza circles (some pizzerias will sell them cheaply or give them to you to make shields). Have students cut a circle of brown kraft paper slightly larger than the pizza circle, snipping the edges at one-inch intervals so it can be folded over the edges, then cut a second kraft paper circle the same size as the pizza circle to paste on the back to cover the folded edges. Wet and crumple the paper, allowing it to dry, then iron it. Draw the design on front, first in pencil, then in permanent marker.

- Lois Rufer of the Brentwood school district in St. Louis County and her husband, Steve, made beautiful shields by collecting willow fronds from trees, soaking them, then forming 18-inch circles that were bound together at the ends. Holes were punched in paper-covered cardboard circles and the willow frames were attached with jute. The shields were decorated with feathers, beads, shells, stones, and other found objects.

Photo 1-4A. *Travelling Tents of the Sioux Indians Called a Tepe* (sic), 1847–48–49, Seth Eastman, watercolor, Purchase: Funds given by Western Electric Company, The Saint Louis Art Museum.

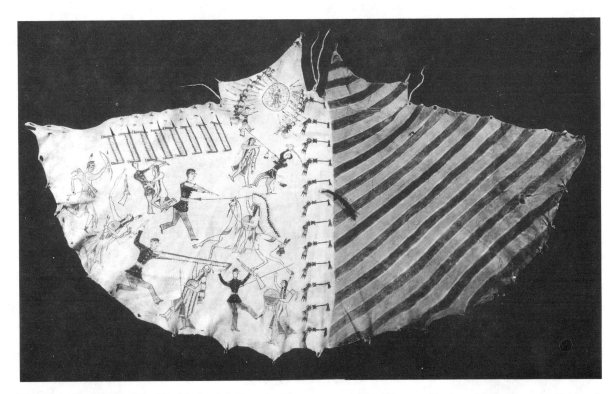

Photo 1-4B. *Little Bluff's Tipi with Battle Pictures,* c. 1904, Kiowa, National Museum of Natural History, Smithsonian Institution.

PROJECT 1-4: **MODEL TIPIS**

MATERIALS

- 24 × 36-inch tagboard
- Unprimed canvas or muslin
- Acrylic paint or tempera mixed with polymer medium
- Pencils
- Leather and string for thongs
- Kraft paper
- Polymer medium or thinned white glue
- X-acto™ knives

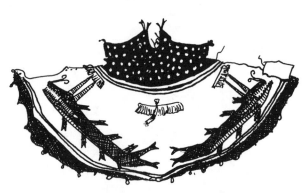

**Drawn from Kiowa Tipi, 1904
Smithsonian Institution**

Model tipis (tepees) were created by Native Americans as toys for children or (mostly) for serious collectors of Indian lore. They are identical to real tipis in every way except their size. A hundred years ago, an anthropologist commissioned groups of old men from the Kiowa and Cheyenne tribes (who had lived in them) to recreate real tipis as models for exhibitions at world fairs. You will be working just as these old men did—in a group.

1. Make a paper pattern in the shape shown here almost as large as the tagboard on which you will glue your canvas. Lay the paper pattern on the canvas, draw around it in pencil, and cut it out. Repeat this process with the tagboard.

2. Starting at the center, apply thinned white glue or polymer medium to the tagboard. Work quickly to apply the canvas to the tagboard, smoothing it from the middle toward all the outside edges. Trim the tagboard so the cardboard does not show underneath.

3. Each member of the group should work on a design. You will want to research tipi designs and decide how to decorate yours. It could have a plain border around the curved edges and up the center and around the top, as shown in one of the examples. Remember that the tipi is shaped like a cone when set up, so sometimes your designs need to be at an angle when you paint them.

4. If you wish to make animal designs, each of you can create a different horse (some with riders) or animal stencil. Trace these to tagboard and carefully cut openings with an X-acto™ knife. *Safety Note: Always make sure your cutting hand is behind the knife when you cut with it.*

5. When you have agreed on a design, share in the painting. Apply the paint with a sponge dipped in paint, dabbed inside the stencils. If not everyone is painting, other group members can make decorative trim and fasteners of leather thongs or canvas. Pieces of bone, beads, feathers, shells, or stones can be added onto the fasteners.

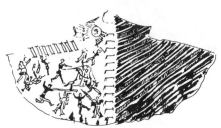

**Drawn from *Little Bluff's
Tipi with Battle Pictures,* 1904
Smithsonian Institution**

**Drawn from Tipi Model, Cheyenne, 1904
Field Museum of Natural History, Chicago**

**Kiowa Battle
Tipi**

PROJECT 1-5: MOIRÉ PATTERNS: ACOMA POTTERY

FOR THE TEACHER

The (mostly) black and white pots made today by Zia, Acoma, and Zuni people come from a long tradition begun by their Mimbres and Anasazi forebears. Women of the Acoma Pueblo have been continually creating pottery for a period of one thousand years. Many of the designs are pure abstractions, while others are taken from recognizable forms from nature or flower-like medallions. Many of the pots have bird designs which became more common in the late 1800s. The strongest design elements are open areas defined by strong lines, and closed areas filled in with parallel lines.

Examples of Southwestern Pots

Bowl, Anasazi, A.D. 1300–1400, Heard Museum, Phoenix, Arizona

Acoma water jar, 1885, Smithsonian Institution

Storage Jar, c. 1900, The Saint Louis Art Museum

Storage Jug, c. A.D. 1050–1250, The Saint Louis Art Museum

PREPARATION

This moiré project is an adaptation of an Op Art project developed by Katie Wendel, who teaches art at Incarnate Word Academy in St. Louis County, Missouri. The moiré effect works as well with the line drawings of a Zuni or Acoma pot as it does with the parallel line paintings of modern artists. The photocopies of line drawings, when taped on top of the original line drawings, give a pleasing moiré effect.

Have pictures or photocopies of some Southwestern pot designs for students to look at. Encourage students to do interesting motifs, surrounding them with fine lines. If they do the first drawing lightly in pencil, then use fine-line marker, they may go back over it later and erase the pencil. Encourage them to incorporate "mistakes" into a design.

ADDITIONAL SUGGESTIONS

- Draw the type of pot made in the San Ildefonso Pueblo by Maria Martinez and her relatives. These black pots were highly polished, with some areas remaining dull black. Apply black wax crayon firmly to create shiny resist designs on the drawing. Cover the design with India ink to create the dull contrast.

- *Sandpaper* in its various colors (black, rust, tan, beige) is an effective and appropriate background for paintings of Native American pots. Have students research pot designs and create a design on sandpaper in any medium, from pastel to tempera paint, using some of the dark red, black, and brown colors favored by Southwestern Native Americans.

Photo 1-5A. *Olla, Storage Jar,* 1100–1250, Pueblo Anasazi, Tularosa, earthenware/pigment, 14-⅜ × 5-⅞ inches, Funds given by the Children's Art Festival, The Saint Louis Art Museum.

Photo 1-5B. *Acoma Vessel,* late 19th century, terra cotta, 12 inches high, Gift of Hennepin County Historical Society, The Minneapolis Institute of Arts.

PROJECT 1-5: MOIRÉ PATTERNS: ACOMA POTTERY

MATERIALS

- Newsprint
- White paper correction fluid
- 8-½ × 11-inch white drawing paper
- Pencils
- Art gum erasers
- Black, brown, and dark red fine-line markers
- Rulers
- 8-½ × 11-inch overhead transparencies

Some of the oldest pueblo pots are from the Anasazi, the ancient tribe that inhabited the four-corners region of Arizona, Utah, New Mexico, and Colorado. In the Navajo language Anasazi means "the ancient ones." This tradition of creating complex geometric designs is continued today by their descendants. Although you will not actually be making a pot in this project, you will be drawing a picture of one. The Acoma Pueblo specializes in pots that have fine black lines painted on a white background.

1. On newsprint, try some simple designs, perhaps using an animal or bird in combination with lines, or separating line patterns to make them interesting.

2. Determine what the general outline of your pot will be. Fold a piece of white paper in half (the same size as the drawing paper) and begin at the fold to draw half a pot that will utilize most of the paper. Then cut through both thicknesses to make a pattern that is perfectly symmetrical.

3. Lightly trace around the outside of the pattern onto the drawing paper. With pencil, lightly divide the pot into sections, as seen on this page. When you have finished, and the ink is dry, pencil lines may be erased.

4. Using a ruler, make straight lines within outlined areas. Avoid having your ruler "drag" the ink marks by always working in the same direction. If you make a mistake, ignore it for the time being and keep going on another part of the pot. When that error has dried, make it part of your design by emphasizing the error by filling in with marker to make an animal or wider line. In extreme emergencies, use white correction fluid to correct it.

5. When your drawing is completely done, copy it onto an overhead transparency film. Tape the transparent copy to the front of your drawing, slightly off-set to give a watery effect (moiré), and mat it in black for display.

PROJECT 1-6: **CERAMIC STORYTELLERS**

FOR THE TEACHER

While Kachina dolls have a long tradition in Southwestern art, and Native American children have always had hand-fashioned dolls, ceramic storytelling dolls are a relatively recent creation. They originated in the 1960s when a Native American artist, Helen Cordova, wished to honor her grandfather, a clown in the Pueblo society. Native American clowns are not like those from a circus; rather, they tell stories to children and pass on traditional lore. She created a ceramic clown storytelling doll surrounded by children. Storytelling dolls today also include animal "storytellers." These charming figures are usually seated, with as few as three and as many as eight small dolls clustered around and on them.

PREPARATION

While students are actually working on their dolls, play tapes of Native American legends—students love them. Challenge students to either write an original story or retell a story. If you do not have a kiln, it might be possible to have these professionally fired by someone who does. Prepare the slip while students are working on their figures so they can easily use it for assembling or for painting afterward.

ADDITIONAL SUGGESTIONS

- As with any three-dimensional project, this could be adapted to make a two-dimensional storyteller collage. Use conté or watercolor to paint the storyteller, then use tracing paper to "fit" children around the large figure. Transfer the smaller figures to paper, painting, cutting out, and gluing them to the storyteller.
- Make kachina wands. Cut cardboard into rectangles (ideally, use wooden shingles with a small rectangle cut from the center of the bottom to allow two handles for the dancer). Have students research kachina dolls, and create an original design for the kachina wand. These can be painted with tempera, acrylic paint, or oil pastels.
- Draw a kachina doll on dark blue or dark brown paper with pastels. The vibrant colors contrast against the dull background. Each student can research and do a different type.

Note: The storyteller project was created by St. Louis storyteller / art teacher, Sue Hinkle, and adapted for secondary students by Linda Bowers of Pattonville High School. It is used with the permission of each.

PROJECT 1-6: CERAMIC STORYTELLERS

MATERIALS

- Red or buff clay (3 or more pounds per student)
- Slip in contrasting colors
- Paint brushes
- Black, white, turquoise, brown, and red terra-cotta underglazes
- Modeling tools or knife

Pueblo storytellers are figures that usually have small forms of the same species clustered around them. While real storytellers were human, of course, sometimes mythical storytelling figures were animals. Although the eyes may be open or closed, the storyteller's mouth is always open because he or she is talking.

1. To get your creative juices going, you will first write a story for your figure. This can be an original story or a retelling of an old story. Name your storyteller, where the storyteller lives, and where he or she is sitting while telling the story. Decide who will be the audience, and then write titles for five possible topics. Write the story from the viewpoint of the storyteller; for example, "The old turtle said . . ." This story should be at least 150 words (no longer than one page) and will be displayed with the figure, so it should be done on a computer or typewriter and mounted on a card.

2. Prepare your clay by wedging. This is most easily done by taking the clay and slapping it vigorously between your palms for approximately 10 minutes, forming a ball. Divide the ball into fourths, keeping the unused portion covered with plastic to prevent it from drying out.

3. To make the torso, form a small ball with one-fourth of the clay. Hold it in the palm of one hand and, with your opposite thumb, push into the center, rotating the ball with the palm and thumb to make a pinch pot approximately ½ inch thick. The pot may be round or elongated. Make a second pot of the same shape and diameter. Roughen the edges with a pencil and apply slip (made by adding water to clay and mixing it until it is approximately the thickness of white glue or cream). Use a knife to make Xs around the seam, place the two halves together, and then smooth the outside of the seam. When you are finished, poke a hole in the bottom with a pencil, and you can gently blow inside it to re-inflate it to its original shape.

4. Make one coil of clay for legs and one coil (not quite so thick) for the arms. Wrap these around the body and attach them with slip, remembering to roughen the places where they will be attached. Smooth them onto the body and create feet and hands on the ends. Make a ball of clay for the head and attach it with slip. Anything thicker than an inch must have a hole in it to allow moisture to escape, or it may explode in the firing. (Use a pencil to make a hole at the bottom of the pinch pot body. The hole in the head can be the open mouth.)

5. The small figures can be simply formed by making balls and coils. Use no fewer than three "little ones." Remember that they must be the same species as the storyteller (baby bears with a large bear, etc.). Attach the small figures to the large one with slip.

6. When the clay is leather-hard, you can begin painting designs on your storyteller with slip in contrasting colors. Most storytellers have a body of a light-colored clay, and are decorated in black, orange-red terra cotta, and white, with an occasional accent of turquoise. These figures are never shiny, so they will be fired only once.

PROJECT 1-7: **PAPIER-MÂCHÉ POTS**

FOR THE TEACHER

This project is fast and easy and does not involve clay, yet allows students to make handsome pots with authentic designs. Having recently seen gourds in New Mexico painted with Native American designs, it occurred to me that not everyone has access to gourds, but that gourd shapes (and pot shapes) could easily be created from balloons of different sizes and shapes. If you have access to gourds, so much the better. Cut off the tops and hollow them out, allowing them to dry. Leave them natural or paint them inside and out with gesso.

PREPARATION

If possible, try this yourself first, as it will give you ideas for shapes that might not have occurred to you otherwise. Libraries have many books featuring pots by Native Americans. If possible, photocopy several different methods of pot decoration, or bring books in for students to look at.

ADDITIONAL SUGGESTIONS

- Have students make a ceramic coil pot as the Native Americans do. They often work with thick coils supported on the inside of a shallow bowl or basket to facilitate turning and handling the pot. After adding two or three coils, paddle the outside of the pot with a ruler or flat stick, supporting the inside with your fingers. When the pot is leather-hard, polish it with a smooth stone or the back of a spoon. (See the directions in the Appendix for coil- and slab-building ceramics.)

- Make a beaded bowl from a very small shallow papier-mâché pot using six thicknesses of paper. When it is dry, brush several layers of melted beeswax inside. Create authentic designs inside the pot by imbedding glass beads of different sizes, using tweezers. While this is time consuming, the results are lovely. Or adapt a Native American design for a small pin by imbedding glass beads in beeswax on a wooden circle (available at hobby shops). A pendant could be made by sewing beads onto a circular piece of leather and attaching it to a leather thong worn around the neck. I recently even saw small model chairs from hobby shops covered with glass beads in Native American designs. While this is not a project for the careless, it is suitable for both genders.

- Paint kachina doll designs on real double gourds, or on papier-mâché "gourds" made by taping a small balloon on top of a larger one, and covering with several layers of papier-mâché. When the papier-mâché is dry, use tempera or acrylic paint.

PROJECT 1-7: **PAPIER-MÂCHÉ POTS**

MATERIALS

- Assorted balloons (12-inch are very suitable)
- Wallpaper paste or Pritt® paste
- Paper grocery bags or kraft paper torn into 1-½-inch pieces
- Cardboard
- Newspaper torn into 1-½-inch pieces
- Shallow plastic containers
- Gesso (black or white)
- Tempera or acrylic paints in rust, black, white, blue, or blue-green

1. Research Native American pots and decide what shape you would like to make. You could make a bowl, a large pot with neck, a pitcher, or an animal pot. Your balloon can be adapted to make it fit the shape you want, but you should know in advance what you are trying to do. Draw the shape you intend to make.

2. Blow up the balloon and tie it, then place it (tied side up) in a shallow container. To make a neck for the pot, cut a 4 × 18-inch strip of tan paper folding it in half lengthwise, then in half again. Cut slits to the fold at intervals of 1 inch. This will give you a long doubled strip to put at the top of the pot. Make the opening any size you wish by overlapping the ends of the strip and placing the circle at the top of the balloon. Hold it in place with pieces of newspaper (approximately 2 × 3 inches) dipped in wallpaper paste (remove excess water from the paper by pulling a piece between your fingers).

3. To make a flat bottom, cut a 3-inch circle of cardboard (or two thicknesses of tagboard) and put the cardboard exactly in the center of the bottom. Hold it in place with masking tape. Completely cover the bottom with papier-mâché, going up onto the sides of the balloon. Totally cover the balloon up to the edge of the neck, leaving the opening of the balloon uncovered.

4. After you have done one complete coat in newsprint, do a second coat in tan paper, a third coat in newsprint, and a final coat in tan paper. This allows you to be sure you have covered the pot evenly. This step will take more than one day.

5. When the pot has dried, pop the balloon and remove it. Hold the pot up to the light and go over any weak spots that allow light to show through. If there are any rough edges inside around the neck, cover them with more small pieces of brown paper dipped in paste.

6. The pot may be painted when it is completely dry. You may allow the tan paper to show as part of the design, or you might choose to apply black or white gesso as a base coat. Make your design authentic by researching and adapting designs and colors used by Native Americans. Most pots had at most two or three colors, depending on clays available.

© 1996 by Prentice-Hall, Inc.

PROJECT 1-8: **NAVAJO FIGURE—COLLAGE**

FOR THE TEACHER

SLIDE #3: *Flower of Las Lunas,* 1987, R. C. Gorman, Navajo Gallery, Taos, New Mexico

R. C. Gorman is a modern Navajo artist who has achieved fame through his artwork, most of which depicts Native American women. He was born in Chinle, New Mexico, and grew up on a reservation. The stark beauty of the area is sometimes reflected in the backgrounds of his paintings. Indeed, the robes that clothe his subjects sometimes resemble canyon walls and rock formations. Often all you can see of his figures is a head, feet (sometimes), and hands. The blankets in which they are wrapped are monumental forms, and his figures dominate the landscape. He creates drawings, lithographs, oil paintings, and sculpture. One particularly beautiful lithograph shows an Indian woman picking up shards of broken pottery in front of Anasazi ruins. The Taos Pueblo is another background he has used for figures.

R. C. Gorman's father was also an artist (and one of the famous Navajo code talkers during World War II). He discovered very early that R. C. had artistic talent. He said,"I never led him by the hand or led him like a teacher. His eyes were his teachers." For a time Gorman painted abstractly, using traditional rug and pottery designs for inspiration. He began painting figures after seeing paintings by the Mexican muralist, Orozco.

Examples of Work by R. C. Gorman

Rainbow Jar, 1982, lithograph, Houston Fine Arts Press

Tortilla Maker, 1978, lithograph, Origins Press

The Spirit of the Foothills, 1982, oil, collection of Goldwater's Department Store, Tucson, Arizona

Danya, 1980, lithograph, Western Graphics

Miriam, 1981, oil, collection of Mr. and Mrs. Herman Deutsch, Long Island, New York

Seated Woman, 1980, oil pastel drawing, Navajo Gallery, Taos, New Mexico

PREPARATION

Discuss with students how much they think an artist is affected by his or her environment. Ask how they would place a figure and use space if they were trying to paint the place where they live. Show the slide that accompanies this project. Ask students to describe what they see. Let them notice that the painting is composed of large open areas. Ask them about composition: Is there a background? How does the subject relate to the use of the page? What are the dominant colors? Encourage them to experiment with watercolor and, while it is wet, loosely drag a brush or piece of paper through the watercolor to make horizontal stripes.

ADDITIONAL SUGGESTIONS

- Have your students imagine they have been asked to participate in a museum exhibition of art by modern Native Americans (such an exhibit takes place at the Heard Museum in Phoenix, Arizona each year). While they may not wish to use traditional "Indian imagery," there still should be some relationship to the Native American heritage and traditions. Many contemporary Native Americans do sensitive, poignant, or ironic artworks that celebrate their heritage. Allow the students to choose any medium from sculpture to collage (including traditional materials) to make a statement about modern life as a Native American.

- If students can't get "into" doing a painting of a person wrapped in a blanket, give them the option of doing an abstract painting running off the edges of the 18 × 24-inch paper, inspired by the designs of Native American pots or blankets.

Photo 1-8A. *Morning Star,* 1981, R. C. Gorman, lithograph, edition of 225, 38 × 28 inches, Courtesy of the Navajo Gallery, Taos, New Mexico.

Photo 1-8B. *Seated Woman,* R. C. Gorman, heroic bronze, edition of 5, Courtesy of the Navajo Gallery, Taos, New Mexico.

PROJECT 1-8: **NAVAJO FIGURE—COLLAGE**

MATERIALS

- 18 × 24-inch drawing paper
- 12 × 18-inch drawing paper
- Pastels or colored pencils
- Watercolors or watered-down acrylic paint
- Flat brushes at least 1 inch wide
- Spray bottle with alcohol or glass cleaner
- Polymer medium or thinned white glue
- Black fine-line marker

Drawn after Summer Storm, 1981
R. C. Gorman
Lithograph, Origins Press
Navajo Gallery, Taos, New Mexico

This project will help you understand how a modern Native American artist reflected his background in his artwork, yet created unique paintings. His monumental figures sometimes fill the page. R. C. Gorman is a Navajo artist famous for his paintings of Native American women. Sometimes he shows two figures seated together, or a mother and child, a single woman against a landscape of rocks or mountains, or a woman seated near a beautiful pot.

1. This painted paper will be used later as part of your collage. Mix watercolor in the lid of the paintbox, adding pigment and water until you have quite a bit mixed. The differences in color as you run out of pigment or add water to the pigment only make it more like the cliffs in the Southwest. Apply the paint in horizontal stripes on 12 × 18-inch drawing paper using a wide brush or a piece of cardboard dipped in paint. You will be making rock-like striations of pigment, so while one "stripe" might be orange, the next one could have a little red or yellow added. After doing two to three inches, and before your pigment dries, spritz it lightly with alcohol or glass cleaner. This causes it to make interesting pigment circles. Set it aside and allow it to dry.

2. Look at the large sheet of drawing paper. Decide how many figures you will have, whether they will be seated or standing, male or female, and what will be in the background. Draw one or more of your classmates wrapped in a blanket. To avoid having all the pictures look alike, some students could stand, while others could be seated, singly or with someone else. These small figure sketches are going to be the basis for your monumental paintings.

3. Observe the folds of the robe and the outside shape. Cut the "robe" from your painted sheet of paper. Apply it onto the background with polymer medium or thinned white glue. Next, draw the head (also hands and feet if you choose) using black marker. When the figure is finished, draw around the outside of it with black marker.

4. If the figure looks strange "floating" on its background, you may use more prepainted collage paper (perhaps a neighbor has a different color) to make a canyon-like background.

PROJECT 1-9: NAVAJO CHIEFS' BLANKETS—COMPUTER STYLE

FOR THE TEACHER

Because traditional weaving is time consuming, I realized that patterns could also be "woven" on the computer and, because of the easily achieved geometric patterns, would actually look like Navajo blankets. The trial and error method is half the fun. Even if students are trying to copy a real design, the limitations and potential of the computer will allow for a great deal of individuality. The earliest chiefs' (wearing) blankets (first phase), woven from the 1850s to 1870s, were simple stripes. The second phase had bands with geometric designs, and the third phase had terraced diamonds and triangles as part of the design. Today's beautifully woven blankets retain many of the same traditional designs and colors, but more elaborate patterns. From the 1870s to 1940s, many blankets were woven for the tourist trade and sold in hotel gift shops and train stations along the route of the Santa Fe railroad. These one-of-a-kind blankets combined traditional patterns with more modern motifs, such as Texaco signs, horses, and trains. The serrated edge on a diamond was a result of Hispanic influence and was not in the earliest blankets. The original blankets were intended to be worn, so incomplete diamonds on the edges would meet at the front, and the two halves would make a complete diamond.

PREPARATION

Try to get several books on Navajo rugs that students may look at and get ideas. Encourage them to start with a truly simple rug, such as one with horizontal or vertical stripes, before they start to elaborate on them. These may be printed out on the computer or photographed in a darkened room directly from the screen, and photocopy enlargements made at a copy store.

ADDITIONAL SUGGESTIONS

- After students have mastered geometric designs, encourage them to experiment with pictorial blankets or rugs. These might contain pictures of trains, covered wagons, animals, flowers, or birds.

- Students could also interpret these paintings on graph paper, using colored pencil or marker. The same instructions would apply.

Photo 1-9. *Serape Blanket*, 1865–1870, Navajo, wool: raveled cochineal-dyed/raveled indigo-dyed/handspun vegetal-dyed/3-ply Germantown yarn, 51-¼ × 69-¾ inches, Purchase: Nelson Trust, The Nelson-Atkins Museum of Art, Kansas City, Missouri.

PROJECT 1-9: **NAVAJO CHIEFS' BLANKETS—COMPUTER STYLE**

MATERIALS

- Computer
- Paper
- Colored pencils

Navajo chief blankets were not actually made just for chiefs but, because they were of such fine quality, those who could afford them were generally more wealthy. Learning to create such a design on the computer is good practice on learning what the computer tools can do for you. The basic "tools" you will use are lines of various thicknesses, rectangles and other geometric shapes, the eraser, and the screen's ruler. If you are using a computer program that has a variety of patterns, you will find experimentation with them interesting.

A few basic suggestions that may make it easier for you:

- If you use grids and rulers, work in half-inch (.50) and fourth-inch (.25) increments.
- If you must erase, click off grids and rulers to make it easier.
- Make erasures as you go along. Don't save them until you are finished.
- If you make a mistake and you click "Undo," it will change the most recent command.
- Your rug will probably not be completely symmetrical, and it isn't crucial. Navajo weavers also made errors.
- Make up your own design rather than trying to copy one exactly. You will catch on quickly to some basic patterns.

1. Create a rectangle you can view in its entirety. It is not important to work particularly large, but make it easy on yourself by being able to see the entire rectangle at a time. The width of your line is particularly important and can be changed at any time. A variety of widths will give a pleasing effect.

2. Make a border by making another rectangle within the first. Find the exact center of the rug design. Although it isn't crucial for the rug to be symmetrical, they generally are.

3. The earliest chiefs' rugs (first phase) were simply red and blue stripes of different widths. Try to make a simple one like this first. The second-phase blankets had stripes that were more elaborate, and the third-phase blankets had triangles.

4. Whether you are working in black and white or color, leave some areas white and some dark, with patterns in some areas. Some traditional color schemes are white, grey, brown, and black, *or* white, grey, black, and red. A modern design might have five or more colors such as medium blue, light blue, light brown, rose, and dark red.

5. When the rug is complete, put "tassels" on the corners or fringe on the two ends. If your rug is printed in black and white, you may use colored markers to enhance it.

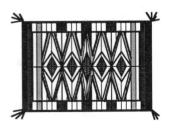

Section 2

COLONIAL ART
(1600 to 1750)

COLONIAL
TIME LINE

	1600	1650	1675	1700	1725	1735	1750
Painting Sculpture Architecture Folk Art	1610 Alphabet sampler	Early Colonial Period, 1630–1670	Theorem Quilting			Genealogical Samplers, 1730	
		Adam Thoroughgood House, 1636–1640		Robert Feke c. 1705–1750	John Greenwood 1727–1792	1738–1815 John Singleton Copley 1738–1820 Benjamin West	
		San Estevan, N.M. 1629	Scrimshaw	William & Mary College by Sir Christopher Wren 1702 John Smibert arrives in America, 1729		Independence Hall, c. 1751 Faneuil Hall, 1740–1742 Charles Willson Peale 1741–1827	
Politics	1607—Jamestown, VA settled 1620—Pilgrims land at Plymouth 1635—Rhode Island settled			1681—Pennsylvania founded by William Penn		The Alamo, 1744 1732—Last English Colony (Georgia) founded George Washington born, 1732	
Literature	1611—King James Version of the Bible			Ben Franklin, 1706–1790 *Poor Richard's Almanack,* 1732			
Science	Halley's Comet sighted, 1531					1727—Death of Sir Isaac Newton 1736—Death of Fahrenheit, creator of the thermometer	
Music				Piano invented by Bartolommeo in Italy, 1710 Philadelphia founded, 1682		Classic era, 1730–1827 Franz Joseph Haydn, 1732–1809	
Current Events	Boston founded, 1630 Harvard founded, 1636 Santa Fe capitol of Spanish Govt., 1610	1673—Marquette and Joliet explore Mississippi River		Captain Kidd hanged in London, 1701 Time of witches in Massachusetts, 1692		Period of Rococo art in Europe, 1697–1764	

EARLY COLONIAL ARCHITECTURE

New England Homes
Wooden homes hewn and pegged
Shingle covering
Lean-to on back
Elizabethan (1558–1603)
Late Medieval features
Steep shingled roofs
Lead-paned casement windows
Symmetrical windows
Eaves close to wall
Tall, central chimneys
Fancy brickwork
Half-timbered houses
Jetty or overhang

Boardman House, 1686
Saugus, Massachusetts

Williams House, 1706–1707
Old Deerfield, Massachusetts

Dutch Colonial Features
Stepped end or straight-sided gables
Gambrel roof
Brick construction

Ackerman House, 1704
Hackensack, New Jersey

St. Luke's Church, East End, 1632
Isle of Wight County, Virginia

Southern Homes
Brick construction
End chimneys
One-and-a-half stories

Adam Thoroughgood House, 1636–1640
Princess Anne County, Virginia

Burlington, 18th Cent.
Charles City County, Virginia

The Alamo, 1744–1757
San Antonio, Texas

Spanish Colonial
Textured adobe
Windowless walls
Flat, timbered roofs
Clerestory windows

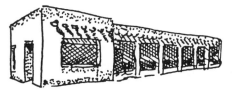

Governor's Palace, 1610–1614
Santa Fe, New Mexico

ARTISTS OF THE PERIOD

PAINTERS

- *Robert Feke* (c. 1705–1750) was a portrait painter, born in Long Island. He was said to have been a sailor and worked in Boston and Philadelphia. It is thought he died at sea.
- *John Greenwood* (1727–1792) was born in Boston, but moved to England at age 25. He was a portrait painter and engraver, and also built organs and lacquered (Japanned) furniture.
- *Gustavus Hesselius* (1682–1755) painted portraits and the first publicly commissioned religious picture in America. He was born in Sweden and came to America in 1712.
- *John Smibert* (1688–1751) was born in Edinburgh, trained in London, and settled in Boston in 1730. He was the first English painter with formal training to immigrate to America. He specialized in portraits.

SCULPTORS

- *Shem Drowne* (1683–1774) was a tinsmith who created the grasshopper atop Faneuil Hall in Boston. Nathaniel Hawthorne thought that Drowne carved America's earliest surviving piece of free-standing statuary, the *Little Admiral* in the Old State House in Boston.
- *Isaac Fowle* (1648–1718), a wood carver, was one of many who carved home interiors and shipwork.
- *Simeon Skillin, Sr.* (1716–1778) was the founder of a dynasty of wood carvers who specialized in fittings for ships such as figureheads and decorative work.
- *John Welch* (1711–1789) was a sculptor who fashioned weathervanes, notably the *Sacred Cod,* which is atop the House of Representatives of the Boston State House.

ARCHITECTS

- *Peter Harrison* (1716–1776), a sea captain, was English born, but immigrated to the United States. Although he was not trained as an architect, he designed a number of major buildings in Newport and Boston.

OVERVIEW OF THE COLONIAL PERIOD IN AMERICAN ART

When the American colonists settled in America (1607 onward), most of their time was spent obtaining shelter, food, and clothing. Creating art was probably the furthest thing from their minds, yet it was not very long before uniquely American art forms began to emerge.

Women began to take over work that men might have done in their former countries (such as weaving) because the men were busy clearing land, hunting, home building, and farming. Just like the Native Americans, many colonists applied decorative details to their tools, clothing, and ultimately their homes. As the character of the colonies changed, merchants and plantation owners had more leisure time and the wealth to support the arts. Furniture makers and house builders refined their designs based on imported pattern books. Immigrants from countries other than England brought art forms and methods of decorating, but perhaps because the English were the first settlers, their traditions strongly influenced early artworks.

PAINTING

For a considerable time portraiture was the basic subject in early colonial paintings. Having portraits painted was a mark of success, immortalizing family members for succeeding generations. The earliest portrait painters were mostly European immigrants or Americans who went to Europe for academic training, such as John White, John Smibert, John Greenwood, Robert Feke, and Gustavus Hesselius. Miniature portraits were often painted, sometimes as a reminder of family members who had to be away for business or war.

Limners (from the word "illuminators") were usually self-taught artists who traveled from town to town painting anything that needed painting, including portraits. Some of these artists were known by name, but most of the "American Primitive" paintings are by unknown artists. Painters were seldom able to support themselves entirely by selling portraits, so they also painted carriages, trade signs, and house interiors.

Landscapes were not uncommon, and sometimes were painted directly onto the walls of the home. Many of these "overmantle" paintings disappeared when they were later painted over or covered with paneling. Landscapes frequently were included in the background of portraits to identify the status of the sitter. For example, a ship's captain might be portrayed with a sailing ship and ocean seen through a window in the background.

Still lifes were seldom used solely as subject matter until the 18th century, although many portraits included perfect still lifes composed of the sitter's tools or belongings.

Examples of Early Paintings

Self Portrait, (date unknown), Robert Feke, Museum of Fine Arts, Boston

Family of Isaac Royall, Robert Feke, 1741, The Harvard Law School, Boston

Pocahontas, c. 1616, artist unknown, National Portrait Gallery, Washington, D.C.

Indians Fishing, 1585, John White, British Museum, London

Saturiba, the Indian Chief, and Rene Laudonniere at Ribaut's Column, 1564, Jacques Le Moyne, New York Public Library

Mrs. Freake and Baby Mary, 1674, unknown artist, Worcester Art Museum, Worcester, Massachusetts

Tishcohan, 1735, Gustavus Hesselius, Historical Society of Pennsylvania, Philadelphia

The Bermuda Group, 1729, John Smibert, Yale University Art Gallery, New Haven

Sea Captains Carousing in Suriname, c. 1758, John Greenwood, The Saint Louis Art Museum

SCULPTURE

Early sculptors had to be versatile to make a living. The original colonists had an immediate need for gravestones, though the earliest surviving ones were carved after 1660. These were simple slabs, sometimes decorated with a rosette or sun design. Eventually a preoccupation with death caused these images to be replaced by winged skulls or crossbones, or sometimes an hourglass to symbolize the swift passage of time on Earth.

Carvers met other needs for trade signs, weathervanes, ships' figureheads, and figures placed outside shops. The most common ones, outside tobacconists' shops, were called "Cigar-store Indians" (at times a female, dressed in a skirt and headdress of tobacco leaves). These figures, and those of African-American slaves, were depicted because they represented "typically American figures."

Carvers often incised designs on chests or cabinets for furniture makers. In the early 1700s, after pattern books were imported, they began doing more elaborate wood carvings for cabinetmakers and home builders.

Examples of Sculpture

Gravestone of John Foster, 1681, sculptor unknown, Dorchester, Massachusetts

Grasshopper weathervane, 1749, Shem Drowne, Faneuil Hall, Boston

Indian weathervane, 1716, Shem Drowne, Province House, Boston

Little Admiral, c. 1750, sculptor unknown (possibly Shem Drowne), Old State House, Boston

ARCHITECTURE

The earliest architecture was rudimentary, yet resembled that from the settlers' homelands. Some of the earliest frame homes in the Eastern colonies featured an overhang based on English medieval architecture. The Dutch brought stepped-gable house fronts and gambrel roofs to America. The steep roofs persisted long after the stepped-gables disappeared. By the 1700s, many homes and public buildings were built of brick, based on classical architecture, with Greek pediments, columns, and Roman porches.

The Germans, Swedes, and Danes brought log-cabin building to America. Adobe homes and Spanish architecture were standard in areas where Catholic priests established missions, such as California, the Southwest, and Florida. Sod homes were sometimes built on the plains where there was little lumber.

Examples of Architecture

Castillo de San Marcos, 1672–1754, St. Augustine, Florida

Governor's Palace, 1609–1614, Santa Fe, New Mexico

San Esteban, pre-1644, Acoma, New Mexico

Cahokia Courthouse, 1737, Cahokia, Illinois

Stanley-Whitman House, c. 1660, Farmington, Connecticut

Hancock House, 1735, Boston, Massachusetts

Colony House, 1739, Richard Munday, Newport, Rhode Island

Drayton Hall, 1738–1742, Charleston County, South Carolina

Palace of the Governors, 1749–1751, Henry Cary, Williamsburg, Virginia

FOLK ART

Folk art consisted of items created by settlers for their personal use in daily living or created by artists who were not academically trained. These artists often compensated for their inability to use perspective or draw anatomy correctly by extreme attention to detail, which resulted in pure, abstract design. American crafts—quilting, scrimshaw, wooden or metal toys, pottery, glass, painted furniture, stenciling, overmantle paintings, mourning paintings, carvings, embroidered samplers, and baskets—undoubtedly had their origins in other cultures, but after a few generations away from original models, they evolved into American designs.

Some immigrant groups such as the Pennsylvania Germans kept alive customs from the old world in such folk crafts as the fraktur (decorated certificate), painted furniture, and painted pottery. Scandinavians decorated their homes with rosemaling (decorative painted flowers and items from nature) in their traditional style. American folk art continues to be created in modern times, with some artists deliberately copying or reviving old techniques, while other very good untrained artists are following their instincts.

Most folk crafts served a useful purpose. Lamps were a necessity and took many forms. Weathervanes were almost the only means of weather forecasting for their time. Whirligigs showed the direction and speed of the wind, but many were also fun to look at. The earliest quilts were created for warmth. Much folk art was created to make homes warm and beautiful to their owners.

Examples of Folk Art

Sampler, 1643, Loara Standish, Pilgrim Hall, Plymouth, Massachusetts

Marriage Chest of Margaret Kernan, 1788, Henry Francis Du Pont Winterthur Museum, Winterthur, Delaware

The Family in the Parlor (scrimshaw), c. 1840, Smithsonian Institution, Washington, D.C.

Cockerel weathervane, 1721, Shem Drowne, First Church in Cambridge Congregational, Cambridge, Massachusetts

Candle sconce (quillwork with pine), 1730, artist unknown, Greenfield Village and Henry Ford Museum, Dearborn, Michigan

Porringer, c. 1655, John Hull and Robert Sanderson, Museum of Fine Arts, Boston

PROJECT 2-1: **PILGRIMS' COLLARS**

FOR THE TEACHER

Common belief (though not always fact) is that the Pilgrims wore plain dress, with the only adornment being shoe buckles for men and plain white collars for both men and women. Large collars were the style of the day, with many colonists other than the Pilgrims wearing lacy collars (including the men).

This project challenges the students to make collars using available materials.

PREPARATION

Start by discussing common objects found around a home and how to use them in a work of art. For example, a necklace could be made of clover or a string of paper clips, but it would be inadequate as a collar unless it could hold its shape. Use tagboard to make a square or oval collar pattern that is approximately 6 inches wide all the way around to help students visualize the approximate size and shape of a collar. In addition to displaying the collars later, plan to photograph each student modeling the collar.

A "given" of this project is that the collar should not cost any money and should be made of found materials. Stress how important imagination and humor are for this project. My students rose to this occasion by making collars of playing cards, rolled up copper foil, squares of colored magazine pages wound around a needle to make beads, a "bathroom collar" constructed of tiny paper cups held together with Band-aids™ and a cut-up sponge. Others were Tinkertoys™, a "Larry Bird" collar made of magazine pictures of Larry Bird attached to a knotted basketball hoop, a decorated cardboard collar with peacock feathers, and, of course, decorated wallpaper. One of the nicest was made of sticks, wire, and large metal washers. As a last resort, a student could decorate just the cardboard collar with colored pencil, but you are not looking for beauty as much as for imagination.

ADDITIONAL SUGGESTIONS

- Have students imagine how it must have been for colonial children not to have toys except those made by their relatives. Suggest they construct a doll of a corncob or cloth, or a pull toy or whirligig of wood scraps.

- Have students research the daily lives of the settlers. Have someone find out how they got their food, did their laundry, built their homes, got cloth for clothing, got leather for shoes, and so on. Assign some to find out how their homes were decorated—what they used on their walls, their tables, their beds. Ask students why they think "country" decorating is so popular and why people collect and cherish handmade objects and folk art.

Photo 2-1A. Student-made collar made from playing cards.

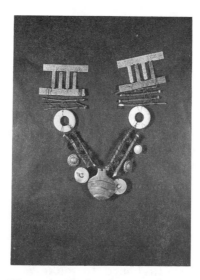

Photo 2-1B. Student-made collar made from washers, sticks, buttons, wire, and miscellaneous metal.

Photo 2-1C. Student-made collar made from rolled metal foil and copper wire.

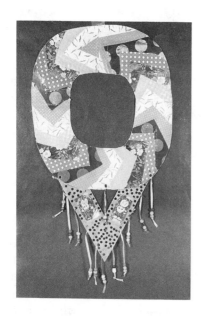

Photo 2-1D. Student-made collar made from wallpaper samples, ribbon, and beads.

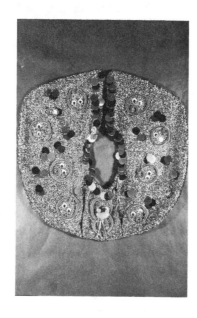

Photo 2-1E. Student-made collar made from metal cloth, goo-goo eyes, and pipe cleaners.

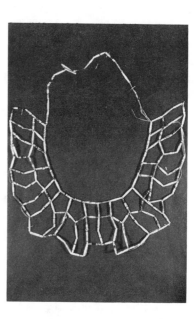

Photo 2-1F. Student-made collar made from cut-up magazine triangles wrapped around a needle and strung together.

PROJECT 2-1: **PILGRIMS' COLLARS**

MATERIALS

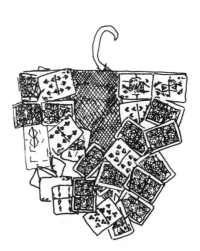

- Found materials
- Cord
- Tagboard
- Colored pencil
- Acrylic paint
- Glue
- 18 × 24-inch black construction paper
- Hangers

The Pilgrims were noted for their plain dress and their white collars, though other colonists had elegant lace and embroidered collars. This assignment is to design a collar with materials you can find around your house. Of course, you can always just decorate a tagboard collar. Originality is important.

1. A tagboard square or oval pattern approximately the shape of a large Pilgrim collar may help you envision the general shape and size of the finished collar. It is possible to color the tagboard collar with colored pencil, or cover it with cloth or wallpaper.

2. Look around your house or where you work for discarded objects suitable for collar material. Examples are playing cards, macaroni, styrofoam cut into shapes, empty film containers, pop tops from cans, cotton balls, corks, workbench finds such as washers or screws, buttons, Legos™, sticks, plastic spoons, or shells. There are unlimited possibilities, but if what you find doesn't seem to be adequate or imaginative, combine it with something else you find.

3. Constructing the project will take time and cannot be done in one session. You may choose to combine everything on a cord, or with wire, or glue it onto a cardboard backing with a glue gun or white glue. Craftsmanship is important. If it all falls apart every time it is handled, you have not done an adequate job of combining everything. You should be able to actually wear it.

4. To display the collar, poke a hole in the exact center of 18 × 24-inch black construction paper. Insert a hanger through the hole, and loosely fold the paper in half, stapling the ends. Arrange the collar on the hanger for display.

PROJECT 2-2: COLORED INK SAMPLERS

FOR THE TEACHER

Although creating cloth samplers was traditionally a method of teaching embroidery to young women, this project is based on pen-and-ink samplers on parchment or fine paper, a sampler variation that was taught to both male and female students.

In the early days of the colonies creating an embroidered sampler, or "examplar," was part of every young woman's education. The tradition grew out of lack of embroidery pattern books in the colonies in the early days. Embroidery, a European tradition, was among the few forms of relaxation for women, so most household linens and female undergarments were embroidered. Young women prepared a trousseau of embroidered linens, which they kept in a hope chest.

Some European cloth samplers were long and narrow (7 × 36 inches) because of the narrow looms on which the cloth was woven. American samplers evolved to become broader and shorter. The oldest existing American sampler was embroidered by Loara Standish, daughter of Myles Standish, in 1654. The sampler originally served as a pattern book for embroidery designs, but in its later years it was used to teach students geography, the alphabet, and math. Although some of the samples were designed by the teacher, most of them were personal.

PREPARATION

Use ¼-inch grid paper to tape under the parchment. You may wish to look up some sayings that appeared on samplers. Some examples are:

- "Learning is an ornament. A portion never to be spent."
- "When land is gone and money spent, then learning proves most excellent."
- "Dunces ever meet with shame and never rise to work or fame."
- "Adorn thyself with grace & truth and learning prize now in thy youth."
- "Modesty is one of the chief ornaments of youth. A contented mind is an inestimable treasure."

Naturally, students will consider sayings such as phrases from their favorite songs more appropriate for their own samplers, but have them get your approval first.

ADDITIONAL SUGGESTIONS

- Do this project on a computer by putting a "grid and ruler" on the screen and working out a design in advance.
- Create a landscape or portrait filling in the grid with "cross stitch" patterns to completely fill the page.

Photo 2-2. This sampler was done with colored marker on an 8-½ × 11-inch piece of parchment, using a grid that could be seen through the parchment.

PROJECT 2-2: **COLORED INK SAMPLER**

MATERIALS

- Colored fine-line markers
- 8-½ × 11-inch parchment or bond paper
- ¼-inch grid paper
- Rulers
- Pencils

The samplers (examplars) you make will be drawn in ink, as male and female students did in the colonial days. Basically you will draw a "cross stitch," which is an X marked in a square. The sampler often had several elements on it such as an alphabet, a verse, a multiplication table, the name of its creator, and a border. Other designs featured houses, buildings, country scenes (including chickens and cows), Adam and Eve, maps, family trees or genealogical details, vines, eagles, anchors, flowers, and trees.

1. Decide what the total composition of the sampler will be. If you are going to make an alphabet or multiplication table, it can go on the top or vertically along the sides. If you select a verse, it will probably be somewhere in the middle, along with your name. Scenes are most commonly across the bottom.

2. Tape a piece of bond or parchment paper on top of the grid paper. You will be able to see it well enough through the paper to use it as a guide. Use a pencil and ruler to lightly draw an even 1-½-inch border all the way around. This will get you started and help in placement of the alphabet. A border gives a finishing touch.

3. To make an alphabet, use five squares down and three squares across for most letters. You will see that some, such as the A, W, and V, need to be wider. It is possible to get all the letters on two and a half lines. If you do this part first, it will help you see how to design the rest of the sampler. Be certain to include your name on the sampler. Errors were commonplace in colonial samplers, so accept it when things don't look quite how you intended or are less than perfect.

4. Lightly pencil in any scene, flowers, or border that you intend to do in cross stitch. An alternative is to use ink to make the "satin stitch," by drawing parallel lines closely to fill in areas. A combination of cross stitch and satin stitch is effective.

5. When you are finished, analyze the composition carefully. If it is not interesting because it doesn't have enough color, or if you cannot read your name or verse, you may need to add emphasis by making the cross lines thicker or by filling in the grid with more color in short parallel lines.

PROJECT 2-3: PENNSYLVANIA GERMAN FRAKTUR

FOR THE TEACHER

The fraktur (hand-written decorated document) is one of the surviving art forms from the early days of the colonies. It was not only beautiful, but also served to record important events. The history of adding pictorial decoration around the edges of a written document goes back to illuminated manuscripts, which used fanciful figures, scrolls, flowers, and animals around the edges.

The frakturs were often completed by the schoolmaster, the minister, or an itinerant artist who traveled around making necessary documents.

Earliest frakturs were individually hand drawn, though later ones might be drawn first, with the text filled in later. Eventually the character of the fraktur evolved to be more uniquely American. Most frakturs are symmetrical and painted in bright colors. Many of the motifs that are used in "country" decorating such as hearts, flowers, birds, and scrolls come from the Pennsylvania German (Deutsch) tradition. Religious song books and bookplates were also embellished by artists.

PREPARATION

Discuss with students what occasions in their families might have caused them to commission a fraktur. Ask if any of them have personal family records such as an old book recording the names of family members and when they were born, died, or married. This is an obvious opportunity for them to do a small genealogical survey of their families. Some might even be moved to do a family tree. One of my students created one to commemorate the death of her goldfish; another, the birth and death of a dog. Another student created a marriage certificate, to be filled in later.

Have students practice writing in calligraphy before they actually decorate a piece of parchment. Most students enjoy calligraphy, as it is a new skill, and they are most impressed to see their own names written with great flourishes. Or a photocopy of an elaborate alphabet can be placed underneath the fraktur and each letter individually traced.

ADDITIONAL SUGGESTIONS

- Pennsylvania German motifs were used to decorate many household items such as furniture, tinware, boxes, panels, tiles, and plates. Have students bring in a "discard" from home such as old furniture or a tray on which they could paint such designs. Or they can paint on "panels" made of gessoed heavy cardboard (do front and back). Libraries and hobby shops have many resources on these designs.

- Research many of the wonderful Pennsylvania German sayings (such as "Too soon old, too late smart") which were written around the edges of plates or tiles. Plain white glazed tiles or plates can be purchased, and designs and sayings painted on with acrylic paint.

- Many computers have beautiful script. Students might prefer to do a fraktur on a computer, printing it on parchment (available by the sheet from photocopy shops), then decorating the border with tempera and gold paint (or fine-line marker and gold pen).

- American calligraphers created pictures of patriotic symbols, such as the eagle, using pen and ink (often brown ink). The same careful strokes that are used for calligraphy can be used to create flowers or trees. Examples of this art may be found in many calligraphy books at your library. Use pencil to lightly outline the shape; then fill in with parallel curving strokes.

Photo 2-3A. Student-made fraktur using the Arabic alphabet.

Photo 2-3B. Student-made fraktur commemorating the student's beloved fish, Bob and Frenchy Bob.

PROJECT 2-3: PENNSYLVANIA GERMAN FRAKTUR

MATERIALS

- Newsprint
- Parchment or bond paper
- Calligraphy markers or calligraphy pens and ink
- Photocopied calligraphy examples
- Pencils
- Rulers
- Watercolor
- Watercolor brushes #4 and #2
- Colored pencils
- Gold fine-line markers

The fraktur is a handwritten and decorated document that records an important event in a family's history such as a birth, baptism, marriage, or death. In Germany these certificates were required by law, and naturally when the immigrants came to the New World, they brought some of their old laws and culture with them. These documents were so important to the Pennsylvania Germans that they have been saved through the years, so you may even have one in your family.

The fraktur you create could record your birth or graduation, or could be given as a gift to a family member to record an important event. If you make only one decorated blank, you can photocopy it for reuse before filling in the information.

1. On the parchment, use a pencil and ruler to draw *very* light horizontal lines for the important information (these can be erased later). To make sure you have spaced things properly, *lightly* pencil in the information such as name, birth date, parents, witnesses, or anything else important.

2. Practice using a calligraphy pen to write your name, numbers, etc. It is important that you learn to write confidently, or your shaky "hand" will show. An alternative is to place a photocopy of an alphabet underneath your parchment and trace individual letters.

3. On newsprint, doodle some of the designs you might use on your fraktur. Rather than slavishly copy what was done 300 years ago, try your own designs, although your designs may resemble the old designs, since many of them were adapted from nature. Some of the motifs used by Pennsylvania Germans, and which you might adapt, include hearts, flowers (particularly tulips), horses, scrolls, people, unicorns (which symbolized purity), and mermaids. The designs were usually balanced, with a geometric design at the center top and other related designs around the edges. Sometimes a single stylized flower might be in a corner. Use your imagination, combining such things as hearts, flowers, and birds. Use curving lines to "tie things together" visually.

4. Lightly pencil designs around the writing. Use watercolor or colored pencil to fill in areas, although you will want to allow the parchment to show through in places. If you later want to emphasize designs with black fine-line marker, you can do so.

5. When the design is complete, use fine-line gold marker or paint to emphasize some areas. Be careful not to overdo the gold—it should be sparingly used just for emphasis.

PROJECT 2-4: **THEOREM PAINTING**

FOR THE TEACHER

Perhaps theorem painting was the reason "'genu-ine' oil painting on velvet" got a bad reputation. This popular craft, done mostly in the early nineteenth century, was relatively short lived, although stenciling has once again become popular. The actual stencil used in painting was called a "theorem." Formulas for colors and designs were sometimes found in ladies' magazines. Most theorem paintings were baskets of fruit painted on velvet, but some landscapes and mourning paintings were also done with the use of theorems. In today's revival of theorem painting, a commonly used background is white velvet that has been antiqued by painting a weak tea solution on it.

PREPARATION

Although preparation for this project is a group effort, each student will have a theorem painting when finished. You may use regular stencil paper, which is about the weight of tagboard, or plastic overhead transparencies. I have used old file folders that I oiled with vegetable oil (allow time for it to dry). A local frame shop may be willing to save velour-finished matboard pieces or colored pieces of scrap matboard that would be suitable for a stenciled background.

Cut the board for the stencil to approximately 4 × 6 inches for various fruits, a basket, leaves, and flowers. Write names of fruit and / or flowers on pieces of paper and allow students to reach into a box to find out what their assignment is; otherwise, you will have an abundance of apples! Suggested fruits are grapes, peaches, apples, pears, melons, cherries, strawberries, and raspberries. Also sometimes included were birds, leaves, flowers, baskets, and vases. It is possible to have more than one student make a specific fruit or flower, but you do want to have a variety.

ADDITIONAL SUGGESTIONS

- After students have completed a fruit or flower theorem, they may find they enjoy stenciling and would like to make more original designs. Cutting out a stencil is not difficult if they have "bridges" to keep it from falling apart. Mourning pictures (a portrait of deceased family members or famous leaders such as George Washington) were a very popular art form. The stenciling was done in different values of black, white, and gray and usually included a figure, a monument or vase, a written tribute, and a weeping willow tree.

- Theorem painting was also done on flat fans used before the days of air conditioning. These were approximately 7 × 9 inches with rounded corners. Stencil a design on tag board, and trim the edges with gold paint or marker, stapling or gluing on a tongue depressor as a handle.

- Sandpaper paintings were done in private schools in the early 1800s. White paper was covered with finely ground marble dust and glue. When dry, landscapes or seascapes were drawn on with charcoal, with fine details sometimes scraped or erased from the charcoal. A satisfactory substitute would be marble dust mixed with polymer medium (available from an art supply house) or actual sandpaper. Black sandpaper could be drawn on with white chalk. These should be spray-fixed to keep them intact.

Photo 2-4A. *Vase of Flowers,* c. 1820–1840, artist unknown, paint on velvet, 22-¾ × 18 × ¼ inches, Purchase: Nelson Trust, The Nelson-Atkins Museum of Art, Kansas City, Missouri. This type of painting was called "theorem painting" because the stencils used were called theorems. It was also popularly known as "Poonah painting" and "formula painting."

Photo 2-4B. *Lafayette at the Tomb of Washington,* early 19th century, silk and wool embroidery on satin, The Saint Louis Art Museum.

PROJECT 2-4: **THEOREM PAINTING**

MATERIALS

- Newsprint or typing paper
- Stencil paper or clear plastic
- X-acto™ knives
- Pencils
- 12 × 18-inch drawing paper or velour wrapping paper
- Acrylic or tempera paint
- Stencil brushes or a sponge cut into small squares

Theorem painting was an accomplishment of educated young people that allowed everyone to make an acceptable (if not particularly original) painting. Theorem painting was based on the use of stencils that could be arranged slightly differently by each person who used them. By working as a group to do this project, each person can cut one stencil, which you may trade with one another.

1. After determining which piece of fruit, flower, leaves, or basket to make, draw it on newsprint as nearly life-size as possible. To keep the stencil from falling apart, remember to leave small spaces between pieces of it, such as in a bunch of grapes.

2. Put a magazine or something underneath the newsprint to protect the table, and tape the stencil paper on top of the drawing. With an X-acto™ knife, carefully cut out the stencil, following the lines. To make a curved cut, work in *short,* repeated strokes until your knife has gone through the stencil. Keep the knife straight, turning the paper. You will find you can make smooth curves. *Safety note: Always keep your "holding hand" behind the one that is cutting with the knife. It is easy to slip and cut yourself.*

3. After the stencil is cut, practice painting on a piece of newsprint before beginning the actual theorem. Hold the stencil carefully in place with one hand, then use a stencil brush or small piece of sponge and carefully stipple (dab) or wipe pigment (if using a sponge), beginning at the outside and working inward. The darkness of pigment at the outside of a piece of fruit and the lightness toward the center give it a rounded effect. To indicate a light source, make one side darker than the other. Mix colors to show differences in value.

4. To begin your theorem, think about how you will overlap some fruit or flowers. Stencil each piece of fruit that will rest on the bottom of the basket if you use an openwork basket, then stencil the basket on top of the fruit or flowers. As you work upwards, leave some fruit incomplete to allow for overlapping. Use a variety of fruit and add leaves; soon you will have a finished theorem painting. One reason for the popularity of theorem painting was that even someone who had never painted before could have an original painting or a bit of "fancy work."

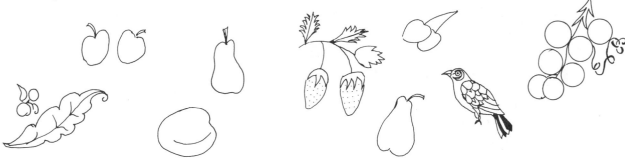

PROJECT 2-5: OVERMANTLE PAINTING

FOR THE TEACHER

Overmantle painting was literally what it sounds like. Often it was done on canvas and then affixed to the wall, but frequently it was done on board and occasionally directly onto the plaster. It was nearly always framed in wood. Most of these paintings were long scenery paintings (sometimes called "rural scene pieces") in proportion to the fireplace, though occasionally an entire fireplace wall would be decoratively painted. Artists advertised that they painted "picture panels over chimney pieces."

As old homes have been torn down or modernized, many of these paintings have disappeared. They were often painted by itinerant painters who traveled from town to town, painting items such as business signs, furniture, home decorations, portraits, and their "landskips." In addition to the overmantle painting, the woodwork sometimes was painted to resemble marble or a fine wood such as mahogany.

Subject matter was serene, often based on the surrounding countryside or town. People, horses, and buildings were frequently included in the scenes of nature, which included the hills, rivers, valleys, and trees. Some were based on English patterns that were used for sampler making, engravings, or imported wallpapers. A few plaster paintings had urns of flowers painted on them as if the flowers were placed on the mantle. Occasionally a patriotic theme was used, showing eagles, George Washington, or homes of famous leaders.

Examples of Overmantles

Van Bergen overmantle, c. 1735, artist unknown, New York State Historical Association, Cooperstown, New York

Overmantle panel, mid-eighteenth century, artist unknown, Old Sturbridge Village, Sturbridge, Massachusetts

Overmantle, c. 1790, Elisha Hurlbut House, Scotland, Connecticut

Overmantle in Set Wetmore House, date and artist unknown, Middletown, Connecticut

Fireboard from East India Marine Hall, 1804, Peabody Museum, Salem, Massachusetts

PREPARATION

Begin with a discussion of the terrain of your local area. Have students use descriptive adjectives for locations in their surroundings (words like flat plains, rolling mountains, muddy river, tree-covered hills, flowering trees, tall houses, crowded city, etc.). Talk about what kind of pictures they might like on their walls that they would be willing to look at every day for the rest of their lives. If you use the back of wide, strippable wallpaper for painting, allow students to determine the length of their painting, then have them apply gesso. It may be necessary to apply gesso front *and* back to avoid curling of the canvas. If you use ordinary paper, cut it so the proportions are much longer than wide, just to challenge students to use a different format than usual.

ADDITIONAL SUGGESTIONS

- Fireboards were used to cover the opening of a fireplace when it wasn't in use. These were normally on boards cut to fit the opening, or on canvas stretched on a frame the size of the opening. These fireboards had various ways of being held upright, but the most common was to cut slots so they fit over the andirons. If students wish to make a fireboard for their own homes, masonite or foam board cut to size are suitable materials. Common subject matter was an urn filled with flowers, scenery, and even a "fireplace interior" made to look like the bricks in an empty fireplace.

- Use two different colors of paint to make a "combed" finish, to marbleize, or to make a wood-grained finish. These faux (false) finishes are used to make inexpensive woods look expensive. Many fine books contain detailed explanations for creating faux finishes. How about a book cover with faux finish paper?

- A long painting such as the one in this project is jokingly referred to by artists as a "sofa-sized painting." A popular competition and exhibit at Washington University titled "Over the Sofa" required artists to submit a proposal to decorate a wall, which was then funded for the exhibit. These decorations were incredibly witty. A friend used garishly hand-painted black velvet and sparkling holiday lights to create a "tasteful" wall. Divide students into groups of four or five to create a *concept* for a modern "over the sofa" wall decoration. Remind them that creativity is paramount. A written proposal complete with sketches would *be* the entire assignment, unless you choose to carry out one of the submissions.

PROJECT 2-5: **OVERMANTLE PAINTING**

MATERIALS

- Wide strippable wallpaper (paint on the textured canvas-like back)
- Gesso or white latex house paint
- Flat wide brushes
- Acrylic, tempera, or oil pastels
- Newsprint
- Pencils

In colonial days, all houses had large fireplaces for heat and cooking. The overmantle painting above the fireplace, often created on canvas, wood, or directly on the plaster, was then framed. This was surely the most beautiful painting in the world to the settlers, as they looked at it every day. The artists painted what they saw around them, including means of transportation (boats, horses and carriages), buildings, ladies in long dresses, men in three-cornered hats, and animals.

1. To prepare your "canvas" for painting, apply two coats of white latex paint or gesso (which is thinned plaster of paris) with a large brush, allowing it to dry between coats. Apply the first coat horizontally; the second, vertically.

2. On newsprint, draw long horizontal rectangles. From your *own* surroundings, draw a small "rough," or thumbnail sketch, as a basis for your overmantle painting. Your landscape might have a river, mountains, trees, and people in modern dress, with modern buildings and cars in the background.

3. After you have decided on your general subject, lightly pencil it on the canvas. Draw the background first, then decide where you want to place the details to make it more interesting. Your painting will have the "feel" of an historic overmantle painting if it is filled with small detail. The most interesting part may be near the bottom and go all the way across.

4. To apply paint, use a larger brush for the background. Overmantle painters sometimes used pieces of sponge to apply leaves for trees and bushes. Practice this technique on newsprint first, using lighter colors of green on the middle to make the trees look rounded.

5. Use a small brush to fill in details. So-called primitive painters love detail and often don't leave anything out. Place your painting on the floor, step away from it, and look at it from a distance to see if your colors are reasonably balanced or if you could add more color in a few places.

**Drawn from Elisha Hurlbut House, pre-1790 by
Winthrop Chandler.**

PROJECT 2-6: **SEPIA LANDSCAPE**

FOR THE TEACHER

European painters, such as Rembrandt, created sketches using reed pen and a sepia wash to work out values (differences in light and dark) for later oil paintings or etchings. Because so many of the earliest American painters were immigrants who had learned to paint in Europe, they naturally continued that tradition. Sepia was a brown inky substance secreted by cuttlefish and adapted for painting, but the color was fleeting, so it was not often used. Today's sepia ink is more permanent. Sepia paintings ranged from very sketchy, loose paintings, to completely detailed paintings, with highlights created with white opaque paint or chalk.

American painters, such as Charles Wimar, created sepia paintings on location as studies for other paintings.

PREPARATION

Have students talk about places they have visited or some they think foreign visitors to America might like to visit. Discuss some of the most famous monuments, cities, landmarks, and natural beauty spots of the continent. Ask them where they would go in North America if they had only one choice. They may use photos, postcards, or magazine photos as resource material, although their interpretation will be created only in brown tones with white highlights. Landmarks might include the Washington and Lincoln monuments, the Brooklyn Bridge, the White House, Mount Rushmore, covered bridges, lighthouses, battlefields, and natural phenomena such as rock formations.

Suggest to students that they practice with ink first, building up color, blotting, and trying the effects they get with various tools such as brushes, pens, sticks, or anything else with which they can make marks.

ADDITIONAL SUGGESTIONS

- Do a small sepia-colored still-life painting based on something simple such as a tool or object in the room.
- A colleague, Timothy Smith, has his drawing students draw trees in a landscape on brown paper using conté crayon in black and white. This simple color scheme is very effective.

PROJECT 2-6: **SEPIA LANDSCAPE**

MATERIALS

- Drawing or watercolor paper
- Sepia ink or brown watercolor
- Watercolor brushes #7 and #10
- Pen nibs and pen holder
- Pencils

Think about and discuss some of the best known "tourist" locations on the North American continent. While many are in the lower United States, others are found in Mexico, Canada, and Alaska. In the early days of the settlers, few people traveled far, and most of what they knew of distant places came from drawings or etchings created by artists.

You may have postcards or photos of someplace you have visited such as Niagara Falls, the Grand Canyon, Yellowstone National Park, Yosemite National Park, San Francisco, New York, Washington, D.C., or other landmarks that you can use as the basis for your sepia painting. Details that add interest include trees, water, mountains, bridges, people, buildings, and animals.

1. On a small piece of paper, practice painting with sepia ink or brown watercolor. Notice how you can make it lighter or darker depending on how much water you use for diluting the ink. You may blot to lighten it, or add more pigment to darken it. While it is wet, you can scratch into it with the point of scissors, or draw into it with a pen and ink. After it is dry, you might go back and draw details with pen and ink.

2. On a larger sheet of paper, use pencil to *lightly* draw a scene you wish to paint. Plan ahead for areas that you intend to make dark and areas that will remain white. Although you can go over areas later with white paint or chalk to make them lighter, it is more effective to plan the light areas in advance, just as you would with watercolor.

3. Keep a scrap of paper next to your actual painting on which to test your brush when you paint. It is better to find out in advance if the color you have is the value (lightness or darkness) you intend it to be. It is easier to add more ink to make something darker than to take it away to make it lighter. If it is darker than you wanted on the paper, dilute it with water and blot with a paper towel.

4. When you think you are done, place the painting on the floor and look at it through squinted eyes. (Squinting your eyelashes helps you see differences in value rather than detail.) You may wish to go back and add detail with pen and ink or a fine brush when you are done with the background.

PROJECT 2-7: **SCRIMSHAW**

FOR THE TEACHER

The art form of scrimshaw emerged in the days when many colonists earned their living by whaling or trading in foreign ports. Sailors whiled away time on long voyages by decorating whales' teeth or bone by scribing (scratching) designs on them. In addition to incising designs, sailors also carved useful items for wives and sweethearts. Fine examples of this craft are in museums today, and include sewing kits, corset stays (to stiffen a corset so women would have tiny waists), wool winders, pie crimpers, jewelry, combs, and thimbles. Details were scratched with a sharp instrument such as a pocket knife, nail, or sail needle. Lampblack (and sometimes chewing tobacco) was rubbed into the design to give a black design on a white background. The subject matter often included ships, maps, flowers, other forms of nature (including the female figure), and, of course, whales.

As sperm whales became more scarce, ivory or bone became acceptable substitutes. One enduring use for scrimshaw is the Nantucket lightship basket (created by lighthouse keepers), and prized today as purses. A lid was decorated with an oval ivory scrimshaw rendering of a ship or whales.

PREPARATION

Various forms of plastic are suitable for scrimshaw, including such items as Friendly Plastic® (available in hobby shops for jewelry), plastic switch plates, and acrylic sheet plastic. For practice, plastic bleach bottles can be cut with scissors or an X-acto™ knife into the outline of a whale's tooth. Students may use an etching tool, T-pin, scratchboard knives, X-acto™ knives, a sharp needle, or nail. Other materials that can be substituted for whales' teeth and baleen are soup bones from the butcher that have been boiled and dried in the sun, horn, antlers, or seashells. To shape bones for scribing, place them in a vise and cut into the desired shape with a coping saw.

Books on American history contain numerous paintings of ship battles. Students can select a portion of one to draw freehand, or a design could be traced from a photocopy. Students would benefit by seeing engraving techniques of any kind to understand how cross-hatching is done. A close look at a dollar bill will give examples of engraving techniques.

ADDITIONAL SUGGESTIONS

- White or black scratchboard is a suitable medium for elaborate scrimshaw designs. For white scratchboard, apply watercolor or dye and allow it to dry before applying India ink to the scratchboard, to allow colors to show through the design. Precolored scratchpaper may be purchased from an art supply store.

- Paintings of merchant ships were proudly displayed on colonists' walls. Do a watercolor or tempera painting of a ship, using magazine photos or reproductions for details, then create the background sky and water from imagination. To avoid having these be direct copies of previous paintings, bring in personal photos of any kind that have skies and seas and paint skies based on the photo. This is not as easy as it sounds, and will challenge students to learn to mix colors.

PROJECT 2-7: **SCRIMSHAW**

MATERIALS

- White bleach or detergent bottles, cleaned and dried
- Candle
- China saucer
- White Friendly Plastic™ or boiled bones
- Scratching instrument: nail, X-acto™ knife, or push pin
- Sandpaper
- Tape
- Scissors
- Oil paint or India ink

Scrimshaw was one of the many colonial crafts, usually done by sailors (called scrimshanders) to while away the time on long voyages. The technique is similar to engraving, which is done by scratching on a metal plate with a needle.

The materials the colonists used were from today's endangered species such as whales' teeth, bones or baleen, or elephants (ivory). Plastic is *not* an endangered material.

1. Make a design on tracing paper based on a colonial painting, such as one of a ship battle. Other suitable subjects are a flower design, trees, maps, or simple animal forms. Avoid geometric design at first, as it is difficult. Do something that allows you to create interesting details with lines. You may want to make a decorative border around your design to give a finished look.

2. The plastic usually comes in a square shape. Use scissors to cut the plastic in the shape you want it to be (possibly an oval or square). With sandpaper, smooth the edges so it will be a finished piece.

3. Transfer your design to the surface by taping it in place and piercing the paper through the lines to make dots on the plastic. When the paper is removed, you should be able to see them well enough to complete the lines. Remove the paper and incise the design by applying gentle pressure with a sharp instrument. It is also possible to draw a design freehand. *Safety note: Always keep your "holding hand" behind the one that is cutting with the knife. It is easy to slip and cut yourself.*

4. To make dark areas in the scrimshaw, make parallel lines close to each other. This can be repeated after you have applied ink if you see areas that should be darkened.

5. When you think you have completed your etching, you may apply black pigment such as oil paint or ink with a fine brush, then rub away the black, allowing ink to remain in the incised areas. You could also use carbon, as sailors sometimes did. Make your own carbon by holding a lit candle under the bottom of a saucer. Use your finger to transfer it to the engraving. To add colored pigment, outline everything in black with a small brush before applying colors one at a time with a brush. Wipe away each color before applying the next.

6. To transform this into jewelry, glue a pin on the back or attach a hanger for a pendant. For a keychain, just drill a hole. To display your finished piece, tape it onto a black fabric or paper background with double-sided tape.

© 1996 by Prentice-Hall, Inc.

PROJECT 2-8: QUILT

FOR THE TEACHER

SLIDE #4: *Album Quilt,* **1848, Mary Ann Hudgins, Eliza Garrett, and Mary Jane Smith, 100-¼ × 100-¼ inches, cotton and sepia ink, Gift of Mrs. Stratford Lee Morton, The Saint Louis Art Museum**

Even though quilting did not originate in America, the homemade quilt is considered as American as "mom and apple pie." It is considered an especially American form of folk art. Crusaders brought the idea of padded layers of cloth sewn together for warmth back to Europe from the Middle East, and the settlers brought the technique to America. The earliest pieced or patchwork quilts were probably made from scraps of worn clothing sewn together and quilted or just tied with string. From simple squares, triangles, and rectangles, an infinite number of patterns was possible, and it was here that the American homemaker showed her ingenuity.

Although one person might piece a quilt top and do the quilting, quilting was often a social occasion, with a number of women getting together to stitch a quilt. Many of the fine quilts seen in museums today were presentation or "friendship" quilts with sections created by a number of different seamstresses. These might be given as a token of esteem to a pastor or local doctor. Sometimes several young women made a friendship quilt to present to a young man on his twenty-first birthday.

Fortunately the art of quilting is admired as much today as it was in the earliest days of the colonies. In addition to traditional geometric patterns, many quilts have been made over the almost four centuries of America's history that illustrate patriotism and pride. The red, white, and blue colors of the American flag, the eagle, Uncle Sam, the Statue of Liberty, George Washington, Abe Lincoln, and other patriotic American symbols have been the subject of many quilts.

Many contemporary artists (men and women) find the quilt to be a wonderful format for expression, both for its size and ease of transportation. A project later in this book is based on quilts created by a modern artist, Faith Ringgold.

PREPARATION

If possible, find books on quilts for students to look at. A magazine such as *Miniature Quilt* has many fine designs that include borders. Point out to students that the overall pattern is determined by patterns created when the triangles and squares are put together. This is a fine project to demonstrate how important differences in value are—that most patterns include both dark and light colors that help define the design. Students will interpret a traditional quilt pattern in watercolor. They will use basically geometric designs, but they may also wish to use a patriotic symbol as part of the design.

ADDITIONAL SUGGESTIONS

- If you have a printing press, you may emboss dampened watercolor or drawing paper in a "quilt" pattern by running it though the press on top of a purchased ¹⁄₁₆-inch thick embossed panel of clear plastic purchased from a hardware store. Have students paint on the back of the paper so that the raised grid will effectively separate the colors.

- Use white glue to make square patterns on the paper to separate colors. Allow the glue to dry before painting.

- Use X-acto™ knives to cut artgum erasers into geometric shapes. Cut approximately ¼-inch down from the top, creating triangles, rectangles, octagons, squares, hectagons, and diamonds. These can be used as stamps to make geometric quilt patterns. Pour tempera paint into damp sponges (or a folded damp paper towel) to create several different colors of stamp pads. Suggest that students first use a ruler to *lightly* make a 1-inch grid on their paper. Students may share shapes. It would be helpful to photocopy a few patterns from magazines or quilt books.

- This is an ideal project for computer graphics experiments. Remember that even if you cannot print out bright colors, you may photograph "quilts" from the screen in a darkened room. If students want an enlarged print of their computer art, it is relatively inexpensive to have color copies of photos made at a photocopy store.

- Cut and share fadeless paper or construction paper to make "Shaker" quilts, known for their strong graphic design, bright colors, and simplicity.

- A traditional Colonial method of creating quilt squares was to use leaves and ferns as stencils, spattering and sponging paint around them. Using fabric paint, each student can create a square on fabric (or use tempera on paper). Place the fern on the square and spatter or sponge paint around the stencil. (Blue or red were the preferred colors.) These squares are then sewn together.

- Crazy quilts were often made of the finest silks, satins, and velvets. They were irregularly cut pieces, sewn together in a haphazard pattern, but with the finest of embroidery holding them together and decorating the patches. Make a crazy quilt from wallpaper samples and fadeless paper by cutting them irregularly to fit exactly, gluing them to white drawing paper (allowing no white to show through), then "embroidering" them with fine-line marker cross stitches to hold them together.

Photo 2-8. *Album Quilt,* **1848, Mary Ann Hudgins, Eliza Garrett, and Mary Jane Smith, 100-¼ × 100-¼ inches, cotton and sepia ink, Gift of Mrs. Stratford Lee Morton, The Saint Louis Art Museum.**

PROJECT 2-8: **QUILT**

MATERIALS

- Watercolor or white construction paper
- White crayon or oil pastel
- ¼- or ½-inch graph paper
- Watercolor paint
- Brushes
- Containers for water

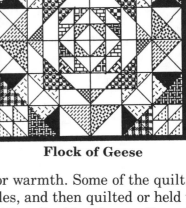

Flock of Geese

In the early days of the colonies, settlers needed quilts for warmth. Some of the quilts were simple patches of old clothes cut into squares, rectangles, and triangles, and then quilted or held together with string. While these evolved sometimes to elaborate patterns with embroidered or appliqued designs, this project is based on geometric shapes such as the triangle or square.

1. Make a 1-½-inch border on the watercolor paper, then use a ruler to make a grid (1 or 1-½-inch squares) with white crayon on white paper. Go over each line twice so the white crayon will act as a resist to the watercolor.

2. On a piece of graph paper, work out a design in pencil, remembering to create a border around the quilt. Fold the paper in fourths, and begin on the fold in the middle, working outward. You may fill in the shapes with numbers such as #1 for lightest, #2 for medium, and #3 for darkest values. It is not necessary to complete the entire graph.

3. Once you've determined a pattern, decide on a color scheme. Related colors such as red, orange, yellow, and white, or a cool color scheme would be effective. You might leave the white of the watercolor paper for one of the "colors."

4. Mix pigment in the lid of the watercolor box. To save constant rinsing and cleaning the brush, paint one color on several of the divisions before you paint the next color. If you make a mistake, just keep going. Southern quilters sometimes deliberately created an error, as they felt only God could make something perfect.

5. After painting the inside of the quilt, start the border. The border acts as a frame to complete the quilt. A curved design or small geometric pattern would be appropriate, or a ½-inch plain edge could be painted on the outer edge, just as a quilt might be finished in a plain edge.

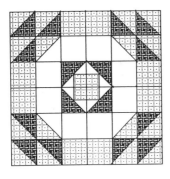

Chimney Sweep

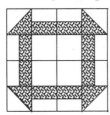

The Wrench

Garden of Eden

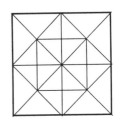

Windmill Pattern

REVOLUTIONARY ART
(1750 to 1800)

REVOLUTIONARY
TIME LINE

	1750	1760	1770	1775	1780	1790	1800
Painting Sculpture Architecture Folk Art	Late Colonial Period 1730–1790	1766–1800s Samplers	Romanticism	Penn's Treaty with the Indians by Benjamin West, 1771	Washington Allston, 1779–1843	Federal Period 1790–1820	Cut-paper love tokens
		Gilbert Stuart, 1755–1828	Monticello 1768–1809		1780–1849 Edward Hicks	Illuminated Fraktur, 1789–1842	"Primitive portraits" c. 1799
		Mount Vernon 1759–1769	Paul Revere (1768) by J. S. Copley	American Flag 1777	Hex Signs 1783–1872 Thomas Sully	Porthole Paintings 1785–1851 John J. Audubon	

| **Politics** | 1754 French/Indian War | 1774, Passage of the Stamp Act | 1773 Boston Tea Party | 1775–1783 Revolutionary War July 4, 1776 Declaration of Independence | 1787 Constitution of U.S. Adopted | 1789 George Washington 1st U.S. President | 1797 John Adams 2nd U.S. President |

| **Literature** | | 1763, Voltaire's Treatise on Tolerance | 1770–1850 Wordsworth 1770 1st Edition of Encyclopedia Britannica | 1776—*Common Sense* by Thomas Paine | | | |

| **Science** | Ben Franklin's kite experiments, 1752 | | Nitrogen discovered by Priestley and Rutherford, 1772 | 1775 Watts invents steam engine | 1775 Hydrochloric and sulfuric acid discovered by Priestley | Eli Whitney invents cotton gin, 1793 | |

| **Music and Theatre** | 1750, Premier of *Beggar's Opera* 1685–1750 Johann Sebastian Bach 1685–1759 George Frideric Handel | 1756–1791 Wolfgang Amadeus Mozart 1752, First Repertory Theatre Lewis Hallam | 1770–1827 Ludwig von Beethoven | | | | |

| **Current Events** | 1769 Daniel Boone in Kentucky | 1770 Boston Massacre | | 1778 Cook discovers Hawaii | 1780 Treason of Benedict Arnold Bald Eagle named national symbol, 1782 | 1789 Storming of Bastille in Paris | |

ARCHITECTURE OF THE REVOLUTIONARY PERIOD

Georgian (named for three King Georges who ruled from 1714–1820)

Middle Georgian (Georgian Colonial) (c. 1730–1769)
Frequently plain exterior
Decorative features often based on Palladio
Palladian window (curved at top)
Double or two-story portico
Giant pilasters (square columns with Corinthian or Ionic capitals)
Raised basement
Hipped roof with balustrades and dormer windows
Shutters on windows

Early Georgian (c. 1700–1750)
Quoins (square stones at corners and under windows)
Unbroken (flat) facade
Symmetrical
Low, hipped roof
Pediments above windows, first floor
Swan's neck pediment above door

Late Georgian (1775–1883)
Broken pediment
Projecting central pavilion

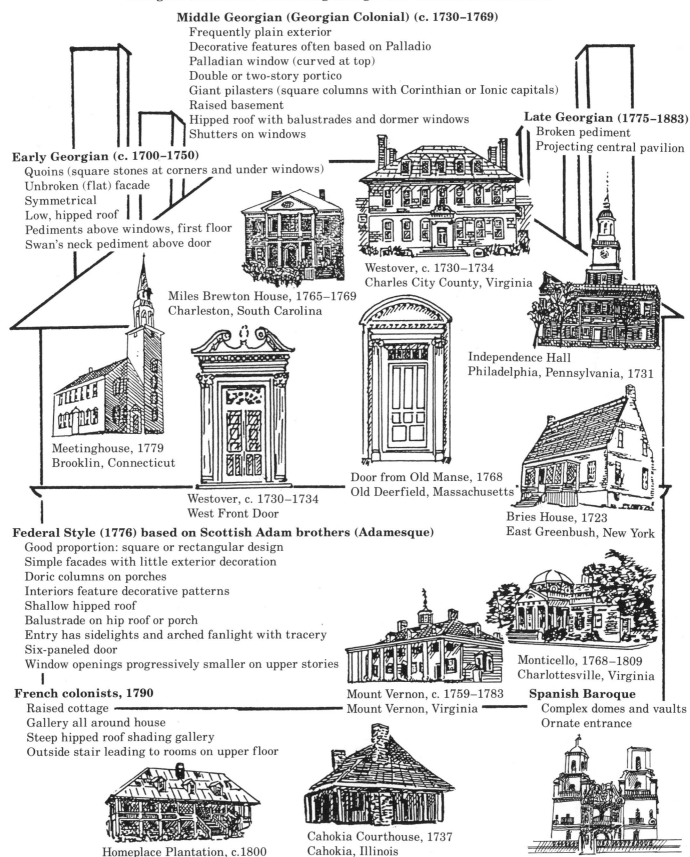

Miles Brewton House, 1765–1769
Charleston, South Carolina

Westover, c. 1730–1734
Charles City County, Virginia

Independence Hall
Philadelphia, Pennsylvania, 1731

Meetinghouse, 1779
Brooklin, Connecticut

Westover, c. 1730–1734
West Front Door

Door from Old Manse, 1768
Old Deerfield, Massachusetts

Bries House, 1723
East Greenbush, New York

Federal Style (1776) based on Scottish Adam brothers (Adamesque)
Good proportion: square or rectangular design
Simple facades with little exterior decoration
Doric columns on porches
Interiors feature decorative patterns
Shallow hipped roof
Balustrade on hip roof or porch
Entry has sidelights and arched fanlight with tracery
Six-paneled door
Window openings progressively smaller on upper stories

French colonists, 1790
Raised cottage
Gallery all around house
Steep hipped roof shading gallery
Outside stair leading to rooms on upper floor

Mount Vernon, c. 1759–1783
Mount Vernon, Virginia

Monticello, 1768–1809
Charlottesville, Virginia

Spanish Baroque
Complex domes and vaults
Ornate entrance

Homeplace Plantation, c.1800
Hahnville, Louisiana

Cahokia Courthouse, 1737
Cahokia, Illinois

San Xavier Del Bac, 1784–1787
near Tucson, Arizona

Section 3.—REVOLUTIONARY ART (1750–1800)

ARTISTS OF THE PERIOD

PAINTERS

- *John Singleton Copley* (1738–1815), like Benjamin West and Paul Revere, was academically trained in England, eventually returning there to live.

- *Charles Willson Peale* (1741–1827) had many occupations, among them being an officer of the Revolutionary War. He studied with Benjamin West in London. A contemporary said of him, "He fit [fought] and painted and painted and fit." He was a naturalist, inventor, and director and curator of his own museum. He was the father of Raphaelle Peale (1774–1825) and Rembrandt Peale (1778–1860), also well-known painters.

- *Paul Revere* (1735–1818) was most famous as a patriot, but was a silversmith and painter as well. His "Revere Bowl" is a classical design that is still widely used.

- *Gilbert Stuart* (1755–1828) was said to have had commissions as early as age 14, moving to London to work and study. He became the most famous American colonial portrait painter, partially because of the many portraits he painted of George Washington. He made 70 copies of his *Athenaeum* painting of George Washington.

- *John Trumbull* (1756–1843) was best known for his small sketches of battles of the Revolutionary War and his landscapes. He was one of America's first romantic painters.

- *Benjamin West* (1738–1820) was one of the first great American painters. After he moved to England, his influence continued as he generously trained many visiting young American artists.

SCULPTORS

- *Samuel McIntire* (1757–1811) was an ornamental carver, but not as skilled with figures as some of his contemporaries. He specialized in carving eagles.

- *George Robinson* (1680–1737) was a Colonial wood carver whose shop specialized in interior design and ships' ornaments.

- *William Rush* (1756–1833), son of *Joseph Rush* (1720–1787), was also a ship's carver. William learned how to carve from his father. He became an officer in the Philadelphia militia during the Revolution. He was famous as a ship's carver before he began carving portrait busts and allegorical figures.

- *John Skillin* (1746–1800) and his brother *Simeon Skillin, Jr.* (1757–1806) originally were ship's carvers, who worked with their father, Simeon Skillin, Sr. Their shop evolved to become important through architectural carving, portraiture, and figures for furniture and gardens. Their style was basically a provincial version of Baroque.

- *John Welch* (1711–1789) was one of the earliest carvers in Boston, specializing in shop and inn signs as well as carving and ship repair.

- *Patience Lowell Wright* (1725–1786) was a colonial "wax modeler," specializing in creating wax figures of well-known people. She went to England and did figures of the aristocracy, including the king and queen. She also made profile wax-reliefs of George Washington and Benjamin Franklin.

ARCHITECTS

- *William Buckland* (1734–1774) was brought to Virginia as an indentured servant. He did all the interiors of *Gunston Hall,* 1758.
- *Thomas Jefferson* (1743–1826), a gentleman / architect, was profoundly influenced by French neo-classicism and Palladian design concepts.
- *Robert Smith* (c. 1722–1777), designed the Capitol Building in Washington, D.C. His drawings for buildings at the University of Virginia were contributions to the evolution of classical architecture in the U.S. He also designed *Carpenters' Hall* in Philadelphia and *Nassau Hall* at Princeton University.

OVERVIEW OF ART DURING THE REVOLUTIONARY PERIOD

By the mid-eighteenth century, the New World's population had increased dramatically. New opportunities were open to the colonists through communication and trade with Europe and the Far East. Major cities such as Boston, New York, Savannah, Philadelphia, and Charleston had thriving ports and a growing middle class. The 13 original colonies came together in one government. Tobacco had become a major crop in the South, which led to large plantations and the use of slaves.

The wealth of the planters and merchant classes enabled them to consider matters beyond mere existence. The American Revolution and formation of a country independent of foreign rule also changed the outlook of Americans.

PAINTING

The great subjects of painting—such as religious, mythological, and historical themes employed by the Europeans—had rarely been interpreted by American painters. Newly built government buildings offered a site for grand-scale paintings of historic moments. The appreciation of art by educated patrons fostered a desire for subjects of this type. Through portraiture we also have records of all our great leaders.

Even those unable to afford fine paintings wished to show their patriotism by hanging paintings of leaders such as George Washington or by displaying patriotic symbols. Many trained and untrained artists did paintings of General Washington. Successful merchants, political leaders, and other professionals had portraits painted of themselves and their families. Some of the most interesting paintings of the time were professional artists' portraits of their own families. Portrait artists were selected for their ability to capture a true likeness, their quick work, and their reasonable prices. Pricing was based on variables such as shaded or unshaded, frontal versus profile, and canvas instead of watercolor paper or vellum.

Horizontal overmantle paintings were an integral part of the architecture, sometimes determining the size of the fireplace. Artists occasionally decorated entire rooms with murals or stenciling.

Examples of Paintings

The Declaration of Independence, 1786–1794, John Trumbull, Yale University Art Gallery, New Haven

Penn's Treaty with the Indians, 1772, Benjamin West, Pennsylvania Academy of the Fine Arts, Philadelphia

The Death of General Wolfe, 1771, Benjamin West, Royal College, London, and National Gallery of Canada, Ottawa

Paul Revere, 1768–1770, John Singleton Copley, Museum of Fine Arts, Boston

Watson and the Shark, 1782, John Singleton Copley, Detroit Institute of the Arts

Washington After Trenton, 1767, Charles Willson Peale, The Metropolitan Museum of Art, New York

The American School, 1765, Matthew Pratt, The Metropolitan Museum of Art, New York

The Bloody Massacre, 1770, Paul Revere, Library of Congress, Washington, D.C.

The Staircase Group, 1795, Charles Willson Peale, Philadelphia Museum of Art

The Surrender of Cornwallis at Yorktown, 1817–1820, John Trumbull, United States Capitol, Washington, D.C.

George Washington, 1796, Gilbert Stuart, Museum of Fine Arts, Boston

The Skater, 1782, Gilbert Stuart , National Gallery of Art, Washington, D.C.

Death of General Mercer at the Battle of Princeton, 1777, John Trumbull, Yale University Art Gallery, New Haven

The Declaration of Independence, July 4, 1776, John Trumbull, Yale University Art Gallery, New Haven

SCULPTURE

As the nation prospered after the Revolutionary War, American sculpture evolved from purely functional forms to decorative forms and "fine art" (beauty for its own sake). The importation of European sculpture, such as the French sculptor J. A. Houdon's portraits of George Washington and Benjamin Franklin, encouraged a similar classicism in American sculpture. Favorite subjects were based on ancient Greek and Roman sculpture. Gravestones began to feature fabric-draped Grecian and Roman cinerary urns. Even the American symbol, Miss Liberty, was clothed like a Greek goddess.

Wood carvers continued to create figureheads, trade-store figures and signs, circus figures, and courthouse or architectural statuary. They also carved classic motifs for cabinet makers to incorporate into their furniture.

A relatively unknown artform today was modeling in wax, mostly done by women. They created fruit and flowers, but also immortalized famous American leaders in small bas-reliefs and portrait busts.

Examples of Sculpture

Sacred Cod, date unknown, John Welch, Boston State House, Boston

Agriculture, Liberty, and Plenty, 1791, John and Simeon Skillin, Jr., Yale University Art Gallery, New Haven

Hope, c. 1790, attributed to John and Simeon Skillin, Jr., Henry Francis DuPont Winterthur Museum, Delaware

Benjamin Franklin, George Washington (wax busts), c. 1725, Patience Lowell Wright, Maryland Historical Society, Baltimore

Governor John Winthrop, 1798, Samuel McIntire, American Antiquarian Society, Worcester, Massachusetts

ARCHITECTURE

In the early days of the colonies, gentlemen were expected to have some knowledge of architecture, and many designed their own homes. A master carpenter might draw up simple working plans for a home, but it wasn't until the late 1700s that architects, such as Robert Smith, designed public buildings. Each group of immigrants imported elements of their former country's style, and American architecture evolved using available skills and materials. The dominant feature of the Revolutionary American style was the use of simple but strong lines. Public buildings generally employed classical features such as Greek columns, pediments, and domes.

Examples of Architecture

Hammond-Harwood House, 1773–1774, William Buckland, Annapolis, Maryland

The "Saron" or Sister's House, 1743, Ephrata, Pennsylvania

First Baptist Meeting House, 1774–1775, Providence, Rhode Island

Carpenters' Hall, 1770–1775, Robert Smith, Philadelphia

Faneuil Hall, 1740–1742, John Smibert, Boston

Virginia State Capitol, 1785–1798, Thomas Jefferson, Richmond, Virginia

Monticello, 1768–1809, Thomas Jefferson, Charlottesville, Virginia

Bank of Pennsylvania, 1798–1800, Benjamin Henry Latrobe, Philadelphia

FOLK ART

Perhaps the spirit of equality in America helped untrained artists to believe that anyone could create art. William Ketchum, in his book *All-American Folk Arts and Crafts* (Rizzol: Intl. Pub., Inc., New York, 1986), said, "Americans considered themselves born artists." Some of the items they created, such as quilts, weathervanes, and whirligigs, show innovation and pride, even though a practical purpose was served. The artists' patriotism often inspired them to use American motifs in their artwork. Heroes such as George Washington and Benjamin Franklin, the Native-American, and symbols such as Miss Liberty, the American flag, Uncle Sam, the eagle, and the Statue of Liberty, were depicted on almost any material that could be decorated. This use of American symbols in artwork continues in modern times (although perhaps with a little less sincerity than during Revolutionary days).

Examples of Folk Art

Rooster Weathervane, 19th century, Smithsonian Institution, Washington D.C.

Lady with Her Pets, 1790, Rufus Hathaway, The Metropolitan Museum of Art, New York

Fraktur Marriage Certificate, 1803, artist unknown, Greenfield Village and Henry Ford Museum

Liberty in the Form of the Goddess of Youth: Giving Support to the Bald Eagle, c. 1800, Abijah Canfield, Greenfield Village and Henry Ford Museum

Peacock Weathervane, c. 1800, collection of Herbert W. Hemphill, Jr.

Navigator, c. 1810, Samuel King, Whaling Museum, New Bedford, Massachusetts

A View of Mount Vernon, the Seat of General Washington (fireboard), c. 1800, National Gallery of Art, Washington, D.C.

Dower Chest, 1803, Philadelphia Museum of Art

PROJECT 3-1: **TEA PARTY**

FOR THE TEACHER

The Boston Tea Party on December 16, 1773 is known to all school children as the Colonists' rebellious act that led to the Revolutionary War. Certainly the high taxes on tea affected how much of this staple people could buy, which increased resentment against England. The teapot was a cherished household item, and many have been passed down through families. Silver teapots constructed by colonial silversmiths such as Paul Revere may be seen in museums.

PREPARATION

This project could be done by two different methods, depending on your facilities. Creating the teapot in cardboard is very satisfactory. If you have access to a kiln, then take the project to the next step, which is to create a teapot in clay. Students would still make a basic pattern in cardboard and try it for fit before cutting out clay slabs.

Before even telling the students what the assignment will be, have them do a five-minute stream-of-consciousness exercise of *writing* a list of nouns (such as animal, house, Volkswagen), and adjectives (haunted, contented, weird) in two vertical columns on one page. I find this helps them realize that they do have ideas that are purely their own.

Demonstrate to students how to make neat fold lines in tagboard by scoring, or making curves by folding and overlapping flaps.

Now discuss the idea of a teapot. Tell students that it must "hold water," have some type of opening for pouring into a cup, and have a handle. It doesn't have to be round or look like a teapot. Many teapots by contemporary artists are built of geometric shapes that are especially appropriate for cardboard or slab building in clay. Have students now look critically at their lists of words and select at least three nouns to draw into the shape of a teapot. They might want to combine nouns or a noun and an adjective to create a teapot. Encouraging students to use unlikely combinations of ideas challenges them to use their imaginations and develops higher order thinking skills (HOTS).

Note: Creating a teapot from cardboard was an assignment given to high school students in a HOTS competition at The Saint Louis Art Museum under the direction of (then) Education Director Pamela Hellwege. This idea is used with her permission and the permission of the Museum.

ADDITIONAL SUGGESTIONS

- Create and decorate a mug in cardboard or clay. This lends itself to interesting ideas, shapes, and decorations.
- Be "designers" for a ceramic factory. A finished drawing of a teapot design or complete tea set could be the project. These could be handsomely done on gray or black paper with pastels or colored pencils.

Photo 3-1. *The Boston Massacre,* 1770, Paul Revere, engraving/partly colored by hand, 19.7 × 21.5 cm., The Saint Louis Art Museum. This engraving was by Paul Revere, one of the great American silversmiths of his time. Revere is mostly known for his famous midnight ride warning of the coming of the British. As can be seen through his engraving, he was also an artist.

PROJECT 3-1: **TEA PARTY**

MATERIALS

For a Cardboard Teapot

- X-acto™ knife
- Glue
- Newsprint
- Tagboard
- Ruler
- Scissors

For a Clay Teapot

- Clay, 2 to 3 pounds for each student
- Rolling pin or 1 × 12-inch dowel
- Battens, 1-½ × 12 inches
- Knives
- Container to make slip

Although this project was developed to commemorate the Boston Tea Party, the teapot is still a very contemporary item, and many exhibits for modern artisans feature only teapots. Creating a contemporary teapot first requires that you come up with an original idea. The shape can resemble almost anything, from a pumpkin to a pyramid. Just don't forget that, whether in cardboard or ceramic, it must have a way to "pour" and a handle.

TO MAKE A CARDBOARD TEAPOT

1. Before beginning your teapot, make several thumbnail sketches on newsprint. Your teapot may be round or oval, or it could be created with flat surfaces to be square or triangular. The requirements are that it have a lid, a handle, and a spout.
2. Make a pattern in newsprint before cutting it from cardboard. Make tabs on each piece for gluing it to another piece.
3. Use a ruler to draw straight edges. To make tabs that fold easily, score along the fold line, using a ruler and the tip of a pair of scissors. After cutting pieces, plan and draw any design on the pieces before gluing them together.
4. Painting the tagboard teapot (with acrylic or tempera) is optional, though you may wish to paint some type of decoration. The teapot may be any color, pattern, and shape you wish to use. As long as it has a lid, handle, and spout, it is still a teapot.

TO MAKE A CLAY POT

Keep clay moist by keeping it wrapped in plastic when not actually working with it.

1. *To make a slab teapot,* roll out a ½-inch thick slab of clay between two battens.
2. Place the tagboard pattern pieces (without tabs) on the slab, and hold a knife vertically to cut out straight pieces.
3. Score (mark with a knife) the areas to be joined, apply slip (clay thinned to the consistency of cream), and smooth the joints from the outside and inside. For greater strength, add a coil of clay inside the joint and smooth it to adhere to the two areas joined.
4. Form the spout and handle separately, allowing all pieces to become slightly firm before scoring and joining them with slip. On the outside of the pot, draw a circle where the spout will be joined. Use a pencil to poke holes within the circle before applying the spout.

1. *To make a coil teapot,* make even coils by rolling the clay with the fat part of the palm just below the fingers. Make a bottom by flattening a ball of clay. Add coils three at a time, making a diagonal cut with a knife when you join one coil to the next. Score the surface of one coil before joining it to another with slip.

2. Use a batten (or ruler) to paddle the outside of the coils while supporting the pot from the inside with your other hand.

3. Complete the shape of the pot before adding the spout or handle. On the outside of the pot, draw a circle where the spout will be joined. Use a pencil to poke holes within the circle before applying the spout with slip.

To finish a clay pot, use either underglazes to apply decorations (while the pot is drying) or finish in one color after a bisque firing. Make the decoration appropriate to the teapot's shape.

**Drawn after teapot, 1796
Paul Revere**

**Drawn after teapot, 1718
J. Lamb and T. Tearle**

**Drawn after teapot, 1764–1785
William Will**

**Drawn after teapot, 1785–1798
William Will**

PROJECT 3-2: GEORGE W.

FOR THE TEACHER

SLIDE #5: *Portrait of George Washington (1732–1799), First President of the U.S.,* 1796, Gilbert Stuart, oil on canvas 48 × 37 inches, National Portrait Gallery, Smithsonian Institution (owned jointly with the Museum of Fine Arts, Boston); Art Resource, NY

The face of George Washington surely is one of the most reproduced and famous faces in history. In addition to being on the one-dollar bill, he has been seen for over 200 years in countless works of art. He was a favorite subject of American pop artists in the 1950s, with individual artists weaving his visage into their contemporary subject matter.

PREPARATION

If possible, find books that have reproductions of Washington's face. Students find it interesting to see how many different media have been used to interpret Washington.

Photocopy a Gilbert Stuart portrait for each student to have. If possible, enlarge or reduce the pictures so each student has the option of creating a serial-image painting, or using it any size, or using it as a reference. Also photocopy at least one portrait onto an overhead transparency so students can project it onto something in different sizes.

Famous Paintings of George Washington

George Washington, 1795, Charles Willson Peale, The New York Historical Society, New York

George Washington in the Uniform of a British Colonial Colonel, 1772, Charles Willson Peale, Washington and Lee University, Lexington, Virginia

George Washington (the "Lansdowne" portrait), 1796, Gilbert Stuart, Pennsylvania Academy of Fine Arts, Philadelphia

The Washington Family, c. 1796, Edward Savage, National Gallery of Art, Washington, D.C.

A Portrait—George Washington, 1796, H. Humphrey, The New York Historical Society, New York

George Washington at the Battle of Princeton, 1780–1781, Charles Willson Peale, Yale University Art Gallery, New Haven

ADDITIONAL SUGGESTIONS

- Bonnie Enos, a colleague, developed a highly successful three-dimensional project using the eagle (at times combined with the flag). Materials available were foam core and cardboard, wire, sculpt-tape, and tempera paint. Each student was challenged to do something different, as long as it was three-dimensional.

- For a fun and challenging group project, provide tagboard, construction paper, staplers, white glue, scissors, and markers or crayons, and have a group of four to six work together to "dress" one of the group members as a historic figure or symbol. Figures such as Uncle Sam, Miss Liberty (who looked like a Greek goddess holding a torch), George Washington, Betsy Ross, and the eagle all have potential. Each member of the group takes responsibility for a portion of the costume, then all work together to dress the model for a picture-taking session.

- Students may design a new currency using their own faces or those of well-known contemporary politicians, musicians, or other heroes. Suggest they think about someone who is visually disabled who would need to be able to feel a difference in denominations. Discuss various commodities that have served as currency such as wampum, gold dust, and trade beads. The money could be two- or three-dimensional.

Photo 3-2A. *George Washington*, 1796, Gilbert Stuart, oil on panel, 27 × 21-¾ inches, The Saint Louis Art Museum.

Students were given photocopies and told to create something completely original using the face of George Washington. Photos 3-2B through 3-2E show the results.

Photo 3-2B.

Photo 3-2C.

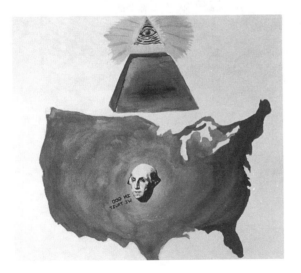

Photo 3-2D.

Photo 3-2E.

The three large student-designed eagles in Photos 3-2F through 3-2H were made as an assignment in the design class of teacher Bonnie Enos at Parkway West H.S., St. Louis County, Missouri. Students were asked to design an eagle, using cardboard or papier-mâché, and painted with tempera.

Photo 3-2F.

Photo 3-2G.

Photo 3-2H.

PROJECT 3-2: **GEORGE W.**

MATERIALS

* Photocopies of George Washington's face
* Overhead transparency of George Washington
* Colored pencil
* Acrylic or tempera paint
* Paper of all sizes and colors
* Collage materials: cloth, cardboard, foam core, sculpt-tape, wood, wire

**Drawn from *George Washington*, 1796
Gilbert Stuart
The Saint Louis Art Museum**

Throughout the history of the United States, George Washington's face has probably been more widely seen than any other image. The great respect shown him by the colonists and the continued respect given the "Father of Our Country" have made him a favorite subject for artworks. You are challenged to use Gilbert Stuart's "Athenaeum" portrait (the one used on the one-dollar bill) in an original artwork. You may reproduce George's face on anything in any size. You are limited only by your imagination, so the more unusual you make this, the better.

1. Begin by looking around your house for suitable material on which to put his face. This could be scrap wood, a jeans jacket, a T-shirt, a mirror, paper, and so on. Your teacher could supply paper and materials for interpreting this.

2. Think about some of the stories of Washington, both those that are historically accurate and those that may be fiction. Some ideas are his wooden teeth, his white wig, the incident with the cherry tree, the legendary designing of the U.S. flag with Betsy Ross, his home (Mount Vernon), and Valley Forge.

3. Any of the following ideas could be used as a "starter":
   * Cut out one or more photocopies of Washington's face and apply them directly to the paper, then fill in around them with other collage materials.
   * Attach a piece of paper or other material to a wall and project an overhead transparency copy of Washington's face onto something with an overhead projector.
   * Paint with acrylic paint onto almost any material.
   * "Draw" it in wire. Then attach the wire to paper, and with a black marker, make a line composition around it.
   * Project it onto wood, and paint with acrylic paint or draw it with oil pastels.
   * Glue the photocopy onto paper, and let George W. be part of a modern musical group.
   * Make an ad selling almost anything using George W.'s face in it.
   * Put George W. on the cover of a magazine.
   * Invent a new kind of money, using George W.'s face on it. It could be any material, shape, or color.
   * Make his face the centerpiece of a patriotic quilt to celebrate the 300th birthday of the United States.
   * Glue the photocopy on paper and make an extension of the photograph, inventing a background such as Washington with his wife, Martha, on horseback, or at Mount Vernon.

PROJECT 3-3: PORTRAIT OF A PATRIOT

FOR THE TEACHER

Before the advent of photography, many of the Revolutionary heroes were portrayed through paintings and portrait busts. The sculptures varied from sophisticated marble carvings and terra cotta to rough folk-art wood carvings.

Students will appreciate the opportunity to make their own distinctive "Revolutionaries," some of whom could be contemporary.*

Examples of Patriotic Portrait Busts

Thomas Jefferson, 1785, Jean-Antoine Houdon, New York Historical Society, New York

Governor John Winthrop, 1798, Samuel McIntire, American Antiquarian Society, Worcester, Massachusetts

Benjamin Franklin, 1785–1790, William Rush (attributed), The Historical Society of Delaware, Wilmington

Andrew Jackson, 1834, John Frazee, The Art Museum, Princeton University, Princeton, New Jersey

Benjamin Franklin, 1778, Jean-Antoine Houdon, The Saint Louis Art Museum

PREPARATION

Discuss some of the leaders of the country—both Revolutionary and contemporary figures. Male and female personalities are equally interesting subjects for sculpture.

Because this project will take several hours, do preliminary work one day, which consists of covering the balloon and preparing the base. Discuss the proportions of the face with students, making them aware of where features are located by having them feel their own faces. If they close their eyes, they feel less self-conscious about doing this. Make them aware of cheekbones and hollows for eyes, size and location of ears, and texture of hair.

Although wheat paste will also work for this project, the commercial pastes listed are easier to mix and cleaner.

As they are working, help them become aware of possibilities for decoration and finishing. These busts are most effective if they are simply stained with diluted brown or black paint and wiped off, or left unpainted.

ADDITIONAL SUGGESTIONS

- Anytime students make a human head, the material seems to have a personality of its own. Terra cotta portraits can be modeled from a solid piece of clay and then hollowed out to a 1-inch thickness, or formed around an egg-shaped "head" made from wadded and taped newspaper. To prevent an explosion during firing, be sure to leave an opening in the bottom for moisture to escape.

- Students may make a painted or oil pastel portrait of themselves in colonial or period costume, or in a uniform. Suggest they select an interior background that tells something about their personalities, such as a still life of personal items on a table or a view out a window that shows where they live. In colonial days, the view in a portrait might show a merchant ship or animals on a farm owned by the subject. Today's students might prefer showing a car, bicycle, or playing field in the background.

Note: This papier-mâché portrait-bust project was developed by Cyndi Shepard of the Cole R1 School District, Russellville, Missouri, and is used with her permission. The life-size busts are most impressive when shown together.

Photo 3-3A. *Benjamin Franklin*, 1778, Jean-Antoine Houdon, plaster, 22-¾ × 17-½ inches, The Saint Louis Art Museum.

Photo 3-3B. This female papier-mâché portrait bust is approximately 30 inches high. It was made using a balloon, cardboard tube, grocery bags, newspaper, and paste.

PROJECT 3-3: **PORTRAIT OF A PATRIOT**

MATERIALS

- Large oval balloons
- Pritt™ or Ross™ art paste or wheat paste
- Newspaper
- Brown paper grocery bags or Kraft paper
- Brown paper roll towels
- Black permanent marker
- 3-inch diameter × 12-inch long tubes (such as mailing tubes or scrap PVC pipe)
- 6 × 11-inch corrugated cardboard rectangles
- Glue gun or white glue
- Scissors
- Masking tape
- Buckets for paste
- Brown or black acrylic paint

   You may want to decide in advance whether to make your portrait bust a man or woman. You will find that each one takes on a personality of its own while you are making it.

1. To make a form for the head, cover a large inflated balloon with four layers of paper. Tear newspaper into strips and dip in paste, removing excess before applying. The next layer can be brown kraft paper (from grocery bags, if you have them). Repeat layers, finishing with brown paper. Allow to dry for at least one day.

2. To create shoulders and base, punch a hole in the center bottom of a brown paper bag, and cut an X just large enough for the (neck) tube to slip through. Cut each corner of the bag halfway up. Insert the tube through the X slit in the outside bottom of the bag, leaving approximately five inches of the tube extended outside. Fill the bag around the tube with crumpled newspaper to hold it straight. Use a glue gun or white glue to attach the cardboard to the bottom of the tube to hold it upright.

3. Turn the bag upside down (making sure the tube is straight), and fold in the sides and ends to make a neat package, a little smaller at the bottom than at the "shoulders." Tape this shut. The package should be stable. Tape the balloon on the tube with masking tape, using enough to make it secure. This is the basis of the portrait bust. Use permanent marker to make a vertical line for the nose, and horizontal lines for eyes (halfway down), bottom of nose, ears, and mouth.

4. Add features by applying paper strips dipped in paste. Fold a strip of paper for the nose and attach it. Make a forehead, cheeks, and chin by loosely wadding paper and holding in place with paper strips. Form the mouth by folding strips and applying horizontally, working down from the nose and upward from the chin. Form eyes by making small balls and holding them in place with folded strips of paper. Form shoulders and neck by pushing in on the paper bag to make rounded shoulders and covering it with paper strips. Collars may be added by folding wet, paste-soaked paper towels. The final layer should be brown paper towels.

5. There are many ways to make hair from paper towels. It can be cut in strips to hang to the shoulder, made into tight curls or ringlets, or loosely attached to make a pony tail. You may want to look at your own hair and that of other students to get ideas for hair styles.

6. The figures may be finished with such accessories as bow ties, ruffles on dresses, or eye glasses (wire covered with paper). The finished busts are most effective left unpainted, although a stain may be made of thinned black or brown acrylic paint, just wiped on. When your entire class has finished, display your portrait busts as a group.

PROJECT 3-4: **THREE CHEERS FOR THE RED, WHITE, AND BLUE**

FOR THE TEACHER

The American flag is a dynamic design. It waves all over the world, on government buildings, and over used-car lots and private homes. For over 200 years it has been incorporated into designs ranging from crests with Miss Liberty and the eagle, to Uncle Sam's clothes and Native American beaded vests or cradle boards. It has been a favorite design for folk artists, and at times they were not too particular about how many stripes or stars it had, or even what the colors were.

On June 14, 1777, Congress declared the flag should have a field of blue and 13 stars. Until then a variety of flags had been used by different groups of citizens. General Washington determined that there should be a standard American flag so that our ships could identify one another. Legend says that he presented the design to the Continental Congress saying, "We take the stars from heaven, the red from our mother country, separating it by white stripes, thus showing that we have separated from her, and the white stripes shall go down to posterity representing liberty."

PREPARATION

Several years ago the San Francisco chapter of the American Institute of Graphic Arts asked 100 designers to interpret the American flag in any medium or color, limiting the size to 12 × 18 inches. Some of the designs were done only in white, others in standard colors but unusual media. A colleague's student interpreted the flag recently in crushed red, white, and blue soda cans. A very famous gate made by a folk artist is constructed of wavy strips of wood, painted red, white, and blue.

Discuss appropriate uses for the flag as design. In 1934 regulations were devised that "govern its formal application, but these do not impinge on the flag as the basis for art." However, the flag at times has been abused and treated with disrespect by social protestors and artists. This is your opportunity to instill the respect the flag merits. Discuss found materials with students, then discuss the design elements of the American flag: the stars, stripes, and field of blue.

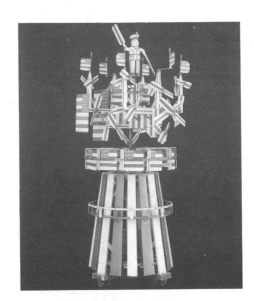

Photo 3-4. *America,* whirligig, c. 1938–1942, Frank Memkus, wood and metal, 80-¾ × 29 inches (with paddle up), Restricted gift of Marshall Field, Mr. and Mrs. Robert A. Kubicek, Mr. James Raoul Simmons, Mrs. Esther Sparks, Mrs. Frank L. Sulzberger, and The Oak Park-River Forest Associates of the Woman's Board, The Art Institute of Chicago.

ADDITIONAL SUGGESTIONS

- Divide the students into small groups and challenge them to design a new flag for their school, city, state, or national government.

- Trade banners were often used outside colonial shops with symbols on them to advertise what was sold within. Have students discuss who the merchants would be in a new town (either a colonial one or some of the "new towns" that are springing up in the nation's suburbs). Each student could design a small trade banner of construction paper by cutting out symbols such as eyeglasses or shoes, and pasting them on a background.

PROJECT 3-4: THREE CHEERS FOR THE RED, WHITE, AND BLUE

MATERIALS

- Newsprint
- Pencils
- Tagboard
- Fabrics and wallpaper
- Glue gun
- White glue
- Tempera paint, acrylic, or oil pastels

It would be relatively easy to make a flag in red, white, and blue by painting it on a piece of cardboard, but why would you want to do something so easy? Instead, try for something really unusual. The American flag design is already created, so all you have to do is adapt it somehow. It has dark and light stripes, a dark field, and shapes that could be stars. Pop artists of the 1950s painted it in shades of white or used it in compositions with other subjects.

1. To get your mind going, begin by making thumbnail sketches on newsprint. Each idea can lead to another. You may wish to combine it with another American symbol such as the eagle, Miss Liberty, or Uncle Sam.

2. Look around your house for materials that could be used: cotton balls, Band-Aids™, cotton swabs, cereal, scrap wood, old crayons, fabric scraps, wallpaper scraps, carpet scraps, jar lids, sea shells, soup can labels, plastic foam meat trays, containers from fast food restaurants, etc. Bring them to school, and perhaps you and other students can trade.

3. Arrange the materials, combining and deciding what can be added, altered, or taken away. Your materials may be sturdy enough to support themselves, but you may need to strengthen them by attaching them to a piece of cardboard with a glue gun or white glue.

4. Your material may not need finishing in any way, or you may want to paint it or paste on "related" items such as words from the Constitution, photocopies of patriotic pictures, or torn pieces of red and blue colors from magazines.

Drawn from *Uncle Sam* Whirligig, late 19th Century Museum of American Folk Art

Drawn from *America*, Whirligig, c. 1938–1942 Frank Memkus The Art Institute of Chicago

PROJECT 3-5: PENNSYLVANIA GERMAN HEX SIGNS

FOR THE TEACHER

Farmers in some counties of Pennsylvania, Virginia, and West Virginia have been painting designs (usually stars within a circle) on their barns for more than 200 years. Whether these "hex" signs are purely decorative or are painted to ward off evil spirits is often debated. Pennsylvania Germans began decorating their (mostly) red barns with these signs shortly after their arrival in the United States. They also sometimes paint white outlines around openings, creating "devil doors" and "witch windows."

Earliest designs were geometric stars of 4 to 32 points, often enclosed within a circle. Most stars have five, six, or eight points, with other decorations or overlapping stars. They generally were painted in four colors. Later designs sometimes had curved points, possibly based on flowers such as the tulip. Sometimes farm animals such as horses or cows were featured.

Modern Pennsylvania German artists create traditional designs as well as elaborate designs based on the fraktur (traditional German official documents). Hex designs are still painted on barns, but are also painted onto metal or masonite circles and sold for decorative use.

PREPARATION

Show students how to make five-, six-, or eight-pointed stars, or make cardboard patterns for students to trace around, as many of the old-time hex-sign painters did. Many of the stars on barns are several feet in diameter, and knowing how to make any size star allows students to work as large as they wish.

Note: Directions were given to me by a colleague, mathematics instructor Dr. Nancy English.

ADDITIONAL SUGGESTIONS

- Purchase or have students save cardboard circles from pizzas. Gesso these on both sides (to keep them from warping), and have students transfer an eight-fold newsprint design onto them. Eight identical designs can be made by folding the paper circle into eighths. A design drawn on one section is repeated eight times by drawing over the back of the design with pencil, then redrawing to transfer it to the next section. After completing the paper design, scribble over the back of it and redraw it onto the pizza circle. Paint it.

- Use acrylic paint to paint a star hex sign on something such as a heavy-duty flat plastic plate, round metal tray, pizza pan, or barrel lid.

PROJECT 3-5: **PENNSYLVANIA GERMAN HEX SIGNS**

MATERIALS

- White 12 × 18-inch drawing or typing paper
- Compass
- Ruler
- Protractor
- Pencils
- Tempera paint

Traditional hex signs were usually stars or flowers within circles. Your hex sign can be a geometric design, birds combined with hearts and flowers, symbols for hobby or sports interests, initials, numbers, or human and animal figures.

To make a "modern" hex sign, fold a circle of paper in half vertically and create an identical ornate design on the two halves. Use pencil to draw first one half, then place it on a lightbox or window and draw over the back of it with pencil, thus transferring the design. Color with watercolor, tempera, colored pencil, or oil pastels.

TO MAKE A FIVE-POINT STAR

1. Draw a circle.

2. Draw diameter AB.

3. Construct diameter CD by placing compass point first at A and then at B, drawing arcs that intersect at E and F.

4. Construct the perpendicular bisector of OB by placing compass point at O, then at B, and drawing arcs that intersect at G and H.

5. Now place the compass point at I (where GH intersects B) and measure the distance to C, then use that distance to make the arc that intersects AB at Q.

6. The distance from Q to C is the length of each side of the pentagon.

7. Use a ruler to draw from point to point to create the star.

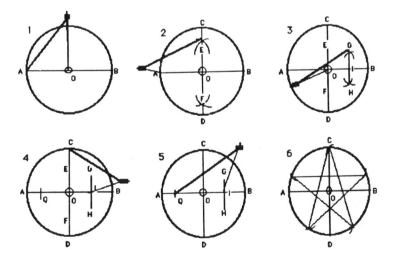

TO MAKE A SIX-POINT FLOWER

1. Use a compass to draw a circle.
2. Without changing the radius of the compass, place the compass point at a point on the circle. Make an arc to mark a point at another point on the circle. Use this method to make six arcs within the circle.

 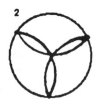 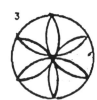

TO MAKE A SIX-POINT STAR

1. Use the method above to mark six points on the perimeter of the circle.
2. Draw a smaller circle in the center, also marking six points on it with a compass. Make a star by using a ruler to draw straight lines from a point on the outside circle to points on the small circle.

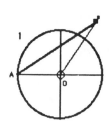 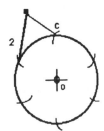 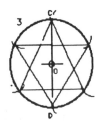

PROJECT 3-6: SCHERENSCHNITTE

FOR THE TEACHER

Scherenschnitte describes paper-cutting the German way. It is a craft still practiced in the United States. It resembles other Pennsylvania German crafts in that it is usually symmetrical. Many of these items were based on Noah's Ark or the Tree of Jesse, both of which involved a variety of animals. In the case of Noah's Ark, a biblical story, the animals always came in pairs. Other designs were flags, the eagle, or sailing ships.

PREPARATION

Have magazines around for students to find photos of animals (or photocopy them from encyclopedias). Some students are good at drawing from memory, but others need references.

ADDITIONAL SUGGESTIONS

- Do this project on white construction paper or watercolor paper, and then paint it with watercolor, a common treatment in Colonial times.
- Create Colonial pinprick pictures by drawing with ink, then pricking from the back of the paper to create textures to enhance fabric or foliage. Almost any subject is suitable for this treatment, including portraits. Frakturs and portraits often were pinpricked from the back.
- Cut silhouettes of each other by having one student sit in front of a light source, such as that of a slide or overhead projector, and trace the student's shadow onto wall-mounted paper. This could be done on black paper, as was traditional, or on roll paper that has been decorated with abstract designs. These will be large, so they could be cut out with scissors. During Colonial days, silhouette portraits were sometimes created on white paper and then painted with watercolor.

Photo 3-6. *Cutout of Animals,* **second quarter 19th century, cut paper and watercolor, 18-¾ × 23-¾ inches, Gift of Edgar William and Bernice Chrysler Garbisch, National Gallery of Art, Washington, D.C.**

PROJECT 3-6: **SCHERENSCHNITTE**

MATERIALS

- Drawing paper or white typing paper
- Pencils
- X-acto™ knives
- Watercolor or colored pencils
- Brushes
- Straight pins

Drawn from Cutout of Animals
Artist Unknown
Second quarter 19th Century
National Gallery of Art, Washington, D.C.

Pennsylvania German paper-cuttings *(Scherenschnitte)* were nearly always symmetrical. Paper was precious, so great care was taken in making a drawing and cutting designs. You will draw the design on one half of a folded piece of paper, and cut through both layers at once. While these cuttings were usually done with very sharp scissors, the X-acto™ knife works better than most school scissors.

1. Fold a piece of newsprint in half. Make an outline that will fit within the drawing paper on which you will trace this design. The outline of the paper-cutting can be heart-shaped, round, square, or irregular.

2. Many paper-cuttings of this type had a variety of animals and plant life on them. On half of the paper, draw up to twenty different kinds of animals (or varieties of the same species such as birds, cats, or dogs). These could be placed in "registers," with several on a top row, several below, etc. Unify the design by having them all perched on branches of a tree, with the trunk in the middle, or on the ground, with trees behind them. Remember to allow each level to be joined somewhere to another level to avoid having everything fall apart. For ease of handling, have one complete piece joined around the edges with openings cut out.

3. If you are going to transfer this to white paper, tape the white paper on top and put them on a window or lightbox to lightly redraw the design on half the paper.

4. Place cardboard or a magazine underneath, and use an X-acto™ knife to cut through both layers at once. To make difficult cuts, remember to keep the knife going straight, turning the paper to make the cuts. *Safety note: Your hand must be behind the knife at all times, as it is easy to slip.* If the knife does not go all the way through, go back later and complete the underside.

5. When the entire paper-cutting is finished, use watercolor or colored pencil on parts of it. Open it up and color each side identically. Allow it to dry, and mount it against a black background.

6. Sometimes these paper-cuttings were further decorated by pricking through the underside with a straight pin.

PROJECT 3-7: **PORTHOLE PAINTING**

FOR THE TEACHER

"Porthole painting" was a term occasionally used in Colonial America to describe the oval or circular shapes that some painters (such as Charles Willson Peale) used for landscapes or portraits. Sometimes a "frame" was painted around a portrait that looked like an actual ship's porthole or an oval stone window. Miniature portraits, which were very popular at that time, were painted in ovals and circles, which perhaps was the source of this painting format. Overmantle paintings or firescreens were often painted in an oval shape, with a square frame around them.

Examples of Porthole Paintings

George Washington, c. 1823 Rembrandt Peale, Terra Museum of Art, Chicago

George Washington, Patriae Pater, c. 1824, Rembrandt Peale, Pennsylvania Academy of Fine Arts, Philadelphia

Porthole View of a Quaker Meeting, 1790, artist unknown, Museum of Fine Arts, Boston

George Washington, c. 1853, Rembrandt Peale, National Gallery of Art, Washington, D.C.

PREPARATION

It is always a challenge for students to ask them to create something in a format other than a rectangle or square. In a circle, a composition might almost appear to "roll" unless it is given weight at the bottom. Students can make oval and round viewfinders of drawing paper to help with composition.

ADDITIONAL SUGGESTIONS

- Students may do a freehand colored pencil minia-ture drawing of themselves in an oval or round format. Or photocopy a school photo, and place the photocopy on a window or lightbox for tracing onto drawing paper. If the photocopy isn't clear, they can refer to the original photo for details.

- Make a foil painting of people or a silhouette by using black acrylic paint on overhead trans-parency plastic film. These can then be backed with aluminum foil. If students choose to color the foil in places, this can be done with permanent marker. Remind them that their picture will be seen backwards when the painted side of the film is next to the foil.

Photo 3-7. *George Washington,* c. 1853, **Rembrandt Peale, oil on canvas, 36 × 29 inches, National Portrait Gallery, Gift of an anonymous donor, Smithsonian Institution/Art Resource, New York.**

PROJECT 3-7: PORTHOLE PAINTING

MATERIALS

- 18 × 24-inch drawing paper
- Compass
- Pencils
- Tempera paint
- Foam egg cartons
- Brushes

Drawn from Poestenkill, New York: Winter, 1868 Joseph Hidley

You could do this project as though looking through a porthole to the outside or inside, depending on whether you want to do a portrait, still life, or landscape. Decide what the subject of your painting will be. In Colonial times, horizontal ovals contained landscapes or historical subjects, while porthole portraits were painted within either a vertical oval, or a circle.

1. For this project, use a piece of 6 × 8-inch drawing paper to make an oval or circular viewfinder to isolate your subject (a "model," scene, or still life) just as if you were taking a photograph. Hold the viewfinder at arm's length and move it around until you see what you want to paint. Use the oval horizontally or vertically and move closer or farther away until you have a satisfactory composition. Keep the viewfinder at hand so you can use it again if needed.

2. With pencil, draw an oval or circle onto a large sheet of drawing paper. Lightly draw what you see through your viewfinder. Don't put much detail in your drawing, as you can add details later in paint.

3. The oval paintings created in Colonial times were sometimes surrounded by a *trompe l'oeil* (fool the eye) effect of real stone or wood. Decide what will be around the outside of your oval painting—it could look like a frame.

4. To paint with tempera, mix paint in egg cartons, and save it for another day by closing the cover. The convenience of tempera paint is that you can mix it just as you would mix oil paint. Make your colors more interesting by darkening colors with something other than black (such as blue, violet, dark green), or adding another color to something you lighten with white. (For example, skies might have just a *touch* of yellow or red [or both] added to the blue before lightening it with white.) You can also paint over an area that has already been painted. Avoid putting tempera on too thickly, however, or it will crack off.

5. When your painting is complete, make a construction paper mat with an oval or round opening to show the painting to best advantage.

Drawn from *George Washington, Patriae Pater,* c. 1824 Pennsylvania Academy of Fine Arts

Porthole View of Quaker Meeting, 1790

PERIOD OF EXPANSION
(1800 to 1870)

PERIOD OF EXPANSION
TIME LINE

	1800	1820	1830	1840	1850	1860	1870

Painting Sculpture Architecture Folk Art

Federal Period 1790–1820

Greek Revival 1820–1860

Gothic Revival 1830–1875

Italianate 1830–1880

Rococo Revival 1840–1860

Egyptian and Renaissance Revival 1860–1880

1845–1926 Mary Cassatt

1801–1848 Thomas Cole

Frontier Art 1800–1850

1836–1910 Winslow Homer

1830–1902 Albert Bierstadt

1848–1892 William Harnett

Frederic Remington 1861–1909

Silhouettes c. 1830–1842

1811–1879 George Caleb Bingham

1830s Theorem paintings

Edward Hicks 1780–1849

Thomas Eakins 1844–1916

George Catlin 1796–1872

Hudson River School, 1825–1870

1816–1872 John Kensett

Audubon's Birds of America, 1827

1850–1888 Currier and Ives

1867–1959 Frank Lloyd Wright

Politics

1803 Louisiana Purchase

1801 Jefferson, 3rd President

1820 Missouri Compromise

1836 Texas becomes Independent Republic

1846 War with Mexico

1850 Fillmore, President

1853 Pierce, President

1857 Buchanan, President

1860 Lincoln, president

Emancipation Proclamation, 1863

1868 U. S. Grant, President

1865 Lincoln assassinated

Civil War ends, 1865

Literature

1820s *Ivanhoe,* Sir Walter Scott

1812–1870 Dickens

1813 *Pride and Prejudice,* Jane Austen

1826 *Last of the Mohicans,* James Fenimore Cooper

1819 *Rip Van Winkle,* Irving

1859 Death of Washington Irving

Uncle Tom's Cabin, Stowe, 1851/52

1855 Walt Whitman

1854–1900 Oscar Wilde

1861 *Great Expectations,* Dickens

1864 *War and Peace,* Tolstoi

Science

1844 Telegraph, Samuel F. B. Morse

1861: Pasteur's theory of germ fermentation

Music

1827 Death of Beethoven

1849 Death of Chopin

Current Events

1815 Napoleon at Waterloo

1822 Simon Bolivar

1804 Lewis & Clark Expedition

1812–1815 War of 1812

1839 Trail of Tears, 13,000 Cherokees to Oklahoma

1848 Gold Rush, California

1858 Bierstadt maps route to Pacific

1857 Dred Scott decision

1867 U.S. buys Alaska

Transcontinental Railroad 1869

Pony Express, 1860

1869 Women's Suffrage

ARCHITECTURE OF THE PERIOD OF EXPANSION

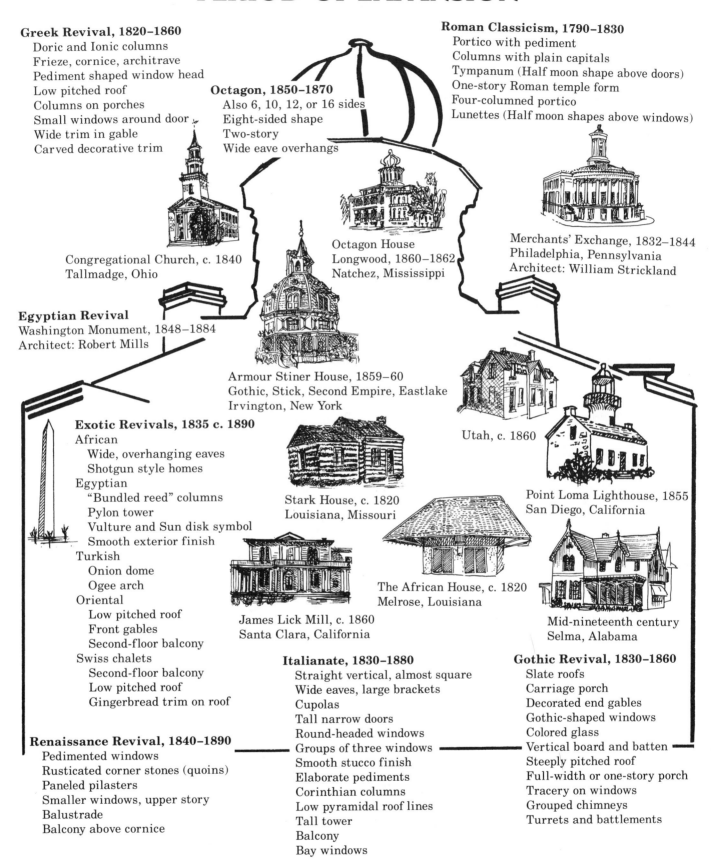

Greek Revival, 1820–1860
Doric and Ionic columns
Frieze, cornice, architrave
Pediment shaped window head
Low pitched roof
Columns on porches
Small windows around door
Wide trim in gable
Carved decorative trim

Octagon, 1850–1870
Also 6, 10, 12, or 16 sides
Eight-sided shape
Two-story
Wide eave overhangs

Roman Classicism, 1790–1830
Portico with pediment
Columns with plain capitals
Tympanum (Half moon shape above doors)
One-story Roman temple form
Four-columned portico
Lunettes (Half moon shapes above windows)

Congregational Church, c. 1840
Tallmadge, Ohio

Octagon House
Longwood, 1860–1862
Natchez, Mississippi

Merchants' Exchange, 1832–1844
Philadelphia, Pennsylvania
Architect: William Strickland

Egyptian Revival
Washington Monument, 1848–1884
Architect: Robert Mills

Armour Stiner House, 1859–60
Gothic, Stick, Second Empire, Eastlake
Irvington, New York

Utah, c. 1860

Exotic Revivals, 1835 c. 1890
African
    Wide, overhanging eaves
    Shotgun style homes
Egyptian
    "Bundled reed" columns
    Pylon tower
    Vulture and Sun disk symbol
    Smooth exterior finish
Turkish
    Onion dome
    Ogee arch
Oriental
    Low pitched roof
    Front gables
    Second-floor balcony
Swiss chalets
    Second-floor balcony
    Low pitched roof
    Gingerbread trim on roof

Stark House, c. 1820
Louisiana, Missouri

Point Loma Lighthouse, 1855
San Diego, California

The African House, c. 1820
Melrose, Louisiana

James Lick Mill, c. 1860
Santa Clara, California

Mid-nineteenth century
Selma, Alabama

Renaissance Revival, 1840–1890
Pedimented windows
Rusticated corner stones (quoins)
Paneled pilasters
Smaller windows, upper story
Balustrade
Balcony above cornice

Italianate, 1830–1880
Straight vertical, almost square
Wide eaves, large brackets
Cupolas
Tall narrow doors
Round-headed windows
Groups of three windows
Smooth stucco finish
Elaborate pediments
Corinthian columns
Low pyramidal roof lines
Tall tower
Balcony
Bay windows

Gothic Revival, 1830–1860
Slate roofs
Carriage porch
Decorated end gables
Gothic-shaped windows
Colored glass
Vertical board and batten
Steeply pitched roof
Full-width or one-story porch
Tracery on windows
Grouped chimneys
Turrets and battlements

Section 4.—PERIOD OF EXPANSION (1800–1870)

ARTISTS OF THE PERIOD

PAINTERS

- *Washington Allston* (1779–1843) was considered the first important American Romantic painter because of the moods depicted in most of his landscapes. He was a European-trained student of Benjamin West.

- *John James Audubon's* (1785–1851) primary interest and life's work was studying and portraying American wildlife. In 1826 his drawings were engraved in England and issued as a collection, *The Birds of America.*

- *Albert Bierstadt* (1830–1902) is best known for his paintings of the American West, based on sketches he did on a surveying expedition. He was born in Germany and returned there to study when he was 23, becoming one of the "School of Dusseldorf" painters (those who were German-born and trained or studied in Dusseldorf).

- *George Caleb Bingham* (1811–1879) was a Missouri artist who also served in the legislature. He is particularly well known for paintings of life on the Mississippi River and portrayals of country political gatherings.

- *George Catlin* (1796–1872), a lawyer until age 27, was a self-taught portrait painter. He became deeply interested in Native American life and eventually lived with 48 tribes, trying to preserve information about their homes, dress, and way-of-life through his drawings and paintings.

- *Thomas Cole* (1801–1848), born in England, immigrated to America at age 18. He was considered the founder and leader of the Hudson River School of painting, which specialized in portraying the beauty and grandeur of America.

- *Edward Hicks* (1780–1849) was raised in a devoutly Quaker home following his mother's death when he was young. He was a coach and sign painter and later became a Quaker preacher. His work often combined historic occasions with biblical quotations painted around the outside.

- *Raphaelle Peale* (1774–1825), eldest son of Charles Willson Peale, studied with his father and specialized in still lifes. In his early career he had been a miniature painter, and this careful attention to detail is shown in the drawing and colors used in his work.

- *Rembrandt Peale* (1778–1860), painted portraits of Washington and Jefferson. His most famous portrait, *Rubens Peale with a Geranium,* painted when he was 23, is of another brother. He had a life-long interest in science and ran the family museum.

- *John Quidor* (1801–1881) specialized in genre scenes. He illustrated popular tales of the day such as *Ichabod Crane Pursued by the Headless Horseman* and *The Return of Rip Van Winkle.* There was not a large market for his type of painting, however, and he supported himself by painting signs, coaches, and fire engines.

- *Frederic Remington* (1861–1909) is known as both a painter and sculptor, most famous for his realistic, romantic subjects of the Wild West. He attended Yale Art School and the Art Students' League of New York. He wrote about and illustrated life on the frontier, and eventually became a rancher.

SCULPTORS

- *Isaac Fowle* (1806–1843) worked in the Skillin workshop. He specialized in figureheads and house carvings.

- *Horatio Greenough* (1805–1852) was the first native-born American sculptor. After study in Europe, he returned to America where he and other young sculptors tried to develop a unique American sculpture based on Greek sculpture.

- *Hiram Powers* (1805–1873) was an extremely successful and well-known sculptor, specializing in the portrait bust and allegorical figures used for building decoration. He eventually became so successful that he was also able to sculpt figures in the classical manner for his own pleasure.

- *William Rush* (1756–1833), a wood and marble carver, was considered the most significant American sculptor who started in the folk-art and figure-carving tradition. He was one of the first directors of the Pennsylvania Academy of the Fine Arts. Many of his works are in Philadelphia.

ARCHITECTS

- *Benjamin Latrobe* (1764–1820) was a professional architect rather than a "gentleman / architect" such as Thomas Jefferson. He introduced the Greek style for public buildings and the Gothic style for homes.

- *Robert Mills* (1781–1855), born and trained in architecture in the United States (through apprenticeship with several prominent architects such as Benjamin Latrobe), was considered a Greek Revival architect.

- *William Strickland* (1788–1854) was a pupil of Benjamin Latrobe, also working in the fashionable Greek mode. He was multi-talented: an engineer, painter, and architect. He worked primarily in Philadelphia and Tennessee.

- *Dr. William Thornton* (1759–1828) arrived in the United States in 1786. Thornton, a physician, had long been interested in drawing and painting. His design for the National Capitol Building was selected and eventually built (with many modifications).

FAMOUS ARTISTS AND "SCHOOLS" OF ART

- *Hudson River School* (c. 1825–1870) was a group of painters whose work reflected their pride in the beauty and grandeur of the American landscape. At times, religious and moral allegories were incorporated into their landscapes of the Hudson valley region. The second generation of this "school" were sometimes called "luminist artists" because of their treatment of light. This group included Thomas Cole (1801–1848), Thomas Doughty (1793–1856), Asher B. Durand (1796–1886), Alvan Fisher (1792–1863), Henry Inman (1802–1846), John Frederick Kensett (1816–1872), and Samuel F. B. Morse (1791–1872). Frederick Edwin Church (1826–1900) and Jasper Francis Cropsey (1823–1900) were also considered members of this painting group.

- *Rocky Mountain School* was a term applied to Western artists who painted views of the frontier and Rocky Mountains in a similar manner to the Hudson River School. Albert Bierstadt (1830–1902), Thomas Hill (1829–1908), and Thomas Moran (1837–1926) were members.
- *Western Painters* George Catlin (1796–1872), Seth Eastman (1808–1875) and Charles Wimar (1828–1862) were especially known for their portrayals of the Native American and frontier scenes. Frederick Remington (1861–1909) became known for his illustrations of frontier life including Native American scenes, landscape, and army-life.

OVERVIEW OF ART DURING THE PERIOD OF EXPANSION

America had become civilized. The capital of the United States had moved to Washington, D.C., and several cities on the Eastern seaboard and in the South were cultured and prosperous. Governmental patronage continued, with artists commissioned to paint murals for state and national capitol buildings, and carvers asked to create statues for public locations. Individuals were interested in having decorative artwork for their homes.

PAINTING

In the early part of the nineteenth century, historical and romantic themes were favored, probably as a result of the influence of such European-trained Colonial painters as John Singleton Copley, Benjamin West, Charles Willson Peale, and Gilbert Stuart. Portraiture continued to be popular, but was no longer the dominating subject.

Art academies and painters' organizations did not come into being until the late 1800s when the leaders of cities such as Philadelphia, New York, and Boston felt a need to bring European culture to their surroundings. Although many painters went to Europe for training, most of the new generation were either apprenticed in fields related to art or were self-taught. One particular aspect of American painting—a use of strong contrasts—may well have come from artists who learned to paint and draw from looking at black-and-white reproductions.

Landscape painting was still considered an "unaesthetic activity," yet it became the form of painting that was most uniquely American. The landscape painters, such as those of the Hudson River School, believed their work had a religious significance, and they depicted the beauty and grandeur of America, with special emphasis on light. Also popular were paintings of the Western landscape—the frontier. The work of American genre painters (artists whose paintings depicted everyday life) was appreciated, though it was considered a cut below the landscape. American narrative painting illustrated popular literature, or depicted great moments in the nation's history. Itinerant painters continued to do portraiture, landscape, and decorative painting. The outlines and flat colors used by untrained artists were appreciated then (and today) by the people who purchased them.

Examples of Painting

The Rising of a Thunderstorm at Sea, 1804, Washington Allston, Museum of Fine Arts, Boston

Great Blue Heron, 1821, John James Audubon, Mercantile Library, St. Louis

Fur Traders Descending the Missouri, 1845, George Caleb Bingham, The Metropolitan Museum of Art, New York

Raftsmen Playing Cards, 1847, George Caleb Bingham, The Saint Louis Art Museum

Moonlit Landscape, 1819, Albert Pinkham Ryder, Museum of Fine Arts, Boston

View from Mount Holyoke, Massachusetts, after a Thunderstorm—The Oxbow, 1836, Thomas Cole, The Metropolitan Museum of Art, New York

Young Omahaw, War Eagle, Little Missouri, and Pawnees, 1821, Charles Bird King, Smithsonian Institution, Washington, D.C.

Washington Crossing the Delaware, 1851, Emanuel Gottlieb Leutz, The Metropolitan Museum of Art, New York

SCULPTURE

By 1800, a gentlemen's society of fine arts might feature collections of plaster casts of ancient sculpture, as well as copies of old master paintings, engravings, and architecture books. Some artists went to Europe to learn to sculpt, but many became sculptors through apprenticeship or learned from family members. American-born stonecarvers mostly learned their trade from stoneyards.

The European tradition of portraits inspired American sculptors to memorialize well-known leaders through the portrait bust. Romantic, draped Grecian figures were carved in wood to decorate furniture. Woodcarving eventually fell out of popularity except for its continued use in folk art, cigar store figures, weathervanes, and shop signs. Sculpture was created in clay, bronze, and marble.

Examples of Sculpture

Water Nymph and Bittern, c. 1828, William Rush, Philadelphia Museum of Art

Andrew Jackson, 1835, Hiram Powers, The Metropolitan Museum of Art, New York

The Greek Slave, 1843, Hiram Powers, Yale University Art Gallery, New Haven

Schuylkill Freed, c. 1828, William Rush, Philadelphia Museum of Art

George Washington, 1814, William Rush, Philadelphia Museum of Art

George Washington, 1832–1841, Horatio Greenough, Smithsonian Institution, Washington, D.C.

John Trumbull, 1834, Robert Ball Hughes, Yale University Art Gallery, New Haven

Daniel Webster, 1858, Hiram Powers, State House, Boston

ARCHITECTURE

In the United States, 1800 to 1870 was a great period of building. The Federal period between 1780 and 1820 had a relatively restrained style. The Greek Revival, or Neo-classical, period occurred at a time when the U.S. government was in the process of building a capitol. Buildings designed by Thomas Jefferson reflected Roman and Palladian designs. Throughout the United States, capitol buildings, bank buildings, and other government buildings reflected the influence of European Neo-classicism from 1820 until the Civil War in the 1860s. Southwestern style continued to be based on that of the Catholic baroque in Spain. Early buildings, such as the Palace of the Governors in Santa Fe, New Mexico, were a blend of Native American adobe pueblos and Spanish architectural styles.

French architectural styles were introduced in the South, and many of these arcaded buildings with their graceful wrought iron balconies can still be seen in New Orleans. French styles with shaded porches were seen as far north as St. Genevieve, Missouri, and St. Louis. Antebellum mansions in the South reflected the interest in Greek and Roman architecture. An influence from the African Continent is seen in the "shotgun" house found (mostly) in the South (so-called because the rooms were usually one behind another, and if a shotgun were fired, it would go straight through from front to back).

Examples of Architecture

Baltimore Washington Monument, 1814–1842, Robert Mills, Baltimore

U.S. Mint, 1829–1833, William Strickland, Philadelphia

Tennessee State Capitol, 1845–1859, William Strickland, Nashville

Trinity Church, 1839–1846, Richard Upjohn, New York City

Renwick Gallery, 1859–1861, James Renwick, Washington, D.C.

Bank of Pennsylvania, 1798–1800, Benjamin Latrobe, Washington, D.C.

The Treasury Building, 1836–1869, Robert Mills, Washington, D.C.

PROJECT 4-1: **AMERICAN NARRATIVE PAINTING**

FOR THE TEACHER

SLIDE #6: *Sea Captains Carousing in Suriname*, **c. 1758, John Greenwood, oil on bed ticking, Museum Purchase, The Saint Louis Art Museum**

From the earliest days of the nation, a few artists were recording America's history in paint. John Greenwood's *Sea Captains Carousing in Suriname* was one of the earliest narrative stories about the Americans. The "Great Themes of Art," which included mythological, historical, and religious subjects, were rarely painted in the first few centuries of the nation. However, by the nineteenth century, many artists were painting events in history and illustrating literature. The literature of Washington Irving (1753–1859), which was published under a pseudonym of Diedrich Knickerbocker *(The Knickerbocker Tales)*, provided rich material for painters such as John Quidor, Asher B. Durand, William Sidney Mount, and Thomas Cole.

Examples of Narrative Paintings

The Legend of Ichabod Crane, c. 1828, John Quidor, Yale University Art Gallery, New Haven

The Return of Rip Van Winkle, c. 1849, John Quidor, National Gallery of Art, Washington, D.C.

The Money Diggers, 1832, John Quidor, Brooklyn Museum, New York

Exhuming the Mastodon, 1806–1808, Charles Willson Peale, Peale Museum, Baltimore

Watson and the Shark, c. 1782, John Singleton Copley, Detroit Institute of Arts

The Buffalo Dance, 1860, Charles F. Wimar (1828–1862), The Saint Louis Art Museum

Prisoners from the Front, 1866, Winslow Homer (1836–1910), The Metropolitan Museum of Art, New York

PREPARATION

Show several slides that illustrate historical or narrative themes and discuss things they have in common (usually they include a number of people in a specific setting). Today's students will appreciate the exaggerated poses and cartoon-like drawing.

ADDITIONAL SUGGESTIONS

- This project would ideally lend itself to a literary illustration. Have students select a favorite passage from anything they are reading and illustrate it. Pencil or charcoal could be substituted for tempera paint.

- Illustrate an actual moment in the recent history of America (or the world). Current events seen in the newspapers daily would make wonderful illustrations. Suggest to students that maybe someday theirs will be the only account that will mark that event. Or suggest this would be for a time capsule to be sent to another planet, telling about life on Earth today.

- Lithographic prints by Currier and Ives chronicled scenes of American lives and current events for 70 years during the nineteenth century. These often homey scenes of rural life and customs continue to be used by decorators. Have students interpret a Currier and Ives winter scene based on what *they* do on a school holiday such as a snow day, spring break, or a day on the beach.

Photo 4-1. *The Return of Rip Van Winkle*, c. 1849, John Quidor, oil on canvas, 39-¾ × 49-¾ inches, Andrew W. Mellon Collection, National Gallery of Art, Washington, D.C. This illustrates the scene where Rip Van Winkle says, "I'm not myself—I'm somebody else—that's me yonder—no—that somebody else got into my shoes—I was myself last night, but I fell asleep on the mountain, and they've changed my gun and everything's changed, and I'm changed, and I can't tell what's my name or who I am."

PROJECT 4-1: AMERICAN NARRATIVE PAINTING

MATERIALS

- Drawing paper
- Tempera paint
- Egg cartons for mixing paint
- Brushes

Your painting may be a "great moment in history"—your own personal history. Think about the things that have happened in your lifetime or in that of one of your relatives. It may help to make a list of some of these events so that you can create a picture in your mind of what that scene looked like and where it took place. It could be something as simple as sitting at a table and having a special dinner, or visiting with friends in a room. Snapshots might help shape your composition.

Narrative drawing generally includes a number of people.

1. Lightly draw the people directly on the drawing paper. Try not to erase, as this affects how the paint will apply to the paper. Group people together, leaving open space. Think of this as a geometric composition, with the people grouped in a circle, triangle (or groups of triangles), or rectangle.

2. Draw the background. Although you want this to be a somewhat crowded picture, some areas should be left without much detail so that the people will be the main attraction.

3. Put a small amount of a complete spectrum of colors in the egg carton cups. Use the brush to take paint from a cup, and mix it with other colors in the lid of the carton (at the end of the day, wash the lid and close the carton to save any leftover paint for the next day). Avoid using any paint straight out of the container. It will be a much more interesting painting if you mix colors. If you want to "gray" a paint, add a complementary color (opposites on the color wheel, such as red-green or yellow-violet). To "model" paint (make it appear rounded), paint it darker on the edges and lighter in the center.

   Don't be afraid to use a color that doesn't exist in nature. If you examine paintings closely, it is amazing how many colors artists use to make something look realistic. Although tempera paint does cover mistakes, try to avoid building it up thickly, as it will flake off.

4. Examine your painting in a mirror or from a distance, perhaps even looking at it upside down or sideways. Flaws in a painting show when you are looking at it this way, and you can usually see how to fix them. When it is finished, mat the painting. The space around a painting given by a mat sets the painting apart and makes it important.

Drawn after *The Return of Rip Van Winkle,* **c. 1849**
John Quidor
National Gallery of Art

PROJECT 4-2: **THE PEACEABLE KINGDOM**

FOR THE TEACHER

SLIDE #7: *Peaceable Kingdom,* **1826, Edward Hicks, 32-½ × 41-½ inches, oil on canvas, Philadelphia Museum of Art, Bequest of Charles C. Willis**

Edward Hicks (1780–1849) trained as a coach, sign, and furniture painter. The flat style of the sign painter is reflected in the manner he used in depicting animals in his well-known allegorical paintings. A Quaker preacher, his work reflects his life, often containing biblical quotations or poetry written around the outside of his artworks in his best sign-painting technique. His paintings were quite popular, as shown by the fact that his funeral was attended by 3,000 to 4,000 people.

In his painting *The Peaceable Kingdom,* Hicks combined his love of painting a historic moment with his enjoyment of painting animals. Around the border is a Bible verse from Isaiah 11:6–9, in which Isaiah prophesizes, "The lion shall lie down with the lamb." He painted more than 100 versions of this one subject. In the background of many of these paintings, there is a scene commemorating Penn's historic 1682 treaty with the Delaware Indians.

Paintings by Edward Hicks

Peaceable Kingdom, 1827, Friends Historical Library of Swarthmore College, Swarthmore, Pennsylvania

The Peaceable Kingdom, c. 1830–1840, Brooklyn Museum, New York

Peaceable Kingdom, 1845, Albright-Knox Art Gallery, Buffalo, New York

The Peaceable Kingdom, date unknown, Abby Aldrich Rockefeller Folk Art Center, Williamsburg, Virginia

The Cornell Farm, 1848, National Gallery of Art, Washington, D.C.

PREPARATION

Compare this Slide #7 with a copy of Benjamin West's painting *Penn's Treaty with the Indians,* Pennsylvania Academy of Fine Arts. Benjamin West (1738–1820) was an academically trained painter, whose work was mostly portraiture and historical subjects. This project could be done using a photograph of almost any subject, or with a drawing done by the student. The involvement of the student with the image is important, because writing about a personal artwork or photo is such a meaningful thing to young people.

Have students select a favorite photograph or drawing and mount it on a white background with a generous border. Suggest that they write either an essay or poem. Because this is not primarily an English project, I strongly suggest that they not attempt a rhyming poem. Ask students to show you the poem or essay before actually transferring it to the artwork. If students choose to write the poem on a computer, the printout could be done or copied onto an overhead transparency, which could then be mounted on top of the artwork (with edges concealed with a mat). If they use glitter, have several box lids over which students can work, both saving on glitter and controlling the mess.

ADDITIONAL SUGGESTIONS

- The "bouquet" of animals unlikely to be grouped together was one of Hicks' specialties. Suggest that students find photographs of animals or reptiles from magazines and use these as inspiration to draw a composition of animals, birds, or fish, crowding or overlapping them. This would be an appropriate subject for a tempera-resist painting or oil pastels.

- Use letters or words only as the inspiration for a composition. They needn't be logical, but could be a combination of the student's initials or one word.

- Students enjoy selecting a favorite saying (such as a line from a song or an inspirational quotation) and writing it with a calligraphy marker. This should be done first on newsprint to allow for perfect spacing.

Photo 4-2A. *Peaceable Kingdom*, c. 1834, Edward Hicks, oil on canvas, 30 × 35-½ inches, Gift of Edgar Williams and Bernice Chrysler Garbisch, National Gallery of Art, Washington, D.C.

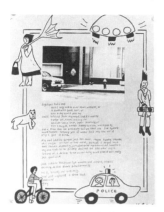

Photo 4-2B. Student poem.

Photo 4-2C. Student poem.

Photo 4-2D. Student poem.

Photo 4-2E. Student poem.

Photo 4-2F. Student poem.

PROJECT 4-2: **THE PEACEABLE KINGDOM**

MATERIALS

- Drawing paper or photograph
- White posterboard
- Mounting tissue, rubber cement, or glue stick
- Fine-line colored marking pens or pencils
- Notepaper or newsprint
- Glitter (if desired)
- Polymer medium
- Brushes

Drawn after *Peaceable Kingdom*, c. 1834
Edward Hicks
National Gallery of Art, Washington, D.C.

Edward Hicks was a Quaker artist who was trained as a sign painter. He often showed off this skill by painting quotations and poetry around the outside of his pictures.

Your assignment is to combine your artwork with written words. You could use a photograph you have taken or a drawing of almost any subject. Although you are not writing a grand novel or epic poem, it should have a minimum of 50 words or several verses to make the writing interesting and contribute to the composition.

1. Look at the picture you will be writing about. On notebook paper, write a story, poem, or "stream-of-consciousness" (one word leading to another) narrative about your subject. You may find that your descriptive words *are* a story or essay. Certainly you can make up a story about this picture from your imagination.

2. Adhere your picture to a matboard background with rubber cement, dry-mount tissue, or glue stick. Carefully write around your picture on the matboard, first in pencil before going over it with black or colored marker. Erase the pencil marks when the ink dries. The story could be below the picture, but it is interesting to write around it or even on top of it, using words as part of the design. The story or poem could be typed on a computer in any size or style, then cut up and pasted around the photograph or painting.

3. With colored marker, you may want to accent some parts of the photo or art and the background—perhaps you could create a border.

4. If you choose to use glitter to accent the composition, use it sparingly. Paint polymer medium on the area you wish to cover, sprinkle glitter on it, and gently shake it to remove excess glitter. This could be applied all around as a border, in stripes across the picture and background, or to accent some drawn designs on the background.

Drawn after *Peaceable Kingdom of the Branch*,
c. 1826–30
Edward Hicks
Reynolda House, Museum of American Art
Winston-Salem, North Carolina

PROJECT 4-3: WASHINGTON CROSSING THE DELAWARE

FOR THE TEACHER

SLIDE #8: *Washington Crossing the Delaware,* 1851, Emanuel Gottlieb Leutz, 149 × 255 inches, oil on canvas, The Metropolitan Museum of Art, Gift of John Stewart Kennedy, 1897

Emanuel Leutz was brought to America as a young child, but his most famous painting, *Washington Crossing the Delaware,* was created in Dusseldorf, where he lived for 20 years. He moved back to the United States in 1859, where he continued to paint. A mural that decorates the stairway of the Capitol in Washington, D.C., *Course of Empire* (1861–1862), was painted by Leutz.

Other Works by Emanuel Gottlieb Leutz

Cromwell and Milton, 1854, Corcoran Gallery, Washington, D.C.

Nathaniel Hawthorne, 1862, National Portrait Gallery, Washington D.C.

On the Banks of a Stream, c. 1860, Corcoran Gallery, Washington, D.C.

PREPARATION

Discuss historic themes in patriotic artworks such as Grant Woods' *Parson Weems' Fable* (the story of Washington chopping down a cherry tree, 1939), John Singleton Copley's *Watson and the Shark* (1782), Paul Revere's *The Bloody Massacre* (1770), Benjamin West's *Penn's Treaty with the Indians* (1772), or Thomas Sully's *Washington at the Delaware* (1819). Encourage students to photocopy their own yearbook pictures and those of their friends and use them as part of this composition. You (or they) could also photocopy Leutz's original *Washington Crossing the Delaware* for creative use as part of the composition.

Project the slide of Leutz's *Washington Crossing the Delaware* and the Larry Rivers's version of the same subject (see Slide #32) onto a screen so that students can see how a modern artist interprets an historical artwork. Although most artists do not work this way, Picasso, Manet, and Rivers were a few who were inspired by the ideas of other artists. Discuss the technique of collage with students, suggesting that they not glue anything down until they are certain that is the way they want it.

ADDITIONAL SUGGESTIONS

- Have students select and paint a very small portion of *Washington Crossing the Delaware* from a black-and-white photocopy. A "modern" color scheme such as magenta, violet, pink, blue-violet, and turquoise could be used to make an abstract tempera based on the black and white values. It would be interesting to display them all on one wall and see if there is any resemblance to the original painting.

- Students could also do a realistic black-and-white rendition of *Washington Crossing the Delaware* from a photocopy, with each enlarging a specific section of the whole. When this is joined together later with tape, it creates an effective mural. It is important that the teacher cut up the photocopy, numbering each section and stapling it to an index card. Make sure the paper used by the students is also numbered and in proportion to the small sections the students are enlarging.

PROJECT 4-3: **WASHINGTON CROSSING THE DELAWARE**

MATERIALS

- 12 × 18-inch drawing paper
- Colored construction paper
- White tissue paper
- Thinned white glue, polymer medium, or rubber cement
- Paint, marker, or oil pastels

Because this is such a well-known work of art, you could interpret it in unrealistic colors and people would still recognize the subject. Or you could photocopy yearbook photos of your friends to use in place of the faces of Washington and his soldiers.

1. Look at a projected slide or reproduction of *Washington Crossing the Delaware,* and use pencil to roughly outline either the entire picture or portions of it on the drawing paper. Do not bother with shading or complete details, as you will cover the drawing with torn paper.

2. Select a color scheme similar to that of the original *Washington Crossing the Delaware* by Emanuel Leutz, or use entirely different colors but limited to approximately seven colors. To do your own interpretation of this artwork, you might use some torn colored paper, filling in some areas with white tissue paper and painting on top of your collage with acrylic paint.

3. Tear paper into approximately 1 to 1-½-inch pieces. You will have better control with small pieces. Put several pieces in place, then glue down a section at a time. Polymer medium may be used as a glue, then brushed over the top of the paper to act as a varnish or (when dry) as a base for acrylic paint.

4. Look at your picture from a distance. You may need to go over some areas with paint, marker, or oil pastels for emphasis or balance.

5. When the projects are finished, display them all together. It will be interesting to see how differently everyone interprets the same subject.

Drawn from *Washington Crossing the Delaware,* 1851
Emanuel Gottlieb Leutz
Metropolitan Museum of Art, New York City

PROJECT 4-4: **FIGURE SKETCHES IN INK**

FOR THE TEACHER

SLIDE #9: *The Jolly Flatboatmen in Port,* **1857, George Caleb Bingham, 47-¹⁄₁₆ × 69-⁵⁄₈ inches, oil on canvas, Museum Purchase, The Saint Louis Art Museum**

George Caleb Bingham (1811–1879) was a painter and portrait artist. He was also a state legislator, treasurer, and adjutant general of Missouri. His work was popular because it showed the rough and rugged frontier life, and at times reflected his political activity. It featured fur traders, hunters, raftsmen, and men relaxing at political gatherings (elections on the frontier were held by voice vote and open ballots, and sometimes went on for three days). He was one of many painters of his time who painted what they saw around them (genre).

To prepare for his beautifully composed oil paintings, Bingham became a master of pen and ink. He did sketches of people, which he used over and over in his (sometimes) crowded compositions. He often placed his figures in pyramidal groups.

Bingham's Masterpieces

The Jolly Flatboatmen in Port, 1857, The Saint Louis Art Museum

Raftsmen Playing Cards, 1847, The Saint Louis Art Museum

The County Election, 1851–1852, The Saint Louis Art Museum

The Verdict of the People, 1855, The Boatmen's National Bank of St. Louis

Fur Traders Descending the Missouri, 1845, The Metropolitan Museum of Art, New York

PREPARATION

Preliminary ink sketches could be done in preparation for a larger composition, but basically this project is simply to do ink sketches. Have students do quick, small, fine-line marker sketches of fellow students on tracing paper. These preliminary sketches should not be graded, and may get students past the point of feeling uncomfortable about making mistakes.

ADDITIONAL SUGGESTIONS

- Students could combine their figure drawings into a larger composition, adding more figures if they wish. This could be painted in acrylic or tempera. If students paint what they know, such as places where they work, these could be exciting paintings.

- Bingham reveled in the beauty of life on the Mississippi. He loved the early morning mists or reflections made by bright sunshine. Have students discuss atmosphere—what it looks like when they are out on a winter or spring morning, the colors of hills and trees in the distance, or the way the sky and water meet at the horizon line. Suggest they paint figures at a favorite time of day.

Photo 4-4A. *The Verdict of the People*, 1855, George Caleb Bingham, oil on canvas, 46 × 65 inches, The Boatmen's National Bank of St. Louis.

Photo 4-4B. *Young Boatman*, George Caleb Bingham, Courtesy of Bingham Sketches, Inc.

Photo 4-4C. *Raftsmen Playing Cards*, George Caleb Bingham, The Saint Louis Museum of Art.

PROJECT 4-4: **FIGURE SKETCHES IN INK**

MATERIALS

- Fine-line markers
- Tracing paper
- Ink
- Pen points
- Brushes
- White drawing paper

Drawn from *Raftsmen Playing Cards*, 1847
George Caleb Bingham
The Saint Louis Art Museum

George Caleb Bingham was a politician and artist. He loved to draw and paint the scenes of the Midwest. Most of his paintings included groups of people, which he often organized in groups of three. He first did ink sketches of people, then used these as references for his paintings.

This project is of people going about their daily work. Think about different types of workers: factory workers, police officers, homemakers, and so on. Think about places where students work: car washes, pizza restaurants, grocery stores, and baby-sitting.

1. Have different people pose for you (some seated, some standing). On tracing paper with fine-line marker do several quick individual figure sketches 6 to 8 inches high. The figures should be roughly the same size. With practice, doing the sketches will become easier. Use at least three of these drawings in the composition. You can reverse the tracing paper if it improves the composition.

2. Cut the tracing-paper drawings into sections. Color over the back of each figure drawing with pencil. Overlap the figures until you come up with an arrangement that is roughly triangular (one figure standing, one seated, one slightly shorter or in front of the others).

3. Before you transfer the figures to a final drawing, draw a background very lightly in pencil. The background might be a restaurant, filling station, classroom, political rally, ticket booth, boat, beach, or concert. Then transfer the sketches to drawing paper by redrawing the fronts of the sketches.

4. Redraw over the pencil lines with fine-line marker or ink pen. If you wish, combine the ink line drawings with ink washes (ink thinned with water), apply the washes first, allowing them to dry before drawing over them with ink. With ink, you cannot erase your mistakes, so don't think of them as mistakes. Just keep making new lines and eventually your figures will look like they should. Instead of fine-line markers, calligraphy markers could be used for variety of line.

5. Look at your composition from a distance. In a black-and-white drawing, you could have 50 percent of the drawing dark and 50 percent white. You can darken in some areas by cross-hatching.

Drawn from *The Verdict of the People*, 1855
George Caleb Bingham
The Boatmen's National Bank of St. Louis
St. Louis, Missouri

PROJECT 4-5: HUDSON RIVER LANDSCAPE POTS

FOR THE TEACHER

SLIDE #10: *The Voyage of Life—Youth,* **1842, Thomas Cole, 57-⅞ × 76-¾ inches, oil on canvas, Ailsa Mellon Bruce Fund, National Gallery of Art, Washington, D.C.**

The Hudson River School of painting was not an actual school, but a group of like-minded painters whose work flourished from 1825 to 1870. It received its name from the many paintings done of the area where the Catskill Mountains rise from the west bank of the Hudson River. The artists viewed nature as a reflection of creation and reverently painted exactly what they saw. They tried to transport the viewer to the actual place—"walking under God's sky."

Although Thomas Cole (1801–1848) was generally considered the founder of the Hudson River School, his close companion, Asher B. Durand (1796–1886), should receive almost equal credit as one of the school's founders. Cole considered his allegorical paintings his most important work. Other original Hudson River School artists were John F. Kensett (1816–1872), Frederick Edwin Church (1826–1900), Jasper Francis Cropsey (1823–1900), Thomas Doughty (1793–1856), Alvan Fisher (1792–1863), Henry Inman (1802–1846), and Samuel F. B. Morse (1791–1872). During the summers these artists painted together in the Catskills, much as the Impressionists often painted together.

Masterpieces by Hudson River School Painters

Kindred Spirits, 1849, Asher B. Durand, New York Public Library

White Mountain Scenery, 1859, John F. Kensett, New York Historical Society

The Oxbow, 1836, Thomas Cole, The Metropolitan Museum of Art, New York

Autumn on the Hudson River, 1860, Jasper Francis Cropsey, National Gallery of Art, Washington, D. C.

PREPARATION

Give students sufficient notice so that each can find a flower pot to bring in. Plastic pots (the larger the better) would be preferable to clay pots. It might be useful for students to have some magazine photos as references for different colors of sky and seasons of the year. It is difficult to paint an atmospheric effect without seeing it.

ADDITIONAL SUGGESTIONS

- This project would ideally be done in ceramics. After forming the pot, students can paint a detailed landscape with underglazes before the final firing with a clear glaze.

- "Hudson Valley Landscapes" could be used to decorate a variety of household items ranging from wastebaskets to bathroom tissue holders, picture frames, or file boxes. Acrylic paint will stick to anything, though it is better to apply gesso first. Ask students to look around their homes for something on which to paint a landscape.

- The United States is filled with natural wonders and monuments that tourists travel across the world to see. Such sights as Niagara Falls, Yosemite, the Grand Tetons, Grand Canyon, the St. Louis Arch, Washington Monument, the Great Lakes, the Painted Desert, the California coastline, and Gulf of Mexico are all beautiful sights. Have students do a painting of surrounding countryside or city scenes in watercolor. Remind them to be aware of how the sky looks at sunrise and sunset, or when it is about to rain.

PROJECT 4-5: **HUDSON RIVER LANDSCAPE POTS**

MATERIALS

- Clay or plastic flower pots
- Newsprint or drawing paper
- Pencils
- Gesso
- Acrylic paint
- Acrylic polymer medium
- Brushes

The Hudson River School artists tried to reproduce the world around them as realistically as possible. They influenced other American landscapists who did not paint in the Hudson River Valley. Select a landscape with which you are familiar rather than one you don't know. Your memory will help you complete details.

1. Make a pattern for the drawing by placing the clay or plastic pot on top of drawing paper. Roll the pot along the paper, drawing along the edges of the pot on the paper. This will give a curved piece of paper that will be an accurate pattern.

2. Make small thumbnail sketches in the general "fan" shape before making the larger drawing. The bottom of the pot will be the land, while the upper part will be sky. Fold the paper in half, then fold the two ends toward the middle to make sure the two sides of your pattern match up on the horizon line.

3. You may use trees, mountains, water, buildings, and people. Write on your design what colors you intend to use. It is not necessary to color this. Apply gesso to the outside of the plastic or clay pot so acrylic paint can adhere to it.

4. Go over the back of your drawing with pencil. Tape the drawing to the pot and transfer your drawing by going over the original design (the pencil will show up if you have gessoed your pot). You could also draw it freehand.

5. Paint the design with acrylic paint. The Hudson River landscapists worked faithfully with color, reproducing nature as exactly as they saw it. However, if you prefer to make unrealistic colors, it will still look like a landscape. Finish the inside and outside of the pot with acrylic polymer medium to make it water resistant. If you use a clay pot, it will last longer if you use it as a decorative cache-pot (hide the real pot inside it).

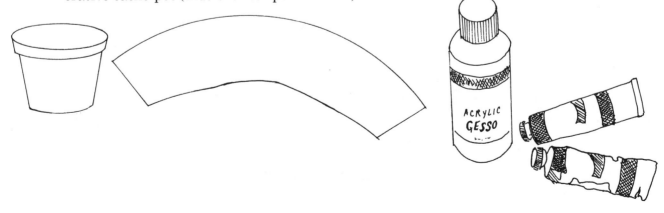

PROJECT 4-6: **BIRDS OF AMERICA**

FOR THE TEACHER

SLIDE #11: *Tricolored Heron,* **(Louisiana Heron), 1821, John James Audubon, 19-½ × 39-½ inches, hand-colored engraving, Mercantile Library, St. Louis**

John James Audubon (1785–1851) came to America from France in 1804 (to avoid conscription into Napoleon's army). Two years later he returned to France and he purportedly refined his drawing skills by spending several months in the studio of Jacques Louis David. He painted portraits, taught, and worked as a taxidermist, but his primary interest and life's work became studying and portraying American wildlife.

Science provided a framework for Audubon's art. He initiated the banding of birds for study. He joined the westward movement and, as he said, "I shot, I drew, I looked on nature only. Beyond this I cared nothing." He usually drew birds in profile, wiring them into life-like positions. His work was romantic, with occasional scenes of the violence of nature, such as a group of birds being attacked in their nest by a snake. He generally completed the bird drawings first, then often allowed his pupils or other watercolorists to draw in the backgrounds.

While in England trying to gain support for publication of his *Birds of America,* he dressed like a frontiersman and apparently was successful at raising money to continue his work.

Examples of Audubon's Art

The Birds of America, 1826, New York Historical Society, New York

Brown Thrasher, 1829, New York Historical Society, New York

Great Blue Heron, 1821, New York Historical Society, New York

Mockingbirds, The Mercantile Library, St Louis

Weeping Crane, The Mercantile Library, St. Louis

PREPARATION

This project can be presented with two different possibilities for interpretation. It can be treated as a scientific representation in the manner of Audubon, or it can be an interpretation of birdlife—bright and anything *but* scientific. Obviously it would be ideal for students to visit a zoo to see and draw (or photograph) exotic birds or animals.

ADDITIONAL SUGGESTIONS

- Scientific representations have been made of all manner of organic life. Beautiful drawings of plants, butterflies, shells, leaves, or fish are all possibilities. Many students will enjoy the absolute adherence to reality that a "scientific" drawing in colored pencil will demand of them.

- Have two students collaborate on a composition, as Audubon did with other artists, with one student creating a background for birds or animals created by the other student. If each student wants a painting to take home, they could collaborate on two similar paintings.

- Students should use crayon or oil pastel to do a colored drawing of birds in their habitat on 12 × 18-inch paper (the entire paper should be covered with color firmly applied). Paint with a coat of black ink, allowing it to dry. Then have students use a nail or other sharp instrument and a ruler to scratch closely and evenly spaced vertical lines through the ink, allowing the background to show through.

Photo 4-6. This 36-inch high papier-mâché blue heron was created by a student of Mary Ann Kroeck.

PROJECT 4-6: **BIRDS OF AMERICA**

John James Audubon, a great naturalist, created scientific drawings of wildlife of America. You may do a "scientific drawing" or an "interpretation" of wildlife.

MATERIALS FOR SCIENTIFIC DRAWING

- Drawing paper
- Drawing pencils or colored pencils
- Photos or photocopies of birds

**Drawn after *Greater Flamingo*
John James Audubon**

1. Because you may have to rely on photographs or photocopies from an encyclopedia, it will be more interesting to make your drawings much larger than your original source. Use an appropriate background (e.g., foliage or branches).

2. Use either a drawing pencil or colored pencils for your illustration. Apply the pencil evenly, working in one direction. Try to show the species you are drawing from more than one angle. When you have finished, label the illustration with the Latin name.

MATERIALS FOR INTERPRETIVE PAINTING

- Drawing paper
- Acrylic or tempera paint (fluorescent colors would be nice)
- Brushes
- Slick-paint™ pens (from a hobby shop)
- Embroidery thread

**Drawn after *Black Billed Cuckoo*
John James Audubon**

This interpretation of birds can be a riot of color. Do huge paintings, and don't be afraid of using color. This project is not a scientific illustration of real birds. John James Audubon would probably roll over in his grave!

Paint in birds and background in bright colors. After the background is done, use a pattern to make a decorative work. Create a very *un*scientific type of artwork using some or all of the following decorative accents:

- Use small dots of contrasting color from a "Slick pen™" to outline a wing or a plant as accent.

- Use a pin to poke small holes on wings or plant leaves, then sew directly on the paper with embroidery thread to create lines.

- Add fake jewels (sparingly) to enhance your picture.

**Drawn after *Wood Duck* (Summer Duck)
John James Audubon**

PROJECT 4-7: THE NATIONAL SURVEY—30,000 FEET HIGH

FOR THE TEACHER

This project is based on the early profession of Albert Bierstadt (1830–1902) rather than on the large romantic landscape paintings of his later career. In 1858 he accompanied the National Survey expedition to the Rocky Mountains and Yosemite Valley. As part of the project, he made sketches which he interpreted into paintings later in his studio.

Bierstadt was born in Germany, but immigrated to the United States with his family as a two-year-old. He studied painting in Dusseldorf, as did many American artists of his generation. He was best known for his romantic paintings of the West and, later, of Native Americans and wild animals.

Examples of Bierstadt's Paintings

The Rocky Mountains, Lander's Peak, 1863, The Metropolitan Museum of Art, New York

The Buffalo Trail, the Impending Storm, 1869, Corcoran Gallery, Washington, D.C.

Thunderstorm in the Rockies, 1859, Museum of Fine Arts, Boston

Storm in the Rocky Mountains, 1866, Brooklyn Museum, New York

PREPARATION

Students will do an abstract watercolor painting based on the patterns seen on a county map or from the window of a plane while flying over North America. The patterns and colors vary considerably depending on the time of year and the region.

You might also cut out aerial views from magazines such as *Smithsonian* or *National Geographic* and post them around the room. Discuss what the countryside looks like from the air. Some of your students who have flown will have noticed the ground patterns created by nature such as rivers, forests, deserts, and mountains.

ADDITIONAL SUGGESTIONS

- Students may do an abstract pencil or charcoal drawing based on an aerial view. Because this is abstract and mostly from the imagination, it does not have to be perfect, and allows for emphasis, repetition, and pattern. Yet the basis on reality gives students a starting point. To give visual interest and unexpected texture, apply gesso to matboard (or drawing paper) with a brush and allow it to dry thoroughly. It is important to stress major differences in dark and light throughout.

- Have students use the watercolor technique to make a giant-scale map of your local area. To be accurate, obtain an actual aerial map or county plat of your region, and divide it for each student to do a portion. Assemble these individual parts on one wall.

- Students can design a monument to commemorate an event that affected your town or area of the country, such as a modern memorial to a hero or heroes. This could be done in pencil, marker, or collage.

PROJECT 4-7: THE NATIONAL SURVEY—30,000 FEET HIGH

MATERIALS

- Rulers
- Compasses
- White construction or watercolor paper
- Watercolor paints
- Watercolor brushes

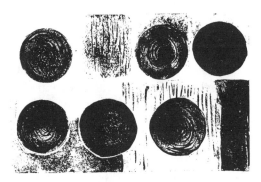

The landscape of America is based on the terrain, but also on logical divisions determined by surveys in the early exploration and settling of the United States. Albert Bierstadt was one of the early surveyors who later painted grandiose Western landscapes. The parceling out of land has resulted in interesting patterns across the landscape as individuals put up fences and hedgerows and chose to grow different kinds of foods. When a plane is 30,000 feet in the air, huge fields look like small squares, and irrigation patterns look like bright circles within the squares. You can see evidence of civilization that adds counterpoint to these (mostly) rectangular and square patterns. Roads slashing through the landscape are seen as thin lines; cities are irregular, patterned shapes. Golf courses, schools with their rows of yellow buses, shopping centers, storage tanks, and railroad tracks, each have a certain "look" from the air. In addition, the season of the year affects the look of the landscape. Freshly plowed fields are dark brown or red, new growth is light green. Mountains look like crumpled paper, sometimes with patches of white on the peaks. Individual trees look like green circles from above, while forests look like oil oozing down hills.

1. Before beginning your abstract aerial landscape, think about what your own surroundings would look like if they were seen from the air. What is the color of the dirt, grass, or hills around you? If you live in a city, think about what the buildings would look like from the air, or how tiny cars would be.

2. Based on areas you have seen, select a geographic location and season. Do a light pencil sketch of how you think the land would look from a plane window 30,000 feet in the air. You might start with mountains, a river, or square patterns of farmland.

3. Look at your abstract drawing and think about how you can add interest. A road, a river, a square farmhouse and outbuildings at a corner of a square, an airport's runways, or crumpled folds of mountains break up the monotony of fields that are all alike.

4. Your general color scheme would probably be earth tones, shades of greens, and violets. Plan ahead for white or light areas by not applying paint in specific areas. To soften your watercolors for painting, apply a small amount of water onto each square or oval of pigment. While the pigment is wet on the paper, crumple plastic wrap and dab with it to make textured effects. You can also scratch white lines into the watercolor with a sharp instrument.

5. After the painting has dried, look at it from a distance and see where you can add differences in value that will add to its interest. You may wish to darken some spots, or go over areas with oil pastel.

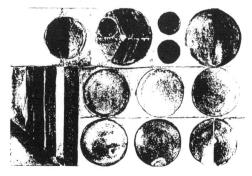

PROJECT 4-8: **CAPITOL BUILDINGS**

FOR THE TEACHER

Capitol buildings throughout the United States seem very similar in design. Most students have seen their own state capitol building or county court house. This project will make students more aware of public buildings—the domes, pillars, and imposing monumentality of the buildings that are constructed for the government.

PREPARATION

Have students find photos of the capitols of several states. They can do individual drawings or tracings from photocopies, then arrange them to make a large collage.

ADDITIONAL SUGGESTIONS

- Have students make three-dimensional domes by doing papier-mâché over a large balloon or by cutting off the top half or third of a ½-gallon plastic soft drink bottle. Make a cylinder of tagboard (or shorten a toilet tissue tube) and tape it over the top of the form. Tear brown kraft paper into pieces approximately 1-½ inches square, and apply them to the dome with wallpaper paste. Dip string or yarn in wallpaper paste and carefully place on the form to create line details. When dry, remove the plastic form or balloon, and apply gesso. Details can be painted on in several variations of white.

- Students can design a mural for the walls or dome of your state capitol as many artists did in the 1800s. This can be done on a piece of drawing paper with colored pencil. Students should consider what the state is famous for, its topography, people, etc. The mural could represent a specific period in history (including current events of interest to students).

PROJECT 4-8: **CAPITOL BUILDINGS**

MATERIALS

- Tracing paper
- Watercolor paper
- Watercolors
- Brushes
- Thinned white glue
- Oil pastels

Nashville, Tennessee

Topeka, Kansas

In the 1800s many of the government and public buildings, such as banks and state capitols, were based on neoclassical architecture. These included columned porches, domes, and architectural details favored by the Greeks and Romans. Research and sketch several buildings done in this style.

1. Make several drawings of state capitol domes or other architectural details on individual pieces of tracing paper. Draw details such as a front porch with pediment and columns, staircases, or decorative sculpture. Make at least five different drawings approximately the same size.

2. Place a large piece of watercolor or drawing paper on a working surface. Move the tracing paper drawings around until you find a balanced arrangement. To transfer these drawings to one piece of paper, pencil over the back of the tracing paper, then redraw over the front. Feel free to overlap or repeat drawings several times (possibly changing sizes).

3. Use watercolors to imaginatively paint these details. Or make a collage by drawing and painting on separate pieces of watercolor paper, moving the pieces around, and then gluing them onto background paper.

4. After the watercolor has thoroughly dried, use oil pastels to "tie it all together." The bright colors of oil pastels will enliven the composition and make it look contemporary. Outline or try "scribble strokes," filling in parts of the background.

University of Missouri, Columbia

New Hampshire

Jefferson City, Missouri, 1906

Salt Lake City, Utah

PROJECT 4-9: COLLAGE OF THE WILD, WILD WEST

FOR THE TEACHER

Frederic Remington (1861–1909) was a cowboy, saloon-keeper, and rancher. He attended Yale University for a year and later the Art Students' League in New York, but was basically a self-taught painter and sculptor. His illustrations and sculpture are as much appreciated today as when he was doing them.

Remington wrote about and illustrated the life of soldiers, cowboys, and Native Americans in the Wild West. His paintings, drawings, and sculpture represented the character of the country and its people. Altogether he produced 25 bronzes and about 2,750 drawings and paintings.

Examples of Remington's Artworks

The Fight for the Waterhole, c.1895–1900, Houston Museum

The Bronco Buster, 1895, bronze sculpture, The Saint Louis Art Museum

His First Lesson, 1903, Amon Carter Museum, Fort Worth

Cavalry Charge on the Southern Plains, 1907, The Metropolitan Museum of Art, New York

PREPARATION

This project could almost be called "What the Wild West Means to Me" because "west" might be Milwaukee to some students, while others are Westerners. Ask students whether they think there still is such a thing as the Wild West. Is there a new frontier? What is a wilderness? Is there one near them? Have they seen horses and cattle? Smelled them? Perhaps the nearest they have come to the Wild West is line dancing. Talk with them about how people dressed, how some of them still dress, and how the Western tradition lives on.

ADDITIONAL SUGGESTIONS

- Students could later use the collage from this project as a printing plate by coating it with ink and pressing fresh white paper on top. With firm hand-pressure or the back of a wooden spoon, many details such as fibers show quite well. If the print is lighter than a student wishes, he or she can draw on it with oil pastel or colored pencil.

- Have students draw a picture of one of Remington's scenes (typically including cowboys, Native Americans, horses or cattle). The picture can then be transferred to copper-colored tooling foil by taping the drawing on top of the foil and lightly redrawing it. Remove the paper and texture the foil using the repoussé method. To give it a "bronze" appearance, wipe it with dark blue-green acrylic paint and wipe off the highlights.

- Using tagboard as a base, have students make torn tissue-paper collages, gluing the paper on with polymer medium or thinned white glue. The theme might be cowboys, horses, animals, forts, or anything else to do with the "Wild West." Finish by doing line drawings over the tissue in India ink.

- Make three-dimensional cowboy boots from construction paper, as demonstrated by a colleague, Sue Trent. With cut-paper contrast inserts, they can be quite effective.

Photo 4-9A. *The Bronco Buster*, 1895, Frederic Remington, bronze, 22-⅞ inches high, Gift of J. Lionberger Davis, The Saint Louis Art Museum.

Photo 4-9B. *The Advance Guard* or *The Military Sacrifice*, 1890, Frederic Remington, oil on canvas, 34-⅜ × 48-½ inches, George F. Harding Collection, The Art Institute of Chicago.

Photo 4-9C. *Teaching a Mustang Pony to Pack Dead Game*, 1890, Frederic Remington, oil on canvas, 20 × 30 inches, Purchase: The Union Pacific Foundation Art Acquisition Fund, The Nelson-Atkins Museum of Art, Kansas City, Missouri.

PROJECT 4-9: **COLLAGE OF THE WILD, WILD WEST**

MATERIALS

- Drawing paper or matboard
- Collage materials: construction paper, yarn, fabric
- Western collage materials: rope, jeans (complete with hobnails, labels, pockets, holes), old leather belt or buckles
- Polymer medium or white glue
- Acrylic paint
- Brushes

Drawn after *Bronco Buster,* **1895**
Frederic Remington
The Saint Louis Art Museum

"Collage" literally means to glue something onto a background. This is to be an impression of the West rather than a literal interpretation of Frederic Remington's paintings. You might select just one item seen in one of his paintings, such as cowboy boots, cattle, a horse, a Stetson™ hat, leather gloves, or adobe buildings, as the theme for your collage. Materials you use for this project could be combined with denim jeans or leather.

1. If you use thin collage materials such as paper or cloth, mount them on paper. If you use heavier materials such as belt buckles or jeans, use a heavier matboard to support the collage. It is also possible to think of this more as a piece of sculpture than a flat painting.

2. Cut or tear the materials into manageable pieces and move them around on the background for awhile before making any definite design. It helps to get the feel of what you are trying for before you glue anything down.

3. Do a rough layout of your idea, perhaps to help you decide what you need to add before doing the final gluing. Check with the teacher for suggestions. Move the materials around a bit more before finally gluing them down. Think about background, line, emphasis, center of interest, and concept. Perhaps adding a bit of yarn or colored paper might give emphasis to your composition. A picture cut from a magazine or one of your own photographs could also add interest.

4. Apply materials with polymer medium or thinned white glue, also brushing the medium on the surface of the collage to act as a varnish. Heavy materials that will not be supported with glue could be attached with brads or stitched onto the paper.

5. If the collage still appears to lack something, select a color such as a dark brown or dark red and paint a few areas. Vary the density, thinly applying paint in some areas to allow the collage to show through, or thickly in some areas to create dark values.

Drawn after *Teaching a Pony to Pack Dead Game*
Frederic Remington
Nelson-Atkins Museum of Art

PROJECT 4-10: AMERICAN FACES IN PLASTIC, PASTEL, AND POLYMER

FOR THE TEACHER

SLIDE #12: *Young Omahaw, War Eagle, Little Missouri, and Pawnees,* **1821, Charles Bird King, National Museum of American Art, 91.8 × 71.1 cm., oil on canvas. Gift of Helen Barlow, Smithsonian Institution / Art Resource, NY**

Throughout the nineteenth century, Native Americans were depicted by several artists who were working partially as painters but also as anthropologists, perhaps to record a vanishing way of life. Charles Bird King (1785–1862) painted a series of portraits depicting members of the Native American delegations that visited Washington in 1821. He was perhaps better known for his *trompe l'oeil* paintings.

George Catlin, one of the most famous western artists, traveled widely, painting hundreds of portraits from four dozen tribes. Many of his paintings were of Native Americans painted for battle and in full regalia. In 1837 he organized a show of his paintings (including live Native Americans). He toured with the show in the United States, England, and France for almost 15 years. His 310 oil portraits and 200 scenes of Native American life were given to the Smithsonian Institution.

Masterpieces by Western Painters

Buffalo Bull's Back Fat, Head Chief, Blood Tribe, 1832, George Catlin, American Museum, Washington, D.C.

Tal-lee, a Warrior of Distinction, 1834, George Catlin, American Museum, Washington, D.C.

Chief Billy Bowlegs, 1861, Charles F. Wimar, The Saint Louis Art Museum

Travelling Tents of the Sioux Indians Called a Tepe (sic), 1847–1849, Seth Eastman, The Saint Louis Art Museum

PREPARATION

Although this project is based on recording Native American life as it was during a certain time period, encourage your students to paint portraits of their own friends, including costumes and hairstyles. They may not realize that today's clothing and hairstyles are unique, but within a few years many changes will occur. The method of drawing on a plastic-covered mirror or holding a piece of plastic in front of the face of a friend and "tracing" with permanent marker allows even the student who "can't draw" to be satisfied with his or her drawing. When these plastic drawings are transferred to paper, students will use their imaginations to complete the drawings and add costumes. Although polymer medium is a water-based material and oil pastels should repel the medium, a layer of oil pastels can be applied, coated with polymer medium, and more pastels added on top. A rich surface is possible with alternate coats of these materials.

Note: This method of drawing faces was presented at a teacher workshop by Louise Cameron of The St. Louis Art Museum, and is used with her permission and that of the museum.

ADDITIONAL SUGGESTIONS

- Have students borrow plastic drawings from each other and put more than one face in a composition.
- Native Americans used a variety of tools to paint, but often only fingers and hands for applying paint to faces. Attach a long piece of kraft paper to the wall or on the floor, and have the students

draw many "face" ovals and profiles. Show examples of Native American faces decorated for special occasions, and have the students decorate faces on the mural using only fingers and hands. (Pour tempera paint on sponges or a pad of damp paper towels for ready access.)

Photo 4-10. *The White Cloud, Head Chief of the Iowas*, 1844–1845, George Catlin, oil on canvas, 22-⅞ × 28 inches, Paul Mellon Collection, National Gallery of Art, Washington, D.C. This painting, with the Chief's face painted with red paint and the green handprint, is one of the most dramatic of George Catlin's paintings of Native Americans.

PROJECT 4-10: AMERICAN FACES IN PLASTIC, PASTEL, AND POLYMER

MATERIALS

- 8-½ × 11-inch plastic (for overhead projector)
- Permanent markers (any color)
- White drawing or pastel paper
- Oil pastels
- Polymer medium
- Brushes
- 12 × 12-inch mirror tiles
- Alcohol
- Paper towels

Just as Charles Bird King, George Catlin, Charles Wimar, and other western painters portrayed Native Americans and their customs, this project is a record of the faces of your generation. Your clothing, hairstyles, and accessories (such as sunglasses or hats) are unique.

1. Tape the plastic on a mirror. With a permanent marker, trace your face onto the clear plastic. Take the time to carefully make details. You can make several drawings, varying them by holding the mirror at a different angle. If you need to make changes, remove the marker with alcohol on a paper towel.

2. Tape the plastic on the back of drawing paper, leaving room for several faces. You may draw your own face several times, or trade with other students. Tape or hold the paper up to a window and trace the faces lightly with pastel onto the drawing paper.

3. The faces are only a starting point. Using oil pastels, color the composition realistically, add accessories, or use your imagination to change it in any way you wish. Make the first coat of color rather loose, working out lights and darks. Apply a coat of polymer medium (don't thin with water), and allow it to dry for approximately 15 minutes. It may pick up some of the pastel, but it will give a glazed effect.

4. After the polymer is dry, apply a second coat of pastel and a second coat of polymer. You may use several alternating coats. For fine details, use colored pencils when the composition is dry.

Faces drawn from portraits by George Catlin

TURN OF THE CENTURY
(1870 to 1900)

TURN OF THE CENTURY
TIME LINE

	1870	1875	1880	1885	1890	1895	1900
Painting Sculpture Architecture Folk Art	Victorian Art 1870–1915 / James Abbott McNeill Whistler, 1834–1903	Gothic Revival Church 1884–1886 / 1870–1890 called The Gilded Age / 1875–1915 American Arts and Crafts Movement / John James Audubon 1785–1851 / George Bellows 1882–1925	Art Nouveau c. 1880–1910 / Weathervanes c. 1860–1885	Trompe L'oeil paintings / John LaFarge 1835–1910 / Winslow Homer 1836–1910 / Mary Cassatt 1845–1926	Charles Burchfield 1893–1967 / Henry Ossawa Tanner 1859–1937 / William Michael Harnett 1848–1892	The Ten / Louis Sullivan 1856–1924	Regionalism 1892–1942
Politics	1872 U.S. Grant re-elected President	1877 Rutherford B. Hayes President / 1877 Nez Perce battle U.S. Govt.		1881 Pres. Garfield assassinated / 1884 Grover Cleveland becomes Pres. / 1888 Benjamin Harrison Pres.	1892 Grover Cleveland elected President / 1890 Women get vote in Wyoming		1898 Spanish/American War / 1896 Wm. McKinley elected President
Literature					Louisa May Alcott (Little Women) 1832–1888	Robert Frost 1874–1963	
Science	1869 Periodic Law	1876 Alexander Graham Bell patents telephone / 1875 Mimeograph	1879 Edison patents incandescent bulb	1885—Gas engine automobile / 1886 Linotype machine / 1887 Contact lens invented		1897 Cause of Malaria found by Ronald Ross / 1899 Aspirin (Felix Hoffman)	
Music	1871 Verdi wrote Aida	Enrico Caruso 1873–1921	1878 H.M.S. Pinafore, Gilbert and Sullivan		Franz Liszt 1811–1886		1888 Irving Berlin born
Current Events	1870–1890 Transcontinental railroads	General Robert E. Lee 1807–1870 / 1871 P. T. Barnum's circus	1885 American Federation of Labor founded		1889 Hull House founded / 1894 Eugene Debs jailed		

134

ARCHITECTURE OF THE TURN OF THE CENTURY

Second Empire
Cornish House, 1886
Omaha, Nebraska

Asymmetrical facades
Steeply pitched roofs
Multi-colored walls
Mixture of styles such as
Italianate, Greek, Gothic
Georgian and Adamesque features

Queen Anne Style
Gray House, 1891
Santa Cruz, California

Second Empire, 1855–1890
Mansard roof with dormers
Classical columns
Veranda-like porches
Decorative cornices
Towers
Paired and triple windows
Quoins (corner stones)
Bay windows
Paired entry doors
Patterned roof
Front and side pavilions

Richardsonian Romanesque
Lionberger House, 1886
St. Louis, Missouri

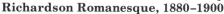

Richardson Romanesque, 1880–1900
Round towers, conical roof
Masonry walls
Asymmetrical facade
Varied colors of stone or brick
Deeply recessed windows
Lines of windows
Fortress-like designs
Broad hip roof
Short, squat chimneys

Queen Anne, 1880–1910
Steep gabled roof
Full width porch
Roof cresting
Finials
Spindlework and beads
Patterned masonry
Corner towers with conical roof
Verandas and balconies
Contrasting building materials
Stained glass
Fish-scale shingles
Horizontal siding

© 1996 by Prentice-Hall, Inc.

Second Empire Style
Renwick Gallery, 1859–1861
Washington, D.C.

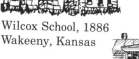

Wilcox School, 1886
Wakeeny, Kansas

Stick, 1860–1890
Straight wooden boards
Square bay windows
Steep roofs
Angular and asymmetrical
Projecting bay
Wide, overhanging eaves
Patterns made with boards
Textures in gables
Squared bay windows

Stick / Eastlake, 1870–1890
Gingerbread millwork added

Folk Victorian, 1870–1910
Porches with spindlework
Gingerbread ornamentation
Combination of styles

Cape Hatteras Light Station, 1871
North Carolina

American Gothic House
Eldon, Iowa

Carpenter Gothic
Pointed arches
Wood painted to look like stone

Victorian Gothic, 1860–1890
Polychromatic exteriors
Pointed arches
High-pitched roof lines
Towers
Tracery
Stained
Vertical board and batten
Contrasting brick and stone

Shingle style, 1880–1900
Shingle covering on most walls
Wavy wall surface
Rusticated stone
Towers
Bay windows—one- or two-story
Gambrel roof occasionally
Round or square headed windows
Horizontal, low buildings
Circular turrets
Verandas

Shingle Style, Low House, 1887
McKim, Meade, and White
Bristol, Rhode Island

Gothic Revival
First Baptist Church, 1884–1886
Lynchburg, Virginia

VICTORIAN ARCHITECTURE

Decorative Scrollwork

Cornice

Frieze
Architrave

Capital

Entablature

Column or Pilaster

Pediments

Shingle styles

Finials

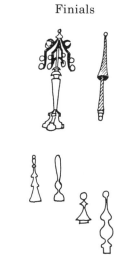

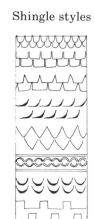

Doors

Windows

Porches

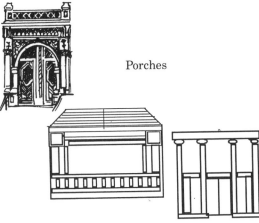

Towers

Section 5.—TURN OF THE CENTURY (1870–1900)

ARTISTS OF THE PERIOD

PAINTERS

- *Mary Cassatt* (1845–1926) was America's foremost Impressionist, and is credited with helping Impressionism become known in the United States. Her best-known subjects are her paintings of mothers and children. Her simplified backgrounds were frequently based on Japanese prints.
- *Thomas Eakins* (1844–1916) was the leading Realist genre painter and portraitist of the nineteenth century in America. He frequently used the (then) new art of photography as a basis for his paintings.
- *William Michael Harnett* (c. 1848–1892) specialized in carefully crafted trompe l'oeil (fool the eye) paintings of tabletop arrangements and on-the-wall still lifes. His "high Victorian" paintings were noted for their smooth brushstrokes and jewel-like colors combined with dark somber tones.
- *Winslow Homer* (1836–1910) worked as a pictorial reporter throughout the Civil War. His realistic paintings depicted contemporary life, frequently hunting scenes. In his later years he became a marine painter working mostly in watercolor.
- *George Inness* (1825–1894) was an American Romantic landscape painter. He was elected to the National Academy in 1868. His early work was realistic, in the tradition of the Hudson River School. His grandiose compositions were filled with minute detail.
- *John Singer Sargent* (1856–1925) was best known for his dramatic portraits of members of high society. Sargent was born in Florence (of American parents), and was trained academically in Italy and France. Although he admired the Impressionists, he could never imagine himself painting without using black, as Monet did.
- *Henry Ossawa Tanner* (1859–1937) was the first well-known African-American painter. He studied with Thomas Eakins in the early 1880s. Tanner's socially-conscious father gave the middle name Ossawa to his son to honor Ossawatamie, Kansas where John Brown was born. Tanner lived most of his life in Europe.
- *James Abbott McNeill Whistler* (1834–1903), an American, studied in Paris where he came in contact with Courbet and the Impressionists. He spent his lifetime in London. His moody, dramatic paintings were often named "symphonies, nocturnes, or arrangements."

SCULPTORS

- *Daniel Chester French* (1850–1931) was referred to in 1905 as the dean of American sculpture. A Massachusetts native, the talented young French was offered his first commission, a memorial for which he sculpted *The Minute Man* (1875). He went to France for further training and, when he returned to America, continued to work in the classical French tradition.

- *Harriet Hosmer* (1830–1908) studied in Rome where she lived the "eccentric life of a perfectly emancipated female" and was the leader of what Henry James dubbed the "White Marmorean Flock," a group of expatriate American women sculptors. She specialized in romantic subjects, and was considered the most famous woman sculptor of her day. Her neo-classical style included full-length statues of historical and mythological figures.

- *Frederick MacMonnies* (1863–1937) went to Paris to study when he was 21. He ultimately lived there for 25 years. He did not sculpt with the neo-classicism of most Americans trained abroad, but his work was naturalistic, reflecting his consciousness of the effects of light and shadow. His *Bacchante and Infante Faun* (a dancing tipsy nude), carved in 1893, was banned in Boston. The Women's Christian Temperance Union (and others) protested its placement in the Boston Public Library building, and it was moved to The Metropolitan Museum of Art in New York.

- *Randolph Rogers* (1825–1892) showed promise as a young sculptor, and his employer financed a trip to Europe, where he ended up settling in Rome. His work was primarily "romantic neo-classicism," and his *Nydia* was so popular that one hundred marble replicas were made of it. He produced the bronze doors for the U.S. Capitol building, which illustrated the story of Christopher Columbus.

- *John Quincy Adams Ward* (1830–1910) assisted Henry Kirke Brown on the equestrian statue of George Washington for Union Square in New York City. His work mostly consisted of life-sized bronze portrait statues for New York City. His work was naturalistic, and he was the "dean of American sculptors from about 1875 on."

ARCHITECTS

- *Richard Morris Hunt* (1827–1895) was a founder and officer of the American Institute of Architects, and primarily known for his designs for sumptuous homes such as *Biltmore House* (1895) in Asheville, North Carolina, and mansions such as *The Breakers* in Newport, Rhode Island. He was often called the "dean of American architecture."

- *Henry Hobson Richardson* (1838–1886) was considered responsible for Romanesque Revival architecture in the United States, which influenced the architects of the Chicago school. He designed churches, a series of small libraries, railroad stations, and many prominent public buildings.

- *Louis Sullivan* (1856–1924) was considered the father of the modern skyscraper, and achieved his goal of designing forms that were original instead of depending on historic styles. He was the first to give unity to a tall building, allowing the vertical supporting structure to be visible externally, and tying the whole together with terra cotta ornamentation. He is also known as the mentor of Frank Lloyd Wright.

- *Stanford White* (1853–1906) was an associate in the firm of McKim, Mead and White which at one time was the largest in the world. Of the 1000 commissions that went through the office, they were responsible for many public buildings such as train stations, libraries, and courthouses, as well as one of the earliest shingle-style homes in Rhode Island.

FAMOUS ARTISTS AND SCHOOLS OF ART OF THE VICTORIAN ERA

- *American Impressionism* began a little later and lasted into the twentieth century. Mary Cassatt was the only American Impressionist, but several others, including

Theodore Robinson (1852–1896), studied under Monet. Their work varied slightly from that of the French Impressionists in that their forms appeared more solid, and they were less obsessed with the appearance of light between them and their subjects.

- *The Ten.* Most of this group of painters had studied in Europe and reflected the popularity of Impressionism in Paris. Their first exhibition, "Ten American Painters," was in 1898, and they continued to show together for 20 years. Members were Childe Hassam (1859–1935), J. Alden Weir (1852–1919), John Twachtman (1853–1902), Willard Metcalf (1858–1925), Edmund Tarbell (1862–1938), Frank Benson (1862–1951), Joseph De Camp (1855–1923), Thomas Dewing (1851–1938), Edward Simmons (1852–1931), and Robert Reid (1862–1929). After Twachtman died in 1902, he was replaced by William Merritt Chase (1849–1916).

- *Trompe L'oeil.* A number of Americans were virtuosos of "deceiving the eye" through their extremely realistic paintings. William Michael Harnett (1848–1892) and John Frederick Peto (1854–1907) were the best known of the American still life painters. At times Peto's paintings were (later) signed with Harnett's name because Harnett's was considered of greater value.

OVERVIEW OF VICTORIAN ART

The art of the late nineteenth and early twentieth centuries reflected the somber attitude of a nation that had survived a major civil war. This period was sometimes referred to as "The Brown Decades" because of the dark, massive architecture and dark colors used by so many of its artists.

PAINTING

There was no one special style of painting such as Impressionism, which had just become popular in Europe, but several of the contemporary artists reflected a European influence. Although most American artists had studied art in New York, Boston, or Philadelphia, many famous American artists continued their studies in France, Italy, England, or Germany.

Most of the artists had turned away from rendering grandiose landscapes and concentrated more on their own surroundings. They portrayed people, places, and objects that reflected a growing pleasure in the out-of-doors.

Examples of Victorian Paintings

The Bath, 1891, Mary Cassatt, The Art Institute of Chicago

The Gross Clinic, 1875, Thomas Eakins, Jefferson Medical College, Philadelphia

The Morning Bell, c. 1866, Winslow Homer, Yale University Art Gallery, New Haven

The Croquet Game, 1866, Winslow Homer, Chicago Art Institute

Portrait of Lady Agnew, c. 1892–1893, John Singer Sargent, National Galleries of Scotland, Edinburgh

Mrs. X, 1884, John Singer Sargent, The Metropolitan Museum of Art, New York

Mrs. George Swinton, 1896, John Singer Sargent, Chicago Art Institute

The Banjo Lesson, c. 1893, Henry Ossawa Tanner, Hampton Institute, Hampton, Virginia

Arrangement in Gray and Black, No. 1: The Artist's Mother, 1871, James Abbott McNeill Whistler, Louvre, Paris

Nocturne in Black and Gold: Falling Rocket, c. 1874, James Abbott McNeill Whistler, The Detroit Institute of Arts

SCULPTURE

Although Victorian sculpture continued to reflect French neo-classicism, an American form of sculpture began to emerge. Equestrian statues and monuments erected to heroes and portraits of presidents and other public figures are seen in our cities and parks today. Decorative sculpture was placed on public buildings, and sculpture on funeral monuments proliferated. A few artists emphasized naturalism in sculpture through the rough surfaces they used, which were not seen in the smooth work of neo-classicists. Several sculptors specialized in portraying the Native American and frontier life.

Examples of Victorian Sculpture

Nydia, the Blind Girl of Pompeii, 1895, Randolph Rogers, Pennsylvania Academy of Fine Arts, Philadelphia

Zenobia, 1858, Harriet Hosmer, The Metropolitan Museum of Art, New York

Daphne, 1854, Harriet Hosmer, Washington University Gallery of Art, St. Louis

Roma, 1869, Anne Whitney, Wellesley College Museum, Wellesley, Massachusetts

The White Captive, 1859, Erastus Dow Palmer, The Metropolitan Museum of Art, New York

The Minute Man, 1889, Daniel Chester French, Concord, Massachusetts

Bacchante and Infant Faun, 1894, Frederick MacMonnies, Philadelphia Museum of Art

George Washington, 1883, John Quincy Adams Ward, Federal Hall National Memorial, New York

Adams Memorial, 1886–1891, August Saint-Gaudens, Rock Creek Cemetery, Washington, D.C.

ARCHITECTURE

Much Victorian architecture survives in the United States and is often cherished because of its ornate embellishments. Many cities such as San Francisco have beautiful frame homes that are maintained in their former grandeur. Public buildings in most cities were built to last, so Victorian city halls, court houses, and banks abound in the United States.

Grandiose palaces such as *Biltmore House* (1895) near Asheville, North Carolina, or "cottages" such as *The Breakers* and *Marble House* (1892) in Newport, Rhode Island, reflected the French Renaissance style, while public architecture featured Second Empire (French) style, or Neo-Romanesque, Neo-Gothic, Neo-Greek, Neo-Roman, and Neo-Egyptian influences (sometimes all at once, it seemed). It was as if the builders in the United States wished to demonstrate a history, even though for the first 200 years of the country's founding, their buildings had sometimes consisted of little more than rudimentary shelter.

Toward the end of the century, technological advances with cast iron and steel allowed the construction of taller buildings. The work of Victorian architect Henry

Hobson Richardson was sometimes compared with the paintings of Thomas Eakins, who was taking painting to new levels. Richardson, who designed the Marshall Field Warehouse in Chicago, was paving the way for architects such as Louis Sullivan and Frank Lloyd Wright

Examples of Victorian Architecture

William G. Low House, 1887, Shingle Style, McKim, Mead and White, Bristol, Rhode Island

The Griswold House, 1863, Stick Style, Richard Morris Hunt, Newport, Rhode Island

The Long-Waterman House, 1889, Queen Anne Style, B. B. Benson, San Diego, California

Terrace Hill, 1869, Second Empire Style, W. W. Boyington, Des Moines, Iowa

State, War and Navy Building, 1888, Alfred B. Mullett, Washington, D.C.

Col. Walter Gresham House, 1887–1893, Nicholas J. Clayton, Galveston, Texas

Marshall Field Wholesale Store, 1887, Henry Hobson Richardson, Chicago

Wainwright Building, 1891, Louis Sullivan, St. Louis

Biltmore House, 1895, Richard Morris Hunt, Asheville, North Carolina

PHOTOGRAPHY

By the turn of the century, photography was well established. It had been used to record the Civil War, and documented the opening of the country. The grandeur of the West became known through photographs. Every family had an important family event, such as a wedding, recorded on film, or the family farm or home shown on a tintype. While the photograph was often considered an artwork in itself, artists such as Thomas Eakins used action studies of male or female nudes as aids in their paintings, much as many contemporary painters use photography as an aid.

Photographic Examples

Steerage, 1907, Alfred Stieglitz, The Saint Louis Art Museum

Female Nude from the Back, c. 1880, Thomas Eakins, The Metropolitan Museum of Art, New York

Portrait of a Woman, c. 1900, Gertrude Kasebier, International Museum of Photography, Rochester, New York

Alice Liddell as Pomona, 1872, Julia Margaret Cameron, The Metropolitan Museum of Art, New York

The Orchard, 1898, Clarence H. White, The Toledo Museum of Art

The Valley from Mariposa Trail, Yosemite, California, 1863, Carleton E. Watkins, collection Daniel Wolf, Inc., New York

MINOR ARTS

Victorian ladies often did paintings such as theorems, or cut stencils in black paper that became part of a framed painting. They created oil paintings on velvet or the back of plate glass, made decorative "pictures" from human hair, and did china painting and fancy embroidery. Young women were often taught painting by copying from old masters.

PROJECT 5-1: **PAINTED LADIES (AMERICAN VICTORIAN HOUSES)**

FOR THE TEACHER

American architecture of the 1870s to 1900s was inspired by many periods and cultures. Any single building could be an incredible collage of styles, and might have resulted from the builder's desire to display his versatility rather than from the disciplined style of an architect. Many homes and public buildings were made of stone and brick with wood trim and "gingerbread." Towers and turrets abounded, and decorative millwork was standard.

San Francisco's elaborately embellished Victorian frame houses are sometimes referred to as "Painted Ladies." The rich colors and extravagant detail recall the opulence of Victorian times rather than the 1920s' Bauhaus design principle of "less is more." Most cities have a number of Victorian homes in various states of repair, but few have been so lovingly cherished as have those in San Francisco.

The following is a list of the major building styles of the period and a synopsis of their characteristics:

- *Italianate:* Straight vertical, tall narrow doors and round-headed windows, elaborate pediments, Corinthian columns on porches, flat or low pyramidal roof lines, sometimes an entrance tower or balcony

- *Stick:* Straight wooden boards used to outline square bay windows, doors, and framework of a house; steep roofs, angular and asymmetrical, projecting bay

- *Stick/Eastlake:* Gingerbread millwork added to stick style

- *Second Empire:* Mansard roof with dormers, classical columns, front and side pavilions or veranda-like porches, paired windows

- *Queen Anne:* Steep gabled roof, corner towers with conical roof, verandas and balconies, contrast of building materials, stained glass, fish-scale shingles, horizontal siding

- *Carpenter Gothic:* Pointed arches, wood painted to look like stone

- *Tudor:* Flattened squared arches

- *Gothic Revival:* Pointed arches, high-pitched roof lines, towers, tracery, stained glass, vertical board and batten, contrasting colors of brick and stone

- *Shingle style:* Shingle covering, round or square-headed windows, horizontal, low buildings, circular turrets and verandas

PREPARATION

If possible, have students do sketches of details of old houses in their own town. These paintings will be much more meaningful and alive if the students actually see local architecture. In lieu of that, however, many books have good photographs that can be photocopied as resource material.

Cut tagboard (manila file folders) into squares, rectangles, triangles, and cones. Students may use the patterns in combination with freehand drawing. They should use different sizes and shapes to design a house as if they were the architect / builder. Any of the media listed here would be suitable for finishing. Or allow students to select any medium at all for completing the project.

- *Black fine-line marker and watercolor:* After drawing lightly on watercolor paper in pencil, outline the building in black fine-line water-soluble marker. Embellish freely. Use watercolor to create a color scheme (five colors should do it). When the watercolor goes over the black marker, the lines will bleed. Students sometimes have difficulty accepting the charming effect this creates, so prepare them to appreciate the "happy accident" in art.

- *Bleach on black paper:* After drawing the house on black construction paper, use cotton swabs or brushes to apply diluted chlorine bleach (⅓ water to ⅔ bleach) along the outlines. Students will quickly see where to create more interest with Victorian embellishments. Remind them to be careful not to spill bleach on their clothing.

- *Chalk or conté crayon:* Draw houses in chalk or with a combination of conté crayon in black, white, and dark red on gray paper.

- *Copy paper and doilies:* Cut out white drawing paper and doilies for the "gingerbread" and mount them on black paper, then draw details with black fine-line marker. Or for a contemporary look, substitute lime, magenta, or orange copy paper, white doilies, and black marker.

- *Eraser stamps:* Each student could make a stamp of a different architectural detail such as lines, curved arches, pointed arches, or "bricks," by cutting the design on the top of an artgum eraser with an X-acto™ knife. Students would share stamps to create individual houses on drawing paper.

- *Grid paper:* Have students make a one-inch grid on drawing paper (or use graph paper). Use marker or colored pencil to design a Victorian house. Color each square individually.

ADDITIONAL SUGGESTIONS

- To make doorstops or bookends, have students paint on gessoed bricks or $2 \times 4 \times 7$-inch boards a tall Victorian house with acrylic paint. This could be varnished with acrylic polymer medium, and felt glued on the bottom.

- Have students make small Victorian house models in foam core. Pieces can be cut on a paper cutter and held together with ¾-inch nails stuck through the bottom of the foam. Decorate with marker or pencil.

- Conceive and design bird houses, as American architects recently did for an auction. These ranged from two-story classical designs to very modern. Although the design itself is the project, these could actually be constructed. Ideally they would be made of wood, but I recently had a family of birds build a nest in a ceramic container, so I know it works. Make sure the hole is the correct size.

PROJECT 5-1: **PAINTED LADIES (AMERICAN VICTORIAN HOUSES)**

MATERIALS

- Tagboard patterns
- Rulers
- Pencil
- Paper
- Tempera paint

Each Victorian house differed from the one next to it as individual owners and their builders decided which of the many styles to use. The size of the lot might have dictated the size and shape of the house. Row houses were often three stories tall and quite narrow. Larger mansions were possible on larger lots or huge estates. Many of the houses were asymmetrical (different on one half from the other), and it was common for them to have bay windows (windows that stuck out from the front of the house to allow in more light).

1. Look around your community for houses that might be as old as 100 years. Notice the roof line, the trim on the windows, the entrance or porch. If you can't find real houses, then look at Victorian houses in books.

2. Decide whether you want to work vertically or horizontally on the paper. Select several cardboard patterns to make the basic outlines of your house. Draw the house from a front-on view. Think about the following items for *your* house:

   - How many stories?
   - Front porch? Sun porches on second and third stories? Steps to the porch? Columns? Railing?
   - Rectangular windows with rounded top? straight across? triangles above them?
   - What kind of roof? Dormers? Turrets? Windows in turrets? Shutters?
   - Pediment? (triangular shape used above porches, windows, or below roof)

3. Draw lightly around a pattern. You may repeat the same pattern several times to make a house three stories high, then select a narrower pattern to put next to those. This will make the house slightly asymmetrical, as most Victorian homes were.

4. Select one color for the major part of the house, then make the trim different values of this color or contrasting colors. Use more than two colors, but fewer than twelve—most "painted ladies" average four to five.

5. Decorations can be purely from your imagination. Popular motifs were shell and scroll patterns, and geometric designs such as squares, triangles, circles, and ovals. Combine these items to make your own "gingerbread" ornamentation. When you paint or draw the house, make these items different in color from the background color.

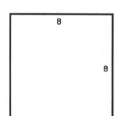

PROJECT 5-2: **WHISTLER'S MOTHER**

FOR THE TEACHER

SLIDE #13: *Arrangement in Gray and Black No. 1: The Artist's Mother,* **1871, James Abbott McNeill Whistler, 57-¼ × 64-¾ inches, oil on canvas, Musee d'Orsay, Paris, France, Giraudon/Art Resource, NY**

Whistler lived in St. Petersburg, Russia, with his father, who went there to design the first Russian railroad. He was educated in the Czar's court, where he learned French. He later returned to the United States where he spent three years at West Point. He left the United States for France, where he studied etching and painting. Whistler exhibited in the Salon des Refusés (the Impressionists' Salon) after his work was rejected by the Paris Salon (the formal French establishment). Whistler worked often in pastels, but became most famous for his portraits and moody, loosely rendered night scenes. He believed in "art for art's sake," which meant that he did not intend his work to carry any social messages, but simply to be appreciated for its beauty.

Masterpieces by Whistler

Portrait of Thomas Carlyle: Arrangement in Grey and Black, No 2, 1872, Glasgow Art Gallery and Museum

The White Girl: Symphony in White No. 1, 1862, Washington, D.C.

Arrangement in Gray and Black, No. 1: The Artist's Mother, 1871, The Louvre, Paris

Nocturne in Black and Gold: Falling Rocket, c. 1874, The Detroit Institute of Arts

PREPARATION

Whistler painted portraits of gentlemen in the same colors and pose as that of his mother. Have students select a partner and practice drawing each other from a side view, including the entire body. It would be interesting to have props such as hats for the young men or long skirts or lengths of cloth or paper to drape as a skirt or shawl for the young women. Have them pay special attention to situating the figure against a background such as a baseboard, wall, or corner. After perfecting the drawings, the students can make a construction paper collage in neutral colors or paint the figure in values of black and white and brown tempera paint.

ADDITIONAL SUGGESTIONS

- A large torn paper collage or painting can be made by hanging a large piece (36 × 48 inches) of paper vertically on the wall. Have a student sit in front of it. Place a projector on a table, and shine the projector toward the student. Another student can draw the silhouette on the paper background. The collage could include patterned wallpaper samples in neutral colors.

- Students could do a "Nocturne" in the manner of Whistler by using only dark pastels to create a nighttime scene of a place near their own home. Blending the pastels, making some areas darker, and adding a few highlights will give a Whistler-like quality to their work.

Photo 5–1. *Nocturne in Grey and Gold,* **1872, James Abbott McNeill Whistler, oil on canvas, 19-⅞ × 29-¹⁵⁄₁₆ inches, Charles Stickney fund, The Art Institute of Chicago.**

PROJECT 5-2: WHISTLER'S MOTHER

MATERIALS FOR COLLAGE

- 18 × 24-inch construction paper, neutral shades
- Scissors
- Rubber cement or white glue
- 18 × 24-inch tracing paper or newsprint

MATERIALS FOR PAINTING

- Drawing paper
- Tempera paint—white, brown, black, yellow, green, red, blue
- Brushes

James McNeill Whistler called his most famous painting *Arrangement in Gray and Black, No. 1: The Artist's Mother.* He was a portrait artist whose paintings were often named after the neutral colors used in them. Have your partner sit so you see only a profile. This will be a full-body portrait. If you have props such as a hat or book, it will make the picture more interesting. Draw objects such as pictures or draperies and a chair, or architectural elements such as windows, doors, or fireplaces to complete your composition.

PAPER COLLAGE FIGURE

1. Draw the figure on newsprint or tracing paper, repeating lines until you are satisfied. As you draw, emphasize shapes of areas where there are differences in value (lights and darks). You will be using different colors of paper to show these values. The face and hands will be a relatively small portion of the finished composition, so it is not necessary to draw them in detail at this time. Use pencil to draw over the back of the paper where the final lines are.

2. Select three to five values of neutral paper. Determine which will be the background. Trace the largest shape (probably the body) onto one color of paper. Wait until you have cut all the pieces before gluing in place. Build up the composition by placing one color on top of another and then glue in place with rubber cement or white glue.

PAINTED FIGURE

1. You will paint directly on the drawing, so do as little erasing as possible. Lightly draw the figure on paper. With paint it is possible to get more detail, so you may wish to draw facial features. Complete your composition by drawing in a background of a room, including details such as a door, window, or picture on the wall.

2. Avoid building up paint too thickly. Try to avoid using black to make dark tones, but use dark greens, blues, and violets to make dark grays. When your brush is loaded with a color, paint that color in various places where it will appear. Many of Whistler's paintings were quite dark, relieved only with flesh tones and delicate additions of colors such as green and blue to grays. If needed, have your model reassume the original pose so you can make necessary changes.

Drawn after Arrangement in Gray and Black, Number 1: The Artist's Mother, 1871 James Abbott McNeill Whistler

PROJECT 5-3: **BULLETIN BOARD**

FOR THE TEACHER

SLIDE #14: *Reminiscences of 1865,* **after 1890, John Frederick Peto, 30 × 20 inches, oil on canvas, The Julia B. Bigelow Fund, The Minneapolis Institute of Arts**

This project is about masters of *trompe l'oeil* (deceive the eye) still lifes that were popular at the turn of the century (as they are again today). Two such masters, John Frederick Peto and William Michael Harnett, often have their work confused because an unscrupulous dealer sometimes signed Harnett's signature on paintings by Peto (Harnett was the more successful, while Peto was largely unrecognized during his lifetime). Harnett is best remembered for his still lifes of such things as pipes, books, and musical instruments, or "back-of-door" paintings that were perfect renditions of guns, a dead rabbit, and hunting clothes. His work was created through the use of shadow, simple colors, and faithful reproduction of what he saw. In 1886 he ran afoul of the law and was arrested because his interpretation of a dollar bill was so realistic. Peto's paintings were not nearly so grand, and he specialized in paintings for offices that resembled bulletin boards. He didn't "prettify" his paintings, so homely, worn objects were reproduced the way he saw them. "Rack" paintings of bulletin boards with letters held in place with ribbon will be the inspiration for the student project.

Masterpieces by Trompe L'oeil Painters

Just Dessert, 1891, William Michael Harnett, oil on canvas, Chicago Art Institute

After the Hunt, 1885, William Michael Harnett, California Palace of the Legion of Honor, San Francisco

Still Life—Violin and Music, 1888, William Michael Harnett, The Metropolitan Museum of Art, New York

The Artist's Card Rack, 1879, William Michael Harnett, Museum of Modern Art, New York

My Gems, 1888, William Michael Harnett, National Gallery of Art, Washington, D.C.

Poor Man's Store, 1885, John F. Peto, Museum of Fine Arts, Boston

Still Life With Lanterns, John F. Peto, Brooklyn Museum, New York

PREPARATION

Have each student do a quick, rough sketch at home of his or her own bulletin board (or refrigerator door), not attempting to capture detail, but simply to notice the things they have thought enough of to save. This probably includes notices, business or appointment cards, photos, or postcards. Students may work individually or in groups. If working in a group, each student may bring in a few objects such as an empty soft drink can, ticket stubs, fast-food containers, pressed corsage, letter, candy wrapper, playing card, or newspaper clipping, and they can work as a group to make a satisfactory arrangement, which they all draw. If feasible, use a flood light to create shadows.

ADDITIONAL SUGGESTIONS

- Each student may interpret one item as realistically as possible, and the drawings will be cut out and grouped together to create a bulletin board or "refrigerator door" (draw a refrigerator door on a long sheet of roll paper). Students could even do realistic drawings of refrigerator magnets to hold things in place.

- Instead of working with their own collections, each student could cut items from a magazine and create a bulletin board from cutouts, adding ribbon and tacks. This should then be drawn in pencil as realistically as possible.

Photo 5-2. *With the Staats Zeitung,* 1890, William M. Harnett, oil on canvas, 14-⅛ × 20-¼ inches, Museum Purchase, The Saint Louis Art Museum.

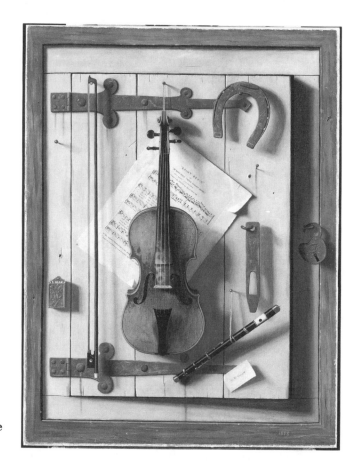

Photo 5-3. *Still Life—Violin and Music,* 1888, William M. Harnett, oil on canvas, 40 × 30 inches, The Metropolitan Museum of Art, Catharine Lorillard Wolfe Fund, Catharine Lorillard Wolfe Collection.

PROJECT 5-3: **BULLETIN BOARD**

MATERIALS

- 12 × 18-inch or smaller drawing paper
- Pencil
- Watercolor
- Photo flood lights (if feasible)

- Push pins
- Ribbon or cloth tape
- Acrylic paint or colored pencil

American artists William Michael Harnett and John Peto specialized in trompe l'oeil (fool the eye) paintings that might be compared to the hyper-realist or super realist paintings of some of today's artists. Your still life items would probably be very different from those of their day. They used pipes, musical instruments, writing quills and ink, leather-bound books, and candles. The items from your desk might include a candy wrapper, baseball, make-up or jewelry, soft drink can, ballpoint pens, book bag, or camera. Harnett's and Peto's "bulletin boards" were strips of painted ribbon into which were stuck photos, letters, cards, and newspapers, that were convincing because of ragged dog-eared edges.

1. Group a number of items on the wall. These could be things you find in your pockets or purse such as homework, a playing card, jewelry, award ribbon or certificate, a comb—whatever is available and personal. The background could be white or colored. Hold items in place with push pins or string. Or use ribbon to hold things in place, as trompe l'oeil painters did.

2. With pencil, *lightly* sketch in the major shapes. If you are working in watercolor, you will not want the pencil marks to show. Include the shadows in your composition because they will make the work look more realistic.

3. To paint in watercolor, tempera, or acrylic, attempt to make everything as realistic as possible. Background shadows may be painted in violet or gray. The background may be something as simple as white paper, or it could be a "wooden" or cork background.

4. If you prefer, this could simply be a still life, with everything painted in the dark, rich tones the Victorians preferred. Rather than using black to make dark areas, try using dark violet, dark blue, and dark green. Try graying colors by adding the complement (such as a touch of green to red, or a little violet added to yellow).

Drawn after *Still-Life—Violin and Music*, 1888
William Michael Harnett
The Metropolitan Museum of Art

Drawn from *A Deception*, 1862
Raphaelle Peale,
Private Collection

PROJECT 5-4: **COLOR WITH MARY CASSATT**

FOR THE TEACHER

SLIDE #15: *At the Theater (Woman in a Loge)* **c. 1879, Mary Cassatt, 55.4 × 46.1 cm., pastel on paper, The Nelson-Atkins Museum of Art, Kansas City, Missouri; Purchase, acquired through the generosity of an anonymous donor**

Mary Cassatt (1845–1926) was the only American who exhibited with the original group of Impressionists. She was born in Pennsylvania, studied at the Pennsylvania Academy of Fine Arts, and went to Paris in 1868 to continue her studies. She exhibited in the Paris Salon in 1872 and 1874, and then exhibited with the Impressionists. She was credited with the wide acceptance and success in the United States of the Impressionists, whom she introduced into the wealthy circle of her family and friends in Philadelphia. Edgar Degas was her mentor, and her skills in oils and pastels were developed when they worked together. She cared for him when he went blind late in life. It is ironic that she also became practically blind in 1914. Her most notable contribution to the Impressionist movement was the obvious influence in some of her works of the Japanese prints that had become so popular in Europe. The simplicity and areas of flat color introduced a new way of seeing.

Well-Known Work by Mary Cassatt

The Loge, 1882, National Gallery of Art, Washington, D.C.

At the Opera, 1879, Museum of Fine Arts, Boston

After the Bath, c. 1907, The Cleveland Museum of Art, Cleveland, Ohio

In the Loge, c. 1879, Philadelphia Museum of Art

Mother and Child, 1900, Brooklyn Museum, New York

The Caress, 1902, National Museum of American Art, Washington, D.C.

Woman and Child Driving, 1879, Philadelphia Museum of Art

Maternal Kiss, 1897, Philadelphia Museum of Art

The Bath, c. 1891, Chicago Art Institute

PREPARATION

Almost any material can be combined with pastels. Pastels come in a variety of types, including traditional hard or soft chalk pastels in stick or pencil form, oil pastels, or oil sticks. Depending on the materials with which the pastels are combined, they can almost resemble oil paintings. One major advantage to pastel, of course, is that it is not necessary to clean brushes, and they are portable. They can be used on any type of paper or canvas.

To open students' minds to the potential of pastel, put out all the materials that can be combined with pastel such as fine-line marker, ink, ballpoint pen, charcoal, watercolor, gel medium, and fixative. Suggest that students experiment on a non-picture with pastel by first making simple marks, then by combining pastel with other materials. Students are not threatened by fear of failure if you assure them that this *must not* be a picture, but just experiments with materials. (Project 5-5 is a second project using photocopied family group photos and pastels to do further experimentation. There is no "For the Teacher" page for Project 5-5.)

ADDITIONAL SUGGESTION

- Have students do a figure study or still life with oil pastel on black paper. The intense colors of oil pastels look wonderful on a dark background.

Photo 5-4. *The Loge,* **1882, Mary Cassatt, oil on canvas, 31-³/₈ × 25-¹/₈ inches, Chester Dale Collection, National Gallery of Art, Washington, D.C.**

PROJECT 5-4: **COLOR WITH MARY CASSATT**

MATERIALS

- Colored pencil
- Pastels
- Oil pastels
- Tissue
- Turpentine
- Markers: fluorescent, fine line, and watercolor
- Ink
- Fixative (or hair spray)
- Paper (drawing, construction, or pastel paper)
- Watercolor
- Charcoal

Drawn after Sketch of
Mother and Daughter Looking at the Baby, **c. 1908**
Mary Cassatt
Maier Museum of Art
Randolph-Macon Womens' College

Although Mary Cassatt painted both in oil and pastel, her colors were soft, and one tends to think of her as a pastel artist. Pastel is a versatile material that can be used by itself or mixed with other media to give many different effects. Mary Cassatt's subject matter often was women, children, or mothers and children together, frequently family members, although she had no children of her own. She often showed her subjects in interior settings or at places with dramatic lighting such as the theater or opera.

1. Before beginning a composition, experiment with several different ways to use pastels from the list given here. This first piece of paper must *not* be a picture or have anything realistic in it. You are just experimenting with making marks.

    - Dark pastel underneath, lighter on top
    - Pastel, complementary colors
    - Pastel over watercolor
    - Pastel sprayed with fixative, then reworked
    - Scumbling (one color on top of another, letting underneath one show through)
    - Pastel pencil underneath, soft pastel on top
    - Oil pastel and turpentine
    - Cross hatching
    - Ballpoint pen and pastel
    - Charcoal and pastel
    - Oil pastels covered with undiluted roughly brushed acrylic medium, then second layers built onto that
    - All strokes going the same direction
    - Pastel combined with charcoal
    - Oil pastel over fluorescent markers

- Ink drawing with pastel on top
- Blending colors with a tissue
- Oil pastel drawn into turpentine
- Pastel on canvas
- Using a palette knife to apply pastel dust mixed with polymer medium
- Working with the side of the pastel
- Pen and ink and pastel

2. On a clean sheet of paper, lightly draw two heads close together. One could be larger than the other, to indicate mother and child, but if you work from your imagination rather than from a model or a photograph, you will be more free to experiment with materials rather than try to make a "likeness." You will find that no matter what your picture looks like, someone will know that it is supposed to be people. If you wish, make more than one drawing.

3. Allow the drawing to dry if you have used wet media with pastel. Place it on the floor or a wall, and look at it from a distance the next day. Continue working, standing off from time to time to see if you could add more color somewhere.

4. Experiment with using pastel and various other media. So many materials work well with pastel, and you may find you can get interesting lines and contrasts through combining media.

Drawn from *The Loge*, 1882
Mary Cassatt
National Gallery of Art, Washington, D.C.

PROJECT 5-5: **FAMILY PORTRAIT COLLAGE**

MATERIALS

- Photocopies of family group photos
- Polymer medium
- 12 × 18-inch heavy watercolor paper
- Pastels
- Newsprint

Mary Cassatt was one of the original Impressionists, whose work was mostly in pastel or oil paint. Her subject matter was almost exclusively portraits of friends or of families with children. Your interpretation of Cassatt's work will be called "appropriationism" because you are using artwork (the photos) created by someone else. Photocopies of your own family photos will be used directly on the paper.

1. Cut or tear the photocopies out and use polymer medium (or thinned white glue) to affix them to the paper. In addition to the photos you have placed on the paper, add some of the leftover photocopy paper to give interesting shapes and texture to the background.

2. While you are waiting for the paper to dry, experiment with "mark-making" with pastel on a piece of newsprint or drawing paper. This experiment will *not* be a picture, but simply trying to see what works when trying out colors next to each other. You may find that you prefer straight lines, while another person will work with the side of the chalk, or another might make curvy, exotic marks or short strokes.

3. When the paper has dried, work directly on the composition by drawing with pastels. You may not wish to draw directly on the faces, and they are only a small part of the composition. Let it show some of the experiments you made when you were making marks with pastels.

4. Because this is a collage, you can add colored paper and objects, continuing to build up until you feel your composition is complete. You can even continue to use new media such as ink, acrylic paint, or whatever else adds to the effect.

PROJECT 5-6: STAINED GLASS/PLASTIC WINDOWS

FOR THE TEACHER

SLIDE #16: (Left) *Hollyhocks,* 1882, 87-¼ × 37-¼ inches, (Right) *Flowering Cherry Tree and Peony,* 1882, 87-¼ × 37-¼ inches, windows, John LaFarge, The Saint Louis Art Museum. Funds given by the Decorative Arts Society in honor of 20th Anniversary of the Friends of The St. Louis Art Museum

Stained glass windows have existed for almost a thousand years and are enjoying a resurgence of popularity. During Victorian times stained glass was used for windows, lamp shades, folding screens, and room dividers.

Louis Comfort Tiffany (1848–1933) and John LaFarge (1835–1910) were well-known artists, whose work in stained glass using Art Nouveau (new art) designs continues to be cherished. Art Nouveau designs incorporated forms from nature and curving sinuous lines. Both artists worked in a manner that differed from Medieval glass artisans in that they used several layers of glass in some places to give a shimmering luminescence to their creations. Their designs reflected the love of nature that was typical of the Victorians. LaFarge showed an Asian influence in his work, based on his travels in the Far East. Tiffany was probably best known for his lamps and vases. Both artists created window designs.

EXAMPLES OF STAINED GLASS BY LAFARGE

Peonies in the Wind with Kakemono Borders, c. 1893, John LaFarge, National Museum of American Art, Washington, D.C.

Peacocks and Peonies I and II, 1882, John LaFarge, National Museum of American Art, Washington, D.C.

Morning Glories, 1878, John LaFarge, Museum of Fine Arts, Boston

Peonies Blowing in the Wind with Kakemono Border, 1889, John LaFarge, Nelson-Atkins Museum of Art, Kansas City, Missouri

PREPARATION

Show students Art Nouveau designs, which may be found in a variety of sources such as poster or wallpaper designs. You may wish to try this project before you teach it, though part of the fun is discovering with the students what happens when you experiment with adding, blending, and removing color. Pure black or colored glue may be purchased, or create your own by adding India ink to white glue and shaking the bottle. The pre-mixed black will be a little richer (use one 4-ounce bottle for four students). Have students try a variety of methods of applying marker.

ADDITIONAL SUGGESTIONS

- Make stained glass by creating a black glue pattern on tagboard, allowing it to dry, painting with watercolor or tempera paint, and then coloring on it with oil pastels. Rich colors will result when the underpainting is allowed to show through. It may be necessary to polish the raised areas of glue with a piece of tissue to make them shiny again.

- Create Art Nouveau patterns by trailing glue on a 4-inch cardboard square. When the glue has dried, brush on ink, and make prints on a 12 × 18-inch piece of drawing paper by repeating the square print inside dark marker lines created to resemble a stained glass window. An alternative is to do this with a 4 × 4-inch lino-cut.

- Frank Lloyd Wright also designed many details using stained glass, but used purely geometric forms such as rectangles and circles, combined with lines. Have students design "Frank Lloyd Wright windows" using rulers, compasses, and brightly colored markers or paper for filling in.

- If real flowers are available, they can be photocopied onto a piece of transparency film. (First protect the surface of the copier with clear transparency film.) Remove any stem and lower the lid of the copier to flatten the flowers as much as possible. These can then be copied and hand-colored with permanent markers or acrylic paint (which will stick to the film). Use permanent black marker to draw around to make it look like stained glass.

- Photocopy any Art Nouveau design onto overhead transparencies and have students fill in areas using acrylic paint on the underside. For shading, use lighter colors first.

Photo 5-5. Student Dawn Citrin's stained glass window done with black glue and permanent marker on overhead projector plastic.

PROJECT 5-6: **STAINED GLASS/PLASTIC WINDOWS**

MATERIALS

- Overhead transparencies
- Black glue (or add ink to white glue)
- Alcohol
- Tissues or soft paper towels
- 8-½ × 11-inch white typing paper
- Pencils
- Permanent markers (6 or 7 basic colors)
- Transparent tape

Drawn after *Hollyhocks,* 1882
John LaFarge
The Saint Louis Art Museum

Victorian stained glass created in the manner of Louis Comfort Tiffany and John LaFarge had a rich shimmering color created by using more than one layer of glass. Your "stained glass" will be created by coloring on both sides of the plastic and blending colors.

1. Try several rectangular thumbnail sketches of a subject such as plants, trees, landscapes, or leaves. Victorian artists were very interested in nature, and a single flower might be the basis for an entire design.

2. Draw your design with pencil on typing paper. Color it, or write what your colors will be. Real stained glass is worked in small sections, with the glass held in place with "lead" or copper channels. Create channels and a border with line, approximately ½ inch inside the edge as if your "window" might be actually used in a house.

3. Tape a piece of plastic on top of your design. Using both hands, hold the bottle of black glue upside down and press to create a line design following your pattern. Allow the glue to dry overnight.

4. Applying the marker is the artistry of this project. Color within the black glue lines. Direction should also be controlled. Protect the working surface with paper, as you will be coloring on the front and back of the plastic right to the edges. Try some or all of the following methods to apply the marker:
   - Make horizontal strokes.
   - Cover with marker, then use a cotton swab to make the pattern.
   - Create a pattern with your finger wrapped in tissue that was moistened with alcohol.
   - Turn the plastic over and use a different color blend on the back.
   - With a tissue, wipe off part of the color.
   - "Spritz" dried marker on the glass with alcohol or glass cleaner in a spray bottle. Let it dry with the spotted effect.
   - Use a pencil eraser, pencil point, or your finger to create pattern.

5. For display, tape on an outside window (or white paper) with clear tape. Tape several together to make an interesting design, or frame by mounting inside a black posterboard mat. Overhead transparency frames may be purchased that are the exact size to display your work.

PROJECT 5-7: **WATERCOLOR LIKE WINSLOW (HOMER)**

FOR THE TEACHER

SLIDE #17: *The Gulfstream,* **1889, Winslow Homer, 28.9 × 50.9 cm., watercolor, The Art Institute of Chicago, Mr. and Mrs. Martin A. Ryerson Collection, 1933**

Winslow Homer (1836–1910) had several distinct periods of art in his life, almost as if he were three different painters. He was a magazine illustrator for *Harpers* during the Civil War. After the Civil War he visited Paris and was elected an associate of the National Academy of Painters before his 30th birthday. On his return from France, he did realistic paintings of contemporary life, often including women and children. From 1875 to 1879 he painted African-American people who were no longer slaves, but still living in poverty. In his later years he became a marine painter working mostly in watercolor and some oil paintings. He painted many hunting and fishing scenes and was as adept at painting animals, scenery, and people as he was at painting water scenes.

Examples of Homer's Paintings

Prisoners from the Front, 1866, Museum of Fine Arts, Boston

Country School, 1871, oil on canvas, The Saint Louis Art Museum

The Croquet Game, 1866, oil on canvas, Art Institute of Chicago

Two Men in a Canoe, 1895, Portland Museum of Art, Portland, Maine

Breezing Up (A Fair Wind), 1876, National Gallery of Art, Washington, D.C.

Two Boys Rowing, 1880, Museum of Fine Arts, Boston

Taking on Wet Provisions, Key West, 1903, The Metropolitan Museum of Art, New York

PREPARATION

Many students have not had much experience with watercolor, so it is important for them to experiment with technique before beginning a composition. Talk about the importance of sketching lightly, then planning white space before painting. Explain about building up intensity of color by glazing, gradually adding pigment. Let them try some of the methods described on the student handout. Inspire them to paint as Homer did, by painting what was around him. He chose subjects of favorite places. Students can relate to this by thinking about places they like to go when they are on vacation or have time to go someplace for a weekend.

ADDITIONAL SUGGESTIONS

- Many students are apprehensive about watercolor, and would like to simply paint non-realistic shapes. Allow them to experiment freely, but from time to time discuss their progress, giving suggestions that might result in an actual composition. While Homer worked realistically, later painters—such as Mark Rothko (1903–1970), Morris Louis (1912–1962), Jackson Pollock (1912–1956), Sam Francis (1923–1994), Frank Stella (b. 1936), and Helen Frankenthaler (b. 1928)—worked loosely with color, still completing paintings that were dynamic compositions.

- Make an abstract landscape simply by working in horizontal lines of color. Encourage students to use color freely, not settling for just a blue sky or green band of trees, but using water freely, allowing one color to bleed into another. They may wish to tilt the paper sometimes, watching for the "happy accident," recognizing it and taking advantage of it. Remind them to allow areas of white to show at times to add sparkle. Discuss how having the paper darker at the top and bottom, and lighter near a horizon line might give depth to the landscape.

- Have students use real leaves as part of their design. Have leaves available, then have students wet their paper and, while it is wet, apply watercolor. Leaves and grass pressed into the watercolor for a time leave a design when the leaf is removed.

Photo 5-6. *The Wrecked Schooner,* **c. 1910, Winslow Homer, watercolor and charcoal, Museum Purchase, The Saint Louis Art Museum.**

Photo 5-7A. *The Herring Net,* **1885, Winslow Homer, oil on canvas, 30-⅛ × 48-⅜ inches, Mr. and Mrs. Martin A. Ryerson Collection, The Art Institute of Chicago.**

PROJECT 5-7: WATERCOLOR LIKE WINSLOW (HOMER)

MATERIALS

- 6 × 9-inch watercolor paper
- Pencils
- Brushes
- Paper towels
- 12 × 18-inch watercolor paper
- Watercolors
- Water bowls (clean and rinse water)

Photo 5-7B. Sample brush strokes.

An American watercolorist such as Winslow Homer depicted nature as realistically as possible. Before beginning your own "nature watercolor," experiment with a variety of methods. Plan ahead to preserve white portions of the paper. Lightly sketch the design on paper before beginning.

- *Dry brush:* On a separate piece of paper, remove most of the pigment from the brush so that when you apply pigment to the watercolor paper, the white will show through. (This might be done on top of an already painted area to give emphasis.)

- *Wet-in-wet:* This technique is often used for clouds or water. Apply water to the portion you want to paint. While it is wet, add pigment to the water and watch it spread. You can add more than one color, and allow them to flow together. You can also blot this if you wish a different effect.

- *Sponging:* Mix color in the lid of the watercolor box. Dip a sponge or wadded plastic wrap into the watery pigment and "print" with it. This is especially effective for trees, grass, or water. One color can be placed on top of another.

- *Blotting:* Blotting wet pigment gives another effect altogether.

- *Paint with cardboard:* With a small rectangle of corrugated or other type of cardboard, dip an end into wet pigment in the top of the paintbox and use it to drag paint across the picture. This is particularly good for painting water or architectural details such as fences or doors. Of course, it makes perfect straight lines for accent.

- *Stipple:* Use just the end of a stiff brush dipped in paint to make dots of color. Closely related colors can be blended together to imply roundness in a form. This is much the same method used by the Impressionist Georges Seurat to do his pointillism.

- *Salt:* Sprinkle Kosher or coarse salt into watercolor. It causes the paint to gather around it for an unusual effect.

- *Lines in watercolor:* Use any sharp instrument to scrape lines into the watercolor to make grass or other lines when needed.

- *Watercolor resist:* Make lines or solid white areas with rubber cement. Allow these to dry, then paint on top of it. When the watercolor has dried, use an eraser or your finger to rub off the rubber cement. White crayon can also be used before paint is applied.

- *Even wash:* Make broad areas of color by mixing a color and applying in even strokes across the page.

- *Graduated wash:* Begin with darker pigment, then gradually dilute it as you go up or down the page.

PROJECT 5-8: **WEATHERVANE**

FOR THE TEACHER

The oldest recorded weathervane was created in the first century B.C. in Greece. Weathervanes were used to tell the direction of the wind, which made them the only means of weather forecasting until the barometer was invented. Weathervanes are considered one of the major American craft forms, and are so valued by collectors that a dealer once took one off a barn by use of a helicopter. The oldest U.S. weathervane is the grasshopper on Faneuil Hall in Boston.

Materials used were iron, wood, tin, or most commonly copper. Many of them were gilded. Designs varied widely, from a simple arrow or banneret to farm animals. The use of a rooster weathervane dated back to the ninth century, when a pope decreed that Christian churches would have a rooster weathervane to remind Christians to pray. The weathervane was used atop public buildings such as libraries and city halls, as well as on farm buildings. Recently several American architects were asked to design weathervanes, and came up with unique, modern designs. Popular design motifs included the arrow, banneret, fish, whales, eagles, ships, mermaids, angels, locomotives, "Miss Liberty," fast horses, sheep, or cows. Silhouette vanes were often made in Victorian times because they were easier to make than the earlier sculptural vanes. They had to balance perfectly to swing in the wind.

Famous Weathervanes

Grasshopper weathervane, 1742, Shem Drowne, Faneuil Hall, Boston

Ship weathervane, last half of 19th century, Smithsonian Institution, Washington, D.C.

Fish weathervane, 1893, Fiske Company, Shelburne Museum, Shelburne, Vermont

Rooster, 1722, First Church, Cambridge, Massachusetts

Angel Gabriel, 1848, Mormon Temple, Nauvoo, Illinois

PREPARATION

Find books with pictures of weathervanes and have students try to draw a design that is personal or of special appeal to them. Suggest that they come up with a symbol that would represent the culture they live in now, or something in which they are especially interested. Twentieth-century weathervanes have been made with trains, cars, and even airplanes.

ADDITIONAL SUGGESTIONS

- Use copper-colored tooling foil. Have students make the same type of design as they would make for a three-dimensional weathervane. Transfer the design to the foil and cut it out. Place the foil on a folded section of newspaper, and use a dull pencil or ballpoint pen to make a repoussé design. Use white glue to mount the finished weathervane to heavy black mount board to display.

- Have students make a three-dimensional weathervane from found objects of wood or metal. This could challenge students' creativity, yet give them a start. The weathervane has to be attached to a stand of some sort, and be seen from both sides.

- Have students cut out a silhouette for a shop sign from cardboard or foam core. These were usually made of wrought iron, so they could be simply painted black, with lighter highlights (foam core is also available in black and other colors). Suggestions would be a boot, top hat, cow's or horse's head, eyeglasses, etc. Hang them from a ceiling at a ninety degree angle to a wall so they will be seen from both sides.

PROJECT 5-8:   **WEATHERVANE**

MATERIALS

- Cardboard
- Heavy-duty aluminum foil *or* copper-colored tooling foil
- X-acto™ knife or scissors
- Thinned white glue or polymer medium
- Ink
- Turquoise acrylic paint
- Straight pins
- ⅛-inch dowels (or wire coat hangers)
- 2 × 6 × 8-inch board with hole for dowel or wire

To make a modern weathervane, try to make something personal: a silhouette of your car, your Zodiac sign, a pet, a girl friend or boy friend, or a building. Early farmers often used simple vanes such as an arrow or a banner, but they also did elaborate ones based on a horse, sheep, cow, eagle, or sailing ship. Many used very elaborate designs, but usually they were meaningful to the person who had it made.

1. Do some thumbnail sketches to get some ideas. The first drawings can be very rough. You may need to do a little research in an encyclopedia to get an idea.

2. When you have decided on a design, draw it carefully on a piece of paper the exact size you intend to make it. It should fit within a 12 × 18-inch sheet of paper. If you intend to have decorative cutouts or designs, draw those also.

3. Go over the back of your drawing with pencil so you can transfer it to cardboard. Trace it onto the cardboard. Carefully cut it out with an X-acto™ knife. You can make a more interesting texture by gluing more layers of cardboard in places on top, or make a line design by gluing yarn in place. You could also make elaborate designs with lines of glue, which you would allow to dry overnight.

4. When the base has dried, spread thinned glue evenly over the entire front of the weathervane and place a layer of aluminum foil on top, smoothing it in place carefully so it adheres to the cardboard. Glue and tape a dowel to the back. Turn the cardboard form on its face and put glue around the back outside edges. Fold the front aluminum foil over the back edges and glue in place. Cut a matching piece of foil to glue on the back, enclosing the dowel and raw edges.

5. Dilute turquoise paint, use tissue to quickly apply it to the foil. Wipe paint off the surface, allowing it to remain in lines. The dowel can be stuck into a base made of 2 × 6 × 8-inch board, or your weathervane could be hung from the ceiling for display.

 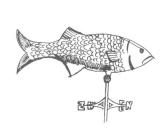  

PROJECT 5-9: **TINTYPE**

FOR THE TEACHER

Photography began about the middle of the nineteenth century. Louis Daguerre (1759-1851), a Frenchman, created a photographic process by coating a silver- or copper-colored plate and exposing a subject directly onto the plate. These plates look "positive" or "negative," depending on how the light hits them. This process was time consuming and expensive, and the resulting images were kept in protective folding cases made of wood, or later of a plastic-like material made of ground sawdust, shellac, and color.

This project allows students to create a daguerreotype lookalike by bringing in old black-and-white family photographs (or baby photos of themselves) to be copied onto an overhead transparency. A less expensive version, the tintype, was printed on tin, and again, usually kept in a frame.

PREPARATION

Photocopy students' old family photos onto overhead transparencies (you can do three to four per sheet), then have them carefully cut apart. If you prefer, you could photocopy from a photography book for them to have "instant ancestor" pictures.

ADDITIONAL SUGGESTIONS

- Mount reduced transparencies of family photos between glass slide holders (available at a photo shop) and create a "lantern-slide" show.

- Reverse painting on glass was a popular Victorian pasttime. Students may paint a scene on clear plastic or window glass with acrylic paint. Remind them to paint the lightest areas first before doing the darkest areas. Back these with white or black paper.

- Silhouettes painted on glass were also very popular at this time, and students may trace around figures cut from a magazine onto white paper. Have them tape clear plastic on top of the paper, and paint silhouettes onto the plastic with black acrylic paint. A watercolor landscape background could then be painted onto a separate piece of white paper before putting the plastic and watercolor together inside a mat.

Photo 5-8. The photocopies of old photos were placed on cardboard with clear overhead plastic on top. The aluminum foil was then tooled and frames made to hold the pictures in place.

PROJECT 5-9: **TINTYPE**

MATERIALS

- Overhead transparencies
- Cardboard (not too thick)
- Heavy-duty aluminum foil
- Copper-colored tooling foil
- Brown acrylic paint
- Ballpoint pens
- Pad of folded newspaper
- Ruler
- Masking tape
- X-acto™ knife

You will be creating a frame for a family photo by doing a technique called repoussé on heavy-duty foil.

1. For this project you will need two pieces of cardboard 1 to 2 inches larger than the photograph. Measure the photograph, and on one of the two pieces, use an X-acto™ knife to carefully cut an opening that is ¼-inch smaller all around than the size of the photograph. *Safety note: When cutting with an X-acto™ knife, work on a magazine or cardboard to protect the table, and always keep the non-cutting hand behind the blade.*

2. Cut a piece of heavy-duty aluminum foil at least 3 inches bigger all around than the outside cardboard dimension. Lay the piece of cardboard with the opening cut in it on top of the foil and trace it inside and outside so the outline is scored in the foil. Place the foil on a pad of newspaper, and work the design in the outlined area with a dull pencil or ballpoint pen. Use a ruler for straight lines. Work on both the back and the front for a three-dimensional design. The design can be made on a piece of paper and traced through with a pencil. The more elaborate the design, the better.

3. Poke a hole in the center of the foil, and cut it on the inside of the frame to ½ inch larger than the opening will be. Cut slits almost to the corners. Fold over the cardboard frame to back inside. On the outside, trim the corners almost to the corner, but leave a little for turning and to allow for the thickness of the cardboard.

4. Center and tape the photocopied photograph, plastic, and aluminum foil of the same size on the plain piece of cardboard (the foil underneath will make it look like a tintype). Place the aluminum covered frame on top of the photo, and fold over the edges on the back of the cardboard, taping them in place.

5. Wipe the outside with thinned brown acrylic paint or brown permanent marker and wipe off, to allow the aluminum to show through. If desired, you could cut a piece of tagboard slightly smaller than the frame and glue it onto the back to cover the taped foil edges.

   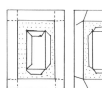

PROJECT 5-10: **SUN GARDENS—VICTORIAN PHOTOGRAMS**

FOR THE TEACHER

Victorians had wide-ranging interests in the world of nature, and some men and women spent leisure time exploring scientific principles. During the mid-nineteenth century, one of photography's pioneers, Sir John Herschel, was making cyanotype prints of natural objects such as wheat, ferns, flowers, and feathers. In Victorian times, an Englishwoman, Anna Atkins, further explored this photographic process, applying the photographic blueprint process to science by exploring and cataloguing plant species. These were sometimes called Algae prints. Sometimes leaves were "anatomized" to show all the cellular structure.* The cyanotype process was fairly complex, involving coating paper with chemicals, then exposing the coated paper to the sun. This project is a simple version of the same process, making prints on blueprint paper in sunlight. No darkroom is necessary.

Author's Note: Although I was not successful at "anatomizing" prints, a call to the Missouri Botanical garden ascertained that this is called "Leaf Clearing," and is done in the fumes of a strong base solution, wearing heavy gloves. Perhaps you might get someone in a science department to work with you to do leaf clearing.

PREPARATION

Blueprints can be made any size, and there are several ways to expose the paper to the sun (or photoflood lamps). It is not possible to give specific times for exposure because this varies considerably with the time of day and the intensity of the sun in various seasons and regions. To know if you have given sufficient exposure, watch the uncovered yellow-coated side of the paper. When the exposed areas turn white, the print is completed. While the Diazo paper can be purchased in long rolls 36 × 1000 feet and blueprints can be made any size, the directions for this are for blueprints approximately 8 × 10 inches. Incidentally, the large roll lasts for years! The paper can be cut in semi-darkness and stored in a black bag (made of black plastic or construction paper). Have students bring natural or man-made objects from home.

ADDITIONAL SUGGESTIONS

- Have students make large 36 × 48-inch blueprints in a darkened room (such as a closet) using an overhead projector in place of sunlight. Tape the blueprint paper onto a wall with masking tape, yellow side up. With the projector approximately six feet from the wall, expose an image taped to the surface of the projector for approximately two hours. This image can be from a Kodalith® transparency (a photographic process made in a darkroom), a fine-line drawing on an overhead transparency, or cut black paper. Develop this in a large box in which approximately two tablespoons of industrial strength ammonia are placed in a bottle cap or similar container. The ammonia fumes will develop the blueprint. *Safety Note: Handle the ammonia carefully! Do not breathe in the fumes.*

- Use black construction paper the same size of the blueprint paper and have students cut designs from it. When this is held in contact with the blueprint paper under glass and exposed, the open areas in the design will remain white; those protected by the black paper will be deep blue. Develop these in large inverted jars with a small capful of ammonia.

- A huge (15 to 20 feet long × 36 inches wide) classroom blueprint can be made by planning ahead. Have each student decide what he or she will place on the blueprint. These can range from drawings on clear transparencies, objects such as shoes, body parts such as legs and feet, heads, hands, keys, cut-outs from black construction paper, or objects from nature. Cut a long piece of blueprint paper in semi-darkness and cut a piece of black roll paper of the same length. Place the black paper on top of the blueprint paper and roll them up together. Find a sunny spot inside the school (or outside on a calm day), and take the entire class and their objects. Unroll the paper, leaving the black paper on top. Have students stand on either side of the paper, ranged along the sides, ready to fling what they have on the paper (sometimes students will lie full length on it). You will have as little as 10 seconds to expose the paper, or as much as several minutes. When the uncovered areas on the yellow paper have turned white, quickly replace the black roll paper on top, roll it up, and carry it back to the room to develop. Loosely unroll the paper in the large "tank" in your room (I used four pieces of plexiglass covered in black roll paper), with a "lid" that consisted of another piece of covered plexiglass. (A large inverted cardboard box would also serve.) Place approximately ⅛ cup of industrial strength ammonia in a low container and place inside the loosely rolled paper. *Safety Note: Take a deep breath before opening the ammonia container and putting it in place.* Leave to develop overnight. The fumes dissipate by morning.

PROJECT 5-10: **SUN GARDENS—VICTORIAN PHOTOGRAMS**

MATERIALS

- Diazo black-line positive dry reproduction paper (available at blueprint supply houses in roll or cut paper)
- Ammonia (standard or industrial strength)
- Large plastic mayonnaise jars
- Bottle lids
- Plate glass or plexiglass
- Ferns, flowers, lace, feathers
- Overhead transparencies
- Black permanent markers
- Black construction paper (same size as paper)

Making photograms or, as the Victorians called them, "Sun Gardens," will challenge you to think about the arrangement of objects as a work of art. Some of the delicate subjects favored by the Victorians were lace, ferns, flowers, leaves, and other natural objects. They sometimes considered these works of art as scientific records of plants, writing the names on the blueprints. If you use leaves, combine written words with the actual plants by writing the names on clear plastic transparency film. Place the film on top of the blueprint paper before putting objects on top.

1. Select the objects you will use. Use several similar objects, such as sheaves of wheat or leaves, combined with something solid in appearance, such as a leaf. It is not necessary to fill the entire composition to make it interesting. Think about the principles of composition: balance, repetition, emphasis, and space.

2. You might prefer to make a "romantic" composition, using objects popular in Victorian times such as lace, feathers, a locket, net, even a black construction paper silhouette (drawn freehand or found in a magazine, glued onto black construction paper and cut out with an X-acto™ knife). *Safety Note: When cutting with an X-acto™ knife, always keep your fingers behind the cutting hand and cut on a soft surface to protect the table.*

3. If you intend to use writing or to combine drawing on a piece of transparency film with permanent marker, do the drawing or writing before you expose your blueprint to the sun. Plan exactly where you will place objects before beginning, as the paper will quickly become exposed. If you do words on a computer, the words can be printed on transparency film directly in a laser printer, or copied in a copy machine from a paper printout.

4. Remove the blueprint paper from its black envelope, put the yellow side up in a sunlit place, and place the objects on the blueprint paper quickly, holding them in place with a piece of glass. Watch the uncovered areas until they turn white, which indicates that the exposure is complete.

5. Place the print (yellow side inward) inside an inverted wide-mouth gallon jar. Pour a small capful of ammonia and place it on a table, then center the jar over it. The fumes from the ammonia will develop the blueprint. When you remove it from the jar, keep the open end of the jar facing downward to keep the ammonia fumes inside. *Safety Note: Take a deep breath before opening the ammonia jar and pouring it. Wash hands with soap and water if you should spill any on yourself.*

6. When the blueprint is fully developed, mount it in a pre-cut mat, on paper, or on a transparency film frame.

EARLY TWENTIETH CENTURY (1900 to 1920)

EARLY TWENTIETH CENTURY
TIME LINE

	1900	1903	1907	1910	1913	1917	1920
Painting Sculpture Architecture Folk Art	Ashcan School 1900—1920 Art Nouveau 1880–1910 Cecilia Beaux 1863–1942 Charles Demuth 1883–1935	George Bellows 1882–1925 Robert Henri 1865–1929 Childe Hassam 1859–1935	Cass Gilbert 1859–1934 Marcel Duchamp 1887–1968 Photo-Secession 1905–1917 Frederic Remington 1861–1909		Armory Show, 1913 Marsden Hartley 1877–1943 Addison Mizner 1872–1933	Dada, c. 1915 American Modernism 1915 Stuart Davis 1894–1964 Maurice Prendergast 1859–1924 Synchromism 1913–1918	John Gutzon Borglum 1867–1941 John Marin 1870–1953 Georgia O'Keeffe 1887–1926
Politics	1901 Taft assassinated; T. R. Roosevelt becomes Pres. Wm. McKinley Taft elected President 1900	1904—T. Roosevelt elected President	1913 Balkan War	1914 Archduke Ferdinand assassinated	1913 Income tax begins	1916 Wilson re-elected	1920 Warren G. Harding Pres.
Literature	1902 *Hound of the Baskervilles*, A. Conan Doyle John Steinbeck 1902–1968			1913 *Pygmalion*, George Bernard Shaw		Jack London 1876–1917 1918 Willa Cather, *My Antonia*	1920 *Main Street*, Sinclair Lewis
Science	1902 Radium discovered, Marie and Pierre Curie		1906 Pure Food and Drug Act 1905 *Theory of Relativity*, Albert Einstein	1906 Wasserman test for syphilis 1910 Gene theory of heredity		1914 Leica camera	
Music and Entertainment	1901 Ragtime Jazz Johann Strauss 1825–1899		Anton Dvorak 1841–1904		1917 "Over There," George M. Cohan	1918—Leonard Bernstein born	1919 Los Angeles Symphony's 1st performance
Current Events	1900 Boxer Rebellion in China	1904 Panama Canal begun	1904 World's Fair in St. Louis 1904–1905 Russian-Japanese War		Execution of Mata Hari as a spy, 1917 1913 Assembly line, Henry Ford	1915 Lusitania sunk 1918 World War I	1920— Prohibition begins

EARLY TWENTIETH CENTURY ARCHITECTURE

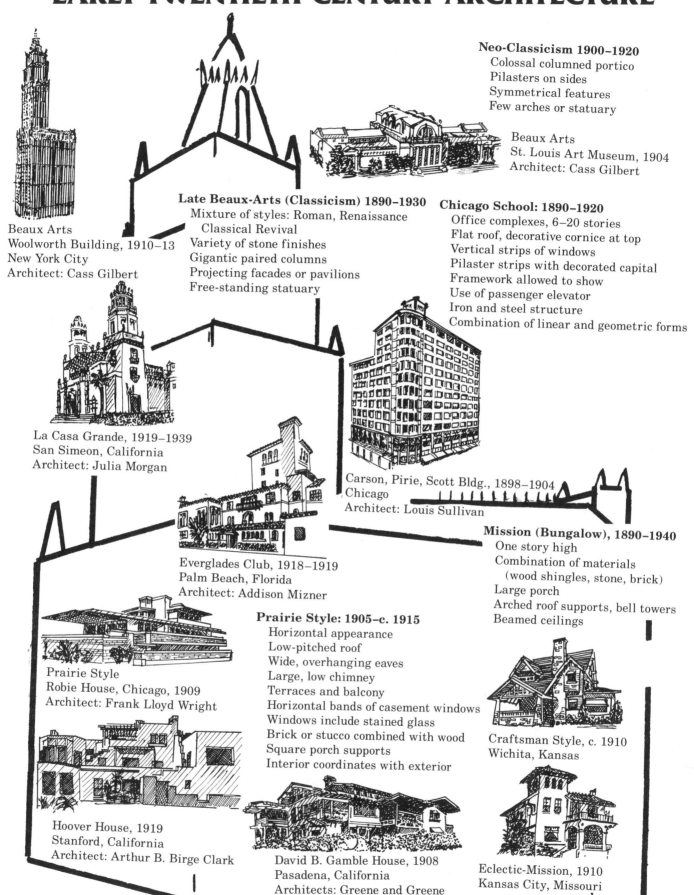

Neo-Classicism 1900–1920
Colossal columned portico
Pilasters on sides
Symmetrical features
Few arches or statuary

Beaux Arts
St. Louis Art Museum, 1904
Architect: Cass Gilbert

Beaux Arts
Woolworth Building, 1910–13
New York City
Architect: Cass Gilbert

Late Beaux-Arts (Classicism) 1890–1930
Mixture of styles: Roman, Renaissance
  Classical Revival
Variety of stone finishes
Gigantic paired columns
Projecting facades or pavilions
Free-standing statuary

Chicago School: 1890–1920
Office complexes, 6–20 stories
Flat roof, decorative cornice at top
Vertical strips of windows
Pilaster strips with decorated capital
Framework allowed to show
Use of passenger elevator
Iron and steel structure
Combination of linear and geometric forms

La Casa Grande, 1919–1939
San Simeon, California
Architect: Julia Morgan

Carson, Pirie, Scott Bldg., 1898–1904
Chicago
Architect: Louis Sullivan

Everglades Club, 1918–1919
Palm Beach, Florida
Architect: Addison Mizner

Mission (Bungalow), 1890–1940
One story high
Combination of materials
  (wood shingles, stone, brick)
Large porch
Arched roof supports, bell towers
Beamed ceilings

Prairie Style: 1905–c. 1915
Horizontal appearance
Low-pitched roof
Wide, overhanging eaves
Large, low chimney
Terraces and balcony
Horizontal bands of casement windows
Windows include stained glass
Brick or stucco combined with wood
Square porch supports
Interior coordinates with exterior

Prairie Style
Robie House, Chicago, 1909
Architect: Frank Lloyd Wright

Hoover House, 1919
Stanford, California
Architect: Arthur B. Birge Clark

David B. Gamble House, 1908
Pasadena, California
Architects: Greene and Greene

Craftsman Style, c. 1910
Wichita, Kansas

Eclectic-Mission, 1910
Kansas City, Missouri

Section 6.—EARLY TWENTIETH CENTURY (1900–1920)

ARTISTS OF THE PERIOD

MAJOR ARTISTS OF THE EARLY 1900S

- *Cecilia Beaux* (1863–1942) painted realistically in the manner of John Singer Sargent. She was principally known for portraits of famous people such as Theodore Roosevelt, Cardinal Mercier, and Clemenceau.

- *George Bellows* (1882–1925), while not an original member of the Ashcan School, reflected their interest, specializing in city life and prize fights. He was a teacher at the Art Students' League in New York and the Chicago Art Institute, and was a participant in the 1913 Armory Show.

- *Charles Demuth* (1883–1935), an American Modernist, studied in Philadelphia and Paris. He was considered a Precisionist, drawing his inspiration from geometric shapes and architecture. His watercolors of flowers, landscapes, and people gave way to industrial subjects, showing elements of Cubism and eventually abstraction.

- *Arthur Dove* (1880–1946) was a painter, represented in Stieglitz's Gallery 291. His early work was as a realistic illustrator. After studying in France and Italy from 1908 to 1910, he returned to the United States and experimented with abstracting nature, while retaining natural colors and forms. He was a contemporary of Georgia O'Keeffe and painted in much the same manner.

- *Marcel Duchamp* (1887–1968), the undisputed master of "Dada" considered himself anti-art. He was born in France, and became a United States citizen in 1955. He was one of the early Cubists, and his *Nude Descending a Staircase No. 1,* painted in 1911, was an especially famous painting of the Armory Show of 1913. He was especially noted for his "ready-mades," purchased items such as a urinal, snow shovel, or bottle washer, which he personally signed.

- *William Glackens* (1870–1938) was an original member of the Ashcan School, a genre painter and illustrator. He lived and painted in France and was a great admirer of Renoir. He helped to organize the Armory Show of 1913.

- *Marsden Hartley* (1877–1943) was a pioneer of modern art in America. He began as an Impressionist painter, then showed "black landscapes" at Stieglitz's Gallery 291. He exhibited with the Blaue Reiter (blue rider) group in Munich and Berlin in 1912, continuing to paint with them from 1914 to 1916. Thereafter, he painted large Expressionist abstractions.

- *Childe Hassam* (1859–1935), an Impressionist painter and illustrator, also did etching and lithography. After studying in Paris, he did paintings of New York and New England. Among his most famous paintings are flag-decorated city scenes with parades.

- *Robert Henri* (1865–1929) was the undisputed leader of the Ashcan School, helping to organize the Independents' show in 1910 and the Armory Show in 1913. Henri studied at the Pennsylvania Academy of Art for one year, then moved to Paris with other Philadelphians to study. On his return, he specialized in portraits and landscapes, and taught in Philadelphia and New York.

- *John Marin's* (1870–1953) work spans several decades of the twentieth century and, like those of several other Modernist painters, features cityscapes, the seashore, and circus scenes. He was essentially an Expressionist, but his work retained Cubist elements. Marin is considered one of the greatest American watercolorists.

- *Maurice Prendergast* (1859–1924) an American landscape painter, was a member of the Ashcan School who had studied in Paris. With his bright yet delicate broad color patches, he was closer to Post-Impressionist painting than any of his American contemporaries.

- *Alfred Stieglitz* (1864–1946), a photographer, strove to achieve recognition for photography as an art form and was a strong supporter through his Gallery 291 of such Modernists as Arthur Dove, John Marin, Marsden Hartley, Charles Demuth, and Stieglitz's wife, Georgia O'Keeffe.

- *Joseph Stella* (1877–1946), a Modernist, was born in Italy. He first exhibited his Futurist (related to Cubism) paintings at the Armory Show of 1913. His later paintings of cities and industrial scenes showed modifications of this style. (Not the father of Frank Stella.)

- *John Twachtman* (1853–1902) became a teacher at Cooper Union and the Art Students' League. He especially delighted in painting pictures of snow. Twachtman was an original member of The Ten.

SCULPTORS

- *Alexander Archipenko* (1867–1964), Russian-born, was a member of the Section d'Or, a dissident Cubist group in France. He immigrated to the United States in 1923, later becoming a citizen. He taught at several American universities. Archipenko had more than 118 one-man shows in his lifetime.

- *John Gutzon Borglum* (1867–1941) used animals and humans in large sculptural groupings, one in Stone Mountain, Georgia, but most notably the portrait heads of four American presidents (Washington, Jefferson, Lincoln, and Theodore Roosevelt) on Mount Rushmore.

- *Alexander Milne Calder* (1846–1923) was born in Scotland. The first of the dynasty of sculptors, he was responsible for most of the sculpture for Philadelphia's City Hall. His best-known work is the 36-foot tall, 26-ton statue of William Penn atop City Hall.

- *A. Stirling Calder* (1870–1915) was the son of Alexander Milne Calder and the father of Alexander Calder. His sculpture was romantic and monumental. He was one of the few sculptors of his day to combine aspects of the new Modernism into his later work.

- *Frederick William MacMonnies* (1863–1937) became best known for the work he did in the 1890s, but worked and taught in the Beaux Arts style during the early twentieth century. He created a set of bronze doors and a statue of Shakespeare for the Library of Congress, and was considered one of the most successful sculptors of his time.

- *Frederick Remington* (1861–1909) was best known as a magazine illustrator of Western scenes. In an exhibition of his paintings and sculpture in 1895, his paintings did not sell well, but his sculpture, *The Bronco Buster,* drew rave reviews. His sculpture of cowboys, Native Americans, and the cavalry are well known to most Americans.

- *Augustus Saint-Gaudens* (1848–1907) was born in Dublin, but brought to America as an infant. He studied sculpture at Cooper Union in New York, then in Paris and Rome. He established the Beaux Arts style in American sculpture. Many of his commissions came from his association with architects McKim, Mead and White.

ARCHITECTS

- *Cass Gilbert* (1859–1934) designed office buildings, stores, clubhouses, homes, and churches. He eventually became a prominent designer of Beaux Arts buildings such as the Arkansas State Capitol, the West Virginia State Capitol, and the U.S. Supreme Court. His Woolworth Building (1910–1913) was an early skyscraper. Gilbert was one of the founders of the Architectural League of New York.

- *Charles Sumner Greene* (1868–1957) and *Henry Mather Greene* (1870–1954) were California architects who were the leading exponents of the Arts and Crafts movement, creating outstanding residences during the first two decades of the twentieth century.

- *Addison Mizner* (1872–1933) became best known for the Mediterranean Revival style he introduced to Palm Beach, Florida. He had previously designed Spanish-style houses while practicing architecture in New York, but eventually moved to Palm Beach, where he designed the famous Everglades Club and villas for many wealthy clients. His influence was largely responsible for the wide use of the Spanish style throughout Florida.

- *Frank Lloyd Wright* (1867–1959) is a world-famous American architect. His revolutionary *Prairie style* architecture created buildings that blended with their surroundings, emphasized by low, horizontal planes, overhanging low-pitched roofs, and rows of casement windows. He developed architectural forms based on geometric shapes such as octagons, hexagons, circles, and arcs. Architecture created by Wright was unified; furnishings, decor, and interior and exterior details all were designed to be seen as part of the whole.

FAMOUS ARTISTS AND SCHOOLS OF THE EARLY TWENTIETH CENTURY

- *The Eight (the Ashcan School,* 1900–1920). They began as the "Philadelphia Realists" (where most of them had been newspaper artists), then moved to New York, and became the "New York Realists." Their paintings depicted daily life in the American urban environment, specializing in people on crowded streets and at the park, theaters, and entertainment spectacles. They first exhibited together in 1908, and were active in the 1913 Armory Show, after which their "new realism" seemed conservative and slightly out of style. The group included George Luks (1866–1933), Robert Henri (1865–1929), John Sloan (1871–1951), William Glackens (1870–1938), Everett Shinn (1876–1953), Ernest Lawson (1873–1939), Maurice Prendergast (1859–1924), and Arthur B. Davies (1862–1928).

- *Dada.* This movement began in France as a revolt against World War I. It was brought to America in approximately 1915 by Marcel Duchamp (1887–1968). "Dada" is a nonsense word (German for hobbyhorse) for a "school" that fostered creativity by rebelling against traditional forms of logic, art, and culture.

- *Futurism/Cubism* (c. 1909). Futurist / Cubist painting was primarily a European movement, but a few painters, primarily Joseph Stella (1877–1946) and Lyonel Feininger (1871–1956), attempted to show the pace and movement of American cities with fractured prisms of light.

- *Photo Secession* (1905–1917). This movement was headed by photographer Alfred Stieglitz (1864–1946), founder of the Little Galleries of the Photo Secession (called Gallery 291). The major exhibitors of the group were photographers Stieglitz and Edward Steichen (1879–1973) and painters Georgia O'Keeffe (1887–1986), Marsden Hartley (1877–1943), John Marin (1870–1953), and Arthur Dove (1880–1946). Gallery 291, which historian Barbara Rose called the largest small room in the world, spearheaded the avant-garde attitude toward art in America.

- *Synchromism* (1913–1918) Synchromist paintings used color to define form and composition. Adherents were Stanton Macdonald-Wright (1890–1973) and Morgan Russell (1886–1943). Their paintings were filled with softly modeled and painted swirling shapes. Macdonald-Wright's were loosely based on the human figure, whereas Russell's were simply abstract shapes.

OVERVIEW OF THE VISUAL ARTS

Several schools of art existed within the first 20 years of the twentieth century—Classicism and Impressionism; stark, earthy Realism; and Modernism. That these three forms of art could evolve simultaneously within a twenty-year span reflects the openness to change in American society. The early 1900s were a time of transition from tradition to innovation. American painters and sculptors continued to feel their educations were not complete without several years spent in Europe studying and working. This European influence was apparent in the artwork of this time. Sculpture continued to be based on classical forms, most of it a direct reflection of French and Italian ideals.

As American society was changing, the artwork created in the opening years of the twentieth century reflected the revolution in politics, industry, and culture. Because of technological breakthroughs, architecture was the artform that differed the most dramatically from the past. Many buildings created in the early 1900s continued to reflect a dependence on classical forms, while others, such as those of Frank Lloyd Wright, were radically different. The Photo Secession movement led by Alfred Stieglitz, which began in 1905, was the heart of the Modernist movement in the United States.

PAINTING

A number of established American artists were still working in the early 1900s, including such luminaries as John Singer Sargent, Winslow Homer, and Thomas Eakins. Paintings by American Impressionists such as Childe Hassam, John Twachtman, and Edmund Tarbell did not differ much in appearance from those of their European mentors. They were fascinated with the depiction of light and the spontaneity of Impressionism.

These paintings contrasted dramatically with the genre interpretations by members of the Ashcan School. Many of the group had originally been newspaper illustrators in Philadelphia and were trained to make quick sketches of daily life. Their artwork reflected the changes taking place in American life following the Civil

War. Although most of them shared a socialist philosophy, their paintings reflected the exuberance of the city, rather than the (sometimes squalid) living conditions of its inhabitants.

This group was instrumental in arranging for the Armory Show in 1913 (which appeared to be the turning point in art from realistic to modern). Their intent had been to provide a showcase for work of serious American artists, but bringing the work of European avant-garde artists to the United States ultimately overshadowed their work. The Armory Show was so drastic and (to many) such a change in how modern art was received that students at the Chicago Art Institute (with the encouragement of the faculty) burned effigies of Matisse and Brancusi! A few artists were greatly influenced by European painting. Some, such as Marsden Hartley and Stuart Davis, were excited about the new Cubism, and ultimately became American Cubists.

MASTERPIECES OF PAINTING

American Impressionists

Across the Room, 1899, Edmund Tarbell, The Metropolitan Museum of Art, New York

Sunlight, 1909, Frank Benson, Indianapolis Museum of Art

The Front Parlor, 1913, William Paxton, The Saint Louis Art Museum

The Union Jack, New York, April Morn, 1918, Childe Hassam, Hirshhorn Museum and Sculpture Garden, Washington, D.C.

Allies Day, May 1917, 1917, Childe Hassam, National Gallery of Art, Washington, D.C.

The Ashcan School

New York Street in Winter, 1902, Robert Henri, National Gallery of Art, Washington, D.C.

The Green Car, 1910, William Glackens, The Metropolitan Museum of Art, New York

Cliff Dwellers, 1913, George Bellows, Los Angeles County Museum of Art

Mrs. Gamely, 1930, George Luks, Whitney Museum of American Art, New York

Central Park, 1908–1910, Maurice Prendergast, The Metropolitan Museum of Art, New York

Sunday, Women Drying Their Hair, 1912, John Sloan, Addison Gallery of American Art, Phillips Academy, Andover, Massachusetts

Stag at Sharkey's, 1909, George Bellows, The Cleveland Museum of Art

Modernism

Battle of Lights, Coney Island, 1914, Joseph Stella, Yale University Art Gallery, New Haven

Brooklyn Bridge, 1917, Joseph Stella, Yale University Art Gallery, New Haven

Chinese Restaurant, 1915, Max Weber, Whitney Museum of American Art, New York

Rush Hour, New York, 1915, Max Weber, National Gallery of Art, Washington, D.C.

Nude Descending a Staircase, No. 2, 1912, Marcel Duchamp, Philadelphia Museum of Art

Nature Symbolized—Connecticut River, 1911, Arthur Dove, Estate of Edith Halpert

Intermezzo, 1915, Arthur B. Davies, Graham Gallery, New York

Four Part Synchromy No. 7, 1914–1915, Morgan Russell, Whitney Museum of American Art, New York

Dada

Fountain (actually a urinal), 1917, Marcel Duchamp, New York Independents Show

Chocolate Grinder, No. 1, 1913, Marcel Duchamp, Philadelphia Museum of Art

The Bride Stripped Bare by Her Bachelors, Even (The Large Glass), 1915–1923, Marcel Duchamp, Philadelphia Museum of Art

SCULPTURE

This period was an expansion of the Beaux-Arts style in both architecture and sculpture, reflecting classical European training. Most of the well-known sculptors such as Daniel Chester French (1850–1931), John Gutzon Borglum (1867–1941), James Earle Fraser (1876–1953), Alexander Milne Calder (1846–1923), and Frederick Mac-Monnies (1863–1937) found themselves creating portrait busts, equestrian and war memorials, stone decorations, and allegorical pieces for public buildings. Expositions such as the 1904 St. Louis World's Fair or the 1893 Columbian Exposition in Chicago were notable for elaborate carved statuary. Borglum created pieces on an especially large scale and began to carve a mountain in Georgia to commemorate General Robert E. Lee. When he died in 1941, he was still working on his best-known work, *Mount Rushmore.* A few modernists such as Elie Nadelman and Alexander Archipenko were simplifying natural forms, eliminating unnecessary details, and reacting against the romanticism of Auguste Rodin, the acknowledged master. Their smooth, stylized pieces were in sharp contrast to the realism of such artists as Daniel Chester French.

Masterpieces of Sculpture

Lincoln, 1922, Daniel Chester French, Lincoln Memorial, Washington, D.C.

Lincoln, 1908, John Gutzon Borglum, Washington, D.C.

End of the Trail, 1915, James Earle Fraser, Brookgreen Gardens, South Carolina

Young Lincoln, 1927, Lorado Taft, Urbana, Illinois

Hostess, 1918, Elie Nadelman, Joseph H. Hirshhorn Collection, Washington, D.C.

Man in the Open Air, 1915, Elie Nadelman, Museum of Modern Art, New York

Woman Combing Her Hair, 1915, Alexander Archipenko, Museum of Modern Art, New York

Dancer and Gazelles, 1916, Paul Manship, Corcoran Gallery of Art, Washington, D.C.

ARCHITECTURE

Possibly the most impressive changes in art in the early part of the twentieth century occurred in architecture. It was about this time that cast iron or steel superstructures became more popular, allowing the building of skyscrapers. Until then, few buildings were taller than two or three stories. Victorian architecture, with its excesses and reliance on historical architectural forms, was nearly at an end. Instead, architects such as Louis Sullivan (1856–1924), Charles McKim (1847–1909), William Mead (1846–1928), and Stanford White (1853–1906) pared buildings to allow the structure to be visible and indeed decorative. Cast iron or carved decorative ornamentation was frequently used both inside and on the exterior.

Frank Lloyd Wright (1867–1959), who had worked with Louis Sullivan, designed residences that were revolutionary. The interior spaces were made to blend with the exterior through the use of large windows, low overhangs, and complementary interior and exterior detailing. His *Prairie Houses* were designed to take advantage of the site, blending the long, low lines with the flat terrain.

MASTERPIECES OF ARCHITECTURE

Carson Pirie Scott and Co. Building, 1898–1904, Louis Sullivan, Chicago

First Church of Christ Scientist, 1909–1911, Bernard Maybeck, Berkeley, California

Robie House, 1909, Frank Lloyd Wright, Chicago

Ward Willitts House, 1900–1902, Frank Lloyd Wright, Highland Park, Illinois

Flatiron Building, 1902, D. H. Burnham and Company, New York

Woolworth Building, 1913, Cass Gilbert, New York

Pennsylvania Station (demolished), 1906–1910, McKim, Mead and White, New York

Cannon House Office Building, 1908, Carrere and Hastings, Washington, D.C.

PROJECT 6-1: ASHCAN SCHOOL PAINTING

FOR THE TEACHER

SLIDE #18: *Snow in New York,* 1902, Robert Henri, 32 × 25-¾ inches, oil on canvas, National Gallery of Art, Washington, D.C.

Robert Henri's (pronounced Hen-rye) father was a riverboat gambler, who left town to avoid being lynched for shooting a local cattleman. He subsequently changed his name and those of his sons. This no doubt made an impact on his son's life! Henri was the acknowledged leader of the Ashcan school (so-called because of the group's propensity for painting realistic scenes of everyday life in New York). Most of the group had been newspaper illustrators before photography was widely used, and they transferred these incisive skills of capturing people-in-motion to their paintings.

Masterpieces by Ashcan School Members

The Masquerade Dress, 1911, Robert Henri, The Metropolitan Museum of Art, New York

New York Street in Winter, 1902, Robert Henri, National Gallery of Art, Washington, D.C.

Cliff Dwellers, 1913, George Bellows, Los Angeles County Museum of Art

Hairdresser's Window, 1907, John Sloan, Wadsworth Atheneum, Hartford, Connecticut

Hammerstein's Roof Garden, 1901, William Glackens, Whitney Museum of American Art, New York

PREPARATION

Have students discuss current events found in magazines and newspapers. Suggest that they bring in a photo based on sports, politics, or any other personal interest. Just as each member of the Ashcan School specialized in a different subject, most students will find that the photos that intrigue them will differ from those of their fellow students. These photos are not for copying, merely to help students identify their interests.

ADDITIONAL SUGGESTIONS

- Painting snow scenes in oil paint or oil pastels will challenge students, as they discover that many colors are used in a supposedly white painting. Suggest that they underpaint the snow-covered ground with orange and ultramarine blue before applying white. The colors will affect the white painted on top, and students will notice how shadows and sunlight appear on snow. The stark contrasts of dark tree trunks, city streets and buildings, paths, and people dressed in winter coats offer subjects for a winter painting.

- Students could tear watercolored paper (which they have previously watercolored) into horizontal strips to make layers of a landscape and glue them onto a background paper. Details may be added with charcoal.

- Select three values of gray construction paper and have students tear the paper to make a collage of a cityscape or landscape. After the paper has been glued down with rubber cement, students can use white, black, and gray conté crayon to draw details on top of the collage, unifying it.

- A favorite game of members of the Ashcan School, most of whom made a living as newspaper illustrators, was played to develop the ability to remember details. One member would leave the room and come back blindfolded to describe as many details in the room as possible—where people were sitting, how their arms were placed, etc.

- A variation of the memory game would be to have several groups of students create a group "found-object" composition on heavy cardboard or foam core. Assign one group to do a "green" board, another to do one in all red, one in all white, etc. They would have to bring objects from home in these colors and pin them on the board. Allow students to look at a board for one minute, then write as many items as they can remember. Or the teacher could prepare just one colored board for a 10-minute exercise.

Photo 6-1. *Boathouse, Winter-Harlem River,* **1918, Ernest Lawson, 25 × 30 inches, Bequest of Marie Setz Hertslet, The Saint Louis Art Museum. This winter scene by Lawson, a member of the Ashcan school demonstrates how a beautiful covering of snow transforms any scene.**

PROJECT 6-1: ASHCAN SCHOOL PAINTING

MATERIALS

- 12 × 18-inch or 18 × 24-inch drawing
  or construction paper
- Brushes
- Pencils
- Tempera, acrylic, or oil paint

**Drawn after *Snow in New York*, 1902
Robert Henri
National Gallery of Art, Washington, D.C.**

Like painters of the Ashcan School, in this project you will paint people where you find them—whether in parks, movie theaters, school, sports events, gossiping while waiting for a bus, or hanging around a mall. The Ashcan School members' paintings tended to be rather dark, sometimes using browns, grays, and blacks, relieved by some bright colors.

1. When you have decided the location of your painting, lightly draw the background first in pencil. After drawing in the background, you will have some idea of the size and number of persons you will need to complete the composition.

2. With the exception of "line 'em up and grin" yearbook photos, you tend to see only portions of bodies of people in a group. Some may have their backs to you, some may be seated, most will overlap others. Newspaper or yearbook snapshots should help you observe this. Lightly draw as many people as you want into the photo. Don't be concerned if they don't look quite like how you envisioned—anyone would know they are people by their general shape.

3. If you are using oil or acrylic paint, do an underpainting in values of brown (sepia) as European-trained oil painters used to do. A painting was "thinly" painted all over, developing areas of light and dark that helped the painter when adding colored pigment. In Ashcan School paintings, many of the painters allowed the brown underpainting to show through.

4. Rather than using color in pure hues, subdue the tone by adding a complementary color (violet to yellow, or green to red, for example). It was the dirty-appearing hues that caused people to call Ashcan School members "the apostles of ugliness" and "the revolutionary black gang." Use bright accent colors sparingly.

PROJECT 6-2: **ON THE BEACH—WATERCOLOR RESIST**

FOR THE TEACHER

SLIDE #19: *Bathers, Verso,* c. 1916–1919, Maurice Prendergast, 35.2 × 50.3 cm., watercolor. Gift of Mr. and Mrs. G. Gordon Hertslet, The Saint Louis Art Museum

Maurice Brazil Prendergast (1859–1924) was a Post-Impressionist and the oldest member of the Ashcan School, with whom he participated in a number of exhibitions. He was born in Newfoundland, but moved to Boston, his mother's home town. He went to Paris at age 30 to study art. Prendergast was somewhat deaf, which caused him to feel isolated.

His paintings usually showed happy scenes of groups of women and children in parks or near beaches in France or Boston. Prendergast frequently used round hats or parasols as focal points in his decorative paintings and tended to arrange his paintings in frieze-like layers.

Mahonri Sharp Young says of Prendergast's work, "He never tired of this lovely toyland where there are no bad things. . . . There must have been rain in Prendergast's three years in Paris, but it rarely rains in his pictures. . . . He believed life was beautiful."

Masterpieces by Prendergast

The Promenade, undated, Columbus Gallery of Fine Arts, Columbus, Ohio

The Swans, 1916–1918, Addison Gallery of American Art, Phillips Academy, Andover, Massachusetts

The Promenade, 1913, Whitney Museum of American Art, New York

Central Park, 1908–1910, The Metropolitan Museum of Art, New York

On the Beach No. 3, 1918, Cleveland Museum of Art

Seashore, c. 1910, The Saint Louis Art Museum

Evening Walk, 1917–1920, private collection, New York

PREPARATION

Prendergast's paintings usually featured groups of people lined up in the foreground, with seashore or park scenes in the background. His frequent compositional device of arranging a picture in horizontal planes should not be difficult for students to understand and emulate; this is one of the things that made his pictures distinctive. His manner of applying color in daubs created a tapestry-like surface (not so different from pointillism, but less exacting).

Explain the concept of resist painting, and encourage students to practice applying paint in daubs, rather than blending.

ADDITIONAL SUGGESTIONS

- Have students select a small segment of a Prendergast painting to interpret in an 8 × 10-inch paper collage. Small pieces of torn construction paper could be glued onto crayon-outlined figures. If students prefer not to do figures in this manner, they could do trees, cityscapes, seascapes, or playgrounds.

- Use the crayon-resist technique to have students do any subject that appeals to them. White crayon on white construction paper, using watercolor, offers all sorts of surprises.

Photo 6-2A. *Beach at Gloucester,* **c. 1918–1921, Maurice Prendergast, oil on canvas, 30-⅝ × 43-⅛ inches, Hirshhorn Museum and Sculpture Garden, Gift of Joseph H. Hirshhorn Foundation, Smithsonian Institution. Photography by Lee Stalsworth.**

Photo 6-2B. Student Millie White's drawing of the track after school was organized by Maurice Prendergast's manner of showing groups of people.

PROJECT 6-2: **ON THE BEACH—WATERCOLOR RESIST**

MATERIALS

- Watercolor
- 12 × 18-inch watercolor paper or light colored construction paper
- White or brown crayon
- Oil pastels

Drawn after *The Flying Horses,* **c. 1902–1906**
Maurice Prendergast
The Toledo Museum of Art

The Ashcan School was the derogatory name given to a group to which Maurice Prendergast belonged. "The Eight," as they preferred to call themselves, specialized in ordinary subjects of the city or country. Prendergast painted mostly faceless people in crowds at the beach or at parks. In contrast to his colleagues, he did not show the seamier side of everyday life through dark colors and sordid backgrounds, but made every painting look like a holiday, with bright colors or soft pastels.

1. Think about a nearby location. It could be a city park, a playing field at school, the seashore, or the place where you live. Consider how it could be divided into three horizontal sections—a foreground, middle ground, and background. The upper third usually will contain sky, perhaps with trees silhouetted against it.

2. Think about what a crowd of people in the foreground might be doing. They could be looking at animals in a zoo, playing or watching baseball, having a family reunion at a park, eating lunch in a cafeteria, watching fireworks at night, or just hanging around a shopping mall or parking lot. Use white or light brown crayon to firmly draw outlines of as many figures as you want. (Prendergast, a rather isolated individual, used crowds of people.) Don't worry about making mistakes—the watercolor will make it better.

3. After you have drawn people, complete the background in the middle third of your painting (again in crayon). This might involve smaller people off in the distance, trees, buildings, carnival rides, umbrellas at the seashore, or a view across the river, with the opposite shore defining the upper third of the picture.

4. Apply watercolor paint to the surface in daubs, rather than blending colors together. For example, on a pink dress, use two or three shades of pink or yellow to make the dress. When you have mixed one color, use it freely in several places on the paper so that you repeat your colors throughout. Prendergast worked in mostly pastel shades.

5. You will notice that the outlines around the figures show up because of the crayon resist. Although Prendergast probably did not actually use crayon resist, most of his paintings have the effect of each figure being encased in an outline. When the painting is dry, use crayons or oil pastel to emphasize certain areas.

PROJECT 6-3: **WATERCOLOR WITHOUT A BRUSH**

FOR THE TEACHER

SLIDE #20. *Weehawken, New Jersey,* 1910, John Marin, 47.6 × 39.1 cm., watercolor, Bequest of Marie Setz Hertslet, The Saint Louis Art Museum

John Marin (1870–1953) was one of the American Modernists whose work was shown at Gallery 291. An architect for four or five years before he studied painting, he worked mostly in watercolor, with his primary subjects based on New York skyscrapers, water, and the circus. He often made pencil sketches at the circus, with lines and squiggles representing the action around him. His paintings frequently had the main subjects clustered in the center, and straight or diagonal lines used to make a border of sorts. Marin frequently wrote about his work, and expressed that the writing and the painting were closely related.

MASTERPIECES BY MARIN

Singer Building, 1921, Philadelphia Museum of Art

Maine Islands, 1922, Phillips Collection, Washington, D.C.

Brooklyn Bridge, 1910, The Metropolitan Museum of Art, New York

Boat Off Deer Isle, 1926, Philadelphia Museum of Art

Lower Manhattan (Composing derived from top of Woolworth), 1922, Museum of Modern Art, New York

Ship, Sea, and Sky Forms (An Impression), 1923, Columbus Museum of Art, Columbus, Ohio

Municipal Building, New York, 1912, Philadelphia Museum of Art

PREPARATION

Show the slide of Marin's painting, and try to find a book that has reproductions of his work. This project challenges students to use painting tools other than a paintbrush. Require students to turn in five index cards with pencil drawings of their surroundings (e.g., fellow students, TV programs, landscape). Emphasize that these are warm-up exercises, but should have definite lines, differences in value, and go almost to the edges of the card (the picture plane). Most students would not be threatened by this exercise, and one of the cards can end up as the subject for the watercolor painting.

ADDITIONAL SUGGESTIONS

- Have students use a paintbrush and loosely paint subjects suggested in the student handout. When it is dry, have them dip cardboard in watercolor and stamp with the edges, emphasizing lines.

- Just as Marin loved to write about painting, display all the paintings on a wall and have students write poetry about a painting. One suggestion is to do a four-line *diamante* about any one of the paintings. In this (literally) diamond-shaped poem, the first line consists of a one-word equivalent of the work (usually the first word that comes to mind). The second line is an action phrase; the third line, a simile or metaphor; and the fourth line, a single-word summation. Ask students to volunteer to read their poems while others try to guess which painting the poem is about. Another stylized poem that could be written about the work is a three-line Haiku poem that consists of 17 syllables: 5 syllables in the first and third lines, and 7 syllables in the second line.

- Use printing ink to make a monoprint. Have students rapidly paint a landscape or seascape on a small piece of plastic and, before the ink dries, lay paper on top of the ink and rub over the back of the paper to transfer the print. If the picture needs more detail, allow it to dry and draw over it with pencil or colored pencil.

Photo 6-3. *Weehawken, New Jersey,* 1910, John Marin, 47.6 × 39.1 cm., watercolor, Bequest of Marie Setz Hertslet, The Saint Louis Art Museum.

PROJECT 6-3: WATERCOLOR WITHOUT A BRUSH

MATERIALS

- Matboard and cardboard strips, ½ to 3 inches wide × 3 inches long
- Watercolors
- Watercolor brush
- Watercolor paper
- Pencil
- Containers for water
- Newspaper or newsprint

Drawn from *Movement No. 2*, 1926
John Marin
Watercolor on paper

John Marin was an early Modernist painter whose work sometimes appears to have been drawn with straight edges. Although his work was mostly abstract, it was still possible to identify his subject, such as a city scene, mountains, or seashore.

1. To get started, do small, quick pencil sketches on five index cards of your surroundings at school or at home that might be used as subject matter for a larger painting. Select one of these cards as your general subject, or combine details from several.

2. Prepare the watercolor pigment for painting by putting a drop or two of water on each color to soften it for a few minutes. The only time you will use a brush in this painting is when you mix generous amounts of paint in the lid of the watercolor box. Apply the paint to the paper by dipping the edge of a piece of cardboard into the paint and stamping with it or using it to drag the paint on the watercolor paper.

3. As a warmup for painting with cardboard, apply watercolor with the edge of a piece of cardboard to make some small detail such as a tree, house, or bridge. On a small piece of paper, experiment with various widths and types of cardboard (matboard, posterboard, corrugated cardboard). By practicing making marks with cardboard, you will discover that you can apply paint in a variety of ways. By twisting, you can make circular marks. You can make long or short lines by dipping the end of the cardboard into paint and printing with it. You can make broad horizontal strokes by dragging the paint. Make combinations of lines—curved and twisting, straight and strong in value (dark).

4. On a fresh piece of watercolor paper, *lightly* draw the subject with pencil. This can be erased after the paint has dried or, if it is light enough, can remain. Your subject can be a local scene—city, mountain, river, seashore, or a place you remember in your mind. This painting is to be abstract with the subject still recognizable, but not painted realistically. Concentrate on developing the center or main focus of the painting in detail before coming out to the edges.

5. Leave some areas of the paper white. The beauty of watercolor is that it is not overworked. Select a color scheme based on how you envision such a place. Most seascapes would be cool colors such as blues, greens, or violets, while you might think of a circus as mostly warm colors. Limit yourself to several hues, mixing variations by adding other colors to those hues.

6. When you think you are finished, place your paper on the floor or pin it on a wall and stand back to look at it. Consider emphasizing the main subject by adding more straight lines with the edges of cardboard. The paintings of Modernist John Marin had an excitement about them created by the directions of the lines. You might also create a "border," as Marin did on his paintings by either leaving them blank around the edges or by making many irregular lines.

PROJECT 6-4: **DESIGN A BUILDING**

FOR THE TEACHER

The early twentieth century was an exciting time for architects. The backbone of most American cities was built at this time, including monumental buildings such as banks, museums, state capitols, railway stations, cathedrals, and private homes.

The invention of the elevator and the use of steel and iron in combination with other materials allowed skyscrapers to be constructed. The typical skyscraper consisted of a two-story-high base, then a vertical shaft in which every story was the same, usually with supports encased in stone or terra cotta, and a cornice, which might have an elaborate frieze on it.

Masterpieces of Architecture

Singer Tower, 1907, Ernest Flagg, New York

Frick Gallery, 1914, Carrere and Hastings, New York

Unity Church, 1906, Frank Lloyd Wright, Oak Park, Illinois

Carson Pirie Scott and Co. Building, 1898–1904, Louis Sullivan, Chicago

The Ayer Building, 1900, Holabird and Roche, Chicago

Flatiron Building, 1902, D. H. Burnham and Company, New York

Woolworth Building, 1913, Cass Gilbert, New York

St. Louis Art Museum, 1904, Cass Gilbert, St. Louis

PREPARATION

This project may take up to two weeks, but is worthwhile. Students get very excited about their architectural models and take great pride in them. Although instructions are given for working with foam board, 14-ply mount board or cardboard could be substituted. (I sometimes obtain foam board scraps and mount board from framing companies, or it can be ordered in large sheets.) Because students are likely to keep and display these projects, avoid having the base any larger than 12 × 18 inches (which would fit on top of a bookcase). Many other materials are suitable for making architectural models. Some that students might use are heavy plastic, balsa wood, cork sheets, and other materials that are available from hobby shops. While you will strive for the best possible craftsmanship, the *idea* is as important as the finished model.

ADDITIONAL SUGGESTIONS

- Encourage students to design furniture or hardware for the interiors of their buildings. Architects such as Frank Lloyd Wright and Louis Sullivan concerned themselves with *every* aspect of a building, not just the exterior.
- Have students design and create a museum, assuming each is the donor of a private collection (theirs). Necessary parts of a museum are easy access for the disabled, restrooms, meeting rooms, storage, elevators, education facilities, lunch room, and galleries that flow easily. A museum could be more than one story. It can be as elaborate as they wish, with paintings glued on interior walls or, at the minimum, a list of their "collection."

Photo 6-4A. This museum, created by student Beth Bennett, is made of posterboard taped together. It includes galleries on both floors.

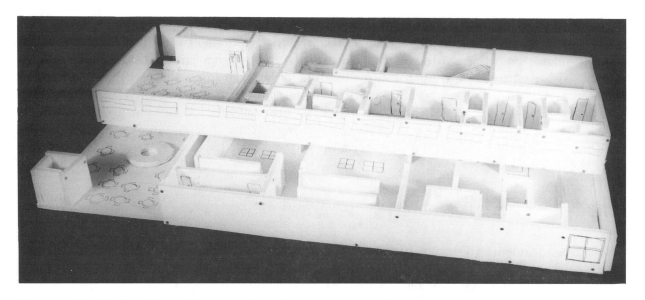

Photo 6-4B. Student Dawn Citrin designed this museum to include public reception rooms, galleries, education and meeting rooms, disabled accessibility. She included a list that described the work that would be in each gallery. It is made of foam core held together with small brass brads.

PROJECT 6-4: DESIGN A BUILDING

MATERIALS

- Foam board
- Paper cutter
- X-acto™ knives
- Graph paper
- Pencils
- Flat-headed nails or brass brads, ⅝ to ¾ inches long

Lovell (Health) House, 1929
Los Angeles, California
Architect: Richard Neutra

Designing your own building will require some research. First, look around where you live. Look at the height of the tallest building in your town, and decide whether you want to build a tall building or a shorter structure. Look at the first story, the middle part of the building, and the roof line. Architects in the early twentieth century designed not only the exterior of the building, but also interior decorative detailing such as murals, carvings, windows, and doors. Decide what purpose your building will serve such as a bank, office, railway station, museum, hotel, or government building.

1. After you have decided on the type of building you will make, do a sketch of it from more than one angle. The roof can be removable or not, as you wish. Decorative details can be added by drawing them in pencil, painting the building with tempera, or adding an extra layer of cut board on the surface. It is not recommended that you attempt to cut out windows or doors, but rather, draw them.

2. Based on your sketch, measure carefully and make a detailed drawing on graph paper of the pieces you will be cutting out. Try to have the base on which the building stands no larger than 12 × 18 inches. The building should be no larger than 9 × 15 inches wide to allow for ease in handling and landscaping. When you make pencil lines for cutting, make them on the inside where they won't show when the building is put together. When measuring, don't forget to allow for the thickness of the board.

3. Carefully cut out the pieces of board with either a paper cutter or an X-acto™ knife. *Safety Note: Always be aware of where both hands are when cutting.*

4. Before joining pieces together, do any decorations that will go on the outside of the building. You can make decorations, such as windows and doors, on drawing paper and glue them on, *or* draw directly on the foam board. If you look at architecture of the early 1900s, you will see that architects gave as much attention to the top of the building as they did to the base and shaft (center area). Contemporary architects are also giving special treatment to the tops of buildings.

5. Join pieces together using brads (small broad-headed nails, approximately ¾ inches long). If you are working with a material other than foam board, you may use white glue for extra security. If you use 14-ply mountboard, pieces may be glued with white glue and held in place with straight pins until they dry.

6. When you are finished, consider landscaping your building by putting foam board shapes of trees or bushes on the base. The roof can be affixed with brads or, if you have finished the inside, leave it removable.

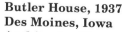

Butler House, 1937
Des Moines, Iowa
Architects: Kraetsch and Kraetsch

Art Deco
Miami Beach, Florida

PROJECT 6-5: SONGS OF THE SKY—CLOUDS

FOR THE TEACHER

SLIDE #21: *The Steerage,* **1907, Alfred Stieglitz, Funds given by Mr. and Mrs. Warren McKinney Shapleigh, The Saint Louis Art Museum**

This project does not involve actual photography, but is based on a theory of photographer Alfred Stieglitz. He said, "My cloud photographs are equivalents of my most profound life experience, my basic philosophy of life. . . . My photographs are a picture of the chaos in the world, and of my relationship to that chaos." The *Equivalents* were small black-and-white photos of clouds that he felt could represent anything.

Stieglitz was born in America, but educated in Germany, where he studied science, later giving that up when he developed his love for photography. After returning to the United States, he became a leader of the Photo Secession movement, a group of photographers who wished to break with tradition. His career encompassed a romantic period, when he did mostly soft-focus photographs of New York; a social-realist period, when he did his most famous photograph, *The Steerage;* and his later, personal style that included his cloud *Equivalents* and many studies of his wife, artist Georgia O'Keeffe. He was the founder of Gallery 291, where many of America's early Modernist painters and photographers were first exhibited.

PHOTOGRAPHS BY STIEGLITZ

Equivalent, 1930, The Metropolitan Museum of Art, New York

Hands, Georgia O'Keeffe, 1920, The Metropolitan Museum of Art, New York

Equivalent, Set C2, No. 3, 1929, National Gallery of Art, Washington, D.C.

Equivalent, Set C2, No. 4, 1929, National Gallery of Art, Washington, D.C.

The Steerage, 1907, The Saint Louis Art Museum

PREPARATION

Save this project for a time when the clouds are interesting and students can go outside or look out a window. Stieglitz's *Equivalents* are mostly quite small (4 × 5 inches). Introduce students to this project by having precut 4 × 5-inch pieces of construction paper for them to practice on. After they have made a number of small drawings, have them make a large composition.

ADDITIONAL SUGGESTIONS

- Since this project is based on the photographs of Alfred Stieglitz, it makes an ideal photographic assignment. Most secondary students have a camera of some sort and might enjoy taking photos of clouds, sometimes including something else such as people, a tree, or a building near the bottom of the picture. Certainly they can look through photos at home and bring in family photos that have interesting cloud pictures.

- Have students mount their six (or more) *equivalent* drawings on white drawing paper. If it would improve their composition, they could cut them further, or intersperse them with strips of black or gray paper to make a collage.

- Cut up a reproduction of *The Steerage,* give each student a small square, and have them use black and white tempera or acrylic paints to enlarge their portion into an 8-inch square replica. When this is finished, join the squares together to make a giant version using only black and white values.

Photo 6-5. *The Steerage,* 1907, Alfred Stieglitz, Funds given by Mr. and Mrs. Warren McKinney Shapleigh, The Saint Louis Art Museum.

PROJECT 6-5: **SONGS OF THE SKY—CLOUDS**

MATERIALS

- Drawing boards (masonite or cardboard)
- Masking tape
- 12 × 18-inch newsprint
- 4 × 5-inch dark gray construction paper
- 12 × 18-inch construction paper: blue, gray, violet, black

- White chalk
- Pastels
- Tissues
- Charcoal

The photographer Alfred Stieglitz went through a period in his career when he preferred to photograph clouds over any other subject. He said, "Clouds and their relationship to the rest of the world, and clouds for themselves interested me."

1. On a day when the clouds are interesting, tape a piece of newsprint to a drawing board and go outside to practice drawing clouds. Tape several 4 × 5-inch pieces of construction paper to the newsprint to hold them in place while you draw with chalk.

2. Notice that clouds are often darker on the bottom than on the top, or that they seem to drift away, lighter in some areas than others. You will get good results working with the side of the chalk as well as the end. Make areas darker by putting in a heavy area of chalk, and use a tissue to pull the chalk out to the edges of the clouds. Avoid outlining clouds—it makes them look like a cartoon.

3. Make at least six 4 × 5-inch cloud drawings. Because the clouds are constantly changing shape, you will have to rely on your memory and imagination. Leave areas of the paper dark and some areas almost pure white. If the white chalk seems inadequate, use charcoal or colored chalk to give different values. Black-and-white photographs have ten different "zones," or values, varying from pure black to white. To make your cloud drawings most interesting, attempt to make as many different values as possible.

4. Select the cloud drawing you like best. Apply that technique to make a larger composition on black or dark construction paper. If the picture is not sufficiently interesting with just clouds, near the very bottom draw a very dark silhouette of something such as mountains, tree tops in the distance, a branch, or even the top of your school.

© 1996 by Prentice-Hall, Inc.

PROJECT 6-6: **COLLAGRAPH PRINT—THE IRON CROSS**

FOR THE TEACHER

SLIDE #22: *Himmel,* **1915, Marsden Hartley, 120.4 × 120.4 cm., oil on canvas with original-painting wood border, Gift of the Friends of Art, The Nelson-Atkins Museum of Art, Kansas City, Missouri**

Marsden Hartley (1878–1943) painted and exhibited with the German Expressionist group, the Blaue Reiter (blue rider), in 1912. His paintings featured the same bright colors and strong shapes as this avant-garde group. After a short sojourn in the United States, he returned to work in England, France, and Germany from 1914 to 1916. He was fascinated by the militarism of German society at that time and, on his return to the United States, painted strong, Cubist compositions that featured imperial colors of black, white, and red and symbols of German militarism such as the Iron Cross. Ultimately, he became a painter of Expressionist landscapes, seascapes, and genre pictures.

Paintings by Hartley

Portrait of a German Officer, 1914, The Metropolitan Museum of Art, New York

Painting, Number 5, 1914–1915, Whitney Museum of American Art, New York

Berlin Abstraction, 1914–1915, Corcoran Gallery of Art, Washington, D.C.

Berlin Ante-War, 1915, Columbus Gallery of Fine Arts, Columbus, Ohio

The Window, 1928, Columbus Gallery of Fine Arts, Columbus, Ohio

PREPARATION

Find a book that contains reproductions of Hartley's work to share with the class. Discuss symbolism with the students. Ask what symbols have been around for a long time that still convey an emotion to some when they are viewed. (Examples include the cross, swastika, peace symbol, hammer and sickle, Statue of Liberty, rising sun, and so on.) Talk about how artists through the ages have used symbolism to convey ideas. Hartley's use of colors and symbols of German Nationalism in 1914 still have the power to invoke in some the emotion that he felt.

ADDITIONAL SUGGESTIONS

- Have students draw a political cartoon about something happening in the world today. Have them start with a stick figure so they realize that the idea is more important than the drawing. Once they have developed an idea, they may find that drawing the people or caricature of a main character is not so difficult.

- Students could do a drawing in pastel, alternating layers of pastel and polymer medium, continuing to build up until it has the thick impasto (texture) of Hartley's work. These should be rather small, so they don't take long.

Photo 6-6A. *The Iron Cross,* 1915, Marsden Hartley, oil on canvas, 47-¼ × 47-¼ inches, Collection, Washington University, St. Louis.

Photo 6-6B. Student work *Teddy,* a collagraphic print made on typing paper. Tagboard was cut and glued down, then the "plate" was varnished, allowed to dry, then inked. Numerous prints could then be made.

PROJECT 6-6: **COLLAGRAPH PRINT—THE IRON CROSS**

MATERIALS

- 9 × 12-inch tagboard (or old file folders)
- White glue
- X-acto™ knives
- Pencils
- Printing ink or acrylic paint
- Polymer medium or spray varnish
- Glass for rolling out ink
- Brayer
- 12 × 18-inch white drawing paper
- Oil pastels

Drawn from *Himmel,* **1915**
Marsden Hartley
Nelson-Atkins Museum of Art
Kansas City, Missouri

You will be making a large print in the manner of Marsden Hartley, an American Cubist painter. Although you needn't use the symbols he used, emulate the *manner* in which he worked, with large irregular shapes, background pattern, and so on, to make an Expressionistic (personal) collagraphic print.

1. Do several thumbnail sketches of a subject that interests you and in which you might use symbols (such as the logo on a car, street signs, school mascots, etc.).

2. Use a piece of 9 × 12-inch tagboard as a base. Cut up and glue on other pieces of board until you have a pleasing composition. It is possible to cut designs (such as circles, checkerboard, or stripes) into some of the tagboard by using an X-acto™ knife. You can build up several layers. Allow the "printing plate" to dry. *Note:* To cut tagboard with an X-acto™ knife, cut over the same area several times until you have cut through to the back. Cut slightly past corners to make them clean. *Safety Note: Remember to place a magazine or cardboard under the board when cutting, and be careful not to cut toward your fingers.*

3. Varnish the plate with diluted white glue, polymer medium, or spray varnish. Allow it to dry. Ink the large collagraph (the plate) by spreading ink with a brayer on a piece of glass, then transferring it to the cardboard plate with a brayer. Use a paper towel to wipe excess ink off some of the top surfaces; this will give a variety of values. It may take several prints to get one that seems right to you. When you get it right, make several prints to trade with friends.

4. To make a print with clean borders, place your plate face down on the center of a piece of 12 × 18-inch drawing paper. Turn the paper over and firmly rub the back of it to transfer the print, giving particular pressure to some of the deeper areas and lines. Pull the print from the plate. Allow it to dry. You can make several prints in this manner, re-inking and wiping the plate each time. When finished, wipe excess ink off the plate.

5. After the print has dried, you may find that it is an attractive composition as is. If not, you could fill in some areas, using oil pastel or acrylic paint in bright colors. Be sure to leave dark outlines showing. If you wish to print in a second color, wipe off as much of the first as you can. When finished, you will find that your plate is a work of art in itself.

Section 7

ART BETWEEN
THE WARS
(1920 to 1940)

ART BETWEEN THE WARS
TIME LINE

	1920	1923	1927	1930	1934	1938	1940
Painting Sculpture Architecture Folk Art	Realism 1920–1940 Precisionism, from 1915 Charles Sheeler 1883–1965 Realism 1920–1940 Romare Bearden 1914–1988 Harlem Renaissance 1919–1929 Jacob Lawrence, b. 1917	Art Deco c. 1925 Social Realism 1920s and 1930s Edward Hopper 1882–1967		German Bauhaus 1906–1933 Grant Wood 1892–1942 American Scene Painting 1930s John Marin 1870–1953	Group F64 photographers Edward Weston 1886–1958 Georgia O'Keeffe 1887–1986 Thomas Hart Benton 1889–1975 Stuart Davis 1894–1964	Alexander Calder 1898–1976 Charles Demuth 1883–1935 Frank Lloyd Wright 1867–1959	
Politics	League of Nations 1920	J. Edgar Hoover appointed to FBI, 1924		1933 CCC Civilian Conservation Corps	1933–1938 New Deal 1935-WPA Works Progress Administration	1936 F. D. Roosevelt president 1935 Social Security Act	1939 Germany conquers Poland
Literature	Eugene O'Neill's *The Emperor Jones*, 1920 1920 Sinclair Lewis *Main Street*	1925 F. Scott Fitzgerald's *The Great Gatsby*	1926 Ernest Hemingway's *The Sun Also Rises*		1934 *Appointment in Samarra*, John O'Hara	*Our Town* by Thornton Wilder, 1938	
Science	1920 Inkblot test Herman Rorschach		1928 Penicillin, Alexander Fleming 1925 The Scopes Trial (also called the Monkey Trial) debate on evolution vs. creation		1932 Nylon and Neoprene, Carothers and Collins 1935 Electronic hearing aid	1938—Photocopy machine, Chester Carlson 1936 Jet engine	
Music	Engelbert Humperdinck 1854–1921	1924 Grand Old Opry formed 1922 Irving Berlin wrote "April Showers"	1923 Bix Biederbecke Jazz Band 1927 *Showboat*, Jerome Kern and Oscar Hammerstein		1934 Cole Porter's "Anything Goes"	George Gershwin 1898–1937	
Current Events	1922 USSR established 1920 Ghandi is elected leader of National Congress of India	Pancho Villa 1878–1923	1927 Lindbergh solos across Atlantic Lenin, 1870–1924	1929 Stock Market crashes	1932 Zuider Zee project completed	1936 Great Dust Bowl	1940 Battle of Britain

ARCHITECTURE BETWEEN THE WARS

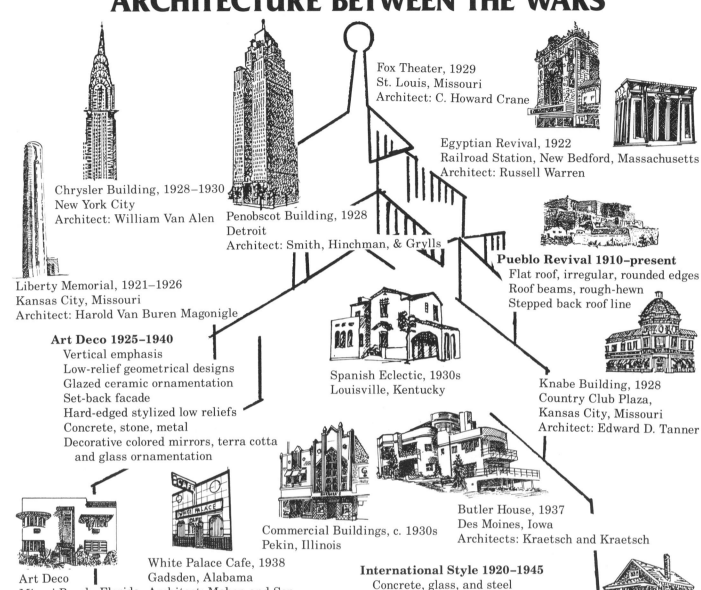

Fox Theater, 1929
St. Louis, Missouri
Architect: C. Howard Crane

Egyptian Revival, 1922
Railroad Station, New Bedford, Massachusetts
Architect: Russell Warren

Chrysler Building, 1928–1930
New York City
Architect: William Van Alen

Penobscot Building, 1928
Detroit
Architect: Smith, Hinchman, & Grylls

Pueblo Revival 1910–present
Flat roof, irregular, rounded edges
Roof beams, rough-hewn
Stepped back roof line

Liberty Memorial, 1921–1926
Kansas City, Missouri
Architect: Harold Van Buren Magonigle

Art Deco 1925–1940
Vertical emphasis
Low-relief geometrical designs
Glazed ceramic ornamentation
Set-back facade
Hard-edged stylized low reliefs
Concrete, stone, metal
Decorative colored mirrors, terra cotta
and glass ornamentation

Spanish Eclectic, 1930s
Louisville, Kentucky

Knabe Building, 1928
Country Club Plaza,
Kansas City, Missouri
Architect: Edward D. Tanner

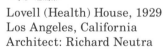

Commercial Buildings, c. 1930s
Pekin, Illinois

Butler House, 1937
Des Moines, Iowa
Architects: Kraetsch and Kraetsch

White Palace Cafe, 1938
Gadsden, Alabama
Architect: Maben and Son

International Style 1920–1945
Concrete, glass, and steel
Exposed steel structural elements
Cantilever
Box-like structure
Flat roof tops
Smooth wall surface
Curtain walls of windows
Eaves boxed in or flush with wall
Natural wooden trim
Little ornamentation
Asymmetrical facade in homes

Art Deco
Miami Beach, Florida

Bungalow, c. 1930s
Crescent, Toronto, Canada

Falling Water, 1936
Bear Run, Pennsylvania
Architect: Frank Lloyd Wright

Lovell (Health) House, 1929
Los Angeles, California
Architect: Richard Neutra

Art Moderne 1930–1945
Horizontal bands of windows
Flat roofs
Smooth wall finish
Curved window glass
Aluminum and stainless steel ornamentation
Circular patterns used on doors or glass

Craftsman 1905–1940
One story high
Low-pitched gabled roof
Roof rafters exposed
Combination of materials
(wood shingles, stone, brick)
Large porch
Tapered porch posts to ground level
Small windows flanking chimney
Cobblestone decorations
Beamed ceilings

Section 7.—ART BETWEEN THE WARS (1920–1940)

ARTISTS OF THE PERIOD

MAJOR ARTISTS OF THE PERIOD BETWEEN THE WARS

- *Ivan le Lorraine Albright* (1897–1983) did surgical illustrations for a medical unit during World War I, which may account for the morbid overtones of his painting. His work has been considered Surrealistic by some and certainly is "beyond reality."

- *Romare Bearden* (1914–1988) tried many forms of art, but did not specialize in a specific style until he was in his fifties. Although he was an African-American who created compositions with African-American people in them, his Cubistic/Abstract/Pop work is considered universal. His work is represented in many outstanding museums and collections.

- *Thomas Hart Benton* (1889–1975) was considered a leader of the Regionalists, a movement he believed was important to the development of a truly American art form. He was a frequent visitor to Gallery 291, and a teacher at the New York Art Students' League. He painted a vast number of murals and later taught at the Kansas City Art Institute. One of his pupils was Jackson Pollock.

- *Charles Burchfield* (1893–1967) was considered a forerunner to the Regionalists because of his subject matter, which was small-town ugliness and squalor. His paintings frequently included evening scenes or dark, moody, romanticized skies.

- *Stuart Davis* (1894–1964) studied with Robert Henri and worked as a magazine cartoonist and illustrator before the Armory Show of 1913. He credited the Armory Show with entirely transforming his way of seeing and painting. His work featured brightly colored abstract forms and bold letters.

- *Lyonel Feininger* (1871–1956), although born in the United States, was raised in Germany, where he painted until he was almost 50 years old. He exhibited with members of the Blaue Reiter group and taught at the Bauhaus. His Cubist/Futurist technique was especially effective for his favorite subjects of cities and sailing ships.

- *Arshile Gorky* (1904–1948), one of the earliest Abstract Expressionists, shared a studio with Willem De Kooning. He immigrated to the United States from Turkish Armenia in 1920. His work is considered Surrealistic.

- *Edward Hopper* (1882–1967) is best known for his paintings of the lonely American landscape. His sensitivity to light transformed ordinary scenes of isolated houses, small-town life, beaches, and nightscapes of hotels and diners. Hopper was a student of Robert Henri, and his choice of Realistic subject matter owes something to the Ashcan School.

- *John Kane* (1860–1934) was a self-taught artist, a "naive" or primitive. Although he lacked formal training, his paintings were just as dynamic as those of some academically trained painters. He had been a house painter and then became a painter, recording scenes around him in painstaking detail.

- *Yasuo Kuniyoshi* (1893–1953) was born in Japan, but came to the United States in 1906 and studied at the New York Art Students' League and the Los Angeles School of Art and Design. His work was somewhat Surrealistic, exhibiting humor and fantasy.

- *Jacob Lawrence's* (b. 1917) long career has been devoted to depicting the social problems and aspirations of African-Americans such as *Frederick Douglass, Harriet Tubman,* and *John Brown.* Other series include *Toussaint L'Ouverture, Harlem,* and the historic migration of African-Americans from the South.

- *Reginald Marsh* (1898–1954) worked as an illustrator and cartoonist after completing his education at Yale. His paintings were based on teeming city life reminiscent of work by the Ashcan School, but Marsh showed urban conditions and was considered a Social Realist.

- *Georgia O'Keeffe's* (1887–1986) work spans several decades in the twentieth century, and is considered a seminal influence in Modernism. She distilled her subject to the essence, whether it was New York buildings, flowers, shells and bones, or the hills of the Southwest. A member of Gallery 291 and the wife of photographer Alfred Stieglitz, O'Keeffe is probably the best-known female artist in the world.

- *Horace Pippin* (1888–1946), a self-taught artist, painted highly personal scenes sometimes based on his World War I experience, and sometimes on his life as an African-American. His work developed at the same time as the Harlem Renaissance, but independently of it. Some of his best-known paintings were of the Abolitionist John Brown.

- *Ben Shahn* (1898–1969) took photographs for the Farm Security Administration during the Depression, and was considered at times "more propagandist than painter." His paintings ranged from Photographic Realism to cartoon-like exaggeration, as in his series on the notorious case of Sacco and Vanzetti which bitterly denounced the American legal system.

- *Charles Sheeler* (1883–1965), a photographer by profession, was known as a Precisionist, primarily for photo-like renderings of the industrial landscape and machinery. His subdued colors made his paintings constrained and unemotional.

- *Edward Weston* (1886–1958), a photographer and member of the F64 Group, Weston was especially well known for his photographs of green peppers and nudes (often his *Green Peppers looked* like nudes).

- *Grant Wood* (1892–1942) was one of the foremost Regionalist painters. His stylized paintings idealized rural life in mid-America. He also satirically illustrated favorite American folk tales and institutions such as the Daughters of the American Revolution.

FAMOUS AMERICAN SCULPTORS

- *Alexander Archipenko* (1887–1964) was Russian-born, but immigrated to the United States in 1923. He worked with the human form, simplifying and ultimately creating holes to make the negative space as important as the positive. He is considered a pioneer of Cubism, and is best known for multimedia sculptures composed of wood, glass, and wire.

- *Jo Davidson* (1883–1952) created bronze portraits of many famous people, including General Pershing, President Woodrow Wilson, and Gertrude Stein. He was trained in New York, but went to Paris for further training. He visited the United States periodically, but spent his life in Europe.

- *José De Creeft* (1884–1974) was born in Spain, coming to the United States in 1929. He was a successful sculptor before immigrating, carving directly in wood and stone. He introduced a method of forming lead sheet with a ball-peen hammer. The curved forms he specialized in were not totally abstract, and his work was considered Moderne.

- *Gaston Lachaise* (1882–1935) was born in Paris, the son of a woodcarver and cabinetmaker. He moved to the United States in 1906. His best-known work is of the exaggeratedly curved female form. He also did decorative sculpture for the American Telephone and Telegraph Building and Rockefeller Center's International Building. He worked for a time for Paul Manship.

- *Paul Manship* (1885–1966), an American-born sculptor, worked in the Art Deco manner, with stylized, streamlined figures and animals. Manship studied for three years in Rome, and his work reflects his fascination with Renaissance and archaic Greek sculpture. His work is always figural, combining the lines of Modernism with realistic interpretation.

- *Elie Nadelman* (1882–1946) was born in Warsaw, Poland, and came to the United States in 1914. He sculpted in a variety of materials, and was considered one of the most sophisticated sculptors during the 1930s. His work was of the human form, often clothed, usually rounded and very smooth and stylized. He was a student of art history, and often was inspired by Greek sculpture.

FAMOUS AMERICAN ARCHITECTS

- *Raymond Hood* (1881–1934) is best known for his work on Rockefeller Center and the Chicago Tribune tower. He spent his career designing skyscrapers.

- *Bernard Maybeck* (1862–1957), whose work was mostly designing private homes in California, felt that architecture should reflect the influence of past cultures, yet his work was quite experimental. His most famous work was the First Church of Christ Scientist (1911) in Berkeley, California. He also designed the Palace of Fine Arts in San Francisco.

- *Julia Morgan* (1872–1957) headed her own architectural office for 46 years, during a time when there were few female architects. She was the first woman ever accepted in Architecture at the École des Beaux-Arts in Paris. She designed more than 800 buildings, and is best known for the *William Randolph Hearst Castle* in San Simeon, California.

- *Richard Neutra* (1892–1970) designed the first completely steel-framed residence in the United States, and was closely associated with the International style. He was born in Vienna and immigrated to the United States in 1925.

- *Frank Lloyd Wright* (1867–1959) was in the vanguard of architecture. While his buildings seldom were taller than two stories, his prairie homes with their unique architectural forms and some of his California architecture remain contemporary.

FAMOUS ARTISTS AND SCHOOLS OF ART

- *Art Deco* (c. 1925). Art Deco referred to applied design that was primarily popular during the 1930s. It was used in buildings, furniture, decorative objects, jewelry, typefaces, and book bindings. It is an enduring facet of design that goes through periods of popularity and is appreciated by contemporary artists.

- *Precisionism* (1915–onward). Precisionist painters were sometimes called Cubist-Realists or the Immaculates. Their paintings were frequently based on photography, transforming cities, the industrial landscape and machinery to flattened shapes and strong shadows, stripped of detail almost to the point of abstraction. Precisionists' work was the precursor of Photo-Realists of the 1970s. The most famous of the group were Charles Sheeler (1883–1965), Charles Demuth (1883–1935), and (at times) Georgia O'Keeffe (1887–1986).

- *Group F64* (1930s). A group of San Francisco photographers shared the belief that a photograph should not imitate a work of art, but simply be what it was—a black-and-white image of the finest possible clarity. The group exhibited together from 1930 to 1935. Several of America's most influential photographers, including Ansel Adams (1902–1984), Imogen Cunningham (1883–1976), and Edward Weston (1886–1958), were part of this group.

- *American Scene Painting* (1930s). American Scene painters thought that American art needed its own typically American subjects and scenes. The best-known painters of this era were Edward Hopper (1882–1967), Charles Burchfield (1893–1967), and regional artists such as Reginald Marsh (1898–1954), and brothers Isaac (1907–1981), Moses (1899–1975) and Raphael Soyer (1899–1987). There is little difference between the American Scene painters and Regionalists, and some of the painters are identified with both schools.

- *Regionalism* (1930s). The Regionalists were genre painters who tried to capture a vanishing America. They painted people at work, American legends, and landscapes, preserving the atmosphere and life-styles of different areas of the country. The best-known Regionalists were Thomas Hart Benton (1889–1975), John Steuart Curry (1897–1946), Grant Wood (1892–1942), and Joe Jones (1909–1963).

- *The Bauhaus (German)* (1919–1933). The German Bauhaus strove to unify art and technology with all the handicraft techniques, and create a total work of art, the "Great Building." When the Nazis closed the Bauhaus School in Dessau, Germany, in 1933, many Bauhaus artists were displaced and immigrated to the United States. They established a short-lived *American Bauhaus* in Chicago in 1938. Widely influential in the field of American modern art and architecture were Bauhaus artists Lázló Maholy-Nagy (1895–1946), Lyonel Feininger (1871–1956), Josef Albers (1888–1976), and Hans Hofmann (1880–1966) and architects Ludwig Mies van der Rohe (1886–1969) and Walter Gropius (1883–1969).

- *Harlem Renaissance* (1919–1929). During the Harlem Renaissance, African American artists in *all* the art forms received recognition. Writers, musicians, painters, sculptors, dancers, and actors portrayed the African American experience in their art, with far-reaching results. Painters Aaron Douglas (1899–1979) and Palmer Hayden (1890–1973) and sculptor Meta Vaux Warrick Fuller (1877–1968) were most closely identified with the Harlem Renaissance, but later major artists who were associated with it are Jacob Lawrence (b. 1917), Romare Bearden (1914–1988), Hale Woodruff (1900–1980), William H. Johnson (1901–1970), Augusta Savage (1892–1962), Lois Mailou Jones (b. 1905), and Archibald Motley, Jr. (1891–1981). Many young African American artists were recruited to paint murals by the government during the Depression. The best known among these were Aaron Douglas, Charles Alston (1907–1977), and Hale

Woodruff. James Van Der Zee (1886–1983) was a well-known documentary photographer of Harlem in the 1920s.

- *Federal Arts Projects* (1933–1943). During the Depression, the Federal Government formed a number of different agencies to aid artists. Among these were PWAP (Public Works of Art Project), the WPA (Works Progress Administration), and the FSA (Farm Security Administration), which employed photographers such as Ansel Adams (1902–1984), Dorothea Lange (1895–1965), and Walker Evans (1903–1975), to record the lives of farmers and the unemployed during this difficult time.

- *Social Realism* (1920s–1930s). The Social Realists used their art to comment on the plight of poor or oppressed Americans. In 1936 they formed an Artists' Congress for the purpose of fighting facism, social inequities, and economic depression through their art. Some of these artists, such as Ben Shahn (1898–1969) and Jacob Lawrence, worked for the government during the Depression. Other Social Realists were Edward Hopper (1882–1967), Phillip Evergood, (1901–1975), and Stefan Hirsch (1899–1964).

- *Magic Realism* (c. 1943). Magic Realist painters fused their imaginary worlds with extremely realistic representations. Ivan le Lorraine Albright (1897–1983), Peter Blume (1906–1992), and Charles Sheeler (1883–1965) were among those whose work went beyond Social Realism. Blume was considered the American artist closest to Surrealism.

OVERVIEW OF THE ART BETWEEN THE WARS

The 1920s were a part of the transition to modern art that had begun ten years earlier and continued through the 1930s. A number of artists who became well known early in the century remained influential through the next several decades as their work evolved. Art appeared to swing from Realism to Modernism, and back to Realism in 10-year cycles—action and reaction. American art had come of age. Although most serious artists still went to Europe to study, generally they began their training in American art schools. Several American collectors, such as Gertrude Vanderbilt Whitney (founder of the Whitney Museum of American Art), Albert Barnes, Alfred Stieglitz, and Walter Arensberg, supported the work of American painters. Between 1921 and 1930, sixty new museums were founded. Many great collectors donated fine examples of ancient art, old masters, and European Modernism to museums.

Although there was not much market for the new work being created, it was an exciting time in the development of art. Established photographers, painters, architects, composers, playwrights, and sculptors found support for their talent through various government agencies. Painters were commissioned to paint murals on public buildings or to supply pictures for small traveling exhibitions and small-town museums. Photographers were hired to record the migration to California caused by weather conditions and lack of work. A number of movements took place during the 1920s and 1930s: American Scene Painting, the Harlem Renaissance, Social Realism, and Art Deco.

PAINTING

Although American Modernism began around the time of the Armory Show (1913), it was almost ten years before the work of major modern painters began to be appreciated. The artists with the most impact were those who developed an intensely personal style and allowed it to mature. In the 1920s in New York, there were two groups of painters—those from "291" and those from the Art Students' League, many of whom were students of Robert Henri and John Sloan. Painters from the Harlem Renaissance did not have any specific style, but to quote one of my professors, Dr. Leon Hicks, "mainly included three themes. They were: the New Negro, the Promise of America, the American Black Experience. . . . It is an art of ambiguities—filled with myths, mysticism, or unique visual symbols."

Examples of Paintings between the Wars

- **Painters from Gallery 291**

  Maine Islands, 1922, John Marin, Phillips Collection, Washington, D.C.

  Fog Horns, 1929, Arthur Dove, Colorado Springs Fine Arts Center

  Acrobats, 1919, Charles Demuth, Museum of Modern Art, New York

  I Saw the Figure Five in Gold, 1928, Charles Demuth, The Metropolitan Museum of Art, New York

  New York Night, 1928–1929, Georgia O'Keeffe, Nebraska Art Association, Sheldon Gallery, Lincoln, Nebraska

- **Precisionist Paintings (Cubist / Realist)**

  The Bridge, 1920–1922, Joseph Stella, Newark Museum, Newark, New Jersey

  House and Street, 1931, Stuart Davis, Whitney Museum of American Art, New York

  Classic Landscape, 1931, Charles Sheeler, The Saint Louis Art Museum

  Early Sunday Morning, 1930, Edward Hopper, Whitney Museum of American Art, New York

- **Social Realist Paintings**

  The Passion of Sacco and Vanzetti, 1931-1932, Ben Shahn, Whitney Museum of American Art, New York

  Nighthawks, 1942, Edward Hopper, Art Institute of Chicago

  The Artist and His Mother, 1926–1929, Arshile Gorky, Whitney Museum of American Art, New York

  Twenty Cent Movie, 1936, Reginald Marsh, Whitney Museum of American Art, New York

- **American Scene Painters / Regionalists**

  The American Historical Epic, 1924–1927, Thomas Hart Benton, Nelson-Atkins Museum, Kansas City, Missouri

  Artists on W.P.A., 1935, Moses Soyer, National Museum of American Art, Washington, D.C.

  Dinner for Threshers, 1934, Grant Wood, Whitney Museum of American Art, New York

  Sun and Rocks, 1950, Charles Burchfield, Albright-Knox Art Gallery, Buffalo, New York

- **Harlem Renaissance Paintings**

  Aspects of Negro Life: From Slavery Through Reconstruction, 1934, Aaron Douglas, Schomburg Center for Research in Black Culture, New York Public Library

Les Fetiches, 1938, Lois Mailou Jones, National Gallery of American Art, Washington, D.C.

Ethiopia Awakening, 1914, Meta Vaux Warrick Fuller, Schomburg Center for Research in Black Culture, New York Public Library

The Mutiny Aboard the Amistad, 1839, 1938–1939, Hale Woodruff, from the *Amistad Mutiny Mural,* Talladega College, Talladega, Alabama

Young Man in a Vest, c. 1939–1940, William H. Johnson, National Museum of American Art, Washington, D.C.

The Janitor Who Paints, 1939–1940, Palmer Hayden, National Museum of American Art, Washington, D.C.

SCULPTURE

Even before the Armory Show in 1913, American sculptors had already begun simplifying and abstracting natural forms. Many American artists had worked in Europe, and a number of European sculptors such as Gaston Lachaise (1882–1935), Elie Nadelman (1882–1946), Jose de Creeft (1884–1974), Alexander Archipenko (1887–1964), and Robert Laurent (1890–1970) had moved to the United States, so the Avant Garde sculpture seen in the Armory Show was already familiar.

The human figure was the primary subject for sculpture during the period between the wars. Until that time, figures had been allegorical, portrait busts, or memorials to famous people, but sculptors of this time were more interested in personal expression. Few of these sculptors were working with Cubism or total abstraction, as many of the painters were, but they were bringing personal insights into their portraits. Rather than working in clay and having assistants create molds and casts in bronze, sculptors were fascinated by direct carving, finding the personal involvement more satisfying.

Examples of Sculpture between the Wars

Floating Figure, 1935, Gaston Lachaise, Museum of Modern Art, New York

Cloud, 1939, José de Creeft, Whitney Museum of American Art, New York

Kneeling Figure, 1935, Robert Laurent, Whitney Museum of American Art, New York

Handlebar Riders, 1935, Chaim Gross, Museum of Modern Art, New York

Indian Hunter with Dog, 1926, Paul Manship, The Metropolitan Museum of Art, New York

Gertrude Stein, 1920, Jo Davidson, Whitney Museum of American Art, New York

Lobster Trap and Fish Tails, 1939, Alexander Calder, Museum of Modern Art, New York

ARCHITECTURE

The period between the wars seemed to spawn an incredible variation in types of architecture. Some of the styles were Frank Lloyd Wright's Prairie Style, the Spanish Revival style of California and Florida, Arte Moderne, revival architecture such as San Simeon in California or the Tribune Tower in Chicago, and the International style that consisted of flat roofs. Skyscrapers abounded, and some of the most beautiful buildings of this period still dominate many American cities.

Art Deco is perhaps the most memorable architectural style of the 1930s. Art Deco buildings were defined by strong vertical or horizontal lines, but still had decorative effects consisting of swirls, shells, sculptured figures, and geometric forms. Molded chrome and etched glass were used in big city skyscrapers and on ocean liners. A resurgence of interest in this sleek, decorative style is apparent in contemporary buildings.

Examples of Architecture between the Wars

Falling Water, 1936, Frank Lloyd Wright, Bear Run, Pennsylvania

La Casa Grande, San Simeon, 1919–1939, Julia Morgan, San Simeon, California

Gulfstream Golf Club, 1923, Addison Mizner, Palm Beach, Florida

William L. Clements Library, 1920–1921, Albert Kahn, University of Michigan, Ann Arbor

House for Dr. Phillip Lovell, 1927–1929, Richard Neutra, Los Angeles, California

Johnson Wax Building, 1936, Frank Lloyd Wright, Racine, Wisconsin

Tribune Building, 1925, Hood and Howells, Chicago

Photo 7-0. *Dining Chair,* **1901, Frank Lloyd Wright. This chair, designed for the Ward Willits House in Highland Park, Illinois demonstrates Wright's characteristic unified architecture that included not only interior and exterior designs, but the furniture as well. Purchase funds given by the Decorative Arts Society, The Saint Louis Art Museum.**

PROJECT 7-1: **THE CHANGING LANDSCAPE: 2-D TO 3-D**

FOR THE TEACHER

SLIDE #23: *Rapt at Rappaport's,* **October 1952, Stuart Davis, 50 × 40 inches, oil on canvas, Gift of Joseph H. Hirshhorn Foundation, 1966, Hirshhorn Museum and Sculpture Garden, Smithsonian Institution. Photography by Lee Stalsworth**

Stuart Davis (1894–1964) was an abstract painter of American scenes. He studied with Realist painter Robert Henri at the New York Art Students' League and exhibited in the Armory Show. He credits this exhibition with being the greatest single influence in his work, and claims that he spent the rest of his career incorporating Armory Show ideas into his work. He tried to convey in his art something of the vitality he felt so keenly in jazz music. He said, "I paint what I see in America, in other words, I paint the American scene." He was one of the earliest American painters to use letters as part of a composition. Straddling the line between reality and abstraction, he is sometimes credited with opening the way for Pop Art.

Major Paintings by Stuart Davis

Report from Rockport, 1940, collection of Mr. and Mrs. Milton Lowenthal, New York

Colonial Cubism, 1954, Walker Art Center, Minneapolis

Lucky Strike, 1921, Museum of Modern Art, New York

Egg Beater, Number 2, 1927, Whitney Museum of American Art, New York

Blips and Ifs, 1963–1964, Amon Carter Museum, Fort Worth

The Paris Bit, 1959, Whitney Museum of American Art, New York

Something on the Eight Ball, 1954, Philadelphia Museum of Art

Visa, 1951, Museum of Modern Art, New York

PREPARATION

The bright colors and details created with letters make Davis's paintings dynamic. Reproductions are available in many different books, and it would be helpful for students to see examples. Demonstrate how to score cardboard using scissors and a ruler to fold it neatly. Assure students that their work won't be an exact copy of a Stuart painting because their interpretation will be a three-dimensional sculpture.

If colored posterboard is not available, tagboard or ordinary cardboard may be used and painted after construction with tempera paint.

ADDITIONAL SUGGESTIONS

- Two-dimensional (flat) collage would be a natural project based on Davis's work. He composed his paintings with line drawings first, then added color "intervals." Fadeless paper would be more fun to use because of its brightness, but construction paper is adequate. Remind students not to throw away any scraps, as sometimes the negative shapes can be used for accent.

- Allow students to select any work of art from an art magazine and interpret it three-dimensionally. This could be done with cardboard, sculpt-tape, papier-mâché, wire, or any other suitable material. Display the original and the interpretation side-by-side.

- Have students interpret their collage by doing a drawing of a small section of it in pencil, creating differences in value through texture.

Photo 7-1A. *Still Life—Feasible #2,* 1949–1951, Stuart Davis, 11-⅞ × 16-⅛ inches, Gift of Morton D. May, The Saint Louis Art Museum.

Photo 7-1B. *Visa,* 1951, Stuart Davis, oil on canvas, 40 × 52 inches, gift of Mrs. Gertrud A. Mellon, Collection, The Museum of Modern Art, New York. Geoffrey Clements, Photography.

PROJECT 7-1: **THE CHANGING LANDSCAPE: 2-D TO 3-D**

MATERIALS

- Colored railroad board or posterboard
- Fadeless paper or construction paper
- Rulers
- Pencils
- Scissors
- X-acto™ knives
- White glue or Tacky™ glue

Blips and Ifs, 1963–1964
Stuart Davis
Amon Carter Museum
Fort Worth, Texas

You will be creating a three-dimensional city landscape from the paintings of Stuart Davis, an artist of the 1930s. Davis often painted portions of buildings and signs as if they were abstract, though his paintings were always based on reality. This project involves transforming a two-dimensional painting into a three-dimensional sculpture, using bright colors and simple forms, enhanced with cut-out letters. A triangular shape, for example, might be made into a pyramid, or a square shape could be a box. Your finished work may bear little resemblance to that of Davis's, but should still be interesting because of the variety of shapes and colors you use.

1. Select at least five pieces of colored posterboard and black or white. Bright reds, greens, blues, and yellows accented with white or black are appropriate for this project. To make cardboard three-dimensional, you will need to make folds and almost create boxes.

2. To score cardboard so it will fold in a perfect line, draw the point of scissors along the edge of a ruler to mark fold-lines on the back of the cardboard, then fold inward. If you want to add letters to the shapes or the composition, use an X-acto™ knife to cut letters from fadeless paper and glue them onto the posterboard. *Safety note: Always keep your fingers behind the knife when cutting, in case it should slip.*

3. When you have made as faithful an interpretation of Davis's painting as possible, insert something of your own. It could be something as simple as cutting out your initials or adding a word or number that means something to you. If you think the picture lacks a point of emphasis, you may want to outline some areas with black marker, add more color, or repeat a color somewhere.

4. Use white or Tacky™ glue to hold shapes together. It may be necessary to use straight pins to hold forms while they dry. Stand back and look at the work and consider whether to add more shapes or letters, or whether additional sculptural material or color could add line for the finish you need.

Rapt at Rappaports, 1952
Hirshhorn Museum and Sculpture Garden
Washington, D.C.

Drawn after *New York—Paris No. 2*
Stuart Davis
Portland Museum of Art, Portland, Maine

PROJECT 7-2: MONUMENTAL FLOWERS IN WATERCOLOR

FOR THE TEACHER

SLIDE #24: *Jack-in-the-Pulpit No. IV,* 1930, Georgia O'Keeffe, 40 × 30 inches, oil on canvas, National Gallery of Art, Washington, D.C.

Georgia O'Keeffe's (1887–1986) long and productive career spanned many "isms," starting with Modernism, when she exhibited at Gallery 291, which was founded by her husband, photographer Alfred Stieglitz. Although some critics say that her work was influenced by the dynamic photography of the 1920s, she had her own unique vision. She was her own most demanding critic, destroying many works she felt were not up to her standards. Although she said she rarely learned anything from her teachers (she later became an art teacher) and she didn't like school, she remembered a high school art class where the teacher brought in a jack-in-the-pulpit and "pointed out the strange shapes and variations in color—from the deep, almost black earthy violet through all the greens, from the pale whitish green in the flower through the heavy green of the leaves." Later she wrote, "So I said to myself—I'll paint what I see—what the flower is to me but I'll paint it big and they will be surprised into taking time to look at it—I will make even busy New Yorkers take time to see what I see of flowers." (From *Georgia O'Keeffe,* Georgia O'Keeffe [New York: Viking Press, 1976, pp. 4 and 23.])

Paintings by Georgia O'Keeffe

Black Cross, New Mexico, 1929, The Art Institute of Chicago

Cow's Skull—Red, White and Blue, 1931, The Metropolitan Museum of Art, New York

From the Faraway Nearby, 1937, The Metropolitan Museum of Art, New York

Music—Pink and Blue I, 1919, Saint Louis Art Museum

Black Iris III, 1926, The Metropolitan Museum of Art, New York

The Mountain, New Mexico, 1931, Whitney Museum of American Art, New York

Yellow Cactus Flowers, 1929, Fort Worth Art Museum

PREPARATION

This project was developed by a colleague, Bonnie Enos. Show students photos of work by Georgia O'Keeffe and point out how she simplified shapes and allowed her subjects to run off the edges. Funeral homes are a great source for fresh flowers (call and tell them your purpose, and they may be willing to hold some discards for you). Another option is to buy silk flowers or have students bring one from home.

ADDITIONAL SUGGESTIONS

- Play music and ask your students to paint to it. Different types of music inspire different types of paintings. O'Keeffe talked about passing by a class at Columbia University where music was playing and students were asked to draw what they heard. She sat down and made a drawing. She said, "This gave me an idea that I was very interested to follow later—the idea that music could be translated into something for the eye." (*Georgia O'Keeffe,* p. 14.) *Music—Pink and Blue I* (1919) was made to express this idea.

- Paint a portion of architecture, such as a barn, house, or skyscraper, in the spare manner of Georgia O'Keeffe's. She eliminated almost everything except doors and windows, painting only simple shapes with shadows and light. At times she painted only a small portion of a building, but allowed it to fill the picture. This would be effective in acrylic, tempera, oil paint, or pastels.

- Use acrylic paint to reproduce a Georgia O'Keeffe painting on a folding metal chair, picture or mirror frame, discarded piece of furniture, or an old plate.

- In several paintings, Georgia O'Keeffe made the small monumental by putting the small object close to the viewer, yet placing it in a vast landscape. A shell or some other small object such as a bone can be the main subject, with a real or fantasy background to complete the composition.

Photo 7-2. *Apple Blossoms*, **1930, Georgia O'Keeffe, oil on canvas, 36 × 24 inches, Gift of Mrs. Louis Sosland, The Nelson-Atkins Museum of Art, Kansas City, Missouri. Photography by Robert Newcombe.**

PROJECT 7-2: MONUMENTAL FLOWERS IN WATERCOLOR

MATERIALS

- Watercolor paper
- Pencils
- Brushes
- Watercolors
- Flowers, real or artificial
- Rubber cement

Drawn from *Two Jimson Weeds*, 1938
Georgia O'Keeffe
Collection of Anita O'Keeffe Young

Georgia O'Keeffe was considered one of the first important female artists. She often painted small objects, such as a flower or shell, so large that it filled the page and ran off it. She painted what was around her, whether buildings in New York, hills and crosses in New Mexico, flowers wherever she was, or a barrel of bones she once had shipped East from New Mexico.

This project is to paint a monumental flower in the manner of Georgia O'Keeffe. The flower you choose will dictate whether you have a dark or light painting. With watercolor, you can build from light to dark color (glazing) by allowing the underneath color to dry first.

1. Look carefully at the parts of the flower, holding it at different angles to see how you will paint it. You can paint it from the side or looking straight down into it. You may paint it more than one time or in combination with another flower or two.

2. Remember that you are painting a monumental flower. You will not paint it in its entirety, but will allow it to run off at least three edges of your paper. Draw it lightly in pencil before you begin.

3. Select a scheme of three or four colors. These should relate to the color of the flower, but you will also use colors that are not on the flower to create value differences, shadows, and background. Your painting could be quite dark, if you choose.

4. Plan to leave at least some portion of the painting white for contrast. If you are afraid you will accidentally paint the white area, apply a rubber-cement resist in that area with a brush, and erase it later. Consider adding a contrasting color to your painting, such as a touch of red in a basically green painting. If you are uncertain about colors, always test them on scrap paper before applying them to the watercolor paper.

PROJECT 7-3: **GREEN PEPPERS**

FOR THE TEACHER

F64 is the camera aperture preferred by a group of photographers in the 1930s, Group F64. It represents the smallest lens opening on a large format camera that will give great depth of field and sharpness. Members of this group exhibited together for only five years, but the work of several of them, such as Imogen Cunningham (1883–1976), Edward Weston (1886–1958), and Ansel Adams (1902–1984), is familiar to most people. They selected similar subjects to photograph—plants, people, twisted wood, scenes in the desert or by the sea—yet the work of each shows individuality. Among other subjects, Weston photographed a series of vegetables, and his (green) *Pepper* photographs are familiar to many.

Masterpieces by the F64 Group

Pepper, 1930, Edward Weston, Los Angeles County Museum of Art

Eroded Rock, Point Lobos, 1930, Edward Weston, The Metropolitan Museum of Art, New York

Clearing Winter Storm, Yosemite National Park, California, 1944, Ansel Adams, University of Arizona, Phoenix

Snake, 1929, Imogen Cunningham, Art Institute of Chicago

Moonrise Over Hernandez, 1941, Ansel Adams, Collection of the Ansel Adams Trust

Two Callas, c. 1929, Imogen Cunningham, Imogen Cunningham Trust, Berkeley, California

PREPARATION

In this project students will really look at a strongly lit subject, such as a vegetable, and draw it in pencil, shading until it is perfect. Discuss photography and mention to students that color photographs were rare until relatively recently. Photographers worked in black and white, and the Group F64 was special because of the contrast with which they printed and the simplicity of their subjects.

Have students bring in something from nature to draw (offer extra credit if they remember within three days). They might have fun (and feel a little foolish) going to the store (as Weston probably did) to select *the one* green pepper, artichoke, or plant that would be the most interesting to use in a composition. Have a few shells or pieces of driftwood on hand for students who forget to bring something. Using photo floods, light the subject from one side, or have students work near a window. Stress making the object larger than life and filling the picture plane.

ADDITIONAL SUGGESTIONS

- Bring in several green peppers. Cut one or two in half crosswise, cut another lengthwise, and leave some whole. Have students do *small,* quick sketches on separate pieces of tracing paper of the peppers from various angles and in various states. Have them move the pieces of tracing paper around, overlapping until they find a pleasing composition, then make a final drawing on one piece of tracing paper. They can then transfer this drawing to larger drawing paper and use marker or watercolor to complete. The colors needn't be realistic—everyone will know they are peppers. (Thanks to Bonnie Enos, a colleague, who developed this project.)

- Have students bring in peppers, onions, cucumbers, apples, and other hard vegetables. Stamp print with them by cutting them in half. Ink them on a paper towel or a sponge soaked with tempera paint or colored ink. Stamp the vegetable onto a piece of drawing paper. Allow students to experiment, using several small sheets of drawing paper. Then challenge the students to make a complete stamped composition on one piece of drawing paper, going over it after it dries with crayon or oil pastels. Extra stampings can be torn or cut out and incorporated into the design by gluing them on.

- This is a perfect photography assignment for students. Carefully look at lighting and make a picture of an object from nature with as small an aperture as possible. If you have even one adjustable camera available, buy black-and-white film and allow each student to take two or three photographs of an object he or she has brought in. (If doing this in black-and-white film, use a gray card [purchased at a camera store] for perfect exposures.)

Photo 7-3. *Water Hyacinth,* **1920s, Imogen Cunningham, platinum print, 11⁷/₁₆ × 8⁷/₈ inches, Purchase: Friends Fund, The Saint Louis Art Museum. This print by Imogen Cunningham illustrates the extreme clarity achieved by using the smallest opening on the camera, F 64.**

PROJECT 7-3: **GREEN PEPPERS**

MATERIALS

- Peppers, flowers, shells, or other natural objects
- Drawing or charcoal pencils
- 8 × 10-inch paper
- Typing paper cover sheet

This project is to render (draw) an ordinary object from nature much larger than its real size. It is based on a group of photographers, Group F64, who brought drama to the objects in their works by filling the frame with an object and printing in strong black and white. You may need special drawing pencils that range from hard to soft, with the soft ones coloring the darkest. Ansel Adams of the Group F64 identified 10 "zones" ranging from white to black in photographs. You should have that many values in your drawing.

1. Make a small 1 × 10-inch value scale by tracing around a ruler. Divide this into 1-inch squares. Leave one end white and make the sections progressively darker until the tenth one is as black as possible. This should not take long and will be a handy reference.

2. Decide what type of background to use for your object. It can contrast dramatically or be of the same general value as your subject. It is not easy to look at a colored object and draw it in black and white. You must look for the lightest areas and the darkest areas. To see this, almost completely close your eyes and squint through your eyelashes. This helps eliminate the colors.

3. When you are drawing with pencil, rest your hand on a "cover" sheet to prevent the drawing from smearing. Do not scribble. Work in smooth, even strokes, filling in the white paper as you go, whether you are pressing lightly or firmly.

4. Stand back and look at your composition from a distance to see if you have sufficient value differences. Continue until you know that some areas are as dark as possible.

Drawn from *Pepper,* 1930
Edward Weston

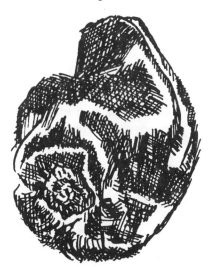

Drawn from *Pepper,* 1930
Edward Weston

PROJECT 7-4: **THE INDUSTRIAL LANDSCAPE**

FOR THE TEACHER

SLIDE #25: *Classic Landscape,* **1931, Charles Sheeler, 25 × 32-¼ inches, oil on canvas, Collection of Mr. and Mrs. Barney A. Ebsworth Foundation, The Saint Louis Art Museum**

A photographer by profession, Charles Sheeler's (1883–1965) paintings incorporated the strong shadows, flattened shapes, and hard edges characteristic of photographs. He tried to simplify forms almost to abstraction, keeping only what he believed to be necessary for the design of the picture. His early work sometimes featured skewed viewpoints of interiors containing simple Shaker furniture. Later he became fascinated by industrial landscape and machinery. He was one of a group of painters called the Precisionists, whose work showed a Cubist influence.

Masterworks by Sheeler

City Interior, 1936, Worcester Art Museum, Worcester, Massachusetts

Barn Abstraction, 1918, Philadelphia Museum of Art

American Interior, 1934, Yale University Art Gallery, New Haven

Architectural Cadences, 1954, Whitney Museum of American Art, New York

River Rouge Plant, 1932, Whitney Museum of American Art, New York

Upper Deck, 1929, Fogg Art Museum, Cambridge, Massachusetts

Americana, 1931, collection of Edith and Milton Lowenthal, New York

PREPARATION

No matter where you live, you will find subject matter that was beloved by Charles Sheeler. He painted barns, skyscrapers, factories, trains, and machinery. Walk around inside the school building or go outside to sketch, having students draw corners, shadows, and intricate relationships between shapes. Try to find photographs of Sheeler's work so students will see how it is possible to tidy up a subject by having sharp edges. Drawing boards for students to use outside the classroom can be made from large pieces of cardboard, foam core, or masonite.

ADDITIONAL SUGGESTIONS

- Use cardboard tubes and empty boxes to create a three-dimensional "industrial complex." This would be an ongoing group project, with students bringing in bathroom tissue and paper towel tubes, shoe boxes, etc. "Gift-wrap" these in pale-colored construction paper, rearranging them onto a cardboard base (glue them together if you wish). Use a flood light to create strong shadows and have students draw or paint from their own "factories."

- Create an abstraction of buildings by allowing students to look through magazines to find pictures of buildings such as barns, houses, or factories. Have them cut these out and make a collage of them, overlapping and repeating a few of the shapes on plain paper. Have them do a painting of these shapes, eliminating almost all details.

- After drawing in basic shapes of a building, students can use a black calligraphy pen-marker to carefully make a variety of textures in the building and its background. It is helpful to have a chart or handout that demonstrates a variety of textures, but students can be surprisingly creative when told that originality and creativity are important.

Photo 7-4. *Classic Landscape*, 1931, Charles Sheeler, 25 × 32-¼ inches, oil on canvas, Collection of Mr. and Mrs. Barney A. Ebsworth Foundation, The Saint Louis Art Museum.

PROJECT 7-4: **THE INDUSTRIAL LANDSCAPE**

MATERIALS

- 18 × 24-inch drawing paper
- 20 × 28-inch drawing boards
- Masking tape (to hold paper on drawing boards)
- Rulers
- Tempera or acrylic paint
- Brushes
- Pencils

Drawn from *Classic Landscape*, 1931
Charles Sheeler
Collection of Mr. and Mrs. Barney Ebsworth
The Saint Louis Art Museum

Charles Sheeler was a photographer who became a painter. He was sometimes called a Precisionist because his paintings were so exact. Many of his paintings related to machinery; industrial complexes such as the Ford Plant at River Rouge, Michigan; skyscrapers; or barns. Because he worked from his own black-and-white photographs, his paintings had subdued colors. He also simplified and eliminated as many details as possible, concentrating instead on forms and shadows.

1. Select a subject like one Sheeler used (trains, boats, factories, ships, barns), working either from your own or family photographs or a magazine. When you have eliminated details and cropped (enlarged a portion of your subject), there will probably be little relationship to the source of your painting.

2. On a piece of drawing paper, lightly draw the subject you will paint. If necessary, use a ruler. Do not allow it to "float" in the middle, isolated; rather, use your imagination to add more buildings, overlapping and sometimes repeating shapes. Complete your composition in pencil.

3. Draw shadows lightly with pencil. If it is late afternoon, shadows will be long and from one direction.

4. Select a subtle color scheme. Paint in several values of one color such as soft beige, blue, or gray. To create shadows, "gray" or darken the area on which the shadow falls. Shade one side of your building. If you want to use a bright color, save it for a place where it will add sparkle to the painting.

PROJECT 7-5: THE LEGACY OF THE HARLEM RENAISSANCE

FOR THE TEACHER

SLIDE #26: *The Library,* 1960, Jacob Lawrence, 24 × 29-⅞ inches, tempera on fiberboard, Gift of S. C. Johnson & Son, Inc., National Museum of American Art, Smithsonian Institution / Art Resource, NY

The Harlem Renaissance took place from 1919 to 1929, and involved all the arts (literature, dance, music, visual arts). Although Jacob Lawrence (b. 1917) was too young to have been part of the Harlem Renaissance, he built on the artistic traditions established by Harlem Renaissance artists such as painters Aaron Douglas (1899–1979) and Palmer Hayden (1890–1973) and sculptor Meta Vaux Warrick Fuller (1877–1968). Lawrence began his career on the Federal Art Project of the Works Progress Administration (W.P.A.) in the late 1930s in New York as soon as he was of legal age. He was furnished materials, paid a salary, and allowed to paint any subject he wished. He created 30 paintings of African-Americans at work and play in the *Harlem* series. He is considered a Social Realist because of his paintings of daily life and the hardships it presented. His work is recognizable by defined shapes, flat colors, and dramatic, simplified design. His paintings were usually small, mostly painted with gouache or tempera. Lawrence said, "My belief is that it is most important for an artist to develop an approach and philosophy about life—if he has developed this philosophy, he does not put paint on canvas, he puts himself on canvas."

Notable Paintings by Lawrence

This Is Harlem, 1942–1943, Hirshhorn Museum and Sculpture Garden, Washington, D.C.

Cabinet Makers, 1946, Hirshhorn Museum and Sculpture Garden, Washington, D.C.

Blind Beggars, 1938, The Metropolitan Museum of Art, New York

In a Free Government, the Security of Civil Rights Must Be the Same as That for Religious (Great Ideas Series), 1976, National Museum of American Art, Smithsonian Institution, Washington, D.C.

John Brown, 1941, Detroit Institute of the Arts

And the Migrants Kept Coming (Series), 1940–1941, Museum of Modern Art, New York, and Phillips Collection, Washington, D.C.

General Toussaint L'Ouverture Defeats the English at Saline, 1938, Amistad Research Center, Tulane University, New Orleans, Louisiana

The Studio, 1977, Brooklyn Museum, New York

Study for the Munich Olympic Games Poster, 1972, Seattle Art Museum

Dreams #2, 1965, National Museum of American Art, Smithsonian Institution, Washington, D.C.

PREPARATION

Although this project is about notable African Americans as painted by Jacob Lawrence, Lawrence's method of painting is applicable to any picture with people in it. Try to get books or slides showing Lawrence's paintings. Point out to students the simple background shapes with which he completed his paintings and his mastery of contrast. Discuss painting without shading (modeling) versus traditional painting methods.

ADDITIONAL SUGGESTIONS

- Using fadeless or construction paper, students can make a cut-paper collage poster to advertise a sporting event such as an Olympic festival (Lawrence did this). This poster should have people of all ethnic backgrounds participating in sports (running, swimming, wrestling, etc.). As a real challenge, students cannot draw on the paper before cutting, but simply cut out shapes with scissors. Nothing should be pasted down until all the pieces are cut out and arranged. Of necessity the cutouts of people will be unrealistic.

- Have students write or tell about someone whose life has inspired them, and why. It might be a parent, relative, public figure, or simply a person who has made a difference in their lives. Have students select one episode in the life of this person and do a pencil drawing, complete with background. Jacob Lawrence's series of Harriet Tubman, an abolitionist, was inspired by admiration for her leadership.

Photo 7-5. *Supermarket—Produce*, c. 1993–1994, Jacob Lawrence, gouache on paper, 31 × 25 inches, Purchase: Museum Minority Artists Purchase Fund, The Saint Louis Art Museum. This is one of a series of supermarket scenes painted near Lawrence's home in Seattle. The strong greens and oranges, the angles and simplified shapes, the effective use of the human figure make this a perfect example of Lawrence's work.

PROJECT 7-5: **THE LEGACY OF THE HARLEM RENAISSANCE**

MATERIALS

- 9 × 12-inch drawing paper
- Tempera paint
- Brushes
- Pencils

Paintings by Jacob Lawrence, a famous African American painter, were notable for their bright colors and simple shapes. Every picture told a story about some aspect of being an African American.

1. Select a public figure of any ethnic background (for example, a politician, actor, or musician). Try to design an environment where you would envision this person. It might be a stage, a workroom, a restaurant, a pool room, a swimming pool, or at home in a living room with family. If this person has some outstanding moment of achievement, you might choose to show that event.

2. Lightly draw the figure (and any other figures you might imagine in this scene). Plan a simple background. An indoor background would have walls, doors, windows—often large, simple rectangular shapes.

3. Your paintings will be more believable if tempera paints are mixed, rather than using colors straight from the container. Select a primary or secondary color, and vary it by lightening it with yellow rather than white, or darken it by adding violet or green. Colors may be grayed by adding the complementary color (a touch of green mixed with red gives more sparkle than black added to red). As an accent, add complementary color to the painting (if you have a violet painting, for example, yellow will give a little life to it).

4. Paint these shapes with almost no shading, leaving the colors "flat." Remember, you are not trying to achieve realistic portrayal here. You are experimenting with another way of applying paint. When your painting is dry, look carefully at it. It might benefit from having a few lines added as accent.

5. If necessary, you can overpaint with tempera, but try to avoid it as much as possible because tempera will flake off if it is put on too thickly.

Drawn from
***Poster Design . . .* Whitney Exhibition, 1974**
Jacob Lawrence

PROJECT 7-6: COLLAGE IN THE MANNER OF ROMARE BEARDEN

FOR THE TEACHER

SLIDE #27: *The Dove,* 1964, Romare Bearden, The Museum of Modern Art, New York

Although Romare Bearden (1914–1988) was born too late to be part of the Harlem Renaissance, he cared deeply about promoting African American artists and their art. Most of his work had a theme, and much of it included African American people. He was a founding member of a group of artists called Spiral who questioned whether African Americans should paint art that referred to their heritage, or could promote the cause of African American artists by simply painting art that was meaningful to them. He was one of the first African American artists to be honored by the Museum of Modern Art with a one-man exhibition.

Although Bearden was first a painter, this project is based on his later work, collages, which combine painted paper, magazine pictures, and some original photos.

Masterpieces by Romare Bearden

The Falling Star, 1980, Estate of Romare Bearden, ACA Galleries, New York

The Piano Lesson, 1983, Estate of Romare Bearden, ACA Galleries, New York

House in Cotton Field, 1968, Estate of Romare Bearden, ACA Galleries, New York

PREPARATION

If possible, try to get original black-and-white photos from photo classes or yearbooks from previous years. Although this project could be done with photocopies of color photos, the photographs' textures will give additional interest. Try to get a variety of colored papers, even wrapping paper, to use as background. Of course, students can also put bright watercolor splashes on their drawing paper and cut it up for part of their collages.

ADDITIONAL SUGGESTIONS

- Cut up photographs and staple or tape them to an 18 × 24-inch canvas board (cardboard would be a substitute). Then use acrylic in different values of one color to tie the photographs together visually with paint. Staples may be used freely as a decorative accent.

- Extend a black-and-white photograph by dry mounting or rubber-cementing the photograph to a much larger 14-ply mountboard background (for example, an 8 × 10-inch photograph on a 22 × 28-inch board). With acrylic paint, colored pencil, or oil pastels, the photograph is extended by continuing lines within the photo almost out to the edges. Although the edges of the photo may be painted, it is more effective to leave it black and white. Obviously, most students have small color photos that could also be used for this exercise.

Photo 7-6. This student-made collage is composed of torn photographs and fadeless paper.

PROJECT 7-6: COLLAGE IN THE MANNER OF ROMARE BEARDEN

MATERIALS

- 12 × 18-inch tagboard or posterboard
- Black-and-white photographs
- Colored fadeless paper
- Rubber cement or glue stick
- Magazines

Romare Bearden began his career as a painter, but his later work was collage. He interpreted scenes of African Americans doing the everyday things most people do: taking a piano lesson, stopping for a cup of coffee before getting back to work, working in the garden with the family, or getting dressed to go out. He usually included a few figures, mostly created with brightly colored cut-out paper (at times incorporating cut-out photographs of humans).

1. Decide what scene in *your* day you want to interpret in collage. You might be participating in sports, sitting at the breakfast table, watching TV, or washing a car (or studying?).

2. Select a warm or cool color scheme, then use the exact opposite color for accent (for example, a dominantly yellow composition might also call for blue and violet). Use bright colors freely. A good composition should have a dominant color, whether it is blue, red, gold, or magenta. Go through magazines and find some areas of plain color used in ads or illustrations. These should only be cut-out shapes with few details.

3. Think about where your event will take place, and plan how to fill the background. Plan where you might want to place another person or two in this composition. You could also cut details of anatomy such as hands, feet, or heads. If black-and-white photographs are available, use these in place of magazine cutouts.

4. Before gluing anything down, make neat edges on the paper. You can tear *or* cut paper into unusual shapes—some large and some small—but don't be sloppy about it. In addition to magazine cutouts, use similar shades of fadeless (very bright) paper. Use the larger blank shapes as background, going clear to the edges of the posterboard.

5. Once you have everything glued down, if you think it will add interest to the composition, paint details with acrylic or tempera, or use oil pastel to give emphasis.

PROJECT 7-7: **ART DECO ELEVATOR DOORS**

FOR THE TEACHER

Art Deco is based on European Modernism and, except in the area of architecture, was slow in being accepted in the United States. One of the identifying characteristics of Art Deco, the ziggurat-like form, came about because New York City passed an ordinance in 1916 requiring skyscrapers to have stepped-back top levels in order to allow more light to filter down. The Public Works Administration (P.W.A.) and Works Progress Administration (W.P.A.) employed artisans in all fields during the 1930s, with sculptors, painters, architects, and craftsmen working together to create buildings that were artistically unified inside and out. Details such as elevator doors, light fittings, mail boxes and radiator covers were important in the design.

The Art Deco style, with its streamlining related to Futurism and its abhorrence of traditional decorative detail such as the acanthus leaf, was firmly entrenched. The Chrysler building was embellished with automotive designs based on hub-caps and radiator ornaments. Incidentally, the spire on the Empire State Building was to be used as a mooring post for blimps (air ships). This was before the Hindenburg burned, and before they realized that updrafts in the city did not make this practical. Many of the major buildings throughout the country, including numerous extravagant movie theaters, were built during the 1930s in the Art Deco manner.

Examples of Art Deco Architecture

Chrysler Building, 1928–1930, William Van Alen, New York

Empire State Building, 1932, Shreve, Lamb, and Harmon, New York

Rockefeller Center, 1931–1940, Raymond Hood and others, New York

Former McGraw-Hill Building, 1931, Raymond Hood, New York

Tribune Tower, 1925, Hood and Howells, Chicago

PREPARATION

Discuss the far-reaching impact of Art Deco in every field of design, including pottery, the movies (which influenced design), jewelry and clocks, automobiles, furniture, typefaces, and advertising. Ask students to bring in examples (pictures or actual objects) of similar design. With the Art Deco revival, contemporary items are available. Books could be photocopied to give ideas.

ADDITIONAL SUGGESTIONS

- Create a three-dimensional Art Deco elevator door design by building up three or more layers of heavy watercolor paper cutouts, with each layer progressively smaller. After cutting out the base (layer #1), trace around outside it in pencil, then make layer #2 a quarter inch smaller than layer #1. Cut out layer #2, and repeat the procedure for layer #3. Place the three layers together to see if more cutting is necessary, or if details should be cut out before gluing them together on a watercolor background. *Safety note: Remind students to have the non-cutting hand behind the knife at all times.*

- Have students use cardboard cartons and cardboard to make models of buildings to wear on their shoulders or heads. A group of famous New York architects once did this for a costume party, with each one wearing the building he had designed.

- Designs for Art Deco textiles and rugs were sometimes created in black and white. Students could create several small marker drawings of motifs based on Aztec, Mayan, Egyptian, or Incan designs, then move these around, combining them with lines, swirls, and circles to create a design for a rug or wall hanging.

- As a major "integrated" design project to be mounted on a large sheet of posterboard, have students make complete details of designs for the lobby of a skyscraper or interior of a cruise ship in the Art Deco manner. Include such things as mail-box slots, dining room chandeliers, carpeting, elevator doors, entrance doors, signs, and decorative sculpture.

- Paint a model of a three-part screen in the Art Deco manner on watercolor paper folded in thirds. This could also be done by scoring heavy posterboard or foam board. A small Art Deco screen of this type could be freestanding on a table.

- Designs could be made for decorative Art Deco windows in the manner of Frank Lloyd Wright. With straight lines and circles, and limited but bright color accents, students can do them on long scraps of posterboard, then mount them on black and display them as a group.

- Creating Art Deco designs is perfect for tooling foil repoussé. In the 1930s, brass and bronze were widely used for decorative detail. Art Deco design, with its swirls, human figures, and relief sculpture, lends itself well to interpretation by students.

- The stylization of animals and humans in the Art Deco manner would be an interesting clay-sculpture project for students. This could be done three-dimensionally or in bas-relief.

- Make Art Deco collagraph prints by gluing successive layers of tagboard using straight lines, circles, and typical Art Deco designs. When finished, have students coat the layers with polymer medium, allowing it to dry before using a brayer to apply ink for printing.

Photo 7-7. *Celestial Sphere,* **1934, Paul Manship, 20½ inches diameter. The figures supporting the sphere are in a typical Art Deco style, and exemplify the work of Paul Manship. The Saint Louis Art Museum.**

PROJECT 7-7: **ART DECO ELEVATOR DOORS**

MATERIALS

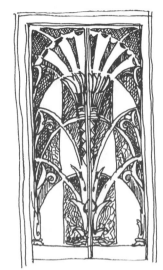

- Drawing paper
- Pencils
- Rulers
- Compasses
- Black fine-line permanent marker
- X-acto™ knives
- Tracing paper
- Black posterboard or construction paper
- Silver or gold wrapping paper
- Glue

Art Deco designs in the 1930s were modern, yet often were from Egyptian, Mayan, Incan, and Aztec designs. The streamlined designs frequently included stylized figures, held together with curving and straight lines. Art Deco design was common in everything from jewelry and clothing to automobiles. You may do the design in several layers glued together, or one layer defined with permanent fine-line black marker.

The skyscraper could have been built only after the invention of the elevator, and elevator doors were an important element of interior design. Elevator doors had two different sections that were related to each other, with identical border designs and identical or slightly varied designs within the borders. The design could consist purely of lines, or could have a motif such as a train, car, person, buildings, or birds (the eagle was popular).

1. Do several thumbnail sketches, then draw your best design on a larger piece of paper. Draw this lightly first in pencil, then go over it with black fine-line marker to make a complete design. Use a ruler and compass for straight lines and curves.

2. If you want to preserve your marker drawing, trace from it by taping it to a window and placing a piece of tracing paper on top. Draw over the back of the drawing on the tracing paper, then transfer it to the front of a sheet of gold or silver colored paper.

3. To protect the table when cutting, place a magazine between the gold paper and the table, and use an X-acto™ knife to carefully cut away portions of the drawing. (If you make a mistake, you can always glue it back on later.) *Safety note: Always be careful to have your fingers behind the knife when cutting.*

4. After the design is cut out and glued together, you can decide whether to emphasize some areas with black marker. Glue the cutout onto black posterboard or construction paper for display.

PROJECT 7-8: **AMERICAN SCENE PAINTING—THE MURAL**

FOR THE TEACHER

SLIDE #28:   Detail, *Social History of the State of Missouri: Politics, Farming, and Law in Missouri*, 1935–1936, Thomas Hart Benton, 55 feet × 14 feet 2 inches, Courtesy of the Capitol Museum, Jefferson City, Missouri

Thomas Hart Benton (1889–1975) is probably the best known of the Regionalists, sometimes called American Scene Painters. Born in Missouri, he was raised in Washington, D.C., where his father was in Congress (a great-uncle had been Missouri's first senator). Although Benton spent several years studying in Europe, he believed that there should be a truly American form of painting. He made a series of sketching expeditions throughout the country, later using his sketchbook images in his monumental mural cycles. His early work was based on Cubism and Synchromism because of his shading and use of bright colors, but ultimately he painted Romantic and nostalgic pictures of American rural life and people at work. Benton was not the only mural painter working during the 1930s, but he was among the best known. At times he would make a three-dimensional clay model of a mural before beginning, arranging figures and working out some colors in advance.

MASTERWORKS BY BENTON

Independence and the Opening of the West, 1959–1962, Harry S. Truman Library, Independence, Missouri

Arts of the West, 1932, New Britain Museum of American Art, New Britain, Connecticut

The New School Mural , c. 1928, New School for Social Research, New York

The Whitney Mural, 1932, New Britain Museum of American Art, New Britain, Connecticut

The Indiana Murals, 1933, Indiana University Auditorium, Indianapolis

America Today, c. 1928, Equitable Life Assurance Society, New York

The American Historical Epic, 1924–1927, Nelson-Atkins Museum of Art, Kansas City, Missouri

Cotton Pickers (Georgia), 1928–1929, The Metropolitan Museum of Art, New York

Hollywood, 1937, Nelson-Atkins Museum of Art, Kansas City, Missouri

PREPARATION

Thanks to photography and the copy machine, creating a mural for a large wall in your building is not so difficult as it used to be. I have been involved in the creation of seven at my school. Decide whether to work directly on the wall for a permanent mural, or on large sheets of brown paper or canvas for something temporary. Our students have done temporary monumental murals for a shopping mall and have also painted gym walls, entry halls, classrooms, cement block locker bays—anywhere there is a large wall. Ask permission first (usually you can get a sponsor to buy the paint). I recommend that *you*, the teacher, measure and do an exact scale drawing of the wall, including drinking fountains, vents, etc. The design or photographs can be photocopied onto overhead transparencies and projected to monumental size and drawn onto the wall with pencil.

Prepare the wall with a fresh coat of white latex paint before beginning (often this can be done by school district painters). Arrange for scaffolding, and cover the floor beneath (either by taping down brown paper or having drop cloths that are folded each day). Select a student who paints well, who is dedicated, and who is willing to be the "resident artist in charge." Several different approaches exist for creating a mural. Here are several we have tried.

1. A "paint-by-number" mural based on yearbook photographs (that were copied on overhead transparencies) was quite successful. It was painted by 100 totally unskilled Seniors. We used seven different hues with five values each. Numbers were assigned to the values (1 being the lightest and 5 the darkest). The paint was premixed to those values and placed in covered, labeled, plastic salad containers (purchased from a grocery store).

2. We also painted murals on walls in two different gyms, where shapes were filled in with areas of flat color (no modeling). The scale of these paintings dictated that color be applied with large brushes by students working on high scaffolds.

3. We have had two different 10 × 40-foot murals designed by professional artists (after meeting with students to decide on a theme); one each by Russell Vanecek and Robert Fishbone. The young artists were "apprentices," with the professionals directing and painting with the students or being helped by them.

4. After school, a National Art Honor Society group painted large tapestries with acrylic wall paint on primed canvas on the floor of an art room. The 17-foot lengths, painted with an environmental theme, were rolled up after drying, until the next painting session.

ADDITIONAL SUGGESTIONS

- Students could do small figure drawings in class, with each student designing a portion of a mural using only two or three figures in a setting. These pencil drawings need never be anything but a "study" for a mural. Thomas Hart Benton did his figure studies while he was traveling, and later placed figures near trees, in buildings, or in a field to complete his compositions. Most of Benton's murals had a theme such as the workplace or the history of a state or country.

- Have students create small plasticine clay figures and make a small scene, as Thomas Hart Benton sometimes did when he was preparing to paint a mural. Students then draw or paint a scene from their maquette.

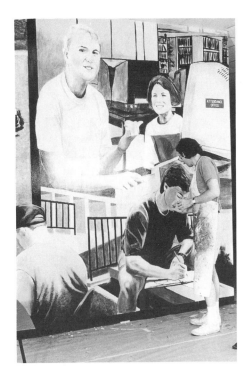 

Photo 7-8A and 7-8B. Mural painted by artist Russell Vanecek with the help of Parkway West students.

PROJECT 7-8: **AMERICAN SCENE PAINTING—THE MURAL**

MATERIALS

- Acrylic or latex wall paint
- Brushes, at least 1 inch, mostly 2 to 3 inches
- Polymer medium
- Overhead projectors
- Pencils
- Colored pencils

- Black fine-line markers
- Photocopies of a scale drawing for the blank wall
- Masking tape
- Overhead transparencies
- Drop cloths or brown kraft paper

Creating a mural in a school needs to be a cooperative effort to complete it in a relatively short time. Think carefully about your subject. Generally it would involve pictures of people (often photocopied onto overhead transparencies), but you need a unifying *appropriate* theme as well such as sports, academics, words combined with student photos, the environment, and so on.

1. Each person involved should create a complete design on 8-½ × 11-inch paper, based on the exact proportions of the wall. Place the drawings together and select the one that seems most appropriate. Chances are you will combine several of them and redraw what the finished product will look like.

2. When the drawing is complete, photocopy it and give each student a copy to fill in with colored pencil. Select the color scheme you want to use, or combine some ideas. Come up with a final color design on small paper before you begin painting a large wall.

3. Have the design *outline* transferred to 8-½ × 11-inch overhead transparencies (by photocopying or drawing with black permanent marker). By taping this onto overhead projectors, you can make the design larger or smaller by moving the projectors back and forth.

4. Draw the entire design onto the wall with pencil. Apply paint, not being afraid to make changes if you are not satisfied.

5. To protect the painting when it is complete, apply two coats of polymer medium with a large brush, allowing it to dry between coats.

6. If appropriate, have a brass label made and have a dedication. Invite staff, students, families, and the press to a formal opening ceremony!

Drawn after *Achelous and Hercules,* 1947
Thomas Hart Benton
National Museum of American Art
Washington, D.C.

PROJECT 7-9: **AMERICAN GOTHIC**

FOR THE TEACHER

SLIDE #29: *American Gothic,* **1930, Grant Wood, 74.3 × 62.4 cm., oil on beaverboard, Friends of American Art Collection, The Art Institute of Chicago**

Grant Wood (1892–1942) painted an idealistic vision of the landscape. With true artistic license, he left out anything that might take away from the vision of a rural paradise. He also painted traditional American folk tales such as George Washington chopping down a cherry tree *(Parson Weems' Fable)* and the *Midnight Ride of Paul Revere.* In recent years Wood's *American Gothic* has become one of the most familiar American paintings through its frequent satiric use in advertising and illustration. The painting, with the sober faces of the farmer and his spinster daughter (in reality, the artist's sister and his dentist), has a universal appeal. The title comes from the Gothic window in the house in the background.

Masterpieces by Grant Wood

Woman with Plants, 1929, Cedar Rapids Art Association, Cedar Rapids, Iowa

Midnight Ride of Paul Revere, 1931, The Metropolitan Museum of Art, New York

The Birthplace of Herbert Hoover, 1931, New York Historical Society, New York

Stone City, Iowa, 1930, Joslyn Art Museum, Omaha

Young Corn, 1931, Cedar Rapids Community Schools, Cedar Rapids, Iowa

Daughters of Revolution, 1932, Cincinnati Art Museum, Cincinnati

Adolescence, 1933–1940, Davenport Municipal Art Gallery, Davenport, Iowa

Parson Weems' Fable, 1938–1939, private collection

PREPARATION

Students enjoy discussing this painting. They quickly see its relationships, contrasts, repetition, and irony. Suggest that they find advertisements, birthday cards, and other items that use famous paintings as the basis for satire.

To save time in this project, a reproduction of the original artwork can be photocopied onto a transparency and projected onto a large sheet of posterboard before students make changes. Humor and original thought are necessities when adapting an artwork for another purpose—otherwise, you are only teaching copying.

ADDITIONAL SUGGESTIONS

- Suggest that students paint a local landscape in the mode of Grant Wood. His paintings usually had a high horizon line, with roads or fields going off to distant hills. He made trees look like round balls, fields perfectly smooth, rows of crops perfectly arranged, and houses like little boxes.

- Just as Grant Wood sometimes worked from photos, divide students into groups to "become a painting." When they have dressed up and found or made a suitable background, take a photo with an instant or regular camera. With prints or slides, you can have multiples made at a copy shop to give everyone a print.

- Make giant "Photo-op" boards of famous artworks that contain one or more groups of people. Give a group of students a postcard or reproduction of famous artworks to be reproduced in cheap tempera on 4 × 6-foot pieces of cardboard (which can be purchased through an art store). Paint outdoors or somewhere where these can be put on a table or floor. Students should not bother painting in faces, but instead use utility knives to cut ovals in the cardboard where the faces would be. (*Safety note: Remind students to keep their hands behind the cutting utensil at all times.*) This would be a good fund-raising project for a school fair, with students offering to take instant photos of people who pose behind the boards.

Photo 7-9. *The Birthplace of Herbert Hoover, West Branch, Iowa*, 1931, Grant Wood, oil on composition board, 29-⅝ × 39-¾ inches, The John R. Van Derlip Fund; owned jointly with the Des Moines Art Center, The Minneapolis Institute of Arts.

PROJECT 7-9: **AMERICAN GOTHIC**

MATERIALS

- Newsprint
- Pencils
- Drawing paper
- Tempera or acrylic paint
- Paint brushes
- Overhead projectors

**Drawn after *American Gothic*, 1930
Grant Wood
The Art Institute of Chicago**

Advertising people are accustomed to thinking up wild ideas—the more unlikely, the better. This assignment is to take something that is apparently serious (the painting *American Gothic* or another well-known American painting) and create an ad from it. When something is as familiar to the American public as this painting, you do not need many details for someone to recognize what you are satirizing.

1. Think what you might like to sell with this painting. It could be something like spaghetti and meatballs, tennis rackets, football helmets, or bubble gum. Let your imagination roam to the local discount store and think of all the things available there.

2. You are the manufacturer of this commodity; therefore, your name needs to be part of the product. Think of where and how your name will be placed, and information on where people can buy this product. Look through a magazine and see how professionals compose an ad so it is eye-catching, yet simple.

3. Do several thumbnail sketches in pencil, then select one and transfer it to a large sheet of drawing paper. Complete your drawing, including lettering, before you begin painting.

4. Mix colors with tempera or acrylic, attempting to match some colors in the real painting *American Gothic*.

PROJECT 7-10: **FOLK ART**

FOR THE TEACHER

For three centuries Americans have appreciated the work of self-taught artists who painted the American Scene. Folk Art is usually realistic rather than abstract, and thus appreciated by those who might not care for abstraction. Some amateur painters were as serious about their art as those who had formal training, and indeed some entered the mainstream of the art world. Anna Mary Robertson (Grandma) Moses (1860–1961) caught the imagination of the country through her lively, people-filled paintings of life in the country as she remembered it. She was one of many naive (or primitive) folk artists whose work developed at about the same time as that of Abstract Expressionists. Other naive painters whose work was popular were Joseph Pickett (1848–1918), John Kane (1860–1934), and Horace Pippin (1888–1946).

Grandma Moses used various resources such as pattern books, needlework designs, and Currier and Ives prints as inspiration, but her composition was uniquely her own. Much of her work is in private collections, but reproductions were widely available to the public through greeting cards and reproductions on fabrics in the 1940s and 1950s.

Well-Known Paintings by Grandma Moses

The Old Oaken Bucket, the Last, 1946, collection of Mr. and Mrs. Garson Kanin

[Untitled] Grazing Cattle, Early Fall, c. 1920, The Bennington Museum, Bennington, Vermont

Home of Hezekiah King, 1942, Phoenix Art Museum, Phoenix, Arizona

Battle of Bennington, 1953, Daughters of the American Revolution, Washington, D.C.

Hoosick Falls, N.Y., in Winter, 1944, the Phillips Collection, Washington, D.C.

Haying, 1956, The Shelburne Museum, Shelburne, Vermont

First Snow, 1957, The Bennington Museum, Bennington, Vermont

PREPARATION

When Grandma Moses painted her pictures, she was a housewife who loved to paint and draw. Her paintings were seldom large, usually 20 × 28 inches. Her childhood memories were of life in the country. Your students will have entirely different childhood memories. This project is about tapping into these memories.

If you actually want to make greeting cards of the students' work, photograph the paintings, taking a "reading" on a gray card (available at a camera store) to get true color. These prints could then be mounted on card stock. Or take the photos to a copy company and have multiple reproductions made of a select few.

ADDITIONAL SUGGESTIONS

- After completing the painting, students can write about their "moment in time." This could be in poetry or prose. (I have found that students enjoy writing about their artwork.)

- If students would like to interpret one season (or four) of the year, they could select something around school and paint it as it would look in that season or other seasons.

- Recently, artists in the South have been painting in the naive style on dried gourds. They depict aspects of life in the country or small towns, filled with detailed paintings of buildings, people, cars, and animals. Some leave the background showing, while others completely fill it in with fluffy white clouds and grass. Smaller gourds are as effective as large ones. One artist outlines first with a wood-burning tool, then fills in with paint. Students can do this project with acrylic paint and then spray varnish it afterward.

Photo 7-10. *Holy Mountain III*, 1945, Horace Pippin, oil on canvas, 25-¼ × 30-¼ inches, Hirshhorn Museum and Sculpture Garden, Gift of Joseph H. Hirshhorn, Smithsonian Institution. Photography by Lee Stalsworth.

PROJECT 7-10: **FOLK ART**

MATERIALS

**Drawn from *Sugaring Off,* 1955
Anna Mary Moses**

- 18 × 24-inch drawing paper
- Tempera or acrylic paint
- Pencils
- Brushes

Folk painting is produced by untrained artists who work instinctively. Their work has been appreciated and collected through approximately 300 years of American history. This project is to make a folk design that will be reproduced as a holiday greeting card, based on your memories of an event from your childhood. Put in it all the people you can remember from your early life.

1. Think about an especially happy holiday event with your family or friends, and try to think of a moment in that day when you might have taken an informal snapshot. The "frozen moment in time" is the subject of your painting and should come from your memory.

2. Picture what the setting would be. It could be outdoors, in a kitchen, at a park, or at a sporting event. Lightly draw the largest objects such as houses, a bridge, lake, or buildings.

3. Complete the composition with distant scenery, then draw people and details in the foreground. You can include animals, cars, or anything that would add to the composition.

4. You will have already thought of the season of the year. Paint the composition with tempera or acrylic paint, using colors that would be appropriate for that season. People would also be appropriately dressed for that season. If it is winter, don't forget that in some parts of the country the snow will cover roofs, trees, and grass.

**Drawn after *The Quilting Bee,* 1950
Anna Mary (Grandma) Moses
Private Collection**

Section 8

ABSTRACT EXPRESSIONISM AND POP CULTURE (1940 to 1965)

ABSTRACT EXPRESSIONISM AND POP CULTURE
TIME LINE

	1940	1945	1950	1954	1958	1961	1963	1965

Painting Sculpture Architecture Folk Art

- Walter Gropius 1883–1969
- Pop Culture, 1945–1965
- Andy Warhol 1927–1987
- Eero Saarinen 1910–1961
- Op Art 1960s
- Richard Anuszkiewicz b. 1930
- Hyper Realists Audrey Flack
- Claes Oldenburg 1929
- Abstract Expressionism 1945–1960
- Alexander Calder 1898–1976
- Jackson Pollock 1912–1956
- Janet Fish b. 1938
- David Smith 1906–1965
- Helen Frankenthaler b. 1928
- Robert Rauschenberg b. 1925
- Color Field Painting 1950–present
- I. M. Pei b. 1917
- Geodesic Dome 1960
- Roy Lichtenstein b. 1923
- Marisol b. 1930
- Morris Louis 1912–1962
- Jasper Johns, b. 1930
- Chuck Close b. 1940

Politics

- 1945 Atomic Bomb World War II ends
- 1950 Korean War
- 1952 D. D. Eisenhower, Pres.
- 1950 McCarthyism
- 1959 Alaska & Hawaii become states
- 1964 L. B. Johnson elected president
- 1948 Israel established
- 1952 Queen Elizabeth crowned
- 1956 Eisenhower re-elected
- 1960 J. F. Kennedy elected Pres.
- 1963 Kennedy assassinated

Literature

- 1940 *For Whom the Bell Tolls* Ernest Hemmingway
- 1941 *Blood, Sweat, and Tears* Winston Churchill
- 1940 *Watch on the Rhine* Lillian Hellman
- 1962 John Steinbeck *Travels With Charlie*
- T. S. Eliot 1888–1965
- 1964 *Herzog* Saul Bellow

Science

- 1942 Fermi splits the atom
- 1940 Plutonium Seaborg and McMillan
- 1949 Einstein's Theory of Relativity
- 1953 Measles vaccine Enders and Peebles
- 1957 USSR launches Sputnik
- 1955 Einstein dies
- 1955 Polio vaccine Jonas Salk
- 1960 Laser
- 1957 Fortran Computer language

Music

- Rachmaninoff 1873–1943
- 1953 Death of Sergei Prokofiev (composer of *Peter & the Wolf*)
- 1962 Beatles become famous
- Cole Porter 1893–1964
- Nat King Cole 1919–1965

Current Events

- 1949 NATO founded
- 1946 United Nations General Assembly
- 1941–1945 World War II
- 1954 Brown vs. Bd. of Education, Topeka
- 1954 Hydrogen Bomb
- 1956 Egypt seizes Suez Canal
- 1957 Sputnik
- 1961 Berlin wall erected
- 1960 13 nations form OPEC
- 1965 Riots in Watts

ABSTRACT EXPRESSIONISM/POP CULTURE ARCHITECTURE

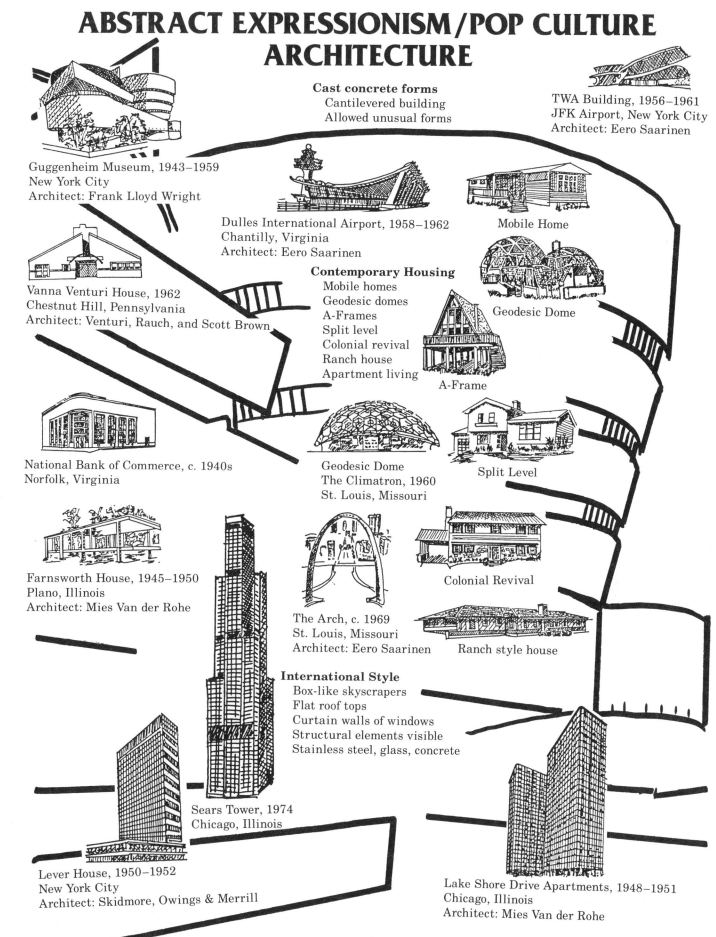

Cast concrete forms
Cantilevered building
Allowed unusual forms

TWA Building, 1956–1961
JFK Airport, New York City
Architect: Eero Saarinen

Guggenheim Museum, 1943–1959
New York City
Architect: Frank Lloyd Wright

Dulles International Airport, 1958–1962
Chantilly, Virginia
Architect: Eero Saarinen

Mobile Home

Contemporary Housing
Mobile homes
Geodesic domes
A-Frames
Split level
Colonial revival
Ranch house
Apartment living

Geodesic Dome

Vanna Venturi House, 1962
Chestnut Hill, Pennsylvania
Architect: Venturi, Rauch, and Scott Brown

A-Frame

National Bank of Commerce, c. 1940s
Norfolk, Virginia

Geodesic Dome
The Climatron, 1960
St. Louis, Missouri

Split Level

Farnsworth House, 1945–1950
Plano, Illinois
Architect: Mies Van der Rohe

Colonial Revival

The Arch, c. 1969
St. Louis, Missouri
Architect: Eero Saarinen

Ranch style house

International Style
Box-like skyscrapers
Flat roof tops
Curtain walls of windows
Structural elements visible
Stainless steel, glass, concrete

Sears Tower, 1974
Chicago, Illinois

Lever House, 1950–1952
New York City
Architect: Skidmore, Owings & Merrill

Lake Shore Drive Apartments, 1948–1951
Chicago, Illinois
Architect: Mies Van der Rohe

243

Section 8.—ABSTRACT EXPRESSIONISM/POP CULTURE (1940–1965)

ARTISTS OF THE PERIOD

FAMOUS ARTISTS OF THE 1940S, 1950S, AND 1960S

- *Willem De Kooning* (b. 1904), born in Rotterdam, Netherlands, immigrated to the United States in 1926. An Abstract Expressionist, his best-known works were huge paintings of women, filled with spontaneous, slashing strokes, often leaving only a face or eyes to indicate the subject. He was a major figure in the mid-1940s and 1950s.

- *Jim Dine's* (b. 1935) earliest contributions to Pop Art were his "Happenings." In later work, he attached objects (such as light switches) to his canvases, inviting viewer participation. His later subject matter is mundane and personal, including objects from a workshop and clothing (as in a series of prints of life-sized bathrobes).

- *Sam Francis* (1923–1994) lived much of his adult life in France. For many years his work consisted of large paint drops and splashes of color around the edges of paintings, leaving an "empty-center." In the 1970s he sometimes painted from the center outwards, demonstrating how the work of an artist evolves, yet has traces of early work.

- *Helen Frankenthaler* (b. 1928) studied with Rufino Tamayo (1899–1991) and Hans Hofmann (1880–1966) before she emerged as a leading Color-Field painter. She poured diluted paint onto canvases, allowing the canvas to show through and creating atmospheric effects. Later work is filled with splotches and daubs, with her most recent work reminiscent of Abstract Expressionist work of the 1950s.

- *Philip Guston* (1913–1980) was an Abstract Expressionist during the 1950s and 1960s. He joined the W.P.A. during the 1930s, painting murals for the U.S. Government. His pre-1948 paintings included realistic figures of children in a dreamlike mood. His work evolved from realistic to symbolic content, frequently painted with clusters of brush-strokes in muted grays, blues, and reds.

- *Jasper Johns's* (b. 1930) work depicts images closely identified with Pop Art, such as the American flag, American maps, targets, and numbers, used in a variety of ways. He resurrected the technique of painting with encaustic (pigment in molten wax), giving rich texture to his work. When asked about his method and purpose, he replied, "Take an object, do something to it, do something else to it."

- *Alice Neel* (1900–1984) did not belong to any school of art, but developed a unique style. A portraitist, she unflinchingly painted people as she saw them. She outlined her subjects with a thick line, portraying them with exaggerated features and simplified contours. The figures dominated the picture plane, often gazing directly at the viewer.

- *Barnett Newman* (1905–1970) was an Abstract Expressionist associated with the Biomorphism (organic rather than geometric shapes) of the early 1940s. He was also considered a Color-Field painter. Ultimately, he painted simple vertical stripes that were a precursor of Minimalism.

245

- *Jackson Pollock* (1912–1956) became the master of the "controlled drip" method of painting large canvases on the floor. He was influenced by the Surrealistic technique of "automatic writing," which supposedly came from the subconscious. However, like most of the Abstract Expressionist painters, Pollock had formal academic training, and his apparently haphazard method of working was deliberate.

- *Robert Rauschenberg* (b. 1925) was one of the major figures of the Pop era. He constructed "combines" of unlikely objects, such as a stuffed goat with an innertube around its middle standing on a large mattress, or a stuffed chicken on top of a box. His assemblages included newspaper photographs based on sports or social commentary.

- *Mark Rothko* (1903–1970) used the Surrealist technique of automatic writing early in the 1940s. His later, most typical works were Color-Field paintings of two or three soft-edged horizontal rectangles within a border. His work has been compared with landscapes with a horizon line, field, and sky.

- *Frank Stella's* (b. 1936) early work was part painting, part sculpture. His huge black canvases with white stripes gave way to large shaped canvases covered with brilliant rainbow-colored stripes following the shape of the canvas. His present-day assemblages take this idea further, with large three-dimensional sculpture/paintings.

- *Andy Warhol* (1927–1987) trained at the Carnegie Institute of Technology in Pittsburgh and was a successful commercial artist before becoming a painter and printmaker. He was flamboyant, a consciously strange personality who became a celebrity. His "campy" subject matter was typical of Pop Art.

- *Andrew Wyeth* (b. 1917) belongs to a dynasty of painters. His father, N. C. Wyeth (1882–1944), was a famous illustrator, and his son Jamie Wyeth (b. 1946) and other relatives carry on the tradition. Wyeth's work is realistic, with subject matter painted near his home of Chadds Ford, Pennsylvania. In common with many well-known artists in America, he goes his own way, little affected by what is happening in the centers of the art world.

FAMOUS SCULPTORS

- *Alexander Calder* (1898–1976) was best known as the originator of the *mobile* and the *stabile*. A mechanical engineer, he was fascinated by movement of the objects he made. His ouvre included such disparate creations as rug designs, designs for the exteriors of Braniff airplanes and BMW cars, paintings, and drawings.

- *Joseph Cornell* (1903–1972) was inspired by Surrealism in the creation of a series of three-dimensional assemblages created within boxes. These other-worldly, highly personal images were created over a forty-year period.

- *Louise Nevelson* (1900–1988) was born in Russia, but came to the United States as a young child. She was famous for found-object assemblages, usually organized within boxes, grouped together and painted black, white, or gold. She used the same assemblage format in other materials such as plastic and metal.

- *Isamu Noguchi* (1904–1988) was born in Los Angeles of an American mother and Japanese father, but spent his childhood in Japan. His sculpture was primarily stone or marble forms, stripped to the essence. He designed lamps, gardens, stage sets for dancers, and was a pioneer of "earthworks."

- *Claes Oldenburg's* (b. 1929) work is always included in major exhibitions of Pop Art. He began with *The Store,* an exhibit in 1961–1962, that featured hand-painted plaster "food." He is especially known for his "soft-sculpture"—such items as drum sets, toilets, and telephones made of sewn, kapok-stuffed vinyl. Many cities feature his monumental public metal sculptures, such as his *Baseball Bat* in Chicago or his *3-Way Plug* in St. Louis.

- *George Segal* (b. 1924) specializes in the human figure, applying sections of his basic material (plaster-impregnated gauze) on living models. After removal of the forms, he reassembles them, placing his "people" in environments such as standing in a doorway, on a bus, on a parkbench, or outside a theater marquee.

- *David Smith* (1906–1965) is best known for his *Cubi* series of polished stainless steel boxes loosely based on the human figure. He learned machine-shop techniques through working at an automobile plant. He was the first American sculptor to use welding techniques.

FAMOUS AMERICAN ARCHITECTS

- *Buckminster Fuller* (1895–1983), an engineer and architect, created the Geodesic Dome which has been adapted to many other uses for buildings throughout the world.

- *Walter Gropius* (1883–1969) was born in Germany, but immigrated to the United States in 1937. He created the Bauhaus in Weimar, Germany which was famous for its dictum "form follows function." He was a primary architect of the "International Style" that featured boxlike forms and little ornamentation.

- *Philip Johnson's* (b. 1906) designs featured walls of glass and boxlike forms, but eventually incorporated historical references such as a Chippendale pediment at the top of the *American Telephone and Telegraph Company Building* in New York City.

- *Ioeh Ming (I. M.) Pei* (b. 1917), born in China, studied under Walter Gropius at Harvard Graduate School of Design. He was considered a pioneer in the use of all-glass curtain walls, and is credited with using precast concrete and cast-in-place concrete in high-rise housing. His *East Building* of the National Gallery of Art in Washington, D.C. and his *Pyramid* for the Louvre are two of his most notable structures.

- *Eero Saarinen* (1910–1961), Finnish-born and an architect like his famous father, Eliel Saarinen (1873–1950), moved to the United States where he worked on the development of Cranbrook Academy. He designed conventional buildings, but is best known for his work with "thin-shell concrete technology" that explored unique forms such as those used in the Washington Dulles *International Terminal*. The stainless steel *Gateway Arch* in St. Louis was also his design.

- *Ludwig Mies van der Rohe* (1886–1969) was German-born, and already a famous architect/designer before he immigrated to the United States when the Bauhaus (of which he was director) was closed in 1933. Box-like buildings created of steel, glass, and reinforced concrete that dominate many city centers are sometimes called "Miesian."

FAMOUS MOVEMENTS AND SCHOOLS OF ART

- *Abstract Expressionism* (1945–1960). Abstract Expressionists conveyed emotion through their method of applying paint to canvas—whether it was random mark-making or specific, repeated forms. It was a coming together of American and European art—the right time, the right artists, the right place (New York in the early 1940s). The movement had its roots in Dada, Surrealism, German Expressionism, and Impressionism. It was also called "action painting." Distinctive approaches were taken by well-known artists, including Jackson Pollock (1912–1956), Hans Hofmann (1880–1966), Arshile Gorky (1904–1948), Willem De Kooning (b. 1904), Lee Krasner (1908–1984), and Franz Kline (1910–1962).

- *Color-Field Painting* (1960s). Color-Field paintings involve few colors, such as those of Mark Rothko (1903–1970), Barnett Newman (1905–1970), and Clyfford Still (1904–1980). These artists were also considered Abstract Expressionists. Stain-painting, as practiced by Morris Louis (1912–1962) and Helen Frankenthaler (b. 1928), might not have existed until acrylic paint came along. Artists poured acrylic paint onto large canvases, creating areas of overlapping color.

- *Happenings* (late 1950s). "Happenings" were "performance art," sometimes involving the audience and art or found objects. These spontaneous theatrical presentations were usually nonverbal and often unplanned. Artists who were known for this particular art form were Red Grooms (b. 1937), Robert Whitman (b. 1935), Jim Dine (b. 1935), Claes Oldenburg (b. 1929), and Allan Kaprow (b. 1927).

- *Hard Edge Painting* (1958–1960s). This referred to the (often) brightly colored paintings where colors were not blended into one another, but flat colors were juxtaposed. This closely followed Abstract Expressionism, and a few artists such as Ellsworth Kelly (b. 1923) and Alexander Liberman (b. 1912) were pioneers in the method. Other Hard-Edge painters were Kenneth Noland (b. 1924) and Frank Stella (b. 1936).

- *Minimal Art* (1960s). "Minimal Art" was a term that applied to a number of art movements, including Op Art, Color-Field Painting, Serial Imagery (related works in a series), Hard-Edge painting, and the shaped canvas. It contrasted with Abstract Expressionism, with its excessive emphasis on the "artist's hand" and brushstrokes. Minimal Art was not concerned with details, but with the overall effect. Ellsworth Kelly's panels of plain color and Frank Stella's shaped canvases were examples of Minimal Art.

- *Op Art* (1960s). Op Art was a version of Hard-Edge Painting in which artists achieved optical reactions by painting colors in the same intensity, but often from opposite sides of the color wheel. The patterns they used (lines, wavy lines, lozenges) caused the eye to move from one area to another quickly and were difficult to view—they tricked the eye. Richard Anuskiewicz (b. 1930) was an American involved in this movement, which began in Europe.

- *Pop Art* (1945–1965). Pop Art was a reaction to the emotional quality of Abstract Expressionism. It began in England, but was quickly adapted and expanded by New York artists. The use of consumer products as the theme and the method of presentation were often direct copies of advertising techniques. The central figures of Pop Art were Andy Warhol (1927–1987), Roy Lichtenstein (b. 1923), James Rosenquist (b. 1933), Jim Dine (b. 1935), Robert Indiana (b. 1928), George Segal (b. 1924), Tom Wesselman (b. 1931), and Richard Diebenkorn (1922–1993). A California-based group of Pop Artists included Billy Al Bengston (b. 1934), Joe Goode (b. 1937), Mel Ramos (b. 1935), and Edward Ruscha (b. 1937).

OVERVIEW OF THE ARTS

Perhaps the government's support of artists during the Depression paved the way for the resurgence of interest in art after World War II. It was a modern world, calling for new ideas. Techniques such as silk screen (developed and supported under the Works Progress Administration during the Depression), photography, and welding became part of the vocabulary of Pop Art. New materials such as plastic, acrylic paint, aluminum, and commercial art's Benday™ dots (a material used for color advertisements) were used in the creation of art. Artists of this period stretched in divergent directions, yet often independently used the same general subject matter (when, for example, several artists in the Pop period were featuring comic book heroes). The line between painting and sculpture became less definite, as painters attached objects to their two-dimensional works to make them three-dimensional. Many wall-hung "paintings" were simply three-sided sculptures in color.

PAINTING

American painting emerged from the 1930s to shake its dependence on European art. Although many European artists had immigrated to the United States during the 1930s, bringing new ideas with them, the art world in the 1940s began to notice the impact of what was happening (chiefly) in New York (and later on the West Coast). There were always artists who did not belong to any school and whose work developed independently and consistently for a lifetime. Meanwhile, Social Realism, Regionalism, and Modernism led to Abstract Expressionism in the early 1940s. By 1945, a reaction against the emotional content and lack of subject common to Expressionistic paintings led to the use of commercial images—Pop Art. Nothing was too banal as inspiration for Pop artists. Road signs, stenciled letters, comic strips, clothing, advertisements, and a combination of any unlikely items were all fodder. Others, however, such as Mark Rothko eliminated specific subject matter altogether.

Examples of Painting from the 1940s to Early 1960s

Mahoning, 1956, Franz Kline, Whitney Museum of American Art, New York

Centre Triptych for the Rothko Chapel, 1966, Mark Rothko, Rothko Chapel, Houston

The Sphinx and the Milky Way, 1946, Charles Burchfield, Munson-Williams-Proctor Institute, Utica, New York

Queen of Hearts, 1943–1946, Willem De Kooning, Hirshhorn Museum, Washington, D.C.

Retroactive I, 1964, Robert Rauschenberg, Wadsworth Atheneum, Hartford, Connecticut

The Subway, 1950, George Tooker, Whitney Museum of American Art, New York

Marilyn Monroe Diptych, 1962, Andy Warhol, Tate Gallery, London

Dreaming Girl, 1963, Roy Lichtenstein, Museum of Modern Art, New York

Monogram, 1955–1959, Robert Rauschenberg, Moderna Museet, Stockholm

Target with Four Faces, 1955, Jasper Johns, Museum of Modern Art, New York

White Flag, 1955, Jasper Johns, Leo Castelli Gallery, New York

Woman and Bicycle, 1952–1953, Willem De Kooning, Whitney Museum of American Art, New York

Blue Territory, 1955, Helen Frankenthaler, Whitney Museum of American Art, New York

SCULPTURE

Abstract Expressionist sculptures featured distortions of form and intense personal emotion. Sculptors found the concept to be fully as important as the form, and few worked realistically. They used traditional media, but the materials of sculpture no longer necessarily dictated what a sculpture would look like. The use of metal had previously been confined to bronze casting. Now, using industrial technology, artists could curve metal rods, weld sheet steel, or have their concepts interpreted by professional metal workers at factories. Suddenly enormous works of art were possible. Sculptors learned they could use outside forces such as motors or the wind to cause portions of their sculptures to move. They took materials to new dimensions.

Abstract Expressionists were Jacques Lipchitz (1891–1973), Isamu Noguchi (1904–1988), Frank Stella (b. 1936), Mark Di Suvero (b. 1933), Alexander Archipenko (1887–1964), and others. Several—such as Claes Oldenburg, David Smith (1906–1965), George Segal, Marisol Escobar (b. 1930), Roy Lichtenstein, and Donald Judd (1928–1994)—were considered Pop artists. Other sculptors such as Joseph Cornell (1903–1973), Louise Nevelson (1900–1988), Alexander Calder (1898–1976), and Louise Bourgeois (b. 1911) had individual, unique styles, and spanned many decades of the twentieth century.

Examples of Sculpture

- **Abstract Expressionist Sculpture**

  Sacrifice II, 1948, Jacques Lipchitz, Whitney Museum of American Art, New York

  One and Others, 1955, Louise Bourgeois, Whitney Museum of American Art, New York

  An American Tribute to the British People, Louise Nevelson, 1960–1965, Tate Gallery, London

- **Pop Sculpture**

  Soft Giant Drum Set, 1967, Claes Oldenburg, collection of Kimiko and John G. Powers, New York

  Two Cheeseburgers with Everything, 1962, Claes Oldenburg, Museum of Modern Art, New York

  Pony, 1959, Ellsworth Kelly, Dayton's Gallery 12, Minneapolis

ARCHITECTURE

After World War II, the city—as it had existed—was greatly changed. As automobiles became available to almost anyone who wanted one, people moved to the suburbs, creating bedroom communities. The European influence of the Bauhaus was felt as architects such as Walter Gropius (1883-1969) and Ludwig Mies van der Rohe (1886-1969) designed buildings for American cities in an International Style that is seen in cities all over the world. For a time, cities erected slab buildings that illustrated the Bauhaus axiom, "Less is more." The skyscraper of the postwar period was boxy, flat topped, and had curtain walls of glass. Some houses were built along the International Style, with the use of glass walls and geometric structure. Architects were much more aware of adapting the home to fit the site and climactic conditions.

Technology allowed architects to cast concrete in various forms that led to innovative structures such as the T.W.A. Terminal at Kennedy Airport. By the late 1950s, buildings were becoming more decorative and interesting.

Examples of Architecture

United Nations Secretariat, 1947–1950, Wallace K. Harrison, New York

Richards Medical Research Building, 1957–1961, Louis I. Kahn, University of Pennsylvania, Philadelphia

T.W.A. Terminal, 1956–1962, Eero Saarinen, Kennedy Airport, New York

Dr. Edith Farnsworth House, 1945–1951, Ludwig Mies van der Rohe, Plano, Ilinois

Johnson House, "Glass House," 1945–1949, Philip Johnson, New Canaan, Connecticut

Lake Shore Apartment Houses, 1949–1951, Ludwig Mies van der Rohe, Chicago

Lever House, 1950–1952, Skidmore, Owings & Merrill, New York

General Motors Technical Center, 1948–1952, Eliel and Eero Saarinen, Warren, Michigan

Marina City, 1959–1964, 1965–1967, Bertram Goldberg Associates, Chicago

Union Carbide Building, 1957–1960, Skidmore, Owings & Merrill, New York

Seagram Building, 1954–1958, Ludwig Mies van der Rohe and Philip Johnson, New York

C.B.S. Building, 1960–1964, Eero Saarinen, New York

PROJECT 8-1: CUBI—TAGBOARD BOX SCULPTURE

FOR THE TEACHER

David Smith (1906–1965) was considered one of the most influential and prolific sculptors of the twentieth century. His knowledge of metal tooling and fine craftsmanship was a result of having worked in a Studebaker automobile plant, where he learned techniques for handling and cutting metals. During World War II he assembled tanks and locomotives in a factory. He began his art career as a painter, studying at the Art Students' League in New York City. At first he simply built up the surfaces of his canvases to a thick impasto; later, he began attaching found objects to the canvases; and ultimately created sculpture, first in wood, then in welded iron. He worked for the Works Progress Administration (W.P.A.) in the 1930s. His work in the 1950s consisted of forged steel "drawings in space." He created fifteen different series of sculptures around a central theme. His *Cubi* series of sculptures featuring cubes and circular forms was begun in 1961. These unique structures of polished steel boxes are the inspiration for this project.

Different Periods in David Smith's Work

Medals for Dishonor, 1937–1940, Hirshhorn Museum, Washington, D.C.

Cockfight, 1945, Saint Louis Art Museum

Hudson River Landscape, 1951, Whitney Museum of American Art, New York

Agricola, 1951, Hirshhorn Museum, Washington, D.C.

Zig, 1960, Lincoln Center, New York

Voltri-Bolton, 1962, Museum of Fine Arts, Boston

Cubi I, 1963, Detroit Institute of Fine Arts

PREPARATION

Discuss how the work of any sculptor evolves and how the material used to some extent dictates what the form will look like. When David Smith began working with welded steel, his work took entirely different forms than he had previously used. His cube forms varied in size and shape, yet were assembled to balance. He sometimes drew his designs in advance, or made cardboard maquettes (models) to achieve balance. Show students how to score cardboard so it will fold straight when they make their boxes.

ADDITIONAL SUGGESTIONS

- Smith also worked on "drawings-in-space," made of steel rods that were bent and welded. Although this method is not normally feasible in an art class, your students can experience working with a malleable material by "drawing" with thick aluminum wire, which could be either suspended from the ceiling or laid flat and attached to a cardboard base. Before working with the wire, students should do thumbnail sketches on which they will base the sculpture.

- Smith also made *Medals for Dishonor,* a series of bas-relief medallions. His medals were first created in wax before casting. Students could carve in microcrystalline wax, or model bas-relief medallions in plasticine or ceramic clay.

- Bas-relief medallions could also be carved from circles of plaster. Make the forms by pouring liquid plaster into paper drinking cups, and peeling away the paper when the plaster has set. Use a paring knife or nail to make a mold.

• Have students make sculpture from found materials through unit repetition. Materials such as small drinking cups (paper cone or waxed), styrofoam balls, tongue depressors, cotton swabs, straws, cross slices of mailing tubes, cotton balls, small jewelry boxes, even recycled soda cans can be joined with white glue or a glue gun. These can be left as is or spray painted.

Photo 8-1. *Cubi XIV,* **1963, David Smith, 122-½ inches high, stainless steel, Purchase: Friends Fund, The Saint Louis Art Museum.**

PROJECT 8-1: CUBI—TAGBOARD BOX SCULPTURE

MATERIALS

- Tagboard
- Cardboard tubes
- Scissors
- Rulers
- Pencils
- Glue (Tacky™ glue, white glue, or a glue gun)
- Straight pins
- Spray paint (silver or white) or tempera, any color

**Cubi XII, 1963
Hirshhorn Museum and
Sculpture Garden**

David Smith created sculpture that was often based on the human figure, yet made of individual welded boxes of polished stainless steel. Working with tagboard, you can get a similar effect and experience a truth in sculpture: it has to balance or it will fall over!

1. Rather than planning the entire project in advance, make a minimum of five boxes of different sizes and shapes. Some should be long and thin, others flat and not very thick, and some perfectly square. Repeat one of the shapes twice or more.

2. To make a tagboard box, you need to measure and cut carefully. Use a ruler and scissors to "score" the tagboard on the inside so it will fold easily. Glue the tabs to the sides.

3. In assembling the sculpture, it is important to balance the composition so it doesn't fall over. If necessary, use pins to hold the boxes in place, and allow two to dry together before you add a third. One possibility for assembling is to attach the boxes to a stand made by attaching a tall round tube or tall rectangular cube to a square base. Glue the boxes to this tall form with white glue, Tacky™ Glue (which dries a little faster), or a glue gun, and hold in place with straight pins until the glue has dried. This time-consuming step may take helping hands from a fellow student. Another idea is simply to attach the boxes to each other rather than using a central support.

4. The polishing of David Smith's stainless steel cubes resembled the abstract painting of his contemporary, Jackson Pollock. You could spray paint your composition in silver, allowing it to dry, then use white spray paint to give a "graffiti-like" surface. Or you could simply paint it abstractly with any color of tempera paint.

Cubi XIX

**Cubi XVIII, 1964
Dallas Museum of Fine Arts**

**Two Circle Sentinel, 1961
Houston Museum of Fine Arts**

PROJECT 8-2: **STABILE**

FOR THE TEACHER

Alexander Calder (1898–1976) came from a line of artists. His father, Alexander Sterling Calder (1870–1945), and grandfather, A. Milne Calder (1846–1923), were famous sculptors. His mother was a painter. Calder created art in the first of his many workshops before he was 10 years old. He trained and worked as a mechanical engineer, but as a young man, moved to Paris and joined other artists. In his long career he created jewelry, wire sculpture, rug and cloth designs, and even surface decorations for airplanes and cars. He began his art career with *Circus,* a collection of miniature animals and acrobats that function mechanically. In his poorer days in Paris, he hired out to "perform" his circus at parties. He was the originator of the *mobile* (named by Marcel Duchamp) and the *stabile* (named by Hans Arp), and often combined stabiles and mobiles. His preferred colors of red, blue, and black were adaptations of the school colors of high school athletic rivals. He said, "The simplest forms in the Universe are the sphere and the circle. I represent them by discs and then I vary them."

Examples of Alexander Calder's Work

Red, Black, and Blue, mobile, 1968, Dallas-Fort Worth Airport, Love Field, Dallas

Lobster Trap and Fish Tail, mobile, 1939, Museum of Modern Art, New York

Flamingo, stabile, 1974, Federal Center Plaza, Chicago

Black Widow, stabile, 1959, Museum of Modern Art, New York

La Grande Voile, stabile, 1966, Massachusetts Institute of Technology, Cambridge

Stegosaurus, stabile, 1973, Alfred E. Burr Mall, Hartford, Connecticut

The Crab, stabile, 1962, The Museum of Fine Arts, Houston

Circus, mixed media, 1932, Whitney Museum of American Art, New York

PREPARATION

Have students recycle their soft drink cans by washing them out and draining them before bringing them in. It would probably be best to assign only a few students to actually cut them up. Have them wear gloves. Pointed five-inch school scissors are adequate for poking a hole on the side and cutting off the tops, bottoms, and seams. Each can will yield a piece of aluminum approximately 4 × 7 inches. Each student should have several pieces. Show them how to flatten the pieces by gripping them at each end and running the curved edge back and forth over the edge of a table. *Safety note: The can edges are sharp; remind students to handle with great care.* Calder actually recycled cans himself in his sculpture, sometimes cutting them up and combining them with wire, not bothering to paint them.

ADDITIONAL SUGGESTIONS

- Have students make portraits of famous people in wire. Calder portrayed many, such as Josephine Baker, Jimmy Durante, and Fernand Leger. These may be hung or mounted for display on 14-ply cardboard. Another option would be to make animals or jewelry in wire combined with metal or cloth.

- Calder's line drawings looked like wire sculpture. They were continuous overlapping lines of circus figures. Students could use fine-line black marker to draw contour drawings of friends in action poses or interpret sports photos from a newspaper or magazine using continuous line only.

- Ask students to "design" an airplane or car, as Calder did for Braniff Airlines and BMW in 1975. He selected the colors and designs to be painted on the outside. His name was boldly signed on his "works of art." For a quick project, photocopy contour drawings of an airplane or car for each student to transform with colored pencils in primary colors. Have students sign them.

- Students can design textiles or rugs with Calder-like shapes such as animals, circles, swirling lines, and adaptations of African designs. Calder's playful shapes and colors were translated into bright prints and carpets made by his wife, Louisa Calder. Colors were pure hues of red, blue, yellow, combined with white and black.

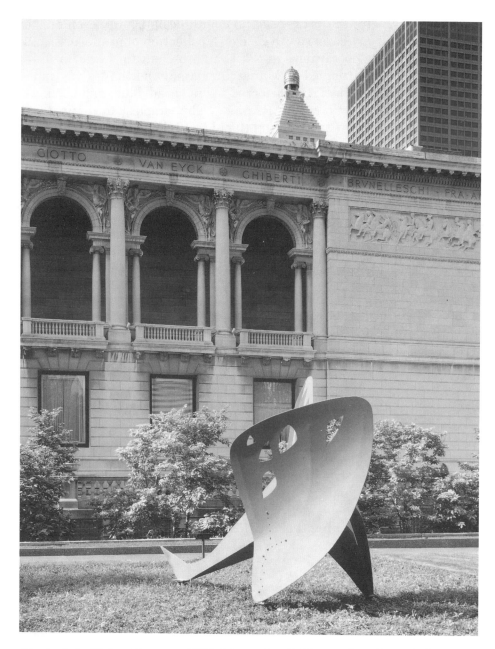

Photo 8-2. *Flying Dragon*, **1975, Alexander Calder, painted steel plate, 365.8 × 579.1 × 335.3 cm., Restricted gift of Mr. and Mrs. Sidney L. Port, The Art Institute of Chicago. Photograph by Thomas Cinoman. This photo shows view #2: McCormick Garden installation view, with strong shadow.**

PROJECT 8-2: **STABILE**

MATERIALS

- Empty soft drink cans, rinsed
- Wire
- Several pairs of cotton gloves
- Scissors
- Paper punches
- Brads
- Spray paint: red, blue, yellow, black, and white
- Tagboard

Drawn after the *Flying Dragon*, 1975
Alexander Calder
The Art Institute of Chicago

Although Alexander Calder designed stabiles that were as high as 52 feet, he usually made a small maquette (model) of aluminum that was enlarged for him at a factory. Aluminum is a quality material, and you will be able to create works of art with recycled soda cans. You will be making maquettes in aluminum, just as he did. Alexander Calder's stabiles frequently were based on animal forms, although they did not necessarily look like those animals.

Safety note: The edges on cut aluminum are very sharp. Use simple precautions in handling. Be careful not to have jagged edges to avoid being cut.

1. Prepare several pieces of aluminum by using the sharp point of scissors to poke a hole in a can near the top. Cut off the top, then down a side, then cut off the bottom. Use cotton gloves while doing this to avoid being cut. To flatten the aluminum, grip a piece on each end, placing the outside of the can next to a table or counter edge, and pull the piece of metal back and forth against the edge of a table until the curve is minimized. After it is roughly cut, use a ruler to draw straight lines on the edges of the aluminum pieces, and cut them carefully to eliminate sharp edges as much as possible.

2. Before cutting your design from the aluminum pieces, make a pattern in tagboard, figuring out how you will join pieces together and where folds will be. Tagboard has approximately the same thickness as aluminum and reacts in much the same way. Trace around your tagboard pattern onto the aluminum. Allow ¼ inch extra for joining seams.

3. You can make a stabile from a single sheet, supported by folding legs in different directions. If two pieces are to be joined, one method is to place the two pieces together and cut them at the same time. Make slits around the edges approximately ¼ inch apart and ¼ inch deep. Alternate folding them first one direction, then the other (as you do to turn in two sheets of paper when you don't have a stapler handy). Or punch holes in the two pieces and hold them together with brads.

4. If you think thick aluminum wire might strengthen or decorate your sculpture, tape the wire to the aluminum with masking tape, then "sew" it on with thinner wire. (Use a nail or hole punch to make holes for attaching.) There are a number of ways to decorate your artwork. The metal is soft enough that you could draw designs on it with a pencil (repoussé designs). You could also make fringe by making cuts along the edge very close together. Calder sometimes created a small wire mobile to attach to the "head" of a stabile.

5. When you are satisfied with your stabile, take it outside and place it on newspaper to spray paint it any of several colors. You could also leave it unpainted, as the designs on the soft drink cans are interesting.

PROJECT 8-3: PAINTING WITH MARBLES

FOR THE TEACHER

SLIDE #30: *Number 1, (Lavender Mist),* **1950, Jackson Pollock, 87 × 118 inches, oil/enamel/aluminum paint on canvas, National Gallery of Art, Washington, D.C.**

This project is designed to give students an appreciation of the types of marks made by Jackson Pollock (1912–1956). Many young people already know Jackson Pollock's work and can't understand how it could possibly be considered art. Yet most major museums own at least one example of Pollock's work. He was an academically trained painter (one of his teachers was Thomas Hart Benton), who occasionally did relatively realistic work, but mostly worked abstractly. Late in his life he went back to loosely figurative painting with black paint applied with sticks or stiffened brushes. (*Note:* I first experienced marble painting in a workshop at the Chicago Art Institute taught by John Rozzelle, and this project is used with his permission.)

Well-Known Paintings by Jackson Pollock

Number 27, 1950, Whitney Museum of American Art, New York

Sounds in the Grass: Shimmering Substance, 1946, Museum of Modern Art, New York

The She-Wolf, 1943, Museum of Modern Art, New York

Cathedral, 1947, Dallas Museum of Art

PREPARATION

Show students books and slides of paintings by abstract artists, encouraging students to talk about this work. They may be confused. Explain that most famous modern painters became well known because they developed a way of working that was unique and recognizable. Imitators of these styles usually went on to something else because they hadn't personally developed this method of working. Help students to understand that an artist who dripped paint onto canvas on the floor from a brush (or a turkey baster, as Pollock did) was creating artwork as much as one who painted with a brush on canvas, or one who today might be drawing on a computer. It is a matter of creativity and attitude toward the work.

Instead of using the handout, it is really interesting to simply hand students the marbles and ink and give no further instructions. They will develop individual ways of using the marbles almost immediately. This project could go on for several hours without them getting bored, although it isn't long before one will request if it would be possible to work with colored ink (let them). As a teacher, you will find it exciting to see the energy that goes into mark-making with marbles. When the project is finished, give each student a marble to take home as a new drawing tool and a souvenir of the experience.

ADDITIONAL SUGGESTIONS

- Have students work as a group of three to each take one of their "marble" drawings and create a wall-hung sculpture. They can manipulate the paper (through folding, rolling, pinning, cutting, curling, etc.) and pin or staple it to a wall. Offer a group grade for this, and you will find an enthusiastic interchange of ideas.

- Push tables together and cover them with newspaper. Place various media on the center of the table. Following the marble painting experience, have students spend at least one hour simply making marks with other materials and tools such as charcoal, conté, oil pastel, ink, brushes, "roll-on" deodorant bottles, sticks. This is a nonthreatening drawing lesson, and even the most timid student will get caught up in the experience. It is a real confidence-booster.

Photo 8-3. *No. 6, 1952,* 1952, Jackson Pollock, oil on canvas, 55-⅞ × 47 inches, Gift of the Friends of Art, The Nelson-Atkins Museum of Art, Kansas City, Missouri. Photography by M. McLean.

PROJECT 8-3: PAINTING WITH MARBLES

MATERIALS

- Marbles
- Sandpaper
- Shallow plastic containers (you may share)
- India ink
- Colored inks (or thinned tempera)
- 18 × 24-inch drawing paper
- Cover-ups for clothing (shirts, plastic bags, etc.)
- Alcohol for cleaning fingers

Although you may not understand the "controlled drip" method of painting used by Jackson Pollock, his work is probably familiar to you. Pollock was an Abstract Expressionist painter, which meant that he painted his feelings. He had been trained as an artist and knew how to draw and paint recognizable subjects, but as his painting style developed, he chose to paint large canvases that he put on the floor and on which he dripped paint. This project does not involve dripping paint, but gives similar results to those of Pollock's paintings.

1. This project has to be done in a standing position and is somewhat uncontrollable, so use an old shirt or paper towel to cover your middle (even a plastic cleaner's bag could be an "apron"). Before beginning, you might want to flatten one of your marbles slightly on one side with sandpaper so it will make more interesting marks.

2. Dip the marble in the ink (pour ink about ¼ inch deep in a small dish). Roll the marble around to cover it with ink. Lift it out and drop it into the middle of the paper.

3. Grasp the paper by the sides and roll the marble around. As it runs out of ink, redip it in ink and continue. Here are some options available:
   - Run the marble around in circles, figure eights, long curvy lines, and straight lines.
   - Fold the paper while the ink is wet and make prints of ink lines.
   - Pour a small blob of ink on the paper and let the marble run in and out of it, re-inking itself in the process and making the blob more interesting as it pulls ink out of it in lines.
   - Crumple your paper before you begin. The cracks make the marble react differently.
   - Place the paper on the floor (on newspaper), dip the marble in ink, and drop it to make dots.
   - Use your inked fingertips to add a little textural interest.
   - If colored ink is available, apply it with either the marble or your fingertips.

4. Here are several options for finishing your work:
   - If most of your design is in the center, make a small mat and move it around until you find the most interesting area to mat.
   - Work with several people as a group to make a "wall sculpture" by folding and manipulating the paper and grouping your sheets together as one composition, pinning them to a bulletin board with straight pins or staples.
   - Use the paper as background for a different type of drawing or collage.
   - Find open areas within the marks you have made, and fill in some areas with color.

PROJECT 8-4: ANDY WARHOL'S BLOTTED LINE

FOR THE TEACHER

When one thinks about Pop artists and images, the work of Andy Warhol (1928–1988) may come to mind first. His serial images of movie stars such as Marilyn Monroe and Elizabeth Taylor, Campbell™ soup cans, Brillo™ boxes, and row-upon-row of Coke® cans or bottles are familiar to most people.

Warhol spent ten years as a successful commercial artist before becoming a painter and print-maker. His first images were of shoes, but he also did illustrations for fashion, travel, and art magazines. He did window displays and table settings for Tiffany, and designed Christmas cards, album covers, and book jackets. Warhol became enamored of making stamps for printing multiple images. At first he carved balsa wood for stamps, then discovered large art gum erasers (he carved images on all six sides), and would fill pages with repeats of the same image, which he later filled in with watercolor. Warhol developed a technique called the *blotted line* that made his drawings unique. He often combined the drawings with watercolor, giving his work a childlike sophistication.

Examples of Andy Warhol's Work

Green Coca-Cola Bottles, 1962, Whitney Museum of American Art, New York

Campbell's Soup Can, 1965, Museum of Modern Art, New York

Marilyn Monroe's Lips, 1962, Hirshhorn Museum of Art, Washington, D.C.

Mona Lisa, 1965, The Metropolitan Museum of Art, New York

PREPARATION

Have students work first on small pieces of paper before beginning a large composition. Warhol drew many subjects including shoes, cats, reptiles, ballerinas, portraits, butterflies, fruit, and musicians' faces. If students prefer not to draw shoes, offer them another option.

ADDITIONAL SUGGESTIONS

- Have students use stamps and watercolor to create a design for small shopping bags on 8 × 10-inch paper. On an art gum eraser, they should cut out at least three line designs with an X-acto™ knife, then combine these designs to create a repeat pattern. Then they can fill in portions of the pattern with watercolor. *Note:* Large eraser stamps can be created from a material called "Soft-Kut Printing Blocks™." *Safety note: Always keep your free hand behind the knife when cutting.*

- A variation of this technique was practiced by Paul Klee who hated to part with his original designs. (Warhol modeled his line technique on that of Klee's.) He traced his original drawing, then painted special black paint (stamp-pad ink—available from your school bookstore—works) on the back of the tracing paper. He then redrew the tracing paper design and painted inside (and sometimes outside) the lines with watercolor.

- Warhol made painted backdrops for a fashion show by using tempera on window shades. Window shades would be inexpensive and adaptable as canvases for large paintings, play backdrops, or murals.

- Warhol went through a "gold period" where he made his broken-line drawings of still life objects and filled them in with gold leaf. (You could use gold paint, gold marking pens, or size and aluminum "gold" leaf—all available at hobby stores.)

- Another "gold period" appropriate for students would be to have students create "crazy golden slippers" as Warhol did when he created 40 shoe styles (based on personalities) for various celebrities such as Kate Smith, Zsa Zsa Gabor, James Dean, and Elvis Presley. These were drawn in ink on white paper, painted in gold, and trimmed with silver or gold doily cut-out decorations.

- Have your students bring in shoes that the family is discarding and challenge them to create something interesting from them. An old shoe can be transformed into a piece of sculpture through covering it with plaster-tape or papier-mâché and found objects. Do drawings of them, or display them as if they were in the window of a shoe store.

Photo 8–4. *Flowers,* **1970, Andy Warhol, Photo Silk Screen. Purchase: The Sidney S. and Sadie Cohen Print Purchase Fund, The Saint Louis Art Museum.**

PROJECT 8-4: ANDY WARHOL'S BLOTTED LINE

MATERIALS

- Drawing paper
- Tracing paper
- Watercolor paper
- Pencils
- India ink
- Pen points and holders
- Watercolors
- Brushes

This project is to draw a side view of a shoe or boot that a famous person might have worn. This could be a historical figure, a musician, actor, or politician. Andy Warhol, a Pop artist, became well known for his blotted-line drawings of shoes when he was a commercial artist.

1. Practice making the blotted line. On a 3-inch square piece of tracing paper, do a simple ink drawing such as flowers or butterflies. Turn this over and place the inked side on a 3-inch square piece of watercolor paper. Allow it to dry for a moment or two, then gently press over the back of it to transfer the ink to the watercolor paper. Remember that the image will print backward from your drawing. It takes a little practice to avoid smearing the ink. You could fill a piece of watercolor paper with a series of small images created in this manner.

2. On regular drawing paper, do a pencil drawing that will be the pattern for your large illustration.

3. Place a piece of tracing paper over your pencil sketch and trace your original drawing in pencil. By working through the back of the tracing paper, you can see exactly where you have been working and align the paper when you transfer a section. On the back of the tracing paper, draw a small section of the original in pen and ink. Do only a small section at a time, or the ink will dry and not transfer.

4. While the ink is wet, turn the tracing paper over, facing the wet side against the watercolor paper. Allow it to set for a few seconds before you gently press the back of the tracing paper to transfer the ink to the drawing paper.

5. When the total drawing has been transferred in ink, allow it to dry, then use watercolor to fill it in. It isn't necessary to stay within the lines.

6. When you are finished, to give it a commercial look, you can write a title or commercial message in ink on the watercolor paper. Warhol allowed his mother to write on his illustrations, since she had "big loopy handwriting" that he admired.

PROJECT 8-5: POP SIGNS AND SYMBOLS

FOR THE TEACHER

SLIDE #31: *American Dream I,* 1960–1961, Robert Indiana, 72 × 60-⅛ inches, oil on canvas, Larry Aldrich Foundation Fund, The Museum of Modern Art, New York

Robert Indiana (b. 1928 as Robert Clark *in* Indiana) is a painter and sculptor whose most famous work is *LOVE* (the image made famous on postage stamps). His paintings and painted wooden constructions were Hard-Edge with solid, bright, sometimes clashing colors, often combined with values of black and white. Like many other Pop artists, he became intrigued with the target format, painting it with letters and numbers. Many of his themes were based on road signs and advertising and his interpretation of aspects of the American environment and way of life. He paid tribute to Charles Demuth's (1883–1935) *I Saw the Figure 5 in Gold* (1928) by using the same imagery in his own work.

Well-Known Works by Robert Indiana

The Demuth American Dream No. 5, 1963, Art Gallery of Ontario, Toronto

Triumph of Tira, 1961, Sheldon Memorial Art Gallery, Lincoln, Nebraska

American Gas Works, 1962, Museum Ludwig, Cologne, Germany

The X-5, 1963, Whitney Museum of American Art, New York

Louisiana, 1966, Krannert Art Gallery, University of Illinois, Champaign

Year of Meteors, 1961, Albright-Knox Art Gallery, Buffalo, New York

The Calumet, 1961, Rose Art Museum, Brandeis University, Waltham, Massachusetts

LOVE, 1966, Indianapolis Museum of Art

PREPARATION

Have students spend two minutes writing single verbs that are meaningful. In *The Demuth American Dream No. 5,* Indiana used five words—Hug, Eat, USA, Err, Die—as a background for his star image and fives. Indiana's work has a format that students will relate to. They can think about the various components of their lives—such as environment, recreation, school, sports, home, work—and come up with words that describe these.

ADDITIONAL SUGGESTIONS

- Create a sculpture with three-dimensional letters combined to make a word. To make three-dimensional letters, give students precut 6 × 8-inch pieces of tagboard, colored railroad board or construction paper, and long strips of the same material 4 inches wide. Have students measure and draw letters carefully, using the full height of 8 inches, then cut two identical 8-inch high letters. Using a ruler, they should mark ½ inch on each long edge of the 4-inch strips. They should score this line with the tip of a pair of scissors, then clip toward it at 1- to 1-½-inch intervals. The tabs are folded and glued to form the sides of the letters. Students can experiment with various ways of combining the letters, which can then be painted in various colors.

- Have students design a postage stamp using letters or any popular symbol. A colleague, Timothy Smith, has his students make sheets of stamps by tracing a small design 12 times. He makes several photocopies of each design which the students then paste up to resemble an actual sheet of stamps, which is then hand-colored using colored pencil. He has also had students do this as a computer graphics project.

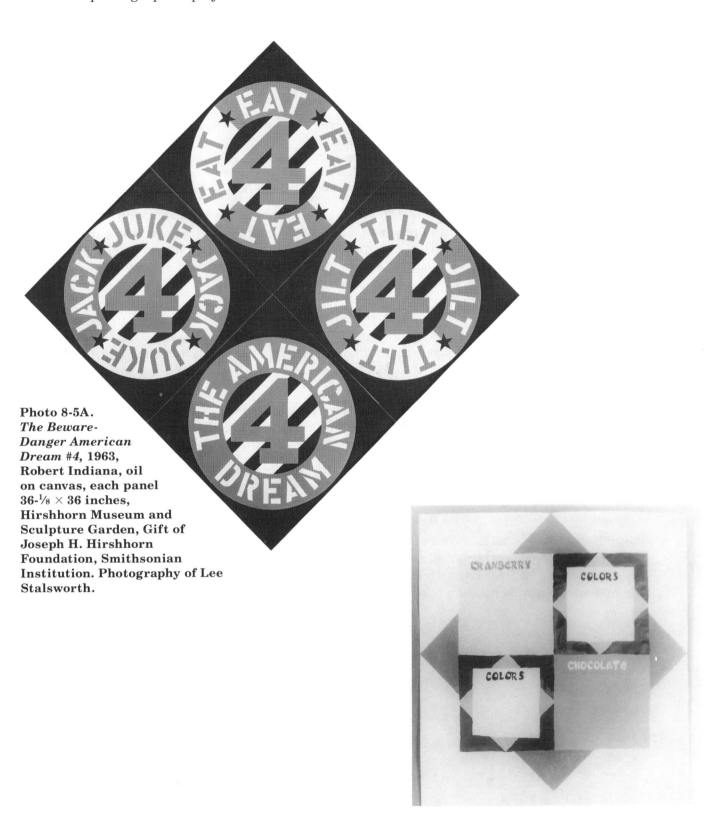

Photo 8-5A.
The Beware-Danger American Dream #4, **1963, Robert Indiana, oil on canvas, each panel 36-⅛ × 36 inches, Hirshhorn Museum and Sculpture Garden, Gift of Joseph H. Hirshhorn Foundation, Smithsonian Institution. Photography of Lee Stalsworth.**

Photo 8-5B. Student work inspired by Robert Indiana.

PROJECT 8-5: POP SIGNS AND SYMBOLS

MATERIALS

- Compasses
- Ruler
- 9 × 12-inch newsprint
- 18-inch square drawing paper
- Tempera paint

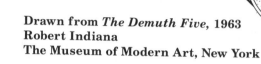

Drawn from *The Demuth Five,* **1963**
Robert Indiana
The Museum of Modern Art, New York

Robert Indiana was a Pop artist who incorporated short words in his paintings and sculpture. His most famous work was *LOVE,* which has been reproduced in many media. It seems such a simple thing to divide a one-syllable word, but it hadn't been done before. His paintings used words arranged within a geometric format. He also used circles, stars, and squares (sometimes turned so they looked like diamonds). The words looked like they had been commercially stenciled.

1. Think about your own life—what issues are important to you? You may be thinking about the environment, dating, work, school, home, and family, or myriad other concerns. On newsprint, write several short words or initials that might be used in a composition. Select up to five or six, and doodle with printing them within a square composition. You could use several together or only one.

2. Make some thumbnail sketches to give you an idea for your painting. The *idea* is more important than the image. You may get your best results by using a compass and ruler and just playing with compositions. What happens when you overlap or combine various geometric figures?

3. When you have decided on the final idea, carefully draw it on the large sheet of paper. Hard-Edge painting requires that work be measured carefully and neatly done. If you look closely at some of the Hard-Edge painting, you will see that even these artists went out of the lines at times, although sometimes they used masking tape to produce exact edges.

4. Select several closely related colors (such as blue, turquoise, green), then add colors from the opposite side of the color wheel (red, red orange). Paint them without any modeling (shading). The flat, bright areas of color were a hallmark of many of the Pop artists. You might choose to separate areas with a wide line of a contrasting color.

Drawn from *The Beware-Danger American Dream No. 4*
Robert Indiana,
Hirshhorn Museum and Sculpture Garden
Washington, D.C.

PROJECT 8-6: "QUOTING" THE OLD MASTERS IN PAINT

FOR THE TEACHER

SLIDE #32: *Washington Crossing the Delaware,* 1953, Larry Rivers, 212.4 × 283.5 cm., oil / graphite / charcoal on linen, The Museum of Modern Art, New York. Given anonymously. Photograph © 1995 The Museum of Modern Art, New York

SLIDE #33: *George Washington Crossing the Delaware* (Stage set for Kenneth Koch's Drama), 1961, Alex Katz, acrylic on wood, oil on wood, china, Gift of Mr. and Mrs. David K. Anderson, Martha Jackson Memorial Collection, National Museum of American Art, Smithsonian Institution

Larry Rivers (b. 1923) has been a flamboyant figure his entire life, as a professional musician in a jazz band, a painter, and a sculptor. He studied art with Hans Hofmann and William Baziotes, expecting to support himself as an art teacher. Rivers was influenced by Willem De Kooning and other Abstract Expressionists, but his work is seen today as a bridge between Abstract Expressionism and Pop Art. His *Washington Crossing the Delaware,* based on the famous painting by Emanuel Leutz, broke away from the Abstract Expressionist concept of painting one's inner feelings and outraged the public by attacking an "institution" such as the heroic painting by Leutz. His figural paintings were combinations of precisely drawn images, letters, blurs, and areas of bare canvas. He sometimes painted the same figure more than once on a canvas. His later work combined sculpture and painting, as he worked with welded metal, plexiglass, and wood.

Examples of Work by Larry Rivers

The History of the Russian Revolution: From Marx to Mayakovski, 1965, Hirshhorn Museum, Washington, D.C.

The Paul Revere Event—Four Views, 1968, New England Merchants National Bank of Boston

First New York Film Festival Billboard, 1963, Joseph H. Hirshhorn Foundation, Washington, D.C.

Berdie with the American Flag, 1955, Nelson-Atkins Museum of Art, Kansas City, Missouri

The Accident, 1957, collection of Joseph E. Seagram & Sons, Inc., New York

Last Civil War Veteran, 1961, collection of Martha Jackson, New York

The Studio, 1956, Minneapolis Institute of Arts

Jim Dine Storm Window, 1965, collection of Larry Rivers

PREPARATION

Compare the Larry Rivers version of *Washington Crossing the Delaware* with that of Leutz's and also of Alex Katz's. Discuss similarities and differences. Rivers's interests were wide ranging, and he often "quoted" masterworks as his basic theme. Unlike many Abstract Expressionists, his theme paintings were often based on people (such as his mother-in-law, Berdie; Napoleon; or Washington), places (a drugstore, a studio), or ideas (patriotism). Begin by standing at a chalkboard and asking students to call out "themes." Write them on the board until you have at least 20.

ADDITIONAL SUGGESTIONS

- Have students use old storm windows or screens as a "canvas." Larry Rivers created a series of compositions within storm windows (as in his *Jim Dine Storm Window,* 1965), either painting directly on the window glass or using cut-up painted cardboard, wood, screen wire, and canvas.

- Have students create a poster for an upcoming event in the loosely painted collage-style used by Larry Rivers in his *First New York Film Festival Billboard* (1963). It is readable as an ad in that it includes pertinent information, most of it done with stencil letters of various sizes. Also included are shapes that might be human figures, a wild variety of colors, some realistic drawings, a few stars, and the names of some foreign-film entries. Instead of stencils, students could use letters of various types that they have made on a computer. If these are too small to read, have them arrange them in a collage on 8-½ × 11-inch typing paper. Photocopy the composition onto an overhead transparency, which can then be projected onto a canvas or paper to make letters of any size.

- Students may project a slide of an original old master painting onto a canvas or large sheet of paper. Have them carefully copy only a portion of it and paint that small area as nearly like the original as possible. Allow the paint to drip, and draw the rest of the painting in pencil, leaving it uncompleted. Small portions of other realistic paintings could be added, or a famous event could be interpreted in an entirely different manner than it was originally depicted (in photographs or paintings). At least six interpretations of *Washington Crossing the Delaware* have been done by famous artists.

Photo 8-6. *Berdie with the American Flag*, 1955, Larry Rivers, oil on canvas, 20 × 25-⅞ inches, Gift of William Inge, The Nelson-Atkins Museum of Art, Kansas City, Missouri.

PROJECT 8-6: "QUOTING" THE OLD MASTERS IN PAINT

MATERIALS

- Drawing paper
- Pencil
- Acrylic or tempera paint

Larry Rivers's large compositions were sometimes based on paintings by famous artists. He never copied them outright, but took their "theme" and sometimes their composition. He then came up with an interpretation that might resemble the original artwork only in its title. Here is your chance to "quote" a famous artist.

1. Begin by selecting a theme. Then randomly cover a piece of drawing paper with pencil sketches. If you are "quoting" a famous painting, draw only small portions of it, or use the general idea of the composition, then put it away and draw variations of your own.

2. You can paint directly on your drawing paper, allowing some of the pencil drawings to show through, or transfer parts of the composition to canvas. The painting should have some realistic areas, some left bare or thinly covered with paint, and other areas that are "painterly" (allowing the marks made by applying paint with a brush to remain unblended).

3. If there are words or portions of words that would give a focal point to the painting or offer a hard-edged contrast, paint or stencil them in. The use of stencils to paint words on artwork was a hallmark of Pop Art painters.

4. Here are a few devices used by Larry Rivers to give added emphasis in a painting:

   - Surround a recognizable figure(s) by wide lines, using two or three bright colors, firmly applied.
   - Repeat recognizable figures more than once (sometimes changing how they are painted, but still making it possible to know they are the same figures).
   - Glue tagboard cutouts onto the background, drawing and painting right over them. The raised edges give variety to a composition.
   - Divide your ground into a grid with pencil. Allow the grid to show through sometimes.
   - Use your knowledge of a foreign language to stencil identifications in that language near the appropriate portions of the human figure.
   - When drawing a face, deliberately leave some of the features "fuzzy," while making others as perfect as possible.

PROJECT 8-7: **THE CARTOON AS FINE ART**

FOR THE TEACHER

Roy Lichtenstein (b. 1923), one of the founders of the Pop Art movement, has remained true to the cartoon-like character of his work over the years, creating a number of series with different themes. His work is filled with hand-painted Benday™ dots (used in color print reproduction in advertising and newspapers) and multicolored lines (staples in the vocabulary of a commercial artist). His paintings were always in brilliant hues, with the characters outlined and flatly colored, often with speech bubbles, like the comics. Many of the paintings incorporated cartoon characters such as Mickey Mouse or Batman. Some of his series included as many as 40 paintings of the same theme, like his *Entablatures* that used motifs from classical architecture. He has always worked on a large scale and, in 1986, completed a 68-foot tall (5 stories high) mural for the Equitable Life Assurance Society in New York.

In his later work, Lichtenstein combines a number of motifs from his earlier paintings and those of other artists whom he admires. Using the artwork of other artists as a springboard for an idea has been commonplace throughout the history of art, and Lichtenstein quotes, appropriates, or restates the work of other famous artists in his own unique style.

Examples of Roy Lichtenstein's Work

Mural with Blue Brushstroke, 1986, Equitable Life Assurance Society building, New York

I Know. . . . Brad, 1963, Ludwig Forum, Aachen, Germany

Blam, 1962, Yale University Art Gallery, New Haven

Popeye, 1961, collection of David Lichtenstein, New York

Calendar, 1962, Museum of Contemporary Art, Los Angeles

Curtains, 1962, Saint Louis Art Museum

Goldfish Bowl II, 1978, Saint Louis Art Museum

PREPARATION

Ask students why they think Pop artists were abandoning the "touchy-feely" painting methods of the Abstract Expressionists and adopting the impersonalism of the consumer mentality. In making all his work look like cartoons, Lichtenstein was commenting on his view of the way a comic book is made—it is a project developed by a committee and could not be considered art. He found it amusing that an individual (himself) could create a cartoon and have it be considered art.

ADDITIONAL SUGGESTIONS

- If students wish to make a very large cartoon-painting (or a mural), have them follow steps 1 to 3 of the project on the student handout, composing the original on 8-½ × 11-inch typing paper. This can be photocopied on an overhead transparency and projected to make any size painting desired, either on canvas, on 22 × 28-inch 14-ply posterboard (be sure to gesso front and back to equalize "pull"), on large roll paper, or onto a wall. To make dots, students may use a stencil; to make stripes, they can apply masking tape to straight areas.

- Following steps 1 to 3 in the directions, students can draw an entire design on tracing paper, then trace over the back of it with pencil and redraw it, transferring the design to black construction paper. They will be able to see the pencil lines well enough to cut it out with an X-acto™ knife. *Safety note: Remind students to put a magazine underneath for cutting, and to keep their hands behind the knife.* Short, repeated strokes are preferable to long strokes, although a metal straight edge may be used for long straight lines. Then they can glue various colors of fadeless paper, wallpaper, magazine cut-outs, or construction paper underneath the openings. Remind students not to glue things in place until they have the entire composition arranged.

- Lichtenstein created sculpture, such as his *Goldfish Bowl II,* in iron and stained glass. Students can make a simple three-dimensional paper sculpture by cutting openings in black paper, gluing colored overhead transparency plastic behind the openings, and joining the two ends of the black paper together.

- A smooth ceramic project such as a box could be decorated in the cartoon technique. Underglazes may be painted on using stencils. Lichtenstein decorated a ceramic female head in this manner; it looked like a wig stand of the type that was popular in the 1950s.

Photo 8-7A. *Goldfish Bowl II,* 1978, Roy Lichtenstein, cast and painted bronze, 39 × 25-¼ inches, Funds given by the Shoenberg Foundation, Inc., The Saint Louis Art Museum.

Photo 8-7B. *Head,* Roy Lichtenstein, ceramic, The Saint Louis Art Museum.

Photo 8-7C. *Mural with Blue Brushstroke,* 1986, 68 feet ¾ inches × 32 feet 5-¼ inches, Courtesy of Roy Lichtenstein, Equitable Building, New York City. This mural, which is five stories high, incorporates images from many of the different series that Lichtenstein did. It also includes "quotes" of other artists such as Fernand Leger, Henri Matisse, Ellsworth Kelly, Jean Arp, Georges Braque, and Frank Stella.

PROJECT 8-7: **THE CARTOON AS FINE ART**

MATERIALS

- 18 × 24-inch drawing paper
- Newsprint
- Tracing paper
- Pencils
- X-acto™ knives
- Colored fadeless paper or construction paper
- Rubber cement
- Colored pencil
- India ink and broad-nibbed pens

Head, 1966
Roy Lichtenstein
The Saint Louis Museum of Art

Roy Lichtenstein has a great sense of humor. He has fun with art, making even the work of great masters look like cartoons. Look at cartoons in the newspaper. Most of them are outlined in black and limited to five areas of bright flat color. Patterns such as stripes and dots show differences in value and give emphasis to negative space. They also have speech "bubbles." This project is to make your subject (whatever it is) look like a cartoon.

1. Use pencil to try many different ideas on newsprint. You may end up combining some of them to make a total composition. You could have a theme, such as fish, flowers, Art Deco designs (as Lichtenstein did), or some other design that is meaningful to you. Another approach is to "quote" other famous artworks, selecting portions of several and combining them with your own ideas.

2. When you have chosen your approach, cut out your newsprint designs, combining and gluing them onto another newsprint background. If you have blank spaces, these could be filled in later with plain areas of color.

3. On a large piece of tracing paper, trace over the entire *newsprint* design. Draw over the back of the *tracing* paper with pencil, then reverse and attach it with tape to the top of your *drawing* paper. Transfer it to the drawing paper by redrawing on the front of the tracing paper.

4. Before adding color, use a broad-nibbed pen and India ink (or a calligraphy marking pen) to redraw the pencil lines in black. Plan to have dots and stripes somewhere within your composition. Leave some areas unpainted or painted with flat color. You may use colored pencil, watercolor, tempera, or acrylic paint to fill in the lines. An alternative is to glue cut-out colored paper or wallpaper onto the background in places, then combine it with your painting.

Goldfish Bowl, 1978
Roy Lichtenstein
The Saint Louis Museum of Art

PROJECT 8-8: **ENCAUSTIC—PAINTING WITH WAX**

FOR THE TEACHER

SLIDE #34: *Map*, 1961, Jasper Johns, 198.2 × 314.7 cm., oil on canvas, Gift of Mr. and Mrs. Robert C. Scull, The Museum of Modern Art, New York. Photograph © 1995 The Museum of Modern Art, New York

The work of Jasper Johns (b. 1930) was considered a precursor for Pop Art, as he abandoned traditional methods of self-expression, choosing instead to use commonplace symbols such as the American Flag, a target, or numbers in his encaustic paintings. He wanted to show the touch of an artist's hand through subtle changes to well-known images. At times these paintings were combined with cast-plaster body parts such as an ear or nose. He also had ordinary objects such as ale cans, or a coffee can filled with paint brushes cast in bronze, which he then hand-painted.

Examples of Work by Jasper Johns

Flag, 1954–1955, Museum of Modern Art, New York

Numbers 0 Through 9, 1961, Hirshhorn Museum, Washington, D.C.

Target with Plaster Casts, 1955, collection of Leo Castelli, New York

Painted Bronze (Ballantine Ale Cans), 1960, Museum Ludwig, Cologne

Target with Four Faces, 1955, Museum of Modern Art, New York

PREPARATION

Jasper Johns's use of encaustic (pigment in wax) can be adapted to the classroom, as anyone who has ever used old melted crayons to do paper batik with students is aware. Encaustic and the use of wax for painting dates back to the Greeks. Powdered pigment and a small amount of damar varnish was added to beeswax. This medium was kept warm and applied with a palette knife.

Do this project by melting wax crayons or oil pastels. I sent home a pile of scrap oil pastels with each student to unwrap, then we sorted them by colors into baby food jars the next day. The jars were set in an inch of boiling water in electric skillets for safety, and small chunks of paraffin added to thin them for easier application. Each jar had its own brush as an applicator (don't attempt to clean these later, just save them for the next time). Wax melters that will hold several colors are available through art supply resources. Try this yourself first, if possible, and experiment touching an encaustic surface with a household iron to make some interesting variations. Another option is to heat a metal palette knife on the surface of an iron for smoothing.

Safety note: Wax will spontaneously ignite if allowed to reach 300 degrees (it will smoke when it gets too hot).

ADDITIONAL SUGGESTIONS

- An effect similar to encaustic can be achieved with the heavy application of oil crayons dipped in turpentine applied to wood or canvas. For further interest, students can use the sgraffito technique of scratching detail through the crayon. These crayon paintings can be varnished to preserve color brilliance and give a new dimension.

- In two of his target compositions, Johns combined the encaustic paintings with casts of various body parts such as partial face casts. Several students could work as a group to make casts of body parts of each other from plaster-tape, then incorporate this into one composition using a commonplace motif of their choice.

• Have students create an all-white collage from wallpaper, magazines, and other found textured materials. The theme could be based on something mundane, or even on the student's name, provided it is well-disguised.

Photo 8-8. *Target with Four Faces*, 1955, Jasper Johns, assemblage: encaustic and collage on canvas with objects, 26 × 26 inches, surmounted by four tinted plaster faces in wood box with hinged front. Gift of Mr. and Mrs. Robert C. Scull, The Museum of Modern Art, New York. Photograph © 1996 The Museum of Modern Art, New York.

PROJECT 8-8: **ENCAUSTIC—PAINTING WITH WAX**

MATERIALS

- Watercolor paper, gessoed on two sides
- Wax crayons, oil pastels, or tempera powder
- Paraffin broken into small chunks
- Wax melter or electric skillets
- Brushes or palette knives
- Paper towels
- Old iron and / or hair dryer
- Soft cotton rags
- Solvent such as mineral spirits
- Palette knives or table knives

Encaustic (colored wax) paintings on wood have existed since the time the Romans occupied Egypt. Wax mixed with color pigment is applied to a surface such as paper, wood, or canvas. Jasper Johns did encaustic paintings of such things as the American flag, targets, and maps. He chose ordinary subjects, feeling that the effect of heavily applied pigment was sufficiently interesting that the subject didn't matter.

1. Select a subject. You may choose, as Jasper Johns did, to do something commonplace such as a stop sign, car, map, stars, or shoes, or you may make a much more complex "painting in wax." The wax has to be relatively hot to apply it, though you will be able to make changes after it is applied by building up color or using an iron to make differences in the surface. *Safety note: Be very careful of the wax. If it is hot enough to paint with, it is also hot enough to burn your skin.*

2. After drawing your subject on the matboard or paper, use a brush to carry pigment to the surface. When you lift the brush out of the wax, hold a paper towel underneath it to avoid drips where you do not want them. If you must, you could use a knife to scrape off an area and do it again.

3. After the wax is applied, use an iron to make changes. A hair dryer could also be used to create varied effects.
   - Heat a knife on the plate of the iron, then use it to smooth the wax.
   - Slide the edge of the iron through the waxed surface like an ice skate to make a variety of lines.

4. To put in detail later, use ordinary crayons dipped in turpentine to add details. You can also scratch through the composition with a nail.

5. To finish the project, polish with a soft cloth or varnish to bring out a satiny sheen.

PROJECT 8-9: POP ART STENCILS

FOR THE TEACHER

This project, also based on the work of Jasper Johns and other Pop artists, is great because it takes away the "fear of drawing" that so many students have. The challenge is for students to use the picture plane effectively, to create differences in value, texture, line, and form, through the repetition of the same letter or number.

PREPARATION

Discuss the use of ordinary everyday objects by such Pop artists as Jasper Johns, Robert Rauschenberg, and Jim Dine. They wished to depersonalize the subject matter of art by taking commonplace symbols— such as letters, numbers, tools, or food—and making them the focal point of their composition. Jasper Johns felt that the surface and the "artist's hand" would be more apparent to the viewer if the subject were of secondary importance. Johns, in particular, used stencil letters and numbers with various media.

ADDITIONAL SUGGESTIONS

- With computers readily available to most students, allow them to make letters on a computer, then cut them up and glue on drawing paper as the basis for a drawing composition. Or let them actually do an entire composition on the computer.

- Use old file folders to make cut-out stencils such as hearts, trucks or cars, hands, birds, or animals. The stencils can be oiled with vegetable oil for frequent use (do them a few days before you actually need them). Challenge students to use the stencils creatively, either with color or black and white.

Photo 8-9. This student work on 18 × 24-inch paper became much more meaningful to the student when she was trying to express what she was feeling at the time.

PROJECT 8-9: **POP ART STENCILS**

MATERIALS

- Purchased cardboard stencils, 6 to 8 inches
- Drawing pencil, black marker, charcoal or conté crayon (black, white, and gray)
- Colored markers
- 12 × 18-inch *or* 18 × 24-inch drawing paper

**Drawn from *Black and White Numerals:
Figure 7*, 1968 Jasper Johns,
The Saint Louis Art Museum.**

This project is based on using ordinary stencil letters, as many Pop artists did. They felt that the subject selected was not particularly important, and that good art could be made with the least imaginative subject. This project will involve a number of experiments, and you will find that you become more creative as you combine materials. You will start with purchased letter stencils, but then you may find that you want to make your own stencils from file folders of such ordinary objects as a heart, a flag, a soda can, a map, etc.

1. Select one stencil letter (perhaps your own initial) to use in the composition. These are some things to think about before you start:
   - Use the whole picture plane, but be aware of the necessity for open space and balance.
   - Give a little more weight to the picture at the bottom to keep it from feeling like it will fall over.
   - Create variety through use of some dark areas, some light, some with pattern.
   - Create some solid areas.
   - Give movement through overlapping, possibly turning the letter on its axis.
   - Create texture through the use of line.
   - Sometimes draw around the outside of a letter rather than filling in the inside.
   - Allow the letters to hang over the edge for variety.

2. Here are some possibilities for making your composition: trace around it with black marker; overlap; swivel it to make a circular effect; turn any direction; or combine it with another letter eventually.

3. Fill in overlapping areas with marker, or emphasize negative space by cross-hatching lines around the letters. A variety of patterns may be used to fill in spaces, or this can simply be the lines created by tracing inside the letters.

4. Try this same project using several colors of conté. You will find that although it is messy, the blending and smearing of the color is very interesting. Also use white conté to give variations that you might not have thought of.

PROJECT 8-10: **THE BLACK OUTLINE: SOAP RESIST**

FOR THE TEACHER

This project is based on the black outline that was used by many of the artists in the 1930s and 1940s. The subjects varied from cityscapes to portraits. Alice Neel (1900–1984) was a portrait artist whose work was distinguished by the strong, honest portrayal of her sitters, and by the strong black or (sometimes) blue outline that she used around her figures. The exaggerated facial features might have been almost like caricatures, but her uncompromising reality neither flatters nor makes fun of the sitter. Her portraits usually are dominated by the person or people looking directly out at the viewer. She also painted nudes, flowers, occasional still lifes, and cityscapes. She painted scenes of Social Realism for the Works Progress Administration in the 1930s, but most of her work was of people in stark interiors. Although most of her work is in private collections, some may be seen in books.

Examples of Work by Alice Neel

Pat Whalen, 1935, Whitney Museum of American Art, New York

Andy Warhol, 1970, Whitney Museum of American Art, New York

The Soyer Brothers, 1973, Whitney Museum of American Art, New York

PREPARATION

This project is suitable for *any* subject such as portraiture, flowers, cityscape, or landscape. Prismacolor Art Stix™ are versatile media, which can be applied in a variety of ways (oil pastel would also work). Because it will look somewhat abstract anyway, encourage your students to work realistically with an actual subject. Collect small pieces of soap (a hotel in your town might save left-over slivers). Experiment with this technique. Have a tray large enough to float the paper in. I used a huge grease tray from the automotive department of a hardware store. You will be surprised at the variety of possibilities.

Note: This project was taught at a National Art Education workshop by William A. Camptin, and is used with his permission. Mr. Camptin suggests that scrap black felt paper (not tar paper) used at construction sites works very well. I have used ordinary construction paper with good results also.

ADDITIONAL SUGGESTIONS

- Students can have a friend sit in a chair, facing them, and do a portrait on black, or dark blue drawing paper in oil pastel. They should do a very light pencil drawing, exaggerating the size of the eyes, hands, or feet (as Alice Neel did). Point out that when someone faces you, the portions of the body closest to you seem much larger. To portray this realistically, students will need to use foreshortening in their drawing. Show them how to hold a pencil in front of them, closing one eye, and estimating size by comparing it on the pencil. Tell students to compare the knees or legs, for example, to the head, which would be farther away, and to paint it the size they see it.

- Have students use a calligraphy marker to do a still life or cityscape. They can draw lightly in pencil, then totally outline the drawing with wide black marker. Then they can fill in within the lines using watercolor or markers and, if necessary, go over the black lines again when they are finished.

- Students can do a composition in oil painting that deliberately "violates the frame." On a piece of 18 × 24-inch paper, they should create a frame by drawing a light pencil line 4 inches smaller than the outside of the paper. Basically they would stay within these lines with the composition, but in one or more places, allow the painting to extend beyond the line (for example, allowing a foot or hand to go into the empty space).

- As a variation of the black picture, students can use black glue on black paper, allowing it to dry completely. When it is dry, they draw with colored chalk inside the lines. They can use a tissue to take chalk residue off the glue lines.

Photo 8-10. This drawing was done with Prismacolor Art Stix™ on black paper. The dark outlines were first put on the paper with soap, which acted as a resist when the drawing was done over it. When rinsed in warm water, the soap disappeared.

PROJECT 8-10: **THE BLACK OUTLINE: SOAP RESIST**

MATERIALS

- Slivers of soap (hotel soap is great)
- Black construction or Arches Cover Stock paper™
- Berol Prismacolor Art Stix™ or oil pastels
- Large tray for dissolving soap
- Warm water
- Newsprint (to put the wet paper on)

If you choose to do a portrait, you might work as Alice Neel did. She was basically a portrait artist who usually outlined her figures with a black or blue line. Her subjects always faced forward, looking directly at the viewer. Using this technique, you could do a portrait of a classmate. Or you might choose instead to do another subject such as a cityscape, landscape, seascape, flowers, a view out the window, or many faces in a crowded setting such as a carnival or a concert.

1. Decide on a subject. Do not use a pencil, but instead draw an outline of your subject directly on the black paper with the corner of a small bar of soap. This soap will act as a resist to preserve the black lines, but will disappear later when the paper is put in warm water. Use it generously.

2. Consider what your color scheme will be. Closely related colors on the color wheel (red/yellow/orange, or violet/turquoise/light blue) give a vibrant look on the black paper. Apply color heavily to the paper. Some suggestions are:

   - Make short, separate strokes, all going the same direction.
   - Color firmly, allowing little of the black paper to show through.
   - Use dark colors as a base, adding lighter colors on top.

3. When you are satisfied, carefully place the paper in a tray containing warm water. The tray should be large enough to allow you to wet the entire paper. If the paper is too large for the tray, you can grasp the paper at both ends, immersing a little at a time by pulling it back and forth. The soap will dissolve in the water, leaving black lines showing. Blot the paper between sheets of newsprint or paper towels.

4. Although you want to keep the black lines, after you allow the paper to dry somewhat, you may continue working on it by using bright colors to highlight areas. Use caution if the paper is still wet. If you build up thick areas, you could make fine details by scratching through the color.

PROJECT 8-11: **INK RESIST AND DRY BRUSH—THE VERTICAL LINE**

FOR THE TEACHER

In his early work, Barnett Newman (1905–1970) did Surrealistic drawings in a manner called *automatic writing,* a form of calligraphy. His work evolved to an Expressionistic style, using circles and straight lines (a form of "Biomorphism"—abstract forms based on shapes found in nature). From 1948 until his death, his work was Minimalist—plain areas of color or black and white divided by one or two vertical lines. These simple paintings were attacked by the art world for being "empty," "decorative," and "fraudulent." Newman's paintings had vast areas of pure color and were the bridge between Abstract Expressionism and Minimalist art.

This project is based on Newman's ink resist drawings. His drawings were concerned with the marks the brush makes when it is almost dry. There was a period when he did not paint; he even destroyed most of his existing work and began again with drawings of this type.

Examples of Paintings by Barnett Newman

Onement II, 1948, Wadsworth Athenaeum, Hartford, Connecticut

Vir Heroicus Sublimis, 1950-1951, Museum of Modern Art, New York

The Wild, 1950, Museum of Modern Art, New York

PREPARATION

Encourage students to experiment and not be concerned about whether something is beautiful or not. Projects of this type take away the fear of drawing for some students because there cannot possibly be a right or wrong. Masking tape of different widths would encourage even further experimentation. Have students do several practice sheets before beginning their full-scale drawings.

ADDITIONAL SUGGESTIONS

- Students can use the masking tape method to do paintings in acrylic. They can leave tape over areas that are to be left bare and, once the first coat is painted, remove that tape and apply tape on top of painted areas. Continue building up areas by applying tape, painting, removing that tape and applying it someplace else, and painting. The variety and textures applied give interesting results.

- Play music in the background for this type of painting. The music selections you choose may lead to different kinds of marks. Encourage students to use different sizes of brushes and other mark-making tools (such as cotton swabs or fingers) to paint, concerning themselves with circles, lines, different widths of strokes, density, direction, and use of the entire page. It takes a little time for them to overcome self-consciousness, but they will begin to start composing.

PROJECT 8-11: INK RESIST AND DRY BRUSH—THE VERTICAL LINE

MATERIALS

- Newspaper
- 18 × 24-inch drawing paper
- Large brushes, 2 to 4 inches
- Small shallow containers for ink
- Black or colored ink
- Newsprint
- Rubber cement
- White candles
- Masking tape
- Alcohol (for cleanup)

These student artworks were done with white crayon and ink in the drybrush technique.

Barnett Newman was fascinated by the marks he could make with a brush. He was a Minimalist, and some of his drawings look like they could have been made in three or four minutes, as they well might have been. He was experimenting—trying to find his way to a new form of art. You will enjoy painting with ink, trying to decide when it is time to quit. In this case, the "less is more" principle of the Bauhaus artists is sometimes important.

1. Practice working with dry-brush on newsprint before making dry-brush/resist paintings on drawing paper.

2. Put masking tape on the drawing paper as a block-out. It can be one long strip or applied completely at random. Even the tears on the ends of the tape will become part of the composition.

3. Apply the ink with the brush. You will get a rich black area where your loaded brush is first applied to the paper. Continue in one motion, allowing the brush to deposit ink until there is no more ink. This dry-brush technique gives interesting differences in your composition by allowing the white paper to show through. After the ink has been applied over the tape and has dried, you may remove the tape.

4. Several other forms of resist are possible:
   - Draw with either the ends or sides of a white crayon or candle; paint ink on top.
   - Paint rubber cement in a pattern. Allow it to dry, then paint ink over it. Rub the cement off with your finger when the ink is dry.
   - Create a small, intensely colored drawing with oil crayon. Brush on ink.

5. Select the best of your compositions to mount. It may be that only a portion of a composition is pleasing to you. Feel free to cut that portion out and mount only a part of your drawing.

LATE TWENTIETH CENTURY
(1965 to Present)

LATE TWENTIETH CENTURY
TIME LINE

1965	1970	1975	1980	1985	1990	1995

Painting Sculpture Architecture Folk Art

Feminist Art Late 1960s–Present

Conceptual Art 1970–present

East Village Art 1980s

Michael Graves b. 1934

Post Modern 1960s to present

Robert Indiana, b. 1928 *Love*, 1966

Wright Brothers at Kitty Hawk, 1903

Red Grooms b. 1937

Louise Bourgeois b. 1911

Photo Realism 1965 to present

Claes Oldenburg, b. 1929 *Giant Hamburger*, 1969

Janet Fish b. 1938

Judy Chicago b. 1939

Edward Keinholz 1927–1994

Duane Hanson 1925–1996

Eight Water Glasses Under Light, 1974

Frank Gehry 1994

Louise Nevelson, 1900–1988

Deborah Butterfield b. 1949

Roy Lichtenstein, b. 1923 *Goldfish Bowl*, 1978

Frank Stella b. 1938

Josef Albers, *Homage to the Square*, 1963
Minimal Painting 1960s

Robert Venturi b. 1925

Keith Haring 1958–1990

Politics

1972 Nixon wins re-election

1976 James E. Carter becomes President

1988 George Bush elected President

1993 2nd woman on Supreme Court

1968 Vietnam War 1888–1976

1973–74 Watergate Nixon resigns

1984 Reagan re-elected

1968 Richard Nixon Pres.

1984 Ronald Reagan becomes Pres.

1992 Bill Clinton elected President

1974 Gerald Ford is Pres.

1980 First woman Supreme Court Justice

Literature

1967 *The Fixer* Bernard Malamud

1983 *The Color Purple* Alice Walker

1988 *Bonfire of the Vanities* Tom Wolfe

1963 *The Reivers* William Faulkner

1961 *To Kill a Mockingbird* Harper Lee

Poet Laureate Howard Nemerov 1920–1991

1986 *Lonesome Dove* Larry McMurtry

Science

1972 Environmental Protection Agency established

1982 AIDS is diagnosed

1986 DNA fingerprinting

1969 U.S. Astronauts land on moon

1978 First test tube baby is born

1984 Compact Disk player

1967 First human heart transplant

1973 First orbiting space lab

1982 First artificial heart implanted

Music

1966 Met. Opera at Lincoln Center

1971 Igor Stravinsky dies

1980 Beatle John Lennon is shot

John Cage 1912–1992

1977 Death of Elvis Presley

1968 Hard Rock Jimi Hendrix

1968 Soul Music Aretha Franklin

Louis Armstrong 1882–1971

Leonard Bernstein 1918–1990

Current Events

1968 Martin Luther King, Jr. assassinated

1979 Islamic State in Iran

1991 USSR dissolved

1982 U.S. recession

Challenger astronauts die in explosion 1986

1966 NOW (National Organization of Women)

1967 Six-day war in Israel

1976 America celebrates Bicentennial

1968 Chinese Cultural Revolution

1979 Iranians seize U.S. Embassy—hold hostages

1973 Vietnam war ends

1995 O. J. Simpson acquitted

1989 U.S. invades Panama

284

LATE TWENTIETH CENTURY ARCHITECTURE

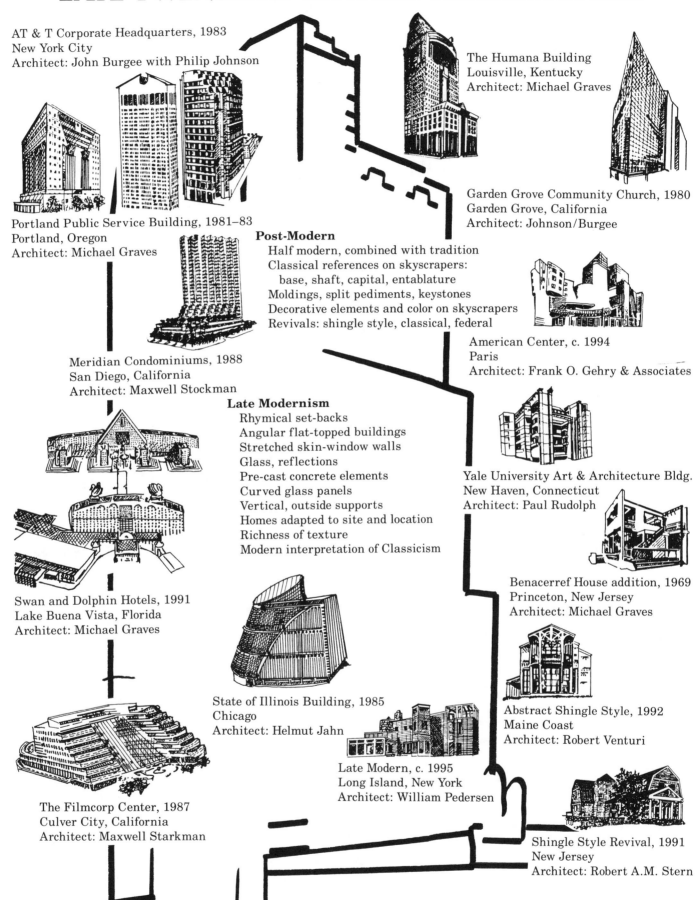

AT & T Corporate Headquarters, 1983
New York City
Architect: John Burgee with Philip Johnson

Portland Public Service Building, 1981–83
Portland, Oregon
Architect: Michael Graves

The Humana Building
Louisville, Kentucky
Architect: Michael Graves

Garden Grove Community Church, 1980
Garden Grove, California
Architect: Johnson/Burgee

Post-Modern
Half modern, combined with tradition
Classical references on skyscrapers:
  base, shaft, capital, entablature
Moldings, split pediments, keystones
Decorative elements and color on skyscrapers
Revivals: shingle style, classical, federal

Meridian Condominiums, 1988
San Diego, California
Architect: Maxwell Stockman

American Center, c. 1994
Paris
Architect: Frank O. Gehry & Associates

Late Modernism
Rhymical set-backs
Angular flat-topped buildings
Stretched skin-window walls
Glass, reflections
Pre-cast concrete elements
Curved glass panels
Vertical, outside supports
Homes adapted to site and location
Richness of texture
Modern interpretation of Classicism

Yale University Art & Architecture Bldg.
New Haven, Connecticut
Architect: Paul Rudolph

Benacerref House addition, 1969
Princeton, New Jersey
Architect: Michael Graves

Swan and Dolphin Hotels, 1991
Lake Buena Vista, Florida
Architect: Michael Graves

State of Illinois Building, 1985
Chicago
Architect: Helmut Jahn

Abstract Shingle Style, 1992
Maine Coast
Architect: Robert Venturi

Late Modern, c. 1995
Long Island, New York
Architect: William Pedersen

The Filmcorp Center, 1987
Culver City, California
Architect: Maxwell Starkman

Shingle Style Revival, 1991
New Jersey
Architect: Robert A.M. Stern

Section 9.—LATE TWENTIETH CENTURY (1965–PRESENT)

ARTISTS OF THE PERIOD

WELL-KNOWN PAINTERS OF THE LATE TWENTIETH CENTURY

- *Chuck Close* (b. 1940) is known for his oversized Photorealistic portraits of friends' faces, created in a variety of media such as inked thumbprints, handmade paper, pastels, paint, and prints. He enlarges his paintings by creating a grid, frequently allowing the grid to become part of the work.

- *Janet Fish* (b. 1938) is a watercolorist who creates realistic still-lifes using mirrors, glass, and flowers in tabletop arrangements. Painted on a giant scale, her artworks reveal her personal sense of order and interests such as gardening.

- *Audrey Flack* (b. 1931) is best known for her Photorealistic paintings. She paints with an airbrush from photographs projected onto canvas. She considers her work to be akin to "vanitas" paintings, the Baroque still-lifes that were reminders of the shortness of life. Her subjects are often objects that are meaningful to her—roses, jewelry, playing cards, even symbols of death such as a stopped watch and melting ice cubes.

- *Keith Haring* (1958–1990) had a short (10 years) but brilliant international career, creating his cartoon-like outlines of people in murals, on a BMW car, on costumes designed for video and an amusement park, and on sidewalks. His large paintings, prints, and sculpture are in collections around the world.

- *David Hockney* (b. 1937) is English, but has made California his home. His paintings frequently feature scenes of swimming pools, California living rooms, or canyons. He also does large photographic assemblages of a single subject in detail, using many views taken from the same location.

- *Joan Mitchell* (1926–1992) was a "second-generation" Abstract Expressionist. After receiving degrees from the Chicago Art Institute, she moved to Paris. She created abstract landscapes, capturing feelings and light-effects in the tradition of American painters.

- *Susan Rothenberg's* (b. 1945) canvases are created with painterly marks, with composition sometimes loosely based on historical artworks such as those of Mondrian. Young minimalist painters of this era were reluctant to paint the human figure, and these ghostly, shimmering images of horses in her early work were her way of creating a subject.

- *Miriam Schapiro* (b. 1923) is best known for her "femmages" (collages that use consciously feminine materials). While teaching an art course for women at the California Institute of the Arts, she and Judy Chicago created an "all-female art environment," *Woman-house* (1971). She uses fabrics to create such images as kimonos or fans, and has done a tribute to the Mexican artist Frieda Kahlo, whom she greatly admired.

287

WELL-KNOWN SCULPTORS

- *Louise Bourgeois* (b. 1911) is fluent in a variety of media including wood and stone carving, Environmental Art, and bronze casting. She was born in France to a family of tapestry artists and studied mathematics at the Sorbonne. Her early work consisted of elongated standing "personages," which she says represented the family she left behind in France.

- *Deborah Butterfield* (b. 1949) is known for her life-sized horses created from diverse found materials. Although she began sculpting horses with steel and plaster, many of her later sculptures were created of sticks and mud.

- *Judy Chicago* (b. 1939) co-founded (with Miriam Schapiro) the Feminist Art Program at the California Institute of the Arts. Her famous work, *The Dinner Party* (1971), was considered one of the landmarks of the Feminist Art movement. A triangular table rested on a tile floor that was inscribed with the names of 999 women. This was created in collaboration with more than 400 women.

- *Dan Flavin* (b. 1933) is probably the best known of the "light sculptors," artists who work with neon tubing. He uses light to transform the appearance of an area, whether it is a box or a room. A Minimalist at first, Flavin gradually began to create more complex color mixtures and reflections. He prefers to call his pieces "proposals" rather than sculpture.

- *Edward Kienholz's* (1927–1994) assemblages often featured life-sized figures within an environment. The themes were sometimes political commentary, or subjects that made the viewer uncomfortable, such as his sculpture *The State Hospital* (1966).

- *Betye Saar* (b. 1926) creates assemblages with an anti-racist theme based on nostalgia for her childhood. She was inspired by the boxes of Joseph Cornell and by Simon Rodia's *Towers* in Los Angeles that were created using found objects.

- *Richard Serra* (b. 1939) has worked with a variety of materials, but is best known for his often controversial environmental sculpture using Cor-ten™ steel. His rusting steel environments can be as large as a city block, and dominate plazas in various cities throughout the United States.

- *Peter Voulkos* (b. 1924) applies Abstract Expressionism to his ceramic sculptures. He is said to have "transformed ceramics as craft into ceramics as art." He continues to work in bronze as well. A teacher at Otis Art Institute and the University of California at Berkeley, Voulkos has "been a major force in the revitalization of California art styles."

FAMOUS ARCHITECTS

- *John Burgee* (b. 1933), in partnership with Philip Johnson, was involved in postmodern architecture. Two of their more famous buildings, the A.T. & T. Building in New York City (1979–1984) and the Republic Bank Building in Houston (1981–1984), specifically remind the viewer of historical buildings in Greece and Holland respectively.

- *Michael Graves* (b. 1934) has become known for his innovative architecture, which sometimes contains decorative elements that are a combination of classicism and modernism. His firm has designed The Swan and Dolphin Hotels at Walt Disney World in Florida, as well as many museums, hotels, and residences, and they specialize in completing the interiors as well as exteriors of their projects.

- *Robert Stern* (b. 1939) is the head of a large group of associates, and works in a number of "quotes" of earlier styles of architecture such as the shingle style or neoclassical, as in his new dining hall at the University of West Virginia. He feels that he and his clients use quality materials, which give a solidity and timelessness to his architecture.

- *Edward Durrell Stone* (1902–1978) designed the Museum of Modern Art in New York and the John F. Kennedy Center for the Performing Arts in Washington, D.C.

- *Robert Venturi* (b. 1925) and his firm design residences and museums such as the Seattle Art Museum and the Sainsbury Wing of the National Gallery in London. His work often incorporates shapes or architectural references from the past. He uses masonry and pattern frequently in his designs.

MOVEMENTS AND SCHOOLS OF ART

- *Conceptual Art* (1970 to present). In Conceptual Art, the *idea* is more important than the artwork. Frequently the viewer will see a drawing of how the artwork might look if it *were* completed. Many 1960s artists sought to eliminate the "product" of art through elimination of a completed project (for example, the artists who produced Happenings). The result is that the location of the artwork is sometimes in the *mind* of the viewer.

- *Earth Art* (1968 to present). Earth Art began when artists used a "new" medium—piles of rocks or dirt to form installations in galleries. Ultimately they went to out-of-the-way places to create their (often impermanent) artworks. Drawings, films, and photographs of the work-in-progress are exhibited and sold. Some of the major American artists involved in this medium are Robert Smithson (b. 1938), Christo (Javacheff, b. 1935), Michael Heizer (b. 1944), Dennis Oppenheim (b. 1938), Patricia Johanson (b. 1940), and Beverly Pepper (b. 1924).

- *Environmental Art* (1960s to present). This term was originally coined in the 1960s when artists transformed entire galleries with materials such as floating helium balloon pillows (Andy Warhol), colored fluorescent light (Dan Flavin, b. 1933), plaster food (Claes Oldenburg, b.1929), and firebrick (Carl Andre, b. 1935). Eventually environmental sculptors transferred their artwork (or earthworks) to outdoor sites. Artists such as Beverly Pepper and Alice Aycock (b. 1946) integrated their artwork into the environment. In the last part of the twentieth century, environmental *artists* are also environmentalists. They are concerned about how humans have changed the environment and are designing artworks for cities and earthworks to reclaim land that has been laid to waste. Artists such as Mel Chin (b. 1951), Newton Harrison (b. 1932), Nancy Holt (b. 1938), and John Roloff (b. 1947) are leaders in the field.

- *Feminist Art* (late 1960s to present). During the early days of Feminist Art, women sought to express themselves through traditional "feminine" materials and techniques. The Feminist Art movement in the 1970s and 1980s sought a more equal balance of the sexes in art museums and galleries. In 1972 the Women's Caucus for Art was formed. Women whose work has become well known, possibly as a result of the efforts of feminist groups, are Judy Chicago (b. 1939), Alice Neel (1900–1984), Audrey Flack (b. 1931), Janet Fish (b. 1938), Nancy Graves (1940–1995), Betye Saar (b. 1926), Mary Frank (b. 1933), Faith Ringgold (b. 1930), Miriam Schapiro (b. 1923), and Alice Aycock (b. 1946).

- *Funk Art* (1950–1960s). Funk Art originated in the San Francisco Bay area. Although painters founded the movement, sculptural techniques and assemblage soon took over. Taboo subjects and materials that would not normally be considered suitable for art became art, much as in the Dada movement. Popular materials were plastic polychromed metal and fiberglass. Ceramist Robert Arneson (b. 1930) and Roy DeForest (b. 1930) were considered Funk artists.

- *Minimalism* (1960s and 1970s). Minimalism featured the use of high-tech materials such as neon, plastic, and metals. Artworks were stripped to the essence, purposely devoid of any "artist's touch." Minimalists included sculptors such as Donald Judd (b. 1928), Dan Flavin (b. 1933), Richard Serra (b. 1939), Carl Andre (b. 1935), Brice Marden (b. 1938), and Larry Bell (b. 1939), and painters such as Agnes Martin (b. 1912) and Mark Rothko (1903–1970).

- *Photorealism* (1965–present). Photorealism could be considered an extension of Pop Art because Pop artists were working from an image already created. The chief difference is that Photorealists worked from their *own* photographs. They projected a slide or worked from a grid to enlarge the photographs, sometimes on a very large scale. Well-known Photorealists were Chuck Close (b. 1940), Don Eddy (b. 1944), Richard Estes (b. 1932), Robert Bechtle (b. 1932), and Audrey Flack (b. 1931).

- *Neo-Expressionism* (1975–present). Neo-Expressionism was basically a German movement, but a number of American artists such as Jeff Koons (b. 1955), Eric Fischl (b. 1948), and Julian Schnabel (b. 1957) are considered part of the movement. The sculptures of Louise Bourgeois (b. 1911) and Judy Pfaff (b. 1946) might be considered New Expressionistic.

- *Post Modern* (1960s to present). American artists considered in the forefront of this period are Julian Schnabel, Judy Pfaff, and Edward Keinholz (1927–1994). It also includes many architects such as Louis Kahn (1901-1974), Michael Graves (b. 1934), and firms such as Kohn Pedersen and Fox, and Johnson and Burgee. Painters, whose work refers to figural sculpture, are Richard Estes (b. 1936), Philip Pearlstein (b. 1924), and Alex Katz (b. 1927). Post Modernism seems to include many "Neos" such as Neo-Classicism, Neo-Expressionism, Neo-Conceptualism, Neo-Romanticism, Neo-Dadaism, Neo-Surrealism, New Perceptualism, New Realism, New Image Art, New Left, etc. In other words, everything old is new again!

OVERVIEW OF THE VISUAL ARTS

The visual arts in the last quarter of the twentieth century strangely resemble those of the first part of the century. Contemporary artists work abstractly, realistically, romantically, or base their work on historical artworks, much as other twentieth-century artists did. There is no one dominant art movement such as Pop Art, Modern Art, or Abstract Expressionism which emerged in other decades. The differences between painting, sculpture, crafts, and environmental art have become blurred, with each medium becoming less distinguishable from the others.

Technology has allowed dramatic changes in the materials available for artists to use in painting, architecture, sculpture, and crafts, yet historical references seem more important than ever. In all the arts one sees "quotes" of the past, as artists appropriate previously used images and ideas.

Photography has become a much more appreciated art form and is a frequent tool of painters. Photography itself has been thoroughly explored and has become more concept oriented as time progresses. Computer-generated images are commonplace in advertising and film, and are also used more frequently in fine arts.

Printmaking continues to play an important part in the visual arts, with many painters also producing prints that allow them greater distribution of their work. Other diverse art forms such as quilting, painting, the treated photograph, and sculpture are being explored.

Businesses, cities, and states have committed themselves to supporting the arts. Public sculpture and murals are visible in most large cities, despite frequent disputes among the citizens on the age-old question, "What is art?" Installations, conceptual art, environmental art, and video are new components of the art field. By the mid-twentieth century, a number of women began to receive recognition in the art field. Among them were painters, environmentalists, and especially sculptors or crafts persons.

Artists who wished to identify with a specific group, such as Feminists, Gays, African American, Asian American, and Native American, sometimes reflected their special interests through their artworks.

PAINTING

The work of many Pop Art and Expressionist master-painters continues to evolve. Figures such as Robert Rauschenberg (b. 1925), Jasper Johns (b. 1930), Helen Frankenthaler (b. 1928), Frank Stella (b. 1936), and Roy Lichtenstein (b. 1923) are still producing important artwork not too different from their 1960s paintings and sculpture. During the 1980s, an inflated art market allowed them and other painters to sell almost as quickly as they painted. The art market experienced a downturn in the 1990s, and this seemed to open the way for young painters to focus on such issues as race, the environment, gender and sexuality, and AIDS. In addition to issues, a renewed interest in realistic landscape and figurative painting is apparent.

Examples of Painting

Eight Water Glasses Under Fluorescent Light, 1974, Janet Fish, Robert Miller Gallery, New York

Holding the Floor, Susan Rothenberg, 1985, Sperone Westwater Gallery, New York

Ocean Park No. 122, 1980, Richard Diebenkorn, Museum of Fine Arts, Houston

Guadalupe Island, Caracara, 1979, Frank Stella, The Tate Gallery, London

A Bigger Splash, 1967, David Hockney, private collection, London

SCULPTURE

Sculpture in the last quarter of the twentieth century seems to have no limits. Materials, techniques, and public support allow artists to work on a heroic scale. A burgeoning of public sculpture parks allows artists to create environmental sculpture on sites where it will be maintained and appreciated. Many contemporary sculptors work in the traditional materials of cast bronze, chiseled marble, and assemblages of found materials, as well as materials such as plastic, metal, wood, and cloth.

Examples of Sculpture

Corridor, 1967, Lucas Samaras, Los Angeles County Museum of Art

Bird E-Square Bird, 1958–1966, Isamu Noguchi, collection of Mr. Carl E. Solway, Cincinnati

Clothespin, Philadelphia, 1976, Claes Oldenburg, Philadelphia

Three Way Plug, Scale A (Soft), Prototype in Blue, 1971, Claes Oldenburg, Des Moines Art Center

Camel VII, Camel VI, Camel VIII, 1968–1969, Nancy Graves, National Gallery of Canada, Ottawa

Sitting Bull, 1959, Peter Voulkos, Santa Barbara Museum of Art, Santa Barbara, California

The State Hospital, 1966, Edward Keinholz, Moderna Museet, Stockholm

The Wait, 1964–1965, Edward Keinholz, Whitney Museum of American Art, New York

Labyrinth, 1974, Robert Morris, Institute of Contemporary Art, Philadelphia

Cantileve, 1983, Whitney Museum of American Art, New York

Depression Bread Line, 1991, George Segal, Sidney Janis Gallery, New York

ENVIRONMENTAL ART

Spiral Jetty, 1970, Robert Smithson, Great Salt Lake, Utah

The City, Complex One, 1972–1974, Michael Heizer, Central Eastern Nevada

Double Negative, 1969–1971, Michael Heizer, Virgin River Mesa, Nevada

Hart Plaza, 1980, Isamu Noguchi, Detroit

Mill Creek Canyon Earthworks, 1982, Herbert Bayer, Kent, Washington

Revival Field, 1990–present, Mel Chin, St. Paul, Minnesota

Isla de Umunnum, The Mound, 1986–1990, Heather McGill and John Roloff, Estuarine Research Reserve, California

SCULPTURE WITH LIGHT

Times Square Sky, 1962, Chryssa, Walker Art Center, Minneapolis

Untitled, 1969, Donald Judd, Hirshhorn Museum and Sculpture Garden, Washington, D.C.

Pink and Gold, 1968, Dan Flavin, Museum of Contemporary Art, Chicago

ARCHITECTURE

Late twentieth-century architecture did not just cease to become one style and suddenly become all new, but was an evolution, a flowing thing. Following the adoption of the Bauhaus theory that "Less is more," most cities had at least one Minimalist building that resembled a box. By the late 1990s, Modernism, which began in the 1920s, had an entirely different interpretation. It was still related to the concept of originality, simplicity, and creativity, but involved new uses of materials. The International-style boxlike skyscraper evolved to have decorative historical elements such as broken pediments, columns, base, shaft, and entablature. Post-Modern and Late-Modern buildings often featured rhythmical set-backs and a stretched skin of mirror-glass.

Architects took advantage of structural materials by repeating precast concrete elements or placing the steel structure on the exterior of the building. Some buildings became quite sculptural, with great aesthetic appeal. In the design of private homes, regional preferences continued to influence the style. In the West and Southwest, the use of adobe and a Spanish influence is still apparent. In the Midwest and East, traditional colonial structures continue to be built.

Examples of Architecture

The Humana Building, 1982, Michael Graves, Louisville, Kentucky

Swan and Dolphin Hotel, 1991, Michael Graves, Walt Disney World, Florida

Portland Public Services Building, 1980, Michael Graves, Portland, Oregon

Whitney Museum of American Art, 1981, Michael Graves, New York

Getty Center, c. 1991, Richard Meyer, Los Angeles, California

Seattle Art Museum, c. 1991, Venturi, Scott Brown, Seattle, Washington

A.T. & T Corporate Headquarters, 1979–1984, John Burgee Architects, New York

Kimbell Art Museum, 1972, Louis I. Kahn, Fort Worth, Texas

Geodesic Dome, 1967, Buckminster Fuller, American Pavilion, Montreal, Quebec

Jefferson Arch, completed 1965, Eero Saarinen, St. Louis, Missouri

Vanna Venturi House, 1963–1965, Robert Venturi, Chestnut Hill, Pennsylvania

Sears Roebuck Tower, 1973, Skidmore, Owings and Merrill, Chicago

John Hancock Center, 1966–1969, Skidmore, Owings and Merrill, Chicago

East Building, National Gallery of Art, 1968-1978, I. M. Pei and Partners, Washington, D.C.

PROJECT 9-1: **RUCKUS: 3-D COLLAGE/ASSEMBLAGE**

FOR THE TEACHER

SLIDE #35: *AARRRRRRHH,* (from "No Gas" portfolio), 1976, Red Grooms, 70.5 × 55.6 cm., lithograph, Gift of William E. Hartman, The Art Institute of Chicago

SLIDE #36: *Hollywood,* 1965, Red Grooms, 31-⅛ × 36 × 12-⅜ inches, construction of acrylic on wood, metal foil, nails, plaster, Gift of Joseph H. Hirshhorn, 1972, Hirshhorn Museum and Sculpture Garden, Smithsonian Institution

When Red Grooms (b. 1937) went on his honeymoon in Italy with wife and collaborator Mimi Gross, they rented a circus caravan and traveled, giving puppet shows to pay their way. The horse that pulled the wagon was named Ruckus. Grooms's best-known "environment" is called *Ruckus, Manhattan: A Sculptural Novel.* This work filled a 6,400-square foot building in New York, and was attended by 150,000 people. His assemblage *Chicago* was created before *Ruckus, Manhattan* and in the same general style. Grooms's sculptural assemblages are whimsical, with buildings deliberately distorted. It has often been called Disneyesque. For a time he was not taken seriously by the art world because of his bizarre sense of humor. He was a pioneer in the field of Happenings. His mature work—while it is always collaborative, with himself as the director of a crew of (sometimes) 20 people—seems like a permanent collection of Happenings. He began as an artist just as pure Abstract Expressionism was phasing out, and perhaps this accounts for the success of his reality-based assemblages.

Examples of Work by Red Grooms

Michigan Boulevard with Mayor Daley, 1978, The Metropolitan Museum of Art, New York

Loft on 26th Street, 1965–1966, Hirshhorn Museum of Art, Washington, D.C.

City of Chicago, 1967, Chicago Art Institute

Tootsie, 1971, Collection estate of Joseph H. Hirshhorn, Washington, D.C.

Mr. and Mrs. Rembrandt, 1971, Cheekwood Art Museum, Nashville, Tennessee

Ruckus, Manhattan: A Sculptural Novel, 1976, collection of the artist, New York

PREPARATION

Explain the idea of a group assemblage. Each student will create an individual piece that will be part of a collage / assemblage. Students may plan together to make something, such as a group of buildings, yet each student needs to take responsibility for only one building. The scale used will depend on display space and materials available. It could be large enough to fill a hall or gallery, or so small it will be displayed on two classroom tables pushed together. Take at least a week to get materials together, working out ideas in advance. Try to get pictures of works by Red Grooms so students will see that they can have fun with the project.

ADDITIONAL SUGGESTIONS

- Have students find an artist's photo or portrait. The artist could be from any field of fine arts such as visual arts, music, theater, or dance. Grooms did a number of artworks based on Matisse, Picasso, Rembrandt, Dali, and other easily recognizable artists whom he admired. Students would then make a portrait of that artist through the use of fabrics and other found objects to create a parody collage of an existing masterpiece. Red Grooms did this with *Mr. and Mrs. Rembrandt.*

Junk sculpture usually shows great wit. Another American, Holly Hughes of Socorro, Arizona, does huge, delightful, "real" sculptures of animals and people from recycled materials of all types. Put out a call to parents for fabric, workbench leftovers, shells, and all the other "good trash" that people don't need and that your students can use to create masterpieces on foam core or cardboard. These paintings / sculptures would be made to hang on a wall.

- *Dali Salad* (1980) was one of Grooms's multiples. It was a humorous three-dimensional print consisting of a variety of "salad greens" printed on plastic cut-outs, with Salvador Dali's head staring up from the center. His eyes were created from ping-pong balls, and the whole "salad" was presented under a clear plastic dome. To make such a composition, have students paint shades of green on acetate with acrylic, then cut it into shapes that could be joined together on a plastic plate to resemble a salad. Rather than putting an image of Dali in the center, have them think of other things they would just as soon not find in a salad. This could make a great display. Other one-dish meals such as spaghetti could also be painted on acetate.

Photo 9-1A. *Maquette for "Way Down East,"* **1978, Red Grooms, mixed media construction, 40 × 106 × 75 inches, Hirshhorn Museum and Sculpture Garden, Gift of Joseph H. Hirshhorn, Smithsonian Institution. Photography by Lee Stalsworth.**

Photo 9-1B. *Ruckus Construction Company,* **1967, Red Grooms and Mimi Gross, mixed media, approx. 365.8 × 762 × 762 cm., City of Chicago, Gift of Mrs. Maggy Magerstadt Rosner, The Art Institute of Chicago. #1 Installation Photography.**

PROJECT 9-1: **RUCKUS: 3-D COLLAGE/ASSEMBLAGE**

MATERIALS

- Glues: white, Tacky glue™, glue guns, epoxy
- Collage materials: cardboard, foam board, burlap
- Paint: tempera, acrylic, house paint
- Wood scraps: broom handles, plywood, etc.
- Papier-mâché equipment: newspaper, brown paper, wallpaper paste
- Tools: hammers, nails, staple guns
- Wire coat hangers and pliers to cut them
- Plaster-impregnated tape (Sculpt-tape™)
- Plaster

Drawn after
Looking Along Broadway Towards Grace Church, 1981
Red Grooms
Marborough Gallery, NYC

© 1996 by Prentice-Hall, Inc.

Red Grooms is an artist/director. He and his large crew of artisans create individual pieces that they put together to make enormous assemblages. They have created two "cities" (Chicago and New York) that include people, streets, cars, crazy distorted buildings, even a subway complete with life-sized riders. His work is brightly colored, cartoon-like, and—above all—humorous. He is always fascinated by the circus and movies, so a circus-like atmosphere with its confusion and bright colors is appropriate for this project.

1. Decide as a class on the theme of your assemblage. If you decide to create the city you live in, think of landmarks, buildings, signs, and places or things you find amusing. Other possible themes are your school, transportation, circus, zoo, grocery store, bakery shop, train station, used-car lot, restaurant, or the prom. Use your imagination, but work together as a group to have a unified assemblage in approximately the same scale.

2. Here are a number of possibilities for creating sculpture:

   - *Cardboard:* Work in layers, with the center being the largest, the actual size and shape you want. On each side glue additional layers working slightly smaller on each side until the form becomes slightly rounded. Paint.

   - *Papier-mâché:* Use tape and newspaper to make forms, or create forms from chicken wire first, then cover with newspaper strips dipped in wallpaper paste. Finish with either paper toweling or torn brown grocery bags or kraft paper.

   - Make a miniature Hollywood-style movie set of just façades. Foam board or cardboard can be cut to shape. Put a brace on the back so it will stand up. Paint it with any type of paint.

   - Cut and twist wire coat hangers. Then wrap them in cloth, or dip cloth in plaster and drape it over the wire shape. Old nylon hose can also be stretched and tied over twisted forms made from hangers, coated with gesso or plaster, then painted.

3. Real objects may be incorporated into the ones you have created and painted. Humor is important here. Try to use objects in a context that is not normal. Allow your viewers to discover how creatively you have used some of the objects.

4. When the individual objects are completed, put them together for an "exhibition." If you have worked on a large scale, allow room between objects so people can walk among them to see them well. Make visual "connections" with what you put on the floor or on the walls behind the assemblage. Don't forget the cartoon-like atmosphere you are trying to create.

PROJECT 9-2: **SERIAL PLANES—CARDBOARD SCULPTURE**

FOR THE TEACHER

Louise Bourgeois (b. 1911) was one of the early modern sculptors whose career continued strongly through the late second half the of twentieth century. She was born in France, where her family had a tapestry business. She studied with Leger, Brancusi, and Giacometti, before moving to the United States in 1938. She worked in many media: drawing, printmaking, carving wood or stone, casting bronze, or creating assemblages. She says that her "personages" represent the family she left behind in France. These stark vertical sculptures are created of wood segments, sometimes carved or painted, sometimes left natural. As a grouping, the personages are dramatic and dynamic. Her work is sometimes considered feminist because of the subject matter and soft contours.

Examples of Sculptures by Louise Bourgeois

Nature Study, 1984, The Whitney Museum of Art, New York

Cell (Eyes and Mirrors), 1989–1993, Tate Gallery, London

Le Defi, 1992, Solomon R. Guggenheim Museum, New York

Cell II, 1991, Carnegie Museum of Art, Pittsburgh

Femme Voltage, 1951, Solomon R. Guggenheim Museum, New York

Sleeping Figure, 1950, Museum of Fine Arts, Boston

Mortise, 1950, National Gallery of Art, Washington, D.C.

Spiral Woman, 1951–1952, Robert Miller Gallery, New York

PREPARATION

This project is based on the sculpture *Spiral Woman* by Louise Bourgeois. It will cost very little, but will take time (it is worth it). Start saving cardboard boxes when supplies are delivered to school early in the year. Cut them with a paper cutter (open the box top and bottom, and insert the resulting square tube into a paper cutter). Storage is no great problem if you cut the boxes as you go.

The serial plane technique was explained by Helen Fleming Stone of Canton, Georgia at a National Art Education Convention, and she gave permission to share it. Her students have done a variety of cardboard sculptures using original colors and shapes.

ADDITIONAL SUGGESTIONS

- Bourgeois also did sculptural carving and molding. Plaster can be poured into any number of containers either to be carved or assembled. Containers such as yogurt cups or milk cartons, balloons, plastic bags, rubber swim caps, rubber surgical gloves, etc., will give interesting shapes. Bonnie Enos of the Parkway District had her students pour plaster into a plastic bag, then encouraged them to drape or support the bag with body contours, such as within an elbow, or clutched with both hands to the abdomen. (*Note:* You, the teacher, must make sure the plaster can be pulled away easily when hardened.) When the plaster has hardened, students should remove the bag and smooth the plaster with paring knives, rasps, and sandpaper. Encourage each student to use a different finish.

- Have students make a set of vertical figures from such things as fence posts, 2 × 4-inch boards, driftwood, broomsticks, tubes from the centers of rugs (carpet stores will save them for you), or anything long. Mailing tubes could be stacked, items added, and so on. Each student could make one figure. A display of these "personages" painted and standing upright and lit with spotlights is very dramatic. Students are quite creative when given a challenge of this sort.

Photo 9-2A. *Untitled,* 1950, Louise Bourgeois, painted wood, 69 inches, on loan to The Saint Louis Art Museum, courtesy of the artist/Robert Miller Gallery.

Photo 9-2B. *The Winged Figure,* 1948, Louise Bourgeois, wood, 70-½ × 37-½ × 12 inches, on loan to The Saint Louis Art Museum, courtesy of the artist/Robert Miller Gallery.

PROJECT 9-2: **SERIAL PLANES—CARDBOARD SCULPTURE**

MATERIALS

- Cardboard boxes cut up
- Wood for base
- Dowel
- Glue
- Utility knives or X-acto™ knives
- Paint
- Sandpaper
- Newsprint
- Paper cutter
- Drill

Louise Bourgeois created many varieties of assemblage, but this project involves creating serial planes. She created one shape, then repeated it as many as 40 times. In her sculpture *Spiral Woman,* a long dowel goes through a hole in the center of each piece, with the pieces rotated slightly to give a spiral effect.

1. Draw various shapes (geometric, free-form, your initial, etc.) on newsprint, then select one and make a cardboard pattern approximately 8 × 8 inches. Choose a design that will allow you to cut at least part of it on a paper cutter.

2. You may do as Bourgeois did, making the same shape but in gradually smaller sizes, or making a gradual change in shape but not in size. Or all 40 planes could be exactly the same. Try not to make this design too complex, as you will be cutting out 30 to 40 identical shapes.

3. After cutting out all the shapes, smooth the edges with sandpaper or a knife, then experiment with stacking them. Options are:
   - Drill a hole in the wood block and glue a dowel upright. Use an electric or hand drill to drill through several cardboard layers at once (the drill bit should be slightly larger than the dowel). After stacking the cardboard pieces on the dowel, experiment with a variety of ways of spiraling them.
   - Stack the pieces one on top of another, simply making a solid block-like form.
   - Stack one on top of another, rotating each piece slightly as you move upward, and gluing as you go.

4. When the figures are finished, either leave them natural or paint them white, black, or a single hue. You could also paint in variations of one hue, ranging from light to dark, or in colors as they evolve in the spectrum.

PROJECT 9-3: WORK WITHIN A FRAME, HISPANIC STYLE

FOR THE TEACHER

Hispanic art in the United States is not a separate entity. However, just as immigrant artists have through the centuries, Hispanic artists brought their own unique cultures to the United States. The work of many Cubans, Puerto Ricans, Mexicans, and South and Central Americans do have commonalities. Certain images such as animals, vegetation, religious images, and references to daily life reflect their cultural background. The work often has in common vibrant colors and, frequently, dark outlines. A number of artists place their work within a frame, either a real one (often painted to match the artwork), or a "frame" painted on the canvas.

Examples of Hispanic Art

Self-Portrait, 1985, Roberto Gil de Montes, collection of Richard and Jan Baum, Los Angeles

The Closing of Whittier Boulevard, 1984, Frank Romero, collection of the artist

Los Marielitos, 1983, Pedro Perez, Museum of Fine Arts, Houston

Our Family Car (an actual painted car), 1985–1986, Gilbert Lujan, collection of Mardi Lujan

Untitled (Animal), c. 1953, Martin Ramirez, collection of Jim Nutt and Gladys Nilsson, Chicago

PREPARATION

This is a wonderful opportunity to talk about multicultural and "group" art in general. In modern American society, many believe there should be no distinctions among groups such as women artists, African American artists, Native American artists, Hispanic artists, and Asian artists. Many such artists create artwork that is in the mainstream of whatever is being done at the time—whether it is Abstract Expressionism, Pop Art, Postmodernism, or another "ism." Other artists who belong to such groups proudly use gender identification or cultural heritage as part of their art. Discuss with students how they think Asian art, for example, looks. Compare it with Hispanic art or Pop Art.

Get as many old picture frames as possible (the larger, the better) by appealing to parents and visiting garage sales and thrift stores.

ADDITIONAL SUGGESTIONS

- *Car Art:* Have students do a drawing of a car and decorate it as if it were a "low rider," a car decorated by an artist such as Gilbert Lujan. Or challenge students to incorporate a representation of their own or a family car into an oil pastel composition. Across the United States many people are creating "art cars" from old cars. These vary from cars covered with found objects to one that is completely covered in growing grass (its owner and friend even had suits to match covered with living grass). As an off-the-wall project, think how much fun it would be to have a group of students paint an actual car with acrylic paint in brilliant colors and designs. Or get car parts such as a door or hubcaps and paint designs on them (Australian Aborigines have been doing this for years).

- Have students do a painting from nature (flowers, animals, landscape) using vibrant colors of oil pastel on black paper, allowing the black to show through. The colors appear more vibrant on a black background.

- Students can create large animals from papier-mâché combined with various other materials such as wood, colored foil, bottle caps, or rope. They can paint their sculptures with tempera or acrylic and use spray varnish to complete.

PROJECT 9-3: WORK WITHIN A FRAME, HISPANIC STYLE

MATERIALS

- Old wooden frames
- Canvas board or masonite to fit frame
- Acrylic, oil, or tempera paint mixed with polymer medium
- Brushes
- Glue
- Materials to glue on frame: wood pieces, other miscellaneous *junque*

Many Hispanic artists of the late twentieth century create their work within a frame. Sometimes it is just a "frame" painted onto the background; other times, it is an actual picture frame. The painting extends out onto the frame, as if there weren't enough room on the canvas, and it had to spill over.

1. Your design could be of houses, people, jungle or desert plants, cars, animals, reptiles, or anything else. Create the design to complement the frame's style (for example, an elaborate design with a fancy frame).

2. Plan ahead how the frame will look, but wait until your actual design is painted before you tackle the frame. You may choose to carve something to attach to the frame or cover the frame with an unusual material such as metal or leather. The frame is almost as important as the painting.

3. Here are several different approaches to using the frame in a composition:
   - If you cannot get actual frames, attach mats of 14-ply matboard before painting, to allow the composition to spill out onto the frame. These are quite effective, with the edge created by the mat giving visual emphasis to the composition.
   - Get a real frame. Paint it or carve it to complement the picture. Things such as snakes, skeleton heads, jaguars, or dogs could be painted on it. Let the design have something to do with the painting.
   - Make a frame of flat boards (batten), 1-¼ × ¼-inch. Attach this to the front of a canvas and paint it black. Paint such Southwestern objects as cacti, flowers, hearts, chickens, and birds on the canvas, then paint some of them out onto the frame. Artist Rudy Fernandez attaches such things to his frames as lead strips, neon lights, and carved objects.
   - Make it fancy. Mount items such as jewelry and doilies to the frame, then spray it gold. Paint a Caribbean carnival scene inside, using people in costume, or jungle scenes and flowers. Allow the composition to spill out of the frame.
   - Paint a line around the outer four edges of your canvas (wood, paper, or foam core could be a substitute for canvas). Use the same colors as you have on the inside composition, but give the frame an edge so it will look like a real frame.

PROJECT 9-4: FACE IN A GRID

FOR THE TEACHER

SLIDE #37: *Robert,* **1973–1974, Chuck Close, 9 × 7 feet, synthetic polymer paint and ink with graphite gessoed canvas, Gift of J. Frederic Byers III, promised gift of anonymous donors, Museum of Modern Art, New York**

The work of Chuck Close (b. 1940) looks as if it might have been a photograph projected onto a screen and drawn. He does indeed photograph his subjects and work from a photograph, but he creates a grid on the photograph and enlarges from the grid. Since 1968 Close has specialized in painting 9 × 6-foot frontal portraits of friends and family. Although his subject matter (the face) has remained the same throughout his career, he is fascinated with different art materials, and has experimented with diverse media from hand-made paper to thumbprinted paintings in ink. In addition to large paintings, he has created compositions in other sizes and media using the same straightforward photographic images.

Examples of Work by Chuck Close

Fanny, Fingerpainting, 1985, National Gallery of Art, Washington, D.C.

Self Portrait / Pastel, 1977, Sydney and Frances Lewis Foundation, Washington, D.C.

Keith, 1970, The Saint Louis Art Museum

Stanley (large version), 1980–1981, Solomon R. Guggenheim Museum, New York

PREPARATION

Students could do a freehand drawing of a friend's face, or of their own face by looking in a mirror. If realism is important, four yearbook photos can be photocopied on one piece of 8-½ × 11-inch transparency film for projecting onto paper that has been taped to a wall. Students lightly draw the projected photograph (taped onto an overhead projector) onto the paper before creating the grid by rubbing candle-wax on the paper.

ADDITIONAL SUGGESTIONS

- Using an overhead projector, students project a transparency photocopy of a personal photo onto a piece of drawing paper mounted on the wall. Then they lightly draw the face in pencil and use a black ink stamp pad and recreate the picture with thumbprints or fingerprints while observing the photo to see value differences. Students really enjoy this technique, and it is a great project for teaching differences in value.

- Students can make a torn-paper portrait on the candle-resist grid by selecting at least 10 different closely related colors of construction paper (for example: pink, red, orange, etc.) or black, white, and several grays. Or an actual textured grid can be made by gluing fish or camouflage net to the paper (this netting can be purchased at a camping or Army/Navy supply outlet). Tear the construction paper (or dry hand-painted watercolor paper) into pieces approximately ½ inch and keep them sorted according to color. The darkest pieces of paper should be applied first, then the lightest, using a brush and thinned glue (or polymer medium). Medium value is next, and students should continue applying pieces of paper, overlapping and building up until the face appears rounded because of value differences. The grid should be allowed to show through in places. The composition could be finished with a border of a contrasting color.

Photo 9-4. *Keith IV—State 1,* **1975, Chuck Close, lithograph, 29-¹⁵⁄₁₆ × 22-³⁄₈ inches, Purchase, National Endowment for the Arts and Anonymous Matching Fund, The Saint Louis Art Museum.**

PROJECT 9-4: **FACE IN A GRID**

MATERIALS

- 18 × 24-inch white watercolor or drawing paper
- Watercolors
- Containers for water
- Brushes
- "Egg crate" plastic ceiling fixture (from hardware store)
- White candles
- Pencils
- 12 × 12-inch mirror squares (taped edges)

Photocopy of Keith IV Lithograph, 1975 Chuck Close The Saint Louis Art Museum

This project is based on a manner of working used by artist Chuck Close. He enlarges through using a grid, creating realistic portraits of monumental size. He has worked in almost all media, using hand-made paper blobs, pastels, ink applied with fingers, acrylic paint applied with an airbrush, and watercolor.

1. Draw an oversized freehand portrait of a face on paper by looking in a mirror or by using a photograph of yourself or a friend. Show only the face and shoulders. An alternative is to project a small photo of yourself from an overhead transparency onto the paper that can be taped on the wall.

2. Place the paper on top of a plastic ceiling "egg-crate" light fixture that has a grid pattern. Tape it in place to avoid having it slip. Use the side of a white candle or white crayon to firmly rub the paper, creating a waxy grid on the paper. Although a small amount of the wax may get inside the grid pattern, it will not show that much on the painting.

3. Soften the colors in the watercolor box by applying a little water to each color. Mix tones in the top of the box. Use a small piece of paper for testing your colors first. You can build up the color by applying watercolor lightly. Start by painting the background first until you have a feel for how much color to mix for a particular area. See what happens when you add a different color to an area that is still wet. The colors blend together. Allow an area to dry, then see what happens when you add a slightly different color to it. The glazing (building up of transparent colors, one on top of another) is what makes watercolors so interesting. You may prefer to have the background repeat colors you plan to use in the hair or flesh. The grid will show through, and give a new dimension to your portrait.

4. Keep a paper towel for blotting areas that may be too dark. Don't be afraid to use color generously. Artists add colors such as blue, violet, orange, yellow, and green to flesh tones and hair to add excitement to their paintings. Stand back from your painting from time to time and look to see where forms appear indistinct, and where more color could be added.

PROJECT 9-5: **TABLETOP REFLECTIONS IN WATERCOLOR**

FOR THE TEACHER

SLIDE #38: *Still Life with Open Book,* **1990, Janet Fish, 48 × 60 inches, oil on canvas, Gift of the William T. Kemper Foundation, Kemper Museum of Contemporary Art and Design, Kansas City, Missouri**

Janet Fish (b. 1938) is a Realistic painter who selects ordinary objects as her subject matter. She has depicted plastic-wrapped fruit and vegetables, and most of her work is based on her fascination with the effects of light and reflections. Her compositions are huge, and the complexity of these arrangements makes ordinary objects come alive. Within her tabletop still lifes, she sets up objects that are a combination of organic materials such as fruit and flowers; seashells of all sizes; shapes; colors; and translucent glass—bowls, vases, water-filled glasses, or mirrored surfaces. She is an avid gardener, and often includes her flowers. Many of her works are oil on canvas, but the subject matter lends itself well to other media.

Examples of Paintings by Janet Fish

Hunt's Vase, 1984, collection of the artist

Chinoiserie, 1984, collection of Paine Webber Group Inc., New York

Painted Water Glasses, 1974, Whitney Museum of American Art, New York

Eight Water Glasses Under Fluorescent Light, 1974, Robert Miller Gallery, New York

Kara, 1983, The Museum of Fine Arts, Houston

PREPARATION

Have students experiment with a variety of watercolor techniques, particularly with painting reflections exactly as they see them, not as they "know" them to be. Either make sure you have light coming in a window or use photo-flood reflectors to get shadows. As Janet Fish says, "looking, just flat-out looking" is how she gets into her "contained world." One of the most exciting parts of Fish's watercolors is their huge size and luminosity. Because large watercolor paper is extraordinarily expensive, I suggest each student be given four to six sheets of white construction or watercolor paper. Have them cut a few of these into straight but irregular shapes, overlapping and gluing several together to create a huge sheet of paper. The irregular shape of the paper and the seams will be an additional challenge to students and should give some delightful results. Because of the size of the paper, students may need to work on tables or the floor. It may be necessary to have several still-life arrangements. Of course, this entire project could be created from one regular sheet of watercolor paper cut up and reassembled, but the large size is what makes Janet Fish's compositions unique.

ADDITIONAL SUGGESTIONS

- Students may make a watercolor painting of their choice. This could be quite abstract as opposed to the Realism of Janet Fish. Purchase gold paint at a hobby store and allow students to use gold paint sparingly as an accent on the finished piece. Encourage them to make one or two shapes of unequal sizes, then to emphasize a few lines with the gold. It is also possible to do this with fake gold leaf by putting the "size" on the paper (the size comes with the fake gold leaf, also available at hobby shops). Allow the size to dry slightly, then use a soft brush to lay the leaf down, brushing off excess. If you use fake gold leaf, then make a "gold-leaf station" (a shoebox) where small pieces may be cut for use and remnants collected for reuse.

• Have students use actual plant material in paintings of plants and flowers. Leaves such as Lunaria (moon plant), grasses, and delicate leaves can be adhered with polymer and painted over, giving an interesting texture to a painting. An alternative to leaves might be to adhere rice paper in a few places. Many of these papers have organic materials in them.

Photo 9-5. *The Blue Pitcher,* 1995. This large watercolor by LuWayne Stark was painted on five pieces of watercolor paper joined together.

PROJECT 9-5: **TABLETOP REFLECTIONS IN WATERCOLOR**

MATERIALS

- Watercolor or white construction paper
- 36-inch wide white roll paper
- Scissors or paper cutter
- Light source (lamps or photo-floods)
- White or Tacky glue™
- Pencils
- Watercolors
- Colored glass bottles, shells, flowers, mirrors, and glass

**Drawn from *Eight Water Glasses Under Fluorescent Light*, 1974 Janet Fish
Robert Miller Gallery, New York City**

Janet Fish is a modern artist who paints watercolors—huge watercolors! Her still lifes are made of objects found around most houses: flowers, vases, jars with water in them, mirrors, shells, and other tabletop decorations. Work together to arrange a large number of objects on a table in the middle of the room, not disturbing it once it has been arranged, as other students will count on things remaining exactly the same.

1. Use three to four pieces of white paper. Cut them into another shape: long, trapezoidal, square, or triangular. Use glue on the underside of a piece and glue it on top of another shape, overlapping approximately 1 inch. Be careful not to get glue on the front of the paper. You will have a very large, irregularly shaped format for your watercolor painting.

2. With pencil, *lightly* draw the objects that will be in your watercolor. You may end up adding things that are not actually in your still life, repeating objects a second time in a different size or color, or painting colors that are not actually in the still life. It is important to repeat colors from one place to another. A warm or cool color scheme, enhanced by an accent of a complementary color, will give good results.

3. With watercolor, faithfully reproduce what you *see*. If you see a reflection, paint it exactly the way you see it. Match colors and shapes as nearly as possible. Realistic painting relies on you not painting what you "know" is there, but what you can *see* is there.

4. When the painting is complete, glue the entire composition to a large sheet of roll paper, and use a ruler to make a straight 1-inch border all the way around the composition. Trim this on a paper cutter or with scissors.

PROJECT 9-6: **TWENTIETH-CENTURY STORYTELLING QUILT**

FOR THE TEACHER

SLIDE #39: *Jo Baker's Birthday,* **1994, Faith Ringgold, 6 × 6 feet, acrylic on canvas with pieced fabric border. Purchase: Museum Minority Artists' Purchase Fund: The Honorable Carol E. Jackson, Mr. and Mrs. Steven M. Cousins, Mr. and Mrs. Lester R. Crancer, Jr., Mr. and Mrs. Solon Gershman, Mr. Sidney Goldstein in memory of Chip Goldstein, the Links, Inc., Gateway Chapter, The Honorable and Mrs. Charles A. Shaw, Donald M. Suggs; Casually Off-Grain Quilters of Chesterfield, Thimble & Thread Quilt Guild, and funds given in honor of Questa Benberry, The Saint Louis Art Museum**

Faith Ringgold's (b. 1930) storytelling quilts are beautiful artworks (often a short African-American history lesson) created by a Feminist working in traditional "women's stuff." She pieces fabric together to frame the outside of a story quilt and both writes and paints on it to tell a story. She often shows paintings with large groups of people, and her stories at times are based on dialogue between them. She mixes her training in the European culture with African Art, frequently incorporating Western Art history as she has in *Jo Baker's Birthday.* The cloth edges around the outside are often pieced vertically, in the tradition of African-American quilts (possibly reminiscent of African Kente cloth).

Examples of Artworks by Faith Ringgold

The Church Picnic, 1987, The High Museum, Atlanta, Georgia

Dancing at the Louvre, 1991, Collection of the Artist, New Jersey

Tar Beach, 1988, Solomon R. Guggenheim Museum, New York

The French Collection, Part I #4 Sunflowers Quilting Bee at Arles, 1991, Collection of Oprah Winfrey

Dancing on the George Washington Bridge, 1988, Collection of Roy Eaton

PREPARATION

This paper quilt should be a little easier to construct and write on than those of Faith Ringgold. It will be important to have a variety of patterned papers and colors, however, to make it effective.
Have students try to reconstruct a favorite childhood memory that involved a gathering of people—relatives or friends. Where did it take place? Who was there? Was food served? Did they sit around a table? What was said? Can they relate it to a similar event from history? Have them write an imaginary conversation or dialogue that could be written around the outside of their composition. The writing and thinking should take place before beginning the quilt.

ADDITIONAL SUGGESTIONS

- As a group project, have each student paint a self-portrait to be grouped around a table as a "family." Ringgold frequently used this device, having everyone painted from the waist or shoulders up, basically facing forward. She painted food on the table and surrounded the table with pieced fabric in stripes. A narrative account might go around the edge, written in black on a light background. This project could be a simple painted paper quilt or an elaborate cloth quilt left to the school as a memento by this class.

- Have students use scrap fabric and create a trapunto (quilted and stuffed) tapestry on watercolor paper. At least one irregular piece of fabric smaller than the paper (several would be better) should be glued or machine-sewn to watercolor paper, leaving a tiny opening for stuffing fiber batting before sewing it shut. One or two significant words may be painted with contrasting acrylic paint onto the stuffed fabric, and possibly more words could be painted onto the background paper. If a sewing machine is available, stitchery may become part of the composition, with lines stitched irregularly over and through the fabric and the paper.

Photo 9-6. *The Dinner Party,* Josephine Baker, Courtesy of the artist.

PROJECT 9-6: **TWENTIETH-CENTURY STORYTELLING QUILT**

MATERIALS

- 36 × 48-inch kraft paper
- Wallpaper sample books or wrapping paper
- White drawing paper
- Pencils
- Black ink or paint, or fine-line black markers
- Glue
- Colored acrylic paint

Faith Ringgold is a modern quilt artist. She sews strips of quilt together to form a border, using a traditional African American quilt-making technique (possibly based on African Kente cloth). Ringgold paints scenes or people on the quilt, using flattened perspective, with most of the people facing front. Her story quilts have writing all the way around the border about real families or famous African-Americans.

1. Select a theme. You might tell a family story you have heard about your ancestors' immigration to the United States, or a story about a family that is immigrating today. Each quilt block around the outside could have a separate story on it about a family member. Or perhaps you would like to make a "quilt" based on some well-known person you admire. Write a story on notebook paper. The story can be lengthy, or only a few sentences, but the writing is an important part of the composition.

2. After deciding on your theme, plan how to make your paper quilt. Use the white paper as a base on which you will glue pieces of paper (or fabric). The story may be written in ink, paint, or markers all the way around the outside of the quilt on white paper and glued on top of the patterned paper used as a border.

3. Select numerous pieces of patterned wallpaper and cut them into approximately 4 × 6-inch strips. Glue them around the outside of the kraft paper in two rows, alternating patterns and sizes to give the effect of pieced fabric.

4. For the center of the quilt, you may continue pasting on pieces of wallpaper in neatly cut shapes, though they could be larger than the strip borders. When the center is complete, paint figures on top of the paper with acrylic paint, allowing the wallpaper to show through in places. Or, paint the figures and table in the center of the quilt on the plain background.

PROJECT 9-7: **GRAFFITI ART**

FOR THE TEACHER

Graffiti art (literal translation: scratching) exists worldwide and generally is not acceptable by any form of organized government. It is a public display created to say, "Here I am, World," or to make a political statement. Graffiti artists are usually writers, often using no more than their names. There are public and private (bathroom-style) graffiti. By its very nature, it is a linear artform, often outlines filled in with brilliant color. This project is not to inspire your students to go write on walls, but rather to try to understand why others do it.

Keith Haring (1958–1990) was a graffiti-inspired artist who began working in the New York subways. In his short ten-year career during the 1980s, he went from being a rebellious street artist to an internationally known artist, creating on-site paintings on five continents. Haring worked very large (when you've learned to paint on walls, your canvases are going to be huge). His graffiti paintings were mostly outlines of human figures, with his images filling every inch of huge canvases, walls, billboards, banners, a blimp, and even a BMW car prototype. Some feel that his work has a relationship to comic-book style, or possibly was inspired by the outlines police officers chalk around bodies at crime scenes.

Examples of Work by Keith Haring

Mural, 1987, Exterior Stairwell, Necker Children's Hospital, Paris

Swatch Watch designs, 1985

New York City Subway Panels, 1984, Fifth Avenue, New York

Mural, 1986, section of Berlin Wall, Berlin

Sculpture installation, 1985, Dag Hammarskjold Plaza, Sculpture Garden, New York

Mural, 1989, Church of Sant'Antonio, Pisa, Italy

Mural, 1984, Collingwood Technical School, Melbourne, Australia

Costuming, 1986, Grace Jones's music video *I'm Not Perfect*

The Ten Commandments, 1985, Contemporary Art Museum, Bordeaux, France

PREPARATION

Talk with students about "outsider" art—why gangs have "Tags," what purpose they feel is served by writing on walls, how it makes a city look to visitors, and whether it is art or vandalism. Students who are not confident of their drawing ability will love trying to draw like Keith Haring. His outlines of the human figure could have been made by even very young children, who would have loved his bright color combinations.

ADDITIONAL SUGGESTIONS

- Although the project is for individual student paintings, a graffiti mural of words could be a great group art project. Put 48-inch brown kraft paper on the wall around the room or on a floor the length of a hallway. First talk about what they want it to say. Remind students that this is to be a work of *art*. If they want to write their names, allow them to write, but they could use bubble letters that could be filled in with patterns such as checkerboards, polka dots, stripes, or zigzags, combining them with solid areas of color to make a cohesive artwork.

- Have students trace the outline of a human figure from a magazine ad, then transfer it to dark colored paper. They may use white paint to "costume" the figure in graffiti-line designs, as Keith Haring did when he painted Grace Jones's body for a music video.

- A circular format is more of a challenge than a square, but Haring designed *Swatch Watch* faces and a record and album cover in which he put his signature figures. Ask students to create a design for a circular wall clock or watch using only line designs.

- Have students bring in any object from home, such as a T-shirt or an old coffee mug, and use acrylic paint to paint it with graffiti art. Design and craftsmanship are important. If they are painting a piece of furniture such as a folding metal chair, they should apply gesso first, then a coat of acrylic paint, then paint with a line painting.

Photo 9-7. Untitled, 1981, Keith Haring, india ink on paper, 38 × 49-3/4 inches, Gift of Mr. and Mrs. Adam Aronson, The Saint Louis Art Museum.

PROJECT 9-7: **GRAFFITI ART**

MATERIALS

- Fluorescent tempera or acrylic paint
- Black tempera or acrylic paint
- Black markers
- Pencils
- Brushes
- Newsprint
- Posterboard

Keith Haring was an academically trained artist, as were several other street artists of the 1980s. Some may have thought they did not receive the public recognition they were entitled to, so used this method of graffiti art to call attention to themselves. Eventually their work made its way into galleries and the mainstream of art.

1. To experiment with drawing the human figure in the manner of Keith Haring, take a sheet of newsprint to practice doodling figures. These figures should be outlines only and can be turned any or all directions. Fill empty spaces with more figures, dashes, dots, or straight and curved lines.

2. Design a poster for an occasion at school, using the method Haring made famous. Make the letters large enough to read, and outline them in black paint. If you wish, fill the area with outlines of human figures or animals, placing them so the lettering is still readable.

3. Use fluorescent paint (if you have it) to fill inside the black outlines or the background, or use the fluorescent paint in combination with regular colors. Sometimes the effect is more startling when the fluorescent paint is only the outline, or is used only for accent.

4. An alternative is to use a 1-inch or larger brush and work only in black on white or white on black with only *one* color-filled shape. Or cut out the posterboard in a shape such as a car or person, and paint graffiti on it. Keith Haring was commissioned to paint the body of a dancer as well as costumes for a video album and a BMW car.

PROJECT 9-8: **ASSEMBLAGE IN A BOX**

FOR THE TEACHER

Betye Saar (b. 1926) grew up in Pasadena, California, but she remembers visiting the Watts neighborhood in Los Angeles, where her grandmother lived, and where Simon Rodia (1879–1965) was working on his famous Watts towers. As a child she collected little shells and bits of glass, and is now best-known for her memory boxes, which are made up of photographs and other mementos from her family. In the 1960s she frequently based her themes on racism against African Americans. Her assemblages were not always in boxes, nor did they always have a racial theme, but it was this that first brought her to the attention of the American public. She has said she was also inspired by the intimacy of the boxes created by Joseph Cornell. She is also a printmaker, and has more recently been working in color Xeroxes.™

Examples of Work by Betye Saar

Indigo Mercy, 1975, Studio Museum in Harlem, New York

Smiles We Left Behind, 1976, Monique Knowlton Gallery, New York

Bessie Smith Box, 1974, collection of Monique Knowlton, New York

Imitation of Life, 1975, collection of the artist

PREPARATION

Have students find boxes! While cardboard is the most accessible, wooden crates sometimes can be used "as is" or cut down. Shallow plastic boxes are fine, or even an old frame can be placed on a background to create a box.

Talk with students about a theme. Printed material such as maps, articles, and art reproductions are appropriate to emphasize the theme. You might even encourage off-the-wall ideas. Stress that humor is important in this project. Have students think of junk that is readily available such as soda can tabs, soup can labels, ice cream sticks, or found items from nature. Give students at least a week to find suitable objects. Offer extra credit to inspire students to bring in items from outside.

Photo 9-8. *My Inheritance,* 1994, Dycie Madsen. This assemblage of hand-cast paper is a tribute to the artist's inheritance from her great-grandmother: a love of nature and gardening, and a steel will and courage. It includes stereopticon slides, rose petals from old love letters, ribbons, lace, antique buttons, and a newspaper giving the sailing dates of vessels in Boston. Courtesy of the artist.

ADDITIONAL SUGGESTIONS

- Have students transform an ordinary cardboard carton (much larger than a shoebox) to make a miniature environment in a "gallery." Most of the top and ⅓ of one side of the box should be cut away so the "set" can be seen and photographed. Students could make colorful environments in the manner of sculptor Judy Pfaff's gallery installations using plastic and shiny mylar. Show students how to cut a circle to make spirals that will hang from the "ceiling," and encourage them to find other miscellaneous materials such as colored wire used in telephone lines, wire hangers, carnival or party supplies, and miniatures made by cutting out faces and patterns from playing cards.

- Have students in groups think about a social issue that is meaningful to them, such as ecology, feminism, racism, AIDS, war, ethnic cleansing, injustice, etc. Encourage them to make a visual representation of this issue, gathering information and presenting it in a dramatic form on a length of roll paper that would go from floor to ceiling. Suggest they avoid having it simply be a collage of magazine or written articles, but instead select symbols that visually represent what they are trying to say. A variety of materials may be used, even to include lights, videos, and sound. This could include written reports, or even a journal that would explain the process the group went through.

PROJECT 9-8: ASSEMBLAGE IN A BOX

MATERIALS

• Container (box) or surface for the assemblage

• Memory materials: old photos, buttons, fabrics, gloves, postcards, or greeting cards that look like old photos

Betye Saar is an African American sculptor who makes "memory boxes" using old photos combined with found materials such as buttons, gloves, lace, and other nostalgic mementos. Look around your house for a variety of items that could be combined in a box to create your personal interpretation of your place in your family.

1. Think about your own family as far back as you know about it. This is a good opportunity to ask your family about stories of their own ancestors. Maybe they will have a story that inspires a theme for a box. These are especially haunting if you use old photographs as a starting point. Photocopy the photos and hand-color the photocopies with brown pencil so you will not damage the original photos.

2. Find a box. Gather materials such as items from sewing or jewelry boxes, or accessories such as handkerchiefs, old gloves, or eyeglasses. If you do not have these in your own home, they can be bought at garage sales or junk shops.

3. If you do not have a box with hinges, you can create your assemblage on an object such as a fan (accordion-pleated wallpaper) or a piece of cloth draped and stapled to a piece of cardboard. Begin with the picture(s). Arrange objects, adding more cloth or objects such as watches, buttons, netting, printed matter or ribbons, etc. Think about the mood you want to create. Related colors might tie found objects together. Attach items with white glue or a glue gun.

4. To give an antiqued look, the objects on the assemblage may be stained sparingly with a thinned burnt umber or deep blue wash of paint. Use a tissue to wipe off excess stain. If you do have an actual box, it might be appropriate to buy a piece of plexiglass to use as a cover, gluing it in place, and putting a hook on the back for hanging.

PROJECT 9-9: **HORSE**

FOR THE TEACHER

SLIDE #40: *Horse,* 1979, Deborah K. Butterfield, 75-¼ × 26 × 96 inches, chicken wire, sticks, mud, paper, dextrine, and grass on steel armature; Purchase, The Nelson-Atkins Museum of Art, Kansas City, Missouri

Deborah Butterfield (b. 1949), a Western potter, once made a series of clay saddles. She eventually settled on life-sized sculptures of horses as her normal theme because of a life-long interest in them. At first she used standard sculpture materials of steel rod armature, clay, and plaster, then progressed to using found materials such as sticks and mud, barbed wire, pipes, fencing, even scrap metal from a destroyed mobile home. The inner structure of her horses became more important as her work evolved. Her early work was always life-sized, but she has also created smaller models. She portrays only mares, as she "sees large male horses as instruments of war."

Examples of Work by Deborah Butterfield

Horse #6-82 (steel, sheet aluminum, wire, and tar) 1982, Dallas Museum of Art

Resting Horse, 1977, Whitney Art Museum, New York

Horse # 9-82, 1982, collection of Ethan and Sherry Wagner

Small Horse (mud and sticks over steel) 1977, private collection

PREPARATION

Have students find examples in history books of statues of leaders on horseback. Discuss why leaders chose to be depicted this way. Point out the problem of making a sculpture balance so it does not fall down, and show how sculptors have solved that problem, such as balancing a horse against a rock. Ask students to try to find a picture of an equestrian statue that is just the horse without a rider. This project could really be fun when you think about the number of materials that are out there that could be used to make a horse. This one should be a modest size that students are comfortable making with the materials they have on hand.

ADDITIONAL SUGGESTIONS

- Have students create other animals using this method. Nancy Graves made life-sized camels covered with burlap. One life-sized animal could be made as a class project. If something like papier-mâché is used as the outer material, be sure to build an inner structure of wood and chicken wire or PVC pipe to support such a large creature. Form the general shape with chicken wire, then cover it with alternating layers of newspaper and brown kraft paper (or grocery bags).

- Students could make paintings of horses, as Susan Rothenberg did. Her horses were unrealistic; often just crude, barely discernible silhouettes. Her work began near the end of the Abstract Expressionist period, so a figure of any type in a painting was avant-garde at that time. Have students apply acrylic or oil paint with a palette knife or "knife" made from 14-ply matboard. The painting could be quite small until students catch on to how to paint with something other than a brush.

- The horse as a painted object could be interpreted in the manner of other famous painters such as Mondrian, van Gogh, Matisse, or Seurat. This project has been done with a number of animals and famous icons such as the *Mona Lisa.* Photocopy an *outline* drawing of a horse onto card stock, giving each student one copy. Discuss unique painting styles of famous artists such as Frank Stella, Seurat, or van Gogh. Have each student select a different artist, and complete the photocopy in the manner of that artist. Mount these together.

PROJECT 9-9: **HORSE**

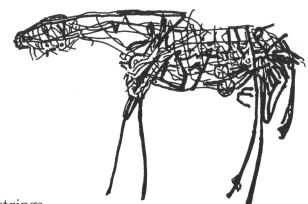

MATERIALS

- Structural base for the horse: chicken wire, stovepipe wire, sticks of all sizes and shapes
- Aluminum foil, approximately 6 feet per student
- Wood, masonite, or cardboard for a base
- Masking tape
- Wire
- Filler: plaster, mud, clay, paper pulp, straw, burlap strings

Some contemporary sculpture is very different from traditional sculpture that makes the viewer want to feel it. Deborah Butterfield's horse sculptures almost say "touch-me-not!" They are rough and prickly, made of unlovely materials such as sticks, wire, and mud. You will make a much smaller version of her life-sized horses.

1. Look around the house, junk yard, fields, and schoolroom for items that can be used to make a horse. Build the horse on a base that will allow you to move it around while working on it. This could be a piece of wood, masonite, or heavy cardboard.

2. Use one long piece of aluminum foil to fashion a crude horse head, torso, and tail. Then tear two equal pieces long enough to be folded over the torso to make four legs. Insert sticks or dowels inside the legs for additional support. Masking tape or wire may be necessary to hold the legs in place until the form is stabilized. Reinforce these legs with more sticks on the outside, binding them together with wire. Although this wire and stick structure will probably show, it will add to the charm.

3. Make up your mind what the horse's position will be before you begin adding materials to it. It doesn't necessarily have to stand on four legs (it could be a reclining horse). Give your horse an "attitude" by the inclination of its head and tail. It could be weary, proud, dejected, or frightened.

4. Disguise the foil by building up the surface with such materials as papier-mâché, sticks and mud, clay, straw, or burlap strings dipped in clay or plaster. The form will have things sticking out of it and will not be smooth. Do not paint the horse because this would detract from the materials you have used.

APPENDIX

Appendix 1.—CLAY TECHNIQUES

INSTRUCTIONS FOR COIL BUILDING

MATERIALS NEEDED

- Clay
- Slip (clay thinned with water to the thickness of cream)
- Plastic for wrapping work in progress
- Scraper
- Paddle (a flat batten board)
- Working surface such as canvas or paper

To test the clay to see if it is in proper condition, form a small roll of clay and drape it over one finger. If it drapes easily, without any cracks, it is perfect for making coils.

Keep any extra clay covered.

Carefully wrap pots while in process. If they need moisture, put a dampened paper towel inside the plastic but preferably not touching the pot.

1. Wedge the clay to avoid air bubbles by forming a ball and gently slapping it between your hands. This will take up to ten minutes, depending on the condition of the clay when you began.

2. Make a base either by flattening a ball or by making a flat coil base. As you start to build upwards, make every effort to keep the bowl completely round.

3. To make coils, use the flat part of your palms just below your fingers to roll a coil on the table. The coil should be the same diameter in its full length. Usually a coil shouldn't be much longer than 12 inches to handle easily.

4. As you build upwards with the coils, score (use a knife to make X marks on each coil before joining the next coil on top of it) and coat it with slip. Make approximately three coils, then take the time to smooth them inside and paddle or use the scraper to smooth the outside. Cut the end of a coil on the diagonal, and the beginning of the new coil also on the diagonal where it will be joined.

INSTRUCTIONS FOR SLAB BUILDING

MATERIALS NEEDED

- Clay
- Plastic for keeping clay moist
- Battens: sticks $\frac{1}{4} \times 1\text{-}\frac{1}{4} \times 12$ inches long

- Rolling pin or 1-inch dowels
- Canvas or paper for rolling slabs
- Knives
- Tagboard (file folders)

1. Wedge the clay carefully and long enough to get rid of air bubbles.

2. Make a tagboard pattern. Slabs can be formed into boxes, rolled and joined on a long edge, and draped over forms of various kinds. Naturally they will need to be thicker if the sides have to support themselves.

3. Put a ball of clay between the two sticks (approximately 10 inches apart), and use the sticks to control a consistent thickness of the slab as you roll it out with the rolling pin or dowel.

4. Place the pattern on the slab. Hold a knife straight up and down and cut around the pattern.

5. To make a box, cut the bottom and four sides, and allow the clay to stiffen slightly before joining the pieces. Score carefully, apply slip, and smooth the inside. To give strength, make a coil of clay to put on the inside of each corner, and carefully smooth it. Use a scraper to clean the edges.

6. If you want to make a lid, make a slab of the correct size. Then cut strips of clay to put on the underside of the lid to keep it from falling off the box and to hold it in place. Again, use slip to join the strips to the lid.

Appendix 2.—"SCHOOLS OF ART" AND CHRONOLOGY OF WELL-KNOWN AMERICAN ARTISTS

COLONIAL ART, 1600–1750

Painting

Robert Feke, c. 1705–1750
John Greenwood, 1727–1792
Gustave Hesselius, 1682–1755
John Smibert, 1688–1751

Sculpture

Shem Drowne, 1683–1774
Simeon Skillin, Sr., 1716–1778
John Welch, 1711–1789

REVOLUTIONARY ART, 1750–1790

Painting

John Singleton Copley, 1738–1815
Ralph Earl, 1751–1801
Charles Willson Peale, 1741–1827
Paul Revere, 1735–1818
Gilbert Stuart, 1755–1828
John Trumbull, 1756–1843
Benjamin West, 1738–1820

Sculpture

Samuel McIntire, 1757–1811
George Robinson the younger, 1680–1737
William Rush, 1756–1833
John Skillin, 1746–1800
Simeon Skillin, Jr., 1757–1806
John Welch, 1711–1789
Patience Lowell Wright, 1725–1786

Architecture

William Buckland, 1734–1774
Charles Bulfinch, 1763–1844
Thomas Jefferson, 1743–1826
Robert Smith, c. 1722–1777

EXPANSIONISM, PIONEER ART, OPENING OF THE WEST, 1800–1870

Painting

Washington Allston, 1779–1843
John James Audubon, 1785–1851
Raphaelle Peale, 1774–1825
Rembrandt Peale, 1778–1860
John Quidor, 1801–1881
Thomas Sully, 1783– 1872

Romanticism

George Caleb Bingham, 1811–1879
Edward Hicks, 1780–1849

American Painters of Indian Life

Karl Bodmer, 1809–1893
George Catlin, 1796–1872
Seth Eastman, 1808–1875
Charles F. Wimar, 1828–1862

Frontier Art: 1800–1850

Eastman Johnson, 1824–1906
Frederic Remington, 1861–1909
Charles Russell, 1864–1926
Albert Pinkham Ryder, 1847–1917

Hudson River School (1825–1870): American Romantic Landscapes

Frederick Edwin Church, 1826–1900

Thomas Cole, 1801–1848

Jasper Francis Cropsey, 1823–1900

Thomas Doughty, 1793–1856

Asher Brown Durand, 1796–1886

Alvan Fisher, 1792–1863

Henry Inman, 1802–1846

John Frederick Kensett, 1816–1872

Samuel F. B. Morse, 1791–1872

Hudson River School (Second Generation)

Albert Bierstadt, 1830–1902

George Inness, 1825–1894

Sculpture

Isaac Fowle, 1800–1853

Horatio Greenough, 1805–1852

Hiram Powers, 1805–1873

William Rush, 1756–1833

Architecture

John Haviland, 1792–1852

Benjamin Latrobe, 1764–1820

Robert Mills, 1781–1855

William Strickland, 1788–1854

Dr. William Thornton, 1759–1828

Richard Upjohn, 1802–1878

Thomas U. Walter, 1804–1887

Photography

Matthew Brady, 1823–1896

Alexander Gardner, 1821–1882

Timothy O'Sullivan, 1840–1882

Carleton E. Watkins, 1829–1916

TURN OF THE CENTURY: VICTORIAN ART, 1870–1900

Currier and Ives, active 1835–1907

John LaFarge, 1835–1910

Albert Pinkham Ryder, 1847–1917

John Singer Sargent, 1856–1925

Henry Ossawa Tanner, 1859–1937

Louis Comfort Tiffany, 1848–1933

James McNeill Whistler, 1834–1903

American Impressionism

Mary Cassatt, 1845–1926

Childe Hassam, 1859–1935

Theodore Robinson, 1852–1896

American Realism

Thomas Eakins, 1844–1916

Winslow Homer, 1836–1910

American Trompe L'Oeil

William Michael Harnett, c. 1848–1892

John Frederick Peto, 1854–1907

Victorian Sculpture

Daniel Chester French, 1850–1931

Harriet Hosmer, 1830–1908

Augustus Saint-Gaudens, 1848–1907

John Quincy Adams Ward, 1830–1910

Olin Levi Warner, 1844–1896

Early Photography

Thomas Eakins, 1844–1916

Gertrude Kasebier, 1852–1934

Edweard Muybridge, 1830–1904

Jacob Riis, 1849–1914

Architecture

Dankmar Adler, 1844–1900

Daniel Hudson Burnham, 1846–1912

Orson Squire Fowler, 1809–1887

Frank Furness, 1839–1912

Richard Morris Hunt, 1827–1895

William Le Baron Jenney, 1832–1907

Charles McKim, 1847–1909

Rutherford Mead, 1846–1928

Frederick Law Olmsted, 1822–1903

James Renwick, 1818–1895

Henry Hobson Richardson, 1838–1886

John Wellborn Root, 1850–1891
Louis Sullivan, 1856–1924
Stanford White, 1853–1906

EARLY TWENTIETH CENTURY: 1900–1929

Painting

Cecelia Beaux, 1863–1942
George Bellows, 1882–1925
Charles Demuth, 1883–1935

The Ten

Frank W. Benson, 1861–1951
Joseph R. De Camp, 1858–1923
Thomas W. Dewing, 1851–1938
Childe Hassam, 1859–1935
Willard L. Metcalf, 1853–1925
Robert Reid, 1862–1929
Edward Simmons, 1852–1931
Edmund C. Tarbell, 1862–1938
John Henry Twachtmann, 1853–1902
J. Alden Weir, 1852–1919
William Merrit Chase, 1849–1916 (a replacement)

American Surrealism

Peter Blume, 1906–1992
Joseph Cornell, 1903–1972
Man Ray, 1890–1976

American Modernism (1915)

John Marin 1870–1953
Joseph Stella 1877–1946

American Dada

Marcel Duchamp, 1887–1968
Man Ray, 1890–1976

Ashcan School (The Eight): 1900–1920

Arthur B. Davies, 1862–1928
William J. Glackens, 1870–1938
Robert Henri, 1865–1929

Ernest Lawson, 1873–1939
George B. Luks, 1866–1933
Maurice Prendergast, 1859–1924
Everett Shinn, 1876–1953
John Sloan, 1871–1951

Painter of Southern Life

Robert Gwathmey, 1903– 1988

Abstract Painting

Stuart Davis, 1894–1964
Arthur Dove, 1880–1946
Lyonel Feininger, 1871–1956
Marsden Hartley, 1877–1943
Hans Hofmann, 1880–1966
Walt Kuhn, 1880–1949
Georgia O'Keeffe, 1887–1986
Max Weber, 1881–1961

Futurism/Cubism, c. 1909

Lyonel Feininger, 1871–1956
Joseph Stella, 1877–1946

Synchromism, 1913–1918

Stanton Macdonald-Wright, 1890–1973
Morgan Russell, 1886–1943

Photo Secession 1905–1917

Edward Steichen, 1879–1973
Alfred Stieglitz, 1864–1946

Photography

Edward Sheriff Curtis, 1868–1952
Lewis Hine, 1874–1940
Charles Sheeler, 1883–1965

Sculpture

Alexander Archipenko, 1867–1964
John Gutzon Borglum, 1867–1941
Alexander Milne Calder, 1846–1923
A. Sterling Calder, 1870–1915
James Earle Fraser, 1876–1953
Frederick William MacMonnies, 1863–1937
Paul Manship, 1885–1966

Elie Nadelman, 1882–1946

Frederick Remington, 1861–1909

Augustus Saint-Gaudens, 1848–1907

Architecture

Cass Gilbert, 1859–1934

Charles Sumner Greene, 1868–1957

Henry Mather Greene, 1870–1954

Bernard Maybeck, 1862–1957

Addison Mizner, 1872–1933

Frank Lloyd Wright, 1867–1959

ART BETWEEN THE WARS: 1920–1940

Painting

Harlem Renaissance, 1919–1929

Charles Alston, 1907–1977

Romare Bearden, 1914–1988

John Biggers, 1924

Aaron Douglas, 1899–1979

Meta Vaux Warrick Fuller, 1877–1968

Sam Gilliam, 1933

Palmer Hayden, 1890–1973

William H. Johnson, 1901–1970

Lois Mailou Jones, 1905

Jacob Lawrence, 1917

Samella Lewis, 1924

Archibald Motley, Jr., 1891–1981

Augusta Savage, 1892–1962

Henry Tanner, 1859–1937

James Van Der Zee, 1886–1983

Hale Woodruff, 1900–1980

Precisionism, 1915–present

Charles Demuth, 1883–1935

Charles Sheeler, 1883–1965

American Modernism, 1930s

Joseph Albers, 1888–1976

Ivan Albright,1897–1983

Elaine de Kooning, 1920–1989

Arthur Dove, 1880–1946

Arshile Gorky, 1905–1948

Marsden Hartley, 1877–1943

Hans Hofmann, 1880–1966

Alice Neel, 1900–1984

Georgia O'Keeffe, 1887–1986

George Tooker, 1920

Max Weber, 1881–1961

Social Realism, 1920s–1930s

Phillip Evergood, 1901–1975

Edward Hopper, 1882–1967

Ben Shahn, 1898–1969

Magic Realism

Ivan Le Lorraine Albright, 1897–1983

Peter Blume, 1906–1992

American Scene Painters (Regionalists), 1930s

Thomas Hart Benton, 1889–1975

George Caleb Bingham, 1811–1879

Charles Ephraim Burchfield, 1893–1967

John Steuart Curry, 1897–1946

Stuart Davis, 1894–1964

Edward Hopper, 1882–1967

Joe Jones, 1909–1963

John Marin, 1870–1953

Anna Mary (Grandma) Moses, 1860–1961

Isaac Soyer, 1907–1981

Moses Soyer, 1899–1975

Raphael Soyer, 1899–1987

Grant Wood, 1892–1942

Andrew Wyeth, 1917

Realism, 1920–1940

George Bellows, 1882–1925

Charles Demuth, 1883–1935

John Kane, 1860–1932

Reginald Marsh, 1898–1954

Horace Pippin, 1888–1946

Charles Sheeler, 1883–1965

George Tooker, 1920

Surrealism

Joseph Cornell, 1903–1972

Arshile Gorky, 1904–1948

Mark Tobey, 1890–1976

Genre and Landscape

Charles Burchfield, 1893–1967

Hale Woodruff, 1900–1980

Photography

Berenice Abbott, 1898–1991

Harry Callahan, 1912

Harold Edgerton, 1903–1990

Walker Evans, 1903–1975

Andreas Feininger, 1906

Arthur Fellig (Weegee), 1899–1968

Laura Gilpin, 1891–1979

Lewis Hine, 1874–1940

Dorothea Lange, 1895–1965

Irving Penn, 1917

Eliot Porter, 1901 – 1990

Margaret Bourke White, 1904–1971

Minor White, 1908–1976

Group F64 Photographers

Ansel Adams, 1902–1984

Imogene Cunningham, 1883–1976

John Paul Edwards, 1883–1958

Sonya Noskowiak, 1900–1975

Henry Swift, 1891–1960

Willard Van Dyke, 1906–1986

Edward Weston, 1886–1958

Sculpture

Alexander Archipenko, 1887–1964

Jo Davidson, 1883–1952

Jose De Creeft, 1884–1974

Gaston Lachaise, 1882–1935

Simon Rodia, 1879–1965

Architecture

Raymond Hood, 1881–1934

Albert Kahn, 1869–1942

Julia Morgan, 1872–1957

Richard Neutra, 1892–1970

ABSTRACT EXPRESSIONISM/ POP CULTURE: 1940–1965

American Bauhaus, est. 1938

Josef Albers, 1888–1976

Lyonel Feininger, 1871–1956

Lázló-Maholy-Nagy, 1895–1946

Hans Hofmann, 1880–1966

Abstract Expressionism, 1945–1960

Milton Avery, 1893–1965

Billy Al Bengston, 1934

Willem DeKooning, 1904

Elaine de Kooning, 1920–1989

Arshile Gorky, 1904–1948

Morris Graves, 1910

Philip Guston, 1913–1980

Hans Hofmann, 1880–1966

Franz Kline, 1910–1962

Lee Krasner, 1908–1984

Agnes Martin, 1912

Robert Motherwell, 1915–1991

Barnett Newman, 1905–1970

Jackson Pollock, 1912–1956

Ad Reinhardt, 1913–1967

Larry Rivers, 1923

New Realism/Pop Art, 1950s–late 1960s

Lee Bontecou, 1931

Richard Diebenkorn, 1922–1993

Jim Dine, 1935

Janet Fish, 1938

Joe Goode, 1937

Robert Indiana, 1928

Jasper Johns, 1930

Jack Levine, 1915

Roy Lichtenstein, 1923

Alice Neel, 1900–1984

Mel Ramos, 1935

Robert Rauschenberg, 1925

James Rosenquist, 1933

Ed Ruscha, 1937

Betye Saar, 1926

Frank Stella, 1936

Andy Warhol, 1927–1987

Tom Wesselman, 1931

Jamie Wyeth, 1946

Andrew Wyeth, 1917

Color Field Painting, 1960s

Sam Francis, 1923–1994

Helen Frankenthaler, 1928

Ellsworth Kelly, 1923

Morris Louis, 1912–1962

Barnett Newman, 1905–1970

Mark Rothko, 1903–1970

Clyfford Still, 1904–1980

Happenings, late 1950s

Jim Dine, 1935

Red Grooms, 1937

Allan Kaprow, 1927

Claes Oldenburg, 1929

Robert Whitman, 1935

East Village Art, 1980s
Hard-Edge Painting, 1958–1960s

Ellsworth Kelly, 1923

Alexander Liberman, 1912

Kenneth Noland, 1924

Frank Stella, 1936

Op Art, 1960s

Richard Anuszkiewicz, 1930

Feminist Art

Judy Chicago, 1939

Elizabeth Murray, 1940

Miriam Schapiro, 1923

Photography

Diane Arbus, 1923–1971

Richard Avedon, 1923

Robert Frank, 1924

Lee Friedlander, 1934

Lázló Maholy-Nagy, 1895–1946

Robert Mapplethorp, 1946–1989

Joel Meyerowitz, 1938

W. Eugene Smith, 1918–1978

Paul Strand, 1890–1976

Brett Weston, 1911–1993

Cole Weston, 1919

Gary Winogrand, 1928–1984

Sculpture

Alexander Calder, 1898–1976

Joseph Cornell, 1903–1973

Mark Di Suvero, 1933

Donald Judd, 1928 –1994

Jacques Lipchitz, 1891–1973

Elie Nadelman, 1882–1946

Louise Nevelson, 1900–1988

Isamu Noguchi, 1904–1988

Claes Oldenburg, 1929

Meret Oppenheim, 1913 –1985

George Segal, 1924

David Smith, 1906–1965

Wayne Thiebaud, 1920

Architecture

Marcel Breuer, 1902–1981

Buckminster Fuller, 1895–1983

Walter Gropius, 1883–1969

Philip Johnson, 1906

Eero Saarinen, 1910–1961

Edward Durrell Stone, 1902–1978

Ludwig Mies Van Der Rohe, 1886–1969

LATE TWENTIETH CENTURY: 1965–PRESENT

Painting

Jennifer Bartlett, 1941

Jean-Michel Basquiat, 1960

Linda Benglis, 1941

Jonathan Borofsky, 1942

Eric Fischl, 1948

Janet Fish, 1938

Leon Golub, 1922

Keith Haring, 1958–1990

David Hockney, 1937

Alex Katz, 1927

Jeff Koons, 1955

Joan Mitchell, 1926–1992

Robert Morris, 1931

Gladys Nilsson, 1940

Ed Paschke, 1939

Philip Pearlstein, 1924

Faith Ringgold, 1934

Susan Rothenberg, 1945

David Salle, 1952

Lucas Samaras, 1936

Frank Stella, 1936

Cy Twombly, 1929

Post-Modern

Edward Keinholz, 1927–1994

Julian Schnable, 1957

Photo Realism / Hyperrealists, c. 1967–1977

Robert Bechtle, 1932

Chuck Close, 1940

Don Eddy, 1944

Richard Estes, 1936

Audrey Flack, 1931

Photography

William Eggleston, 1939

Annie Leibovitz, 1949

Cindy Sherman, 1954

Jerry Uelsman, 1934

Conceptual Art, c. 1970–present

Joseph Beuys, 1921

Christo (Javacheff), 1935

Richard Serra, 1939

Robert Smithson, 1928–1973

Sculpture

Magdalena Abakanowicz, 1985

Carl Andre, 1935

Louise Bourgeois, 1911

Deborah Butterfield, 1949

John De Andrea, 1941

Mark DiSuvero, 1933

Marisol Escobar, 1930

Nancy Graves, 1940-1995

Red Grooms, 1937

Duane Hanson, 1925–1996

Richard Hunt, 1935

Edward Kienholz, 1927–1994

Judy Pfaff, 1946

Betye Saar, 1926

Kenny Scharf, 1984

Ernest Trova, 1927

Minimalism

Larry Bell, 1939

Dan Flavin, 1933

Brice Marden, 1938

Richard Serra, 1939

Funk Art

Robert Arneson, 1930

Roy deForest, 1930

Ceramics

Maria Montoya Martinez, 1887–1980

Peter Voulkos, 1924

Earth Art / Environmental Art

Alice Aycock, 1946

Mel Chin, 1951

Newton Harrison, 1932

Michael Heizer, 1944

Nancy Holt, 1938

Patricia Johanson, 1940

Dennis Oppenheim, 1938

Beverly Pepper, 1924

John Roloff, 1947

Robert Smithson, 1938

Architecture

Denise Scott Brown, 1931

John Burgee, 1933

Charles Eames, 1907–1978

Michael Graves, 1934

Louis I. Kahn, 1901–1974

Ioeh Ming Pei, 1917

Robert Stern, 1939

Robert Venturi, 1925

NOTES